Vera Buch at age 19

Vera Buch Weisbord

A RADICAL LIFE

INDIANA UNIVERSITY PRESS

Bloomington and London

Published in Canada by Fitzhenry & Whiteside Limited, Don Mills, Ontario

Manufactured in the United States of America

Library of Congress Cataloging in Publication Data

Weisbord, Vera Buch, 1895—
A radical life.

Includes index.
1. Weisbord, Vera Buch, 1895— 2. Communists—
United States—Biography. 3. Communism—United States—
History. 4. Trade-unions and communism—United States—
History. I. Title.
HX84.W42A37 1977   335.43'092'4[B]   76-28276
ISBN 0-253-34773-4   1 2 3 4 5 81 80 79 78 77

To my parents

NELLIE AMELIA LOUISA CRAWFORD *and* JOHN CASPER BUCH

who did so much for me

and for whom I could do so little.

ACKNOWLEDGMENTS

SINCERE THANKS ARE DUE TO CAROLYN ASHBAUGH FOR EXTENSIVE HELP IN getting material, especially on Gastonia; to Rosalyn Baxandall for steady support; to Joan Chase for material on the coal industry; to Sara Heslep for competent help in revising the first three chapters; to Dan McCurry for some Southern material; to Charles Voss for material in the *Daily Worker*; to Susan Fernandez and John Gallman of Indiana University Press for their warm-hearted and sympathetic support. Of course, my husband and partner was always ready to help when called on.

Contents

Introduction

By *Paul Buhle and Mari Jo Buhle*

VERA BUCH WEISBORD'S AUTOBIOGRAPHY IS AN IMPORTANT DOCUMENT OF American radical history. Her story is significant far beyond her own personal history. Political and industrial insurgency of the 1920s, and specifically the early period of American Communism, remain virtually unexplored social movements. Beneath the placid surface of American prosperity and bourgeois self-confidence bubbled an uneasiness both economic and cultural, a discontent that would spill over in the next decade into a major protest against the political order. Vera Weisbord was there, amid strikes whose dynamism foreshadowed the rise of industrial unionism. But her memoirs reflect an even more unique and less understood aspect of twenties radicalism: the experiences of women. She recalls her hopes and personal disappointments, her self-doubts and her own perceptions of women's role in American radicalism of the time, as has no Communist writer before. The product is not a conclusive political document but is instead a narrative rich with information and interpretation.

The pioneer era of American Communism was a difficult one. Labor and the Left stood between the high hopes of the pre-1920s on the one hand and the revival of mass social movements during the 1930s on the other. The very vision of socialism and the deep confidence in its inevitability which had been shared by hundreds of thousands of Americans from all walks of life was shaken by world war and shattered by the precipitous decline of the radical movement. Communists observed with anguish the employer counteroffensive against hard-won labor gains, the "open shop" drive and the strong-arm tactics against workers in mass production, judicial decisions against labor organizing, and the general public hostility toward reforms. They found strength in their new faith, Communism, and in the vision of the Workers' Fatherland in Russia. But their very ideological convictions deepened their sense of isolation within America. As they sought constituencies outside the social stasis the Lynds described in *Middletown*, Communists gave decisive shape to their movement.

American Communism had initially grown out of a unique combination of labor insurgency and Left political crisis shortly before 1920. From the outbreak of the First World War, strike activity reached unprecedented levels in the United States, as millions of workers gained the union recognition and shorter hours sought for generations. "New Immigrants" from Southern and Eastern Europe were emboldened to sympathize with and work for the liberation of their homelands. City general strikes, massive demonstrations of workers and soldiers even suggested here and there that revolutionary institutions were being created parallel to existing ones. For a moment, the Russian Revolution seemed to many to supply the key. If Europe followed Russia into world revolution, and America Europe, then surely the future belonged to the "Soviets" (workers' councils) and to the dedicated vanguard at the head of the mass. But in reality the appearance of an American Bolshevism only served to dramatize the paralysis of the American Left. Socialists and proto-Communists locked in a fierce internecine struggle, while federal and state governments accelerated a program of arrests, imprisonment, and deportation. Meanwhile workers flocked to the unions, which extreme revolutionists denounced as hopelessly reactionary, and willingly followed individual radical leaders for economic gains while showing little interest in the political side of unionism.

The youthful, zealous Communist movement therefore spent much of its energy "underground," issuing revolutionary proclamations with little concrete application for the labor movement. For many potential enthusiasts, like Vera Buch, this Left was hard even to locate, let alone join and engage. For Communists who survived the political experience it offered the traumatic lesson outlined by Lenin in *Left-Wing Communism: An Infantile Disorder*. As veteran Communists recalled in later years, they had to abandon the evangelical belief that workers could be converted by slogans and the promise of leadership.

The realization that revolution would not be achieved by open advocacy of radical principles was a watershed in the modern Left-wing movement. In one sense or another, the whole range of pre-1920 strategies had rested upon the older belief. Socialists envisioned a patient education conducted through the ballot with the support of the trade union movement. The Industrial Workers of the World (IWW) believed proletarians would be educated to the "One Big Union" idea, the economic organization as a revolutionary nucleus, ready to replace the existing state apparatus. American Communists through 1921 had guessed that if they proclaimed the revolutionary imperative and offered proper leadership, the masses seething with unrest would finish off capitalism. Instead, Lenin suggested, Communists had to compensate for their minority status by the tactic of maneuver—adroit shifting within the existing non- and anti-Communist political and economic institutions. The revolutionary party had to nurture its strengths, allocate its resources, and prepare constantly to leap into the arenas of decisive struggle.

In the early and mid-twenties, Communist gains promised greater success. Acting vigorously for a fighting program within the fading American Federation of Labor, Communists won over several important unions and scores of local city federations to their programs. Concurrently, they worked through political channels of the burgeoning farmer-labor movement for a national opposition to the two-party monopoly. Thousands of former Socialists and IWWs who had hitherto held back now joined the Communists. Communists saw themselves as the source of strength and guidance for democratic and radical forces within existing unions, an ideological bellwether of a vast political alliance against Capital.

By 1925, however, these advances were cut off. As the constituency for labor and political insurgencies dwindled, important allies of the Communists drew back to cut their own losses. Communists responded with intensified propaganda campaigns, exposing themselves to conservative attack. Leaders in the American Federation of Labor covered their failures with cries against the "Red Menace," while Robert La Follette headed a Progressive Party campaign from which Communists were avowedly excluded. Communism in America had entered a period of "splendid isolation."

Moreover, the effort of American Communists to master Russian-style Bolshevism encouraged a self-defeating internal strife. In what they perceived to be the Leninist spirit, Party leaders divided into tight political groupings and fought tooth and nail over major and minor issues. Many local activists and sympathizers were confused by differences which, indeed, often broke down to little more than justification for a power struggle. Events in the Soviet Union and in the Comintern fueled factionism in the United States, and decisions made by the leaders often resulted in sudden, sometimes unexpected, shifts in strategy. With each sharp turn American Communists lost part of their claim to a sincere dedication to the labor movement that their actual agitation on behalf of workers had rightfully earned. Within the Left, mutual suspicions became endemic, a certain cyncism grew evident in the internal decision-making process. Unused to recruiting new members, they doubtless lost opportunities, treated individuals unfairly, and called upon local groups to advance or retreat in what appeared to observers a crazy-quilt fashion of running a revolutionary movement.

Yet, for all these limitations, Communists confronted the great issue of the day: the crisis of the labor movement, above all of the millions of unskilled, unorganized workers. Labor dynamism of the 1920s came from the poverty-stricken, hard-pressed workers outside the craft unions, especially from those workers in "sick" economic sectors like textiles and coal where low profits encouraged employers to cut the already near-starvation wages and to allow the miserable working conditions to deteriorate further. Through the Communist apparatus, a young, talented, and energetic woman like Vera Buch could find fulfillment and purpose among the greatest struggles of the day.

Vera Buch Weisbord participated in one of the greatest innovations of the radical labor movement in the 1920s–1930s: the shop paper. Previously, socialist newspapers had been written mostly for the autodidact craftsman. Philosophical, concerned with general knowledge, such papers had little meaning to the unskilled worker. By contrast, Communist papers staged a direct, continuous offensive over wages and the conditions on the factory floor. Such papers, ultimately published by non-Communists as well, became in the 1930s an important link between the intimate concerns of day-to-day agitation and the larger objectives of industrial unionism.

Vera Weisbord was also on the scene in the key struggles for the democratization and revitalization of the United Mine Workers. The Save the Union committees were combatted by the iron-fisted John L. Lewis and ultimately abandoned by Communists themselves. Nevertheless, such agitation kept the fires of militancy burning for another day. When Arnold Miller defeated the successors to the Lewis machine in the 1970s, more than a few veterans recalled the committee's labors of a half-century earlier.

Finally, Vera Buch Weisbord was an important figure in the strikes at Passaic and Gastonia. Although unique in themselves, these outbursts provided continuity between the first mass uprisings before 1920 and the successful industrial union drives during the thirties. Whether recent immigrants or native-born Southerners, the work force demonstrated that community involvement and support was the key to victory. Vera Weisbord's experiences were evidence that the potential for all-out struggle had not been squelched by the decade's much-touted prosperity and social consensus.

She also shared, less consciously perhaps, in an experience which has been relatively ignored by scholars and participants alike: that of a woman in the modern Left. This aspect of the narrative has a tinge of tragedy, most of all because the constrictions on women's role in the Communist movement were barely recognized, let alone discussed, as a burning theoretical or practical question. In the 1920s radical women were heirs to a collapsed feminist tradition.

From the early decades of the nineteenth century, women had participated in the great reform movements. Abolitionism, temperance, populism, American socialism—all had witnessed women as a prominent constituency and more than once a dominating force. Within these movements women had established their own prerogatives and considered their agitation as an extension of the work they did in the name of Woman's Rights. As agents in the historical movement for their emancipation, women reformers envisioned women's freedom tantamount to the transformation and purification of American society at large. No reform movement graced the pre-1920 world without the question of woman's rights and woman's place or role considered, at one time or another, by its constituency.

By the 1920s the force that made such recognition possible had dissipated, and the women's movement was a mere shadow of its former self. In part, this collapse has been traced to the passage of the "Susan B. Anthony" Amendment, for generations the rallying cry of feminists and by the 'teens the issue around which millions of women were organized. But even amidst the suffrage triumph, the most compelling features of the nineteenth-century women's movement were fading. The autobiographical accounts of the earlier generation reveal deep feelings about the political experience, what it meant in terms of a personal awakening, and especially the importance of friendships gained as women broke their emotional isolation or domestic confinement. This was a genuine social movement, a woman's cultural experience expressed in political terms— what we might today call a "sisterhood." By the 'teens, the element of sorority had virtually disappeared. To be sure, the number of outspoken feminists had increased and the intellectual respectability of feminism made it almost a mark of sophistication in contemporary consciousness. But the other side of the advance was an unmistakable tenor of individualism.

In 1927, journalist Dorothy Dunbar Bromley compiled several tenets of what she called "Feminist—New Style." One of her most revealing descriptions read:

FEMINIST—NEW STYLE professes no loyalty to women *en masse*, although she staunchly believes in individual women. Surveying her sex as a whole, she finds their actions petty, their range of interests narrow, their talk trivial and repetitious. . . .*

The commitment to women's equality and right to self-determination is here abstracted from the notion of a collective struggle and in many ways suggests the quality of feminism popular in the 'teens and 'twenties—a rather ironic outcome to a century-long social movement.

The prewar Socialist Party had been deeply influenced by the women's rights movement. Women who were leading agitators and organizers in the party had entered radical activity via suffrage, the purity crusade, or temperance. In turn, they pushed other socialists, male and female, to take up woman's cause in the name of socialism and to elicit the participation of other women, whether urban factory worker, professional, or rural housewife. Only the most narrowly "proletarian" radicals hostile to the Party's electoral strategy openly scoffed at the socialist commitment to women's equality.

By the time of the Russian Revolution little remained of the older tradition. A few socialists tried, with limited success, to transfer agitational energies from suffrage to "working-class" issues like birth control and the price of goods. Such a move paralleled the practical emphasis of many socialists upon the trade unions rather than political education as such. But whereas unions brought workers together and imparted a sense of distinct identity to each member, working-class women remained atomized, in their homes, reached only by virtue of membership in the proletarian family. Even those women with radical sympathies remained for the most part politically inert, save in strike campaigns or political affairs where men's role was foremost.

American Communism inherited this situation and was without the benefit of an organized and self-consciously militant feminist constituency to influence its politics and practices. Most women entered the movement through the traditional auxiliary role to foreign-language revolutionaries. They made the meals, scrubbed the pots, raised money for the newspapers and defense funds, provided comfort, and imparted domestic dignity to the organizer and agitator. While the Socialist Party had from 1910 regularly included a few women in its top leadership and many in its regional hierarchies, among Communists prominent women were scarce.

More important, even as the Communists emerged from the "underground" in the earlier 1920s, special work among women had already been

---

*"Feminist—New Style," *Harper's Magazine*, 155 (October 1927), 556.

blessed by Lenin's writings. The Comintern's International Woman's Secretariat directed the establishment of national departments resulting in the creation of a Woman's Bureau of the American Party in 1922. In turn, the Woman's Bureau formed a United Council of Working Class Women (sometimes known as the United Council of Working Class Wives), encouraging local affiliates like the Mothers' League of Boston and Detroit Proletarian Women. That same year, International Woman's Day was celebrated as a supremely proletarian holiday, with a special section of the *Worker*, the Party organ, devoted to the "woman worker" and the "mothers of the proletariat."

The implications of this policy were enhanced by the utter hostility toward all forms of women's activities not consciously "proletarian." Stokes, who was perhaps the most authoritative Communist woman, attacked the class blindness of the "pure feminist" in 1922 and lavished praise upon female proletarians united with "strength and courage in the battle for the workers' control of America."* That this policy of forming women's battalions for such purposes only was unsuccessful is demonstrated by an appeal from the Women's Department of the American Party to the Comintern in 1929 for "an instructor for work among women in the U.S.A.†

Nevertheless, individual women made significant contributions. Among the most important activities were those described by Vera Buch Weisbord. At Passaic, for example, she and other radicals carried on the style of work pioneered in the 'teens. Following the efforts of Socialists and IWW agitators in the Lawrence and Paterson strikes, they educated wives to the essential roles they could play as members of the community and household. They organized women to meet domestic crises, like the shortage of money, clothing, and food, for the duration of the strike. And they established collective childcare facilities, so that mothers could participate in strike activities. They were preparing for the practices of women's auxiliaries and emergency brigades during the sitdowns of the 1930s.

The experience of Vera Buch Weisbord was certainly not that of a "typical" Communist woman of the twenties, if indeed such a prototype exists. There are, however, elements in it suggestive of larger difficulties and triumphs. Lacking a supportive milieu of political women, she was repeatedly isolated and dependent on the direction of the Party on the one hand, and on her relationship with Albert Weisbord on the other. In

---

*"Women and Revolution," *The Truth* (Duluth, Minn.), June 23, 1922.

†Quoted in Theodore Draper, *The Roots of American Communism* (New York, 1957), 167.

this tragic but familiar double bind, to lend herself fully to either was to rob herself of the other possibility. These dilemmas were only at one level specifically those of a woman in an isolated and factionalized Communist Party; at another level they were shared by women radicals throughout the twentieth century. We hear Vera Buch Weisbord's story because she was not and is not overwhelmed by all the evident difficulties. We believe her voice will call out others.

Although we specifically do not share the interpretation Vera Buch Weisbord has made of the Communist movement of the 1920s and her assessment of many events and personalities, our disagreements are not so important as to hide from us and from others the revelations of her life.

CHRONOLOGY

Vera Wilhelmine Buch

August 19, 1895: Born in Forestville, Conn. Parents were Nellie Amelia Louisa Crawford (descended on her mother's side from William and Elizabeth Tuttle, who came from England in 1635) and John Casper Buch, whose grandparents probably came to America from Germany around 1848. (His mother, Wilhelmine Schelling, was born in Hamilton, Canada, where there was a German settlement. She came to the U.S.A. at age ten. My grandfather Buch, born in New York City, fought in the Civil War.)

Around 1899: Family moved to New York. Entered kindergarten probably at age four.

February 1908: Graduated from grade school; was valedictorian.

1908–1912: Hunter High School.

1912–February 1916: Hunter College. Won three first prizes in French competition among colleges in U.S.A. and Canada.

April 1916–April 1917: In TB sanatorium. Through friend became acquainted with socialist movement.

Spring 1918: Family moved to Caldwell, N.J., for my health. Spent next three years commuting between New York City and Caldwell.

Early 1919: Became connected with left wing of Socialist Party, New York, and attended its meetings. Joined IWW. Joined Communist Party when it first formed in 1920. Was briefly underground. Worked for Central Committee of Russian Cooperative Unions in New York.

Early 1922: Family moved to a country home outside Dover, N.J. Stayed there for recuperation until early 1925, then returned to New York City. Taught French in high school. Joined Workers (Communist) Party.

1926: Passaic Strike. Met husband. Organized women.

Early 1927: Various Party activities in New York. Went to Philadelphia when my husband was made assistant district organizer and began contacts with coal miners. Took part in Sacco-Vanzetti demonstrations.

Fall 1927: Went with my husband to Detroit, where he was made district organizer. Got job in auto plant and was part of committee working for a union in the auto plants. Was editor of factory newspapers.

Spring 1928: Was sent to coal fields of Pennsylvania by Party Central Committee to do "women's work." Was associated with the women's auxiliaries of the United Mine Workers, building Save the Union Committees.

Fall 1928: Returned to New York. Underwent induced abortion. National Textile Workers Union formed.

April 5, 1929–late October 1929: Gastonia strike and trials.

Late 1929 and 1930: Lived in New Jersey. Worked in large textile mill in Newark. Separated from Communist Party.

1930–1935: In New York. Was active member of group called Communist League of Struggle and associate editor of its paper, *The Class Struggle* (reprinted in Greenwood editions).

1935: Moved to Chicago.

LIST OF ORGANIZATIONS

Afro-American Committee
Allgemeine Union (German left
  socialist group)
American Civil Liberties Union
  (ACLU)
American Federation of Labor (AFL)
Associated Silk Workers (ASW)
Brotherhood of Electrical Workers
Central Committee of Russian
  Cooperative Unions
  (Centrosoyus)
Civilian Conservation Corps (CCC)
Central Executive Committee
  (CEC)
Communist International
  (Comintern, CI)
Communist Labor Party (CLP)
Communist League of America
  (Cannon group)
Communist League of Struggle
  (Weisbord group)
Communist Party (CP)
Communist Party (Majority or
  Lovestone group)
Conference for Progressive Labor
  Action (CPLA; Muste group)
Congress of Industrial Organizations
  (CIO)
Congress of Racial Equality (CORE)
Farmer Labor Party (FLP)
Federated Textile Unions (FTU)
Fellowship of Reconciliation (Muste
  group)
Full Fashioned Hosiery Workers
  Union (FFHWU)
Industrial Workers of the World
  (IWW)

International Hat, Cap and Millinery
  Workers Union
International Labor Defense (ILD)
International Ladies Garment
  Workers Union (ILGWU)
International Press Correspondence
  (Inprecor)
International Upholsterers Union
National Industrial Recovery Act
  (NIRA)
National Textile Workers Union
  (NTWU)
Needle Trades Workers Industrial
  Union (NTWIU)
Proletarian Party (PP)
Public Works Administration
  (PWA)
Red International of Trade Unions
  (Profintern)
Socialist Party (SP)
Socialist Labor Party (De Leon's
  group)
Trade Union Unity League
  (TUUL)
United Council of Workingclass
  Housewives (UCWH)
United Front Committees of Textile
  Workers (UFC)
United Mine Workers (UMW)
United Textile Workers (UTW)
Workers (Communist) Party
  (WCP)
Workers Party (WP)
Workers International Relief (WIR)
Workingwomen's Councils (WC)
Works Progress Administration
  (WPA)

Though cowards flinch and traitors sneer,

We'll keep the Red Flag flying here.

—"The Red Flag"

I

The Skies Are Empty

TO THE LITTLE GROUP HUDDLED BESIDE THE VAN IN THE SHADOWED EMPTY street, the scene was like the edge of night. Above them a building loomed, tall, blank, its summit merging with the faint, starless sky. At the very top two squares of light held their eyes.

"Look girls," said the mother. "That's where we're going to live, way up there. That's our new home."

For the younger one, age four, the first clear, keen perception blurred quickly into sleepiness and the memory of jelly bread eaten hours before at a round table with strange people.

"I want to go to bed," she said.

And now out of nowhere, out of the stillness, came a rumbling, then a roar, as with ear-shattering noise to their left a train crashed by. They glimpsed for the first time the iron supports of the high tracks on the nearby transverse street. The L train thundered its full length, finally sweeping on.

"He didn't tell me about *that*," said the mother.

Meanwhile, the father had been bustling about unloading the van. Now he called out crossly from the stoop: "Come on, come on, we ain't got all night."

So for the first time the little family started up the four flights to their high-perched new home.

In the dining room stacked with furniture, a raw flaring gas flame overhead disclosed other rooms all empty. Mattresses were placed on the floor, blankets were found. The two little girls fell immediately asleep, so too the father, who began to snore.

His wife Nellie beside him turned away in aversion. The marriage bed had never brought her joy, and now every inch of her body ached in fa-

3

tigue. Her numb brain fretted through a well-worn channel; how he had thrown up his job to celebrate when they first got married, so that they had to leave their first home on a good street in Bristol, opposite her sister's, and go to live in the scrubby outskirts of a smaller town; how he had refused to carry water from the well, so that hauling it herself tore loose a kidney that would torment her all her days; how he sulked that Sunday morning when the first child's birth was imminent: "Yes, and spoil my day off for me." Well, here they were now in the big city. New York held opportunities for education; here her girls might have a better life than hers. She would see to that. Late in the night with this consolation she was able to fall asleep.

When the Buch family arrived at the turn of the century in this newly opened neighborhood in the Bronx, between two large parks there were vacant lots, even a farm remaining. John thought its semirural nature would appeal to Nellie, who had never in her life lived in anything but a small town. John too, though born in New York, had lived mostly in small places; they were country people. Although Nellie felt strange at first, living up so high amid the noise of the L trains and trolleys, she quickly got used to it. Having a train near by was a relief for John, who had had to tramp five miles each way between Forestville and his job in Hartford, Connecticut. He soon found work in his trade of woodcarving from among the many furniture and piano factories. The big city had always lured him; he hoped to provide better for us all. With sister Ora, going on seven, placed in P.S. 4 just three blocks away, and with Mother pleased to find a nearby Presbyterian church, the family quickly settled into urban life.

I, too, the tot of four, gradually fitted into my own niche as basic facts of my origin and environment built up my little world. "When you were born," Mother often said, "Ora felt so bad. 'You don't like me any more,' she'd say. 'You only like that *little* baby.' " She also would tell how she wasn't hungry and couldn't eat before I was born. "You were born like a skeleton. I was afraid to bathe you, your little bones might break." This uningratiating picture of myself she modified a little. "Oh, you plumped up later. Never seemed to have much appetite though. Cornmeal mush was about all I could get you to eat." Luckily, I was breastfed at the start, this quaint substitute for the bottle being still in vogue in those remote times.

In that quiet interlude when I was home with Mother all day, Ora at school and Papa at work, the days were lit as though with an inner sunlight. I spent hours on the dining room floor with my treasures: the favorite rag doll Susie, a flat shiny piece of onyx, some letter blocks, and a frayed picture book. Mother taught me the letters and would read to me when she had time. I had a favorite ditty, "There was a frog lived in a bog, a frog of high degree. . . ."

Mother had tales of me as a spunky three-year-old. When I got mad, I'd jump up and down, my jumps just as high as I was. In spite of a certain physical frailty I liked to run and jump, and I was a good climber. When sunburnt in summer, my skin was darker than my then blonde hair. Once, when Mother was making me a pink dress, I said I wanted to be a boy. " 'If you were a boy, you couldn't wear your new pink dress.' 'Yes,' says you, 'but I could wear pink pants.' " Affectionate and demonstrative, often I climbed into Mother's lap to kiss and hug her. Once she said as she clasped me close, "This little girl is about the only comfort her poor Mother has."

Quickly we fitted into the ways of our building and the block. On the second floor under us lived the Dolls with two children, Marcelle, my age, and Charlie, about ten. The Dolls were Alsatian, he a machinist, a sallow, bent-over man in a greasy gray work apron, his wife thin, hollow-eyed, and stoop-shouldered, too. They were poor people like us. Mamma and Mrs. Doll together would contrive a child's dress or pinafore (always worn over the dress in those days) out of Mother's discard, or make the sheets last longer by splitting them and stitching the outside edges together. Charlie Doll used to take me sleigh-riding in the winter: I didn't whimper from cold like the other kids, he said. In a four-room flat at the side lived the Benzes with two small children, Frieda and three-year-old Max. Across the street on the top floor was a family named Bolte. Little Charlie, their youngest, used to call up from the street, "Wilhelmine," and would have a banana for me. So they teased me, "Willie's got a fellow! Look, she's blushing." I would run down at his call. Around the corner were the Buchsbaums; their daughters, Nellie and Ethel, also became our playmates. On the third floor rear lived the Barrys, and little Helen Barry and I played together.

"The Barrys are Irish, they're *Catholic*," Mother enlightened me.

"What's Catholic, Mamma?"

"Well, it's like they pray with *beads* and make a lot of the Virgin Mary and have a lot of images in their church. It says in the Good Book, 'Thou shalt not make unto thee any graven image.' "

"Are they bad?"

"Why, no, I don't know as I'd say they're bad. We had nothing but Irish back in Forestville. People called it Dublin Hill. Just shanty Irish. Oh, they were nice enough if you got to know them. They spoke Gaelic. Ora picked up a few words of it from the children. Always a raft of kids they had. No, I wouldn't say the Catholics are bad, they're just *different*."

Some hint of disapproval lurked behind her words, as when she would say the Dolls were *Alsatian*, the Benzes *German*.

A scene comes to mind of Helen Barry and a very small person that was myself enacting certain scenes in a nearby vacant lot. A few trees grew there, and a high board fence cut it off from Third Avenue. The L trains roared overhead but we paid no attention. We were lying on the grass and weeds under the trees with our dresses lifted up. Surely we must have worn underpants, but they had evidently been discarded, our shoes and stockings also. With glee and a tingling sense of daring, we were displaying our nude little bodies.

"Once a mosquito bit me right here," I invented, indicating the very center of that secret part that always had to be covered, was never given any name, and that somehow or other one was often aware of. "Naughty, naughty, *bad*," Mamma would say, jerking away any little hand that might want to linger there. Two five-story buildings faced us, overlooking the lot. Were there people behind those blank windows? Helen, pale and flat of face, blue-eyed, frowsy-haired, lifted her dress high and paraded. Imitating, I followed suit. How old were we, four? five? Innocent little animals, yet wily enough to be secretive, we indulged in these antics only beyond range of the watchful maternal eye.

After a happy year in kindergarten, entering grade one at five, I started up that long, toilsome ladder. "What's your name?"

"Willameanbush."

"Spell it."

"W-i-l-h-e-l-m-i-n-e."

"B-u-s-h?"

"No, B-u-c-h."

So it went through the grades. Each morning we would start out together, Ora and I, never with eagerness, just reluctantly dragging our feet. "Aw, Mamma, why do we have to go to school?"

"Everybody goes to school. You don't want to grow up ignorant, do you?" The dreary routine of reading, writing, and 'rithmetic, the cramping of active little bodies for hours behind their desks, seemed as inevitable as sunrise in the morning and darkness at night.

Because this was before World War I, first grade did offer German lessons. Every morning Herr Hülshof, a kindly middle-aged gentleman, appeared to teach us little songs, proverbs, and common words. Could I ever forget *O Tannenbaum, O Tannenbaum, wie grün sind deine Blätter* and such homely bits of wisdom as *Salz und Brot macht Wangen rot*, and *Aller Anfang ist schwer*?

One unforgettable day when we passed a certain vacant lot on the way to school, a man stood among the weeds. In one hand he had a cat. Holding it by the hind legs, he slammed its body hard against the side of a building, slam after slam until at last there were no more cries. Then he flung it away to the other side of the lot. A numb, sick feeling remained with me all day. Mother said, "It's dreadful. There are people like that in this world. They just don't care, they're cruel." I couldn't forget the poor cat, its cries, that awful man.

Mother must have had great adaptability to fit as easily as she did into the new surroundings. For all her native American conviction that foreigners were irremediably inferior, she quickly made friends and everybody liked her. But she hated the saloons. There was one in our house below us, another on the corner diagonally opposite. Some women's husbands squandered their pay there. At the 10:00 P.M. closing time, especially on Saturdays, drunks lining the sidewalk would bawl out songs like *Sweet Adeline* and *Clementine*. Sometimes a woman would silence them by dousing them from above with a dishpan full of water.

For Mother, religion was a fundamental part of life, her only solace at times. As early as we could talk, she taught us a bedtime prayer. Sundays, with Papa staying behind in skeptical amusement, we three betook ourselves to the small Scotch Presbyterian church down Washington Avenue. I was in the infant class in Sunday school, where stout, gray-bearded Mr. Fox encouraged our infant piety with Bible stories and hymns like "Jesus Loves Me." His image of the Christ child whom I must love became a little confused with my rag doll Susie. Using the Golden Rule, Mother did her best to live up to her Christian duty to teach her children to be good. She resorted often to Bible quotations: "Judge not, that ye be not judged" to restrain our name-calling; or "Blessed are the meek, for they shall inherit the earth" when we boasted; or "Sufficient unto the day is the evil thereof" if tomorrow worried us. Slowly a picture of God was built up, a remote aging gentleman not unlike Mr. Fox residing in far distant skies, who knew if a little girl even *thought* something wicked, and was ready to strike in punishment when she was naughty, despite his failure ever to appear and explain his will.

Mother was the one who was always home, Father a figure scarcely known.

Early in the morning six days a week there would be steps in the kitchen, sometimes a muttering as he stirred about, an odor of burnt grease, of fried potatoes, of warmed-up coffee. Then the kitchen door would close, and the day would be well spent before Papa returned. He would peel off his jacket and take his place at the oilcloth-covered table. Not yet thirty, he was already bald, his blond hair fringing the sides and back of his head. He had blue eyes, a fleshy nose, and a wide full-lipped mouth. If not too tired, he would talk of whatever happened in the shop that day, sometimes harangueing about the foreigners, those Eyetalians who were driving down his trade, ready as they were to work for nothing, satisfied to eat bread and garlic for their dinner and live ten to a room like animals. Mother said little, generally assenting to her husband's opinions. After supper Papa would sit in his shirt-sleeves to read the paper, by the window in summer, at the table in winter. Ofter he would fall asleep so, with his head drooping down on his chest.

On Sundays he would put on his good suit, and after dinner, observing the day of rest, we would all just sit around, or perhaps go for a walk. Sometimes in summer the family would visit the zoo in Bronx Park. Invariably Papa would become cross and stalk angrily ahead, we three trailing him, depressed and silent. Never did we know what had set him off. At such times I would quietly sing a hymn or just tell myself Jesus loved me, a consoling thought. When at home we all felt stiff and unnatural on Sundays. Even reading other than the Bible was not encouraged. It was only later that Sunday discipline was relaxed to include the newspaper with its funnies: "The Katzenjammer Kids," "Happy Hooligan," "Desperate Desmond," "Alphonse and Gaston."

The Sunday papers also carried stories of the high and mighty rich— the Vanderbilts, the Carnegies, the Rockefellers, the Astors, Goulds, and Morgans—which we read with zest, in mixed envy and contempt. A picture of John D. Rockefeller, the original moneymaker, showed a skinny, shriveled, aged man with a face like a death's head. "If I had a mug like that, I'd keep it out of the paper." "Money don't add anything to good looks," we would say. Mrs. Hetty Greene, the richest woman in the world, "had a face to stop the town clock." Sometimes we would figure out on what tiny percentage of their income we would consider ourselves rich.

While the humble routine of our days lent a certain security, I learned early that my life was not an easy, carefree one. First of all there was Papa. Ordinarily his conduct was fairly typical of a hard-working family man. Surely it was not his fault that his long hours of work excluded him from home life. Sometimes he was better-natured, even jolly, and our spirits lightened. Then he would sing a little song:

> O, Mrs. McSauley, she'd fine purty twins.
> Two fat little divils they we-ere.

But all this had nothing to do with the outbreaks that occurred at times, eventually forming a permanent pattern, casting a shadow over the home.

Ordinarily, when he came home at night, John would give just a touch to the bell. At times, however, the bell would sound long, hard, insistently.

This was a signal. Mamma would give a start, her face would darken, her forehead contract; the three of us would look at each other apprehensively. Then he would fling the kitchen door open violently, his face flushed, his look wild. If he answered our "Hello, Papa," it would be with a snarl. Or he would brush us aside and stalk straight through the full length of the flat to the front room to sit in a silence loaded with foreboding. We knew now what we were in for: *Papa was mad!* Understanding was beyond us children; my chief reaction at these times was fright.

"Come, children," Mother would say, as she dished up the supper. "Looks like we'll be eating by ourselves tonight."

Trembling, with lumps in our throats, we would gulp down the meal. Mamma would clear the table. Suddenly Papa would spring up yelling and rush back to confront us. A lot of loud rough words came from him. He seemed to be very angry at Mamma, and at us children too, as if he didn't like us and didn't want us there at all. This commotion alternated with periods of silence in which he sat by the front room window. Mamma never answered. Tight-lipped, she would bend over her sewing, her fingers jerking nervously. This would go on far into the night. Ora and I would lie trembling in bed until the early morning, when we might sleep a little.

That was all. It was only one night, and only once in a while. But for days we would go about silently, a stone in our chests, our throats dry. There were no words for this menace, this sudden intrusion of violence into our lives. One afternoon, after one of those terror-filled nights, coming home from school we found Mother looking agitated. She stopped sewing, took off her glasses and wiped them. We saw she had been crying. "I've been thinking. Mebbe I'd do better to take you kids and just leave. Rent one little room downtown where the other poor people live. Mebbe I could manage to support you." We couldn't answer. The matter was never mentioned again. It was clearly unfeasible for her to earn enough or for our education to continue. For her daughters' sake she would have to endure these nights.

Something else concerning Papa affected our life in the most drastic manner. After some months of working regularly, turning over his week's wages to Mamma as the manager of the economy, one day he would come home carrying his tool kit. "I'm laid off. Oh, don't worry. I'll look, I'll find something," he would reassure Mother, always optimistic. With the greatest dispatch, he would go out the next morning to make the rounds of the shops of his trade. Sometimes he found another job. And sometimes he did not. Woodcarving was seasonal even in the best of times.

Mamma would share her worries with us, her efforts to save, the necessity now of doing without needed shoes and nutritious but expensive food like eggs and fresh milk. "I'll try to put in more time on the collars, to earn a little more." Like Mrs. Doll and other neighborhood women, she had for some time been taking in sewing. A downtown factory jobbed out this work to a Mrs. Bell, who in turn jobbed out bundles to her neighbors. Mother did collars and jabots, a then-stylish frill to attach to one's collar front; the work was part machine, part hand sewn. Now Ora and I started to help: I learned to thread needles, Ora sewed a little. Later I also began the hand finishing. The collar had to be pinned to the counterpane. As I sewed, leaning forward to the bed sitting on a little stool, my back would ache, but I felt proud to help Mamma. In good times we children kept what we earned for spending money. In the bad times often this tiny return from the sewing was all we had for food. And the house was always littered with the collars; with so many demands on her, Mamma could not keep it clean. The unkempt house and the collars became part of the bill of grievances when Papa got mad.

When Papa was laid off, finding twelve dollars for rent each month was the big problem. Sometimes in desperation Mother would write her sister Anna Squire in Connecticut, who never failed. At other times, overcoming her pride, she would borrow five dollars from Mrs. Buchsbaum. In those days rents were collected in person by the owner of the building. I can never forget the time our bald, portly landlord, Mr. Cohen, came in on his rounds and sat down. Mamma remained standing by the kitchen door; she had to tell him she didn't have the money. She started to speak, then stopped. I looked up to see her wiping tears from her cheeks with a corner of her apron; then she began uncontrollably to sob. I hid my face in her long skirts and cried with her. Mr. Cohen got up abruptly, muttered something, and left. It was thanks to the charity of this good man that we were allowed to be in arrears for months at a time.

"Laid off, out of work" were the words that menaced our life from the beginning. How many mornings did I open the hall door cautiously in order not to frighten away the fairies who might have left a basket of food for us . . . but there never was even a paper bagful. Later, when religion was firmly implanted in me, how fervent were my prayers. "Please God, please help us, please make someone give Papa a job." Weren't we good people, didn't Mamma go to church every single Sunday?

Eventually there would be a job once more. Debts would be paid, the tension would ease, we could again afford simple luxuries like corned beef and cabbage or beef pot roast for Sunday dinner, jelly and butter on our bread, and milk. Our daily meals were simple enough: bacon gravy over a plateful of hot mealy potatoes, or fried cornmeal mush with stewed beef heart and gravy; in summer a cooked vegetable and a plateful of lettuce leaves with it.

The street was always our second home. The sidewalks of New York—how many lives have been nurtured in this vile yet stimulating setting! Released from the trammels of school we could shout and run. The vacant lots offered air and sunlight as well as space to play. Among the trash, bottles and shards from yesterday's kitchens, grass and weeds grew abundantly, even humble flowers like dandelions and pink knotweed, and those tiny seeds people fed to canaries.

While little boys like Charlie Bolte or cross-eyed Maxie Benz might be part of the girls' games, the big boys like Charlie Doll kept to themselves. For me an unfavorable aura hung about them, reflecting Mother's disparagements: "Little boys are nice, but I don't like *big* boys," as though warning us, with that peculiar furtive look she had when telling something bad about Papa. I never did get to find out what was wrong with the big boys; in any case, they had no appeal.

Besides hopscotch and jacks, the game of follow-master, taking us into unexpected and even dangerous places, was a favorite. I loved also the old singing games of English origin, such as "Have you any bread and wine, for we are the Romans." A favorite was a sad little ballad which began:

> Water, water, wild flower, growing up so high,
> We are all young ladies, and we are sure to die.
> Wild flower, blush for shame,
> Turn your back and tell your beau's name.

Sometimes on Third Avenue, a tall blond man would go by, a Boer from South Africa, as rumor had it. With this romantic background and the strangeness of his appearance, his passing each time was an event. A very big man, erect and proud, he walked bareheaded with long taffy-colored locks hanging down to his shoulders. A large collie on a leash preceded him, the two walking deliberately and with dignity, the man looking always straight ahead as though oblivious to his surroundings. Always the pair would be followed by a group of children, while the rest of us would stare, carried away for the moment into some world other than our own.

Romantic, too, were our feelings when in autumn we might be allowed down after supper. The air held a little nip of cold, the skies above were black, shadows filled the street, and the vacant lots were fearsome. At twilight a man came around with a ladder to light the gas lights. Sticks of carbon would be found by the lamp posts in the morning. Now the lamps cast a mellow glow over the pavement. When the L train roared by we would stand looking up at it, fascinated by the lighted windows and the crowds of people inside coming home from work to those other lights of kitchens and dining rooms which soon would warmly envelop them. Washington Avenue, the next block, was the farthest we were allowed to go after dark. There in a drug store window big globes filled with colored liquids glowed in the radiance of the street lamp with beautiful ruby red, blue, or amber light.

In autumn too came Halloween; no masquerading or begging then, it was just a time for romping and pranks. The boys would run wildly about, marking storefront windows with chalk and swatting the girls with long black stockings, the toes filled with flour or ashes.

Then in November came the election eve bonfires. The boys would save orange crates and other wooden boxes, storing them in the cellar. On election eve the flames rose high; the warmth was good in the chilly air, the sparks sprayed the street. We roasted sweet potatoes in the ashes, and white potatoes we called "mickies." One time Ora and I, forgetting Mother's prohibitions and lured by one fire after another, strayed farther than we had ever gone after dark. Mingled with the sense of adventure of that evening was a warmth of companionship we rarely enjoyed.

It was on Thanksgiving Day that the children went around in costume wearing masks and soliciting treats. Since our mother didn't approve of begging, this was not permitted us.

When winter really came on, how bitter it was to get up in the morning, the windows thick with frost! The stove in the parlor next to our bedroom never had a fire in it except possibly on Sundays. The frost patterns were so beautiful, glistening with blue and golden sparkle as the streetlight hit them. Still, we couldn't linger; grabbing our clothes, we would scurry out to the kitchen where Mother had a coal fire going. Quickly dressed, a dash of water on our faces at the kitchen sink, a dab with the limp gray towel, our long hair braided by Mamma, and we were ready. A slice or two of bread with Karo corn syrup, a cup of cocoa, then bundled up off to school we went. The snow crunching under our feet, our faces tingling, our fingers and toes becoming numb, we would run most of the way.

Fearsome things in the streets spiced our playtime with fancied dangers. Such as the Chinese laundry on Third Avenue, always closed. It was rumored the Chinese stole children, even ate them. On Third Avenue too on winter evenings we went for bundle-wood. Hastily we ran down a flight of steps, with a glimpse into a dark cavernous place, slipped the swarthy Italian man his nickel, and then—squeezing the round flat bundle to our chest—clambered fearfully back up the steep, dark stairs.

Most of all we feared the Rooneys, the Irish couple who were our janitors. They occupied rent-free the worst flat, the first floor rear, a place where not one room ever had sun or even full daylight. Mrs. Rooney cleaned the stairs, mopped the marble floor in the vestibule, polished the glass door and the brass doorknob, and finally swept off the stoop. She was a big powerful woman in a dirty apron and torn sweater, her gray hair pulled back tight into a bun at the back from a broad face often flushed very red. Shaking her broom as she towered above us, she would hurl angry words in a piercing high voice as she chased us off the stoop.

Her husband's share of the work was to tend the hot water boiler in the cellar. He also worked at some job or other, coming in at irregular hours carrying a dinner pail. He wore a shabby brown suit and a slouch hat; an auburn beard covered most of his face. What little could be seen of his skin was dull red. Bushy eyebrows hid his eyes. Rooney never talked; there was never a more silent man than he. Still, we were afraid of him. Was it his red beard, his silence, the aura of liquor that hung about him, or just the fact that he was a *man* . . . ?

Once in a great while when we came home from school, our mother would be out. The doors of our flat were never locked, but how to get in downstairs? Ring some other bell? Oh no! We had been trained to be self-reliant, not to bother people. There was one way: through the cellar. Sometimes Ora would say, "You go down, Peggy. I'll hold your books." Down the narrow flight of steps, littered and dirty, already a close, earthy smell. . . . Shutting the cellar door behind me, I was at once in thick utter darkness. I knew the layout of the place. To the right, partitions dividing the tenants' compartments (we had one where we kept coal in winter, a trunk, and other oddments); to the left a cement wall, which I could touch to guide myself as I walked straight ahead, right hand outstretched. Toward the back at the left was the furnace room. The big question was: *Was Mr. Rooney there?* His hours were uncertain. His liquor odor, and a rank tobacco odor too, hung always about the place. If these Rooney smells were very strong, he was likely to be there. Cautiously, my palms sweating, my heart thumping in my bony little chest, I groped my way in the murky silence. Far ahead, the faintest sort of glimmer indicated the glass panel of the back door, my goal. Now in the open warm space around the furnace the darkness showed a tiny red gleam, I heard a slight creaking sound—his pipe, his chair—! Like one possessed, my heart pounding wildly, I ran. Mr. Rooney never uttered a word, never moved. . . . It was his mere presence that was sheer terror. When at last I could close that

church, with frequent socials where a Scotch woman used to sing "Bonnie Prince Charlie" and a man with a rich baritone would intone "Larboard Watch, Ahoy."

It was in church and Sunday school—and surely I was no more than nine years old—that I had my first love affair. Robert Vollbrecht was a few years older than I and sang in the choir. I first knew my love at a Christmas performance when in his richly-toned voice he read the Bible story of the birth of Christ. His voice thrilled me. Would he ever notice me? A girl named Hazel MacDonald lived right next to the church. I asked her, just to say his name, did she know Robert? "Robbie Vollbrecht? Why, of course . . . We're old friends. Many a time he slept over in my house." What joy, what privilege was hers! . . . and certainly they went to parties and places where a poor child like me was never invited. For years, literally years, I nursed this hopeless, secret love.

Each spring Mother's sister Anna Squire from Bristol, Connecticut, came to visit us. Aunt Anna was a nice lady, better dressed than Mamma, with brown hair and eyes and a space between her front teeth. A dressmaker, she came to purchase materials and check the fashions. When she came Papa was banished to a chair and bolster bed in the parlor. The two women would stay awake very late whispering as they lay in bed together. For a week everything was in a hubbub with trips downtown and constant talk about dressmaking problems and materials such as serge and worsted, outing flannel and canton flannel, of dimity and voile, lawn and organdy, gingham and percale, unbleached muslin, plush and velveteen; of linings, plackets, guimpes and yokes, selvages and bias, and tailor tacks.

Once while she was there I exploded a paper bag "balloon." When Mother's heart started to palpitate at the loud bang, Aunt Anna took her little sister Nellie on her lap to comfort her, shooting an exasperated look at me. "Oh, that child!" I felt she didn't like me, only Ora. I retreated to the slate-fronted washtub in the kitchen and chalked a picture of a child with wings that was Ora, labeled "Angel" and a queer little thing that was me, labeled "Slop Jar."

In those early days sometimes I used to run away from home. Some nameless hurt, some obscure feeling of being unappreciated, a wish to punish those who didn't love me enough, would send me off thinking, now they'll see how they can get along without me! Once I went to the park and walked farther than I had ever gone. Always there was the expectation that something would happen—the old fairy-godmother myth—to resolve the situation.

Another time the outcome was rather comical. It was a winter evening when I put on my things and left without a word. I remember the dark, completely empty streets. It was cold, and I walked fast, speeded by the motor of my own passions, again expecting supernatural intervention. I had got as far as the Presbyterian Church, some four blocks away, when nature rather than supernature intervened. I needed to urinate. Even with not a soul in sight, not for anything would I do such a thing in the street. I turned and ran home at top speed. Later, defeated but unrepentant, I was standing alone in the dark by the bedroom window when Mother came and put her arm around my shoulder. "Can't you think," she asked gently, "how bad Mother feels when her little girl runs off like that? What makes you do it?" Though I was sorry I had hurt her, I could not answer, for I did not know why, having no words for the obscure turmoil that was within me.

I was a generally docile child, but capable of perverseness at times. Some impulse beyond my control would take hold of me, which seemed almost to belong to someone else. Once I refused Mother's request to pick up my toys before supper. As disobedience could not go unpunished, she tied me under the table. The feelings that filled me then, nameless as always, would probably be called frustration and childish rage. Did Mother weaken? Probably not; her discipline was firm, though not extreme. She rejected her own mother's literal following of Solomon's edict, "Spare the rod and spoil the child." When I had swallowed my pride and said I was sorry (it was only for having got myself into this fix), she untied me. To Mother this second self in me was a little devil that I must try to subdue.

Her big problem, which she considered uniquely hers, was that her two children were so different. "What can anybody do if they have two that are complete opposites?" Ora was aggressive, assertive, demanding. I was secretive but of strong feeling, usually good-natured, shy, and affectionate. Of course, Ora and I fought. Mother would gently say, when we screamed at each other, "A soft answer turneth away wrath, but grievous words stir up anger." To soothe us she might recite a poem I loved very much:

> Backward, turn backward, oh time in thy flight.
> Make me a child again just for tonight.
> Mother, come back from the echoless shore.
> Hold me again in your arms as of yore.

My sister Ora's "spells" were a mysterious occurrence of those early years. She would be lying on the big bed with her eyes open, humming, yet plainly unaware of her surroundings. Mrs. Doll would be called in to confer. Should they apply a cold compress to her head or a hot water bottle to her feet? Eventually Ora would come out of her spell.

For everyone in that building a doctor was the last resort. Mother kept a big, shabby green "Doctor Book" on the top shelf of the kitchen cupboard supposedly out of reach of little hands. It was a complete illustrated work on anatomy with diagnoses of common ills. She also had Dr. Humphrey's Specific Remedies, tiny white pellets in little numbered bottles. A catalog directed which to take for various ailments from scarlet fever to dysmenorrhea. Dissolved in water, the pills all had the same sweetish taste.

In the spring we took a pungent mixture of sulfur and molasses to "purify the blood." Father drank sassafras tea all his life. As a laxative we took licorice powder in water or chewed licorice sticks. As a skin emollient a piece of mutton tallow wrapped in a soiled piece of paper was kept in the kitchen cabinet. A hot water soak for feet and a mustard plaster on the chest were routine for colds. Witch hazel relieved small injuries. Mother used to tell how her own mother's cure for all ills was the bitter herb boneset brewed into a tea. God knows what ailments we really had . . . we did survive, after all. Mother was diagnostician, practitioner, and nurse.

One thing we always loved was for Mother to tell about her family, the Tuttles. "Now I want you children to understand that we aren't just ordinary people. We're descended from Irish kings named Tuthill. Then the family lived a long time in England. Young John and Elizabeth Tuttle came here in 1635, in a ship called the Planter, to the New Haven Colony. Later on Tuttles owned the land where Yale College now stands. Then in 1848 Orris Tuttle went out to Illinois and plowed virgin prairie and cut down trees to build a farm."

"Tell us about the Indians, Mamma."

"Well sir, I was born in Camden, in Oneida County, New York. One of our ancestors, Noah Tuttle, came there with the first settlers in 1795. There was an Indian reservation nearby; we learned things from them, like plants good to eat, wintergreen berries, dockweed, and purslane (they called it 'pusley'). They had a way of putting on a shawl over the forehead and folded down over the cheeks and neck.

"When I was ten we moved out to Iowa. Then it was all the West. We went by railroad but people still were going in wagons—prairie schooners we called them. We lived in Orient, Iowa, just a little place. People plowed virgin land; we called it "paraira." There was prairie dogs there in burrows underground, and prairie hens. Houses were far apart; if you wanted to go someplace you just jumped on a horse. Grandmother Tuttle rode horseback in her eighties. If she'd ever see one of us girls slumping over she'd tap us on the shoulder and say, 'Try and be as straight as Grandma is anyway.' "

We loved the family picture album with the uncles and grandfathers in their long beards. There was Grandma Amelia Tuttle Crawford, with her hair slicked back and eyes penetrating as gimlets. She ran a strict religious household with daily Bible reading and prayers. "Our father was kind and good, but our mother would meet us at the door after school to lay out work for us. That wasn't all. She'd come into our bedroom at night and beat us and often we didn't know what for. 'You know what you did,' she'd say. I made up my mind then, if I ever had children, I wouldn't be cruel to them." Another photograph showed Grandmother with her four girls. Already touched with the melancholia that started with her menopause, she looked gloomy indeed. The three older sisters were stiff, grim-faced, like her. Our mother, the youngest, on the other hand was round-cheeked, clear-eyed, a fine-looking girl.

As for Papa's background, we used to have an old musket standing in a corner of the front bedroom which had belonged to Papa's father, who had fought in the Civil War. Enlisting very young as a drummer boy to avoid having his age checked, he had said he was born in Germany (it was really New York City). Every month Papa went to the lodge meeting of the Sons of Veterans of the Civil War. He too had been born in New York City, but his family later moved to Washington, New Jersey, and finally Bristol, Connecticut. Papa's mother had been born in Hamilton, Canada, where many Germans lived who came over in 1848. She had come down to Connecticut at age ten all alone from Hamilton. Her maiden name was Schelling, and we sometimes went to see Papa's cousins of that name who lived in Highbridge.

Grade school settled into a dull routine, relieved by a few bright spots such as weekly cooking lessons. We learned basic sewing right at our desks, but Mother taught us much more at home: embroidery, knitting, crocheting, running our foot-powered Singer sewing machine. Handwriting was my weak point; countless times I was kept after school to copy sentences, but it never helped. Geography was fascinating; I mused over the names . . . Susquehanna, Monongahela, Siberia, Damascus; above all, the names evoking the brilliant tales of the Arabian Nights, the Gulf of Aden, the Straits of Babel-Mandeb. In reading too and in composition and spelling I shone.

One day I discovered, several blocks from home, a large imposing building with columns at its entrance, overhead a sign saying "Public Library." How did one get to go in and read all the wonderful books that must be in there? "Why don't you ask your teacher?" Mother advised. Approach Teacher, the big lady sitting behind the desk, on such a foreign subject as the library? I could not; the stronger the attraction of the place, the greater my inhibition. Over and over I read the books we had at home: *The Arabian Nights*, Longfellow's *Hiawatha* and *Evangeline*, the

Golden Fairy Book, The Deerslayer, and Holland's tale of colonial days, *The Bay Path.* In the parlor, a plain bare room, uncurtained and uncarpeted, we kept certain special treasures. The large, well-bound copy of Dante's *Purgatory* and *Paradise,* with Gustave Doré illustrations, was a treat to look at on Sunday afternoons. The heavy photo albums filled with Tuttles were here, too, and Mother's well-worn family Bible, with the names of three generations of children scarcely legible on the flyleaf. On the mantelpiece stood two tall plaster casts, one of the Venus de Milo, the other of a Greek athlete; on the wall hung a plaster cherub's head, probably one of Della Robbia's, its wings folded around its curls. Such things were an inspiration to my native artistic bent, and when not reading I was always drawing.

Mother schooled us in strict Protestant values. Beyond rudimentary manners, such as saying please and thank you, or not interrupting while older people talked, she stressed most honesty and keeping one's promises. To distinguish between right and wrong, the fundament of the Protestant conscience, also received great emphasis. The Ten Commandments were another standby. Forgiveness was a Christian virtue constantly stressed. "Love your enemies; be kind unto them that do despitefully use you" was hard to learn. Ora was so mean, how could I have this good sweet feeling toward her?

Sunday school and church were still the high point of the week. Lustily I would join in the hymn singing. My favorite was

> 'Tis midnight and on Olive's brow
> The star is dimmed that lately shone.
> 'Tis midnight in the garden now
> The suffering Savior prays alone.

The final, awe-inspiring lines of one hymn moved me most of all: "When the awful summons hearing/Heaven and earth shall pass away." Infinity and nothingness, dreadful concepts, clashed in those words; for one devastating moment I would get a glimpse of both. Hymns were always with me. Often, of a Sunday evening, I would sit alone in the dark parlor at the rounded corner window that overlooked the L. High above was a patch of distant night sky, with perhaps a few faint stars. As I sang my favorites quietly to myself, I would think of what lay beyond that sky, of God, of infinite space and eternity. I was learning to be philosophical, stoical. Now in the frequent hard moments of my life I would tell myself: this will pass; it must be endured just for the moment.

My sister's resentment of me was part of the pattern into which I was born. While her scornful rejection of me hurt, I responded by fighting her back, returning taunt for taunt, blow for blow. She was two years and nine months older and a lot bigger; still, being nimble and quick I could hold my own in fights and I developed a sarcastic tongue. Poor Mother— our fighting wore her out. "Girls," she would plead, "why can't you be nice to each other? Birds in their little nest agree, but here are you two fighting like wild animals!"

Actually we were not always fighting; interludes of sisterly companionship would occur, on our way to school or the park together. Sometimes when we were little we would lie on the bed tickling each other, exploding in giggles and shrieks of laughter. Craft work was another bond. Besides the perpetual needlework, whenever she could afford to, Mother bought us leather and brass work materials. We also had a narrow loom on which we wove beads. Evenings we would read the same book, alternating chapters.

As my sister and I grew, our sleeping together on the three-quarter-sized bed became impossible. We fought for space and blankets on the cheap, caved-in straw mattress. The solution was removing me to a chair bed. Three chairs were set up side by side at night in the parlor; over them was laid the bolster from the big bed. At first, the bed was dismantled each morning and set up at night, but after a while this got to be too much trouble. Besides, no one ever came into the parlor anyway. We had few visitors; the plain fact was, we were ashamed of our home and couldn't invite anyone.

Mother's big treat was to go once a month to her Ladies' Aid Society at the church. She would do up her hair, dark brown showing a few gray hairs already, in a pompadour with a "rat" inside it, adding her "switch" to the knot at the back. There were still some of the roses in her cheeks, and with her gray-blue eyes and her best dress, to me she looked lovely. Sometimes, one of the ladies would invite the others to her home, but because Mother could never return the invitation, she couldn't go.

What seemed to be the very basis of our lives was the seasonal nature of Papa's employment. How we envied the Buchsbaums, who enjoyed the privilege of a steady job! Mr. Buchsbaum drove a milk wagon; whatever his wage, it was forthcoming every week, year in, year out. In those times $25 a week was considered a good wage or salary for a family. Papa generally received $12 for his long week of 66 hours. There was one factory, however, that paid him $18. I remember well the time they sent someone to call him there. When Mamma answered the knock on the door, the envoy merely said, "They want John to come in tomorrow." What elation, what real joy these few words brought us! When Papa came we were lined

up and Mamma said simply, "I've got good news, John. Soschecht called."
How his face lighted up as he stopped short! She had to repeat every word
of the message.

"Well, I'll have to go back to get my tools," he said, "but I'll hop over
there right away. It's not far; I'll get in a day tomorrow."

"If it'll only hold out a while, I'll be able to save some money,"
Mamma gloated. "We only owe ten dollars on the back rent."

"Maybe we can splurge a little. Do you need a new dress?" he asked
her as we were eating supper. "Get them something new," he added, looking at us children.

During this prosperity period, as a surprise to Papa we renovated the
dining room. We bought a new table spread, all green and gold, soft and
thick, and a cheap cotton rug. We cleaned and polished everything: furniture, floors, windows, the carved oak clock from the Sessions factory in
Bristol where Mamma used to work, the two large engravings of deer in
a snowy scene, the photo of Mamma all dressed up with the other Ladies'
Aid members in its frame hand-carved by Papa. The dining room looked
so lovely that when Papa came in he turned back, actually thinking he
had got into the wrong flat.

The Soschecht job held out for nearly a year, long enough for Mamma
to save up $50, for us a large sum and for her a real triumph. We were
just beginning to feel some ease, some security, some real hope. Then
came that familiar, dreaded day when Papa brought his tools home. So we
fell back into the old on and off rhythm. The $50 had to be reluctantly
given up, bit by bit, for rent and food.

The years brought growth to us children; otherwise they effected
change without improvement. The neighborhood grew but changed for
the worse. Once construction started in earnest, the section quickly lost
its open, semirural character. Drilling and blasting, without which there
is no building in New York, went on apace. The clatter of the drill and
the loud explosions blended with the roar of the L trains, the jangling of
the trolley cars, and the pounding of horses' hooves.

As buildings were finished, they quickly filled with newcomers from
only one source: New York's lower East Side. Our Bronx neighborhood
became a second-stage stop for the immigrants who were then swarming
into the country. They would live first on Rivington Street, Hester Street,
Grand Street, Houston, Delancey, or countless others of those gloomy,
dirty, crowded ratteries. To move to our neighborhood was a big advance.
But in a few years our area too became densely packed, dirty and noisy,
another slum.

Automobiles were beginning to appear; we children followed them, slow as they were, hollering "Get a horse!" The saloon on our corner was gone, to Mother's great relief, though the one across Third Avenue remained. A vegetable store run by Italians took its place, with big counters outside on the street in summer.

The large Third Avenue store of the Great Atlantic and Pacific Tea Company remained, with its delightful smells of coffee, spices, sawdust on the floor, and its beans, crackers, and other staples in great bins. The little store of the Weismans, who gave us credit, remained too. We still had our bakery around the corner, where I would buy an "eight-cent loaf of homemade bread," but cookies were no longer handed out to small children.

Now our old playground, the Third Avenue vacant lot, was filled in by a big tenement building. A fine new candy store displayed its temptations, and next to it was a nickelodeon showing moving pictures for five cents. It was far more thrilling than the Buchsbaums' stereopticon with its flower garden slides. Here people laughed, jumped around, and made faces, actually *moved*, and then a train came right at you. They had stories, too, generally ending in a wedding accompanied by piano music played by a big-bosomed, high-pompadoured young woman.

With the immigrant invasion pushcart peddlers began to clutter Third Avenue under the L tracks. Those with no licenses would look anxiously about and at the first sign of the policeman on the beat would push off. The sidewalks were littered now, there were always people about, screams of children and adult voices added to the general din. Now came the beginnings of hostility. As the immigrants of many European countries swarmed into the neighborhood, fights would break out among the children. The oldtimers banded together to drive out the newcomers with screams of "You dirty Wop!" "Sheeney!" "Dirty Irish Mick!" "Why don't you go back to Hester Street where you came from?" Gone were the old innocent days of our singing games.

The better-off families left. A Jewish family and an Italian family moved into our building. New smells of garlic and olive oil permeated the hallway. In summer the Italians tried to dry cut-up tomatoes and green peppers on the roof. Great was their disappointment when the vegetables simply rotted. When a new baby was born in that family, to my mother's indignation it was bound up in swaddling clothes. There was a mystery concerning the Jewish family. Every Friday a sound of chopping, loud and long-continuing, came from there. What in the world were they doing? We had never heard of gefüllte fish. Was it something connected with their religion? At last they moved away, the mystery unsolved. The solidarity and cooperation that the years had built up among the permanent tenants was strengthened by the worsening of the environment. Misfortune aroused quick sympathy. When Marcelle Doll was sick with typhoid, Mother made ice cream for her. When Frieda Benz was stricken with spinal meningitis and the doctor stayed with her for hours, the building held its breath until the word spread that the child was out of danger.

Crime was not yet part of our immediate world. One evening during my early years, as I was going to bed, a newsboy was bellowing the evening papers down below. "Extry, horrible murder."

"What's a harblemurder, Mamma?"

"It's where somebody kills somebody—oh, it's nothing, he's just trying to sell his papers. Say your prayers and go to sleep."

The Black Hand was something everybody was aware of: a mysterious something lurking one knew not where, referred to with condemnation and awe. Once for several days the newspapers told of a little girl who had disappeared somewhere in lower New York, her body finally discovered stuffed into a chimney. At last crime reached us close by. A man designated as a "Jack the Ripper" attacked several neighborhood women and girls with a knife. We were cautioned in school not to loiter but to run straight home; children living on the other side of Crotona Park were escorted home by a policeman. For a few days until the fellow was caught we enjoyed the biggest sensation of our lives.

Ordinarily, excitement was provided at infrequent intervals by a fire, by someone taken to the hospital, a child run over, a wedding, or a funeral. At such times all the inhabitants of the block would be at their windows, missing no details of the event. "It's better than to go on suffering, if you can't get well." " 'Tis the will of God, 'tis not for us to know all his ways." "She'll never be happier than now." So life was summed up in platitudes full of poignancy for the poor people of that block.

Natural phenomena such as a great electric storm in summer would be a sensation. Ora would be frightened, and Mother, having once been in a building struck by lightning, hated storms, but I always loved them—the heavy winds blowing the heat away, the great flashes of lightning, the loud peals of thunder: all this stirred something very deep in me, a feeling of kinship with the violence of nature, a feeling of wonder and excitement, an intimation of the richness of life.

Once a cloudburst occurred—such a storm as I have never since experienced. In a darkness like night, the water poured down in a solid mass with lurid flashes of lightning and dreadful thunder crashes. Then, at a sudden noise from the hall, Ora and I ran out: the roof door had swung open and a huge stream of water accompanied by a cold wind was pouring down the stairwell. Really frightened now, we rushed for protection to our mother, who was standing white and shaken in the kitchen. "Only your Heavenly Father can help you now, my children," she said solemnly, rolling her eyes ceilingward as she sheltered us in her arms. For a long time afterward damp mold clung to the walls in the hall.

As the building deteriorated, vermin increased. Mice, roaches, and bedbugs were numerous and persistent. Our mother toiled unceasingly, sprinkling powder for the roaches, dousing the beds with kerosene and other evil-smelling liquids. "There's somebody in the place that don't care and won't fight 'em, so we all have to suffer," groaned Mother. In the old days when mice were few, she'd set traps for them, while I in my perversity liked to feed them. I'd put bread crumbs and bits of bacon by the kitchen range. Curled up on the oilcloth, I'd wait for them. Plump, sleek, little gray creatures with their beady eyes, they would nibble at my snack.

Sometimes our trap caught one that had to be beaten to death with the poker, Mother the reluctant executioner. Finally she discovered their hole behind the woodbox and nailed a flattened tin can over it. . . . Everything was so different now.

Mother was becoming more and more worn in the unending struggle against dirt and poverty. The innate gentility and refinement that were part of her New England inheritance were becoming eroded, though never entirely washed away. She didn't put on her hat and gloves in summer any more when she went out. The sewing on the collars continued, year in and year out. Though no pressure was put on us children to help, we still sewed after school. Sunday rest was no longer adhered to.

A heavy chore in those days was the weekly washing. An old copper boiler on the kitchen stove was filled with cold water carried by pails from the sink. The clothes were stuffed into it, half a bar of shredded yellow soap added, a little borax too. A steamy acrid odor soon filled the house. The boiling clothes had to be punched with a gray wooden stick ending in two prongs, then lifted out a little at a time into the dishpan, and dumped for rinsing into one of the washtubs. Ora and I helped as soon as we were old enough.

Rubbing on the washboard was the next stage, a heavy job that Mother always did. One time perhaps she was more tired than usual and some black marks of the bedbugs stained the sheets. Frantically she rubbed, getting more and more nervous and distraught. She was thin and pale now, her hair turning gray, her face already lined. "I ain't no slut," she said as she furiously rubbed. This wasn't the way she talked; she must have meant to express her desperation at this degraded life, at this hopeless trap in which she found herself caught.

Summer evenings we'd go up on the roof to cool off, while the people from the lower floors sat out on the stoop. Summer nights were a punishment in those New York tenements where the bricks held the heat all night. The bedbugs alone could make sleep impossible. I would lie counting my bites.

As we grew older Mother confided more in us. She explained our father's "mad" spells: the Italians he worked with drank wine and sometimes invited him, but not being used to it, he quickly got drunk. She still dwelt on her grievances of Forestville days; John's refusal to carry water from the well, his callousness when the baby was coming, and so on. "Oh, if girls only knew what it is to get married, they'd stay single. That's why I want you girls to be teachers, to have a good steady job so's you can be independent. Aunt Anna was so anxious for me to get married. I was going to have it so fine. Oh, yes, I did have it fine," she would add in bitter recrimination, as though hinting of things too terrible to tell.

Relations between parents are only dimly perceptible to a child. Certain scenes come back: Mamma sitting in the kitchen dejected, Papa smoothing her hair. "What's the matter, Nellie, don't I work hard, don't I bring you all my pennies, all I earn?"

"Yes, but sometimes you speak so cross to me it 'most breaks my heart." Papa abruptly turned away without another word. . . .

Another time, as we came up from the street for supper, Mother met us saying: "Now I want you both to go into the parlor. Papa is there. He feels very bad. As he was coming home he saw some children running to meet their Papa. He feels you don't love him. Go in there and kiss Papa and tell him you love him." She looked agitated, strange and furtive. We went into the parlor, where our father sat motionless by the window, his elbows on his knees, his face buried in his hands. Timidly, wanting so much to comfort him, I put my hand on his shoulder and lightly kissed his forehead. "Papa. . . ." I choked up and couldn't speak. He didn't seem to know we were there.

Another time: Mother, hysterical, overwhelmed by her difficulties, throwing herself on the floor weeping and exclaiming, "Help me, my Father, my punishment is more than I can bear." Mutely I suffered with them at these times, unable either to help or to understand.

Mother's best memories were of her girlhood in Iowa. After grade school she had taken a three-month teacher training course and on the strength of that taught in a little one-room rural school.

She had had a sweetheart there in Iowa, one she really loved. They were engaged. Then they had quarreled, and she had returned East to stay in Bristol, where her sister Anna was already married. The young man had married someone else. In Bristol Nellie had worked in a clock factory. Papa had seen her on the street once; she had such blooming red cheeks, he had said, "That's the girl I'm going to marry." Bringing back these old times would agitate Mamma; we could see her trembling and almost crying as she went on with her sewing.

For all her disparagement of her husband, she had nothing but praise on one subject: John's artistic talent. He had wanted to be an artist, but having no appreciation, his family had put him to work in a factory at age twelve. In a drawer at the bottom of the bedroom closet, Papa had a portfolio full of his drawings. When he was mad, he would drag this out, carry it to the kitchen, and dump it all in the woodbox. Mamma never touched it. It would lie there until a couple of days later when Papa, crushed and shamefaced, would retrieve it and return it to the drawer. Sometimes of a Sunday we were allowed to look at the drawings. One of Benjamin Franklin, which Papa had done when he was twelve years old, we thought was wonderful.

While my father never seemed as close to us as Mother, still there was some companionship, like our clamming excursions to Pelham Bay. We always went there at low tide (Papa checked this in a newspaper), so I saw the beach empty of water, the great naked piles of the pier green with bilge, the exposed jagged rocks brown and slippery. I would take off my shoes and stockings, hiding them among the reeds beside a boulder. With chilled bare feet I would trot along beside Papa on the hard-packed, damp sand. We would proceed slowly watching until somewhere a slender spout of water would arise. Then quick, quick, to run over the wet sand, then to dig with my little shovel, and finally to pull up the treasure, the tightly closed little-neck clam, and drop it into the pail.

Though we talked little on these excursions, there was a comforting feeling of having a father. Papa spoke gently then when he did speak, as though he liked to have me with him. I could almost forget those other times when all he said was so hateful.

In these years, the prepuberty years, curiosity about where babies came from was satisfied not by asking Mamma, who would probably have said, "The stork brings them." I had a better way: the doctor book! It was simply a question of being alone in the house. . . . Quivering with anticipation, I would climb up to the shelf above the kitchen cupboard to drag it down. Now the wicked joy of the forbidden. . . . Thumbing the pages, I would read a little about the stomach or the kidney. But what I really wanted was the part about the uterus, the fetus, the penis, and all those secret things which grown-ups never mentioned. With a nameless feeling of great attraction and excitement, I gloated over the pictures, read a little here and there, never daring to linger very long. . . .

Interest in boys was awakening. I actually used to misspell words in school in a mixed class so that I could sit next to a dark, hook-nosed boy in the rear who liked me and brought me candy. Feelings for girls became warmer too. I became close with one schoolmate, Grace McDermott, a small child with round black curls. She was poor like me; she invited me to her home. Her mother wasn't there; she had to go out working every day. We could understand each other, and when I left, spontaneously we embraced. This friendship was lost when I was skipped a grade for the second time.

My closest friend was always Marcelle Doll, the quiet gentle little girl on the second floor with whom I had grown up. She was more like a sister than Ora, who was becoming increasingly hostile. Once Marcelle and I were walking in Crotona Park after school. "Wilhelmine," she said suddenly, stopping, "Do you know where babies come from?"

Recalling the doctor book, I proceeded to enlighten her. She just stood there in the path, with a look in her deep-set gray eyes as though she had grown older in those few minutes.

"I don't believe it," she said.

"It's true. I read it in a book." Marcelle said nothing more as we walked on.

Then one fine spring day—I may have been ten years old—a group of us girls were rambling in the park of a Saturday morning. One of us picked up a folded sheet of paper with handwriting visible. "A love letter!" she exclaimed. Giggling, we unfolded the sheet and read. It began, "My dearest girl," and described in great detail a sex act. We read looking over each others' shoulders and passing it from hand to hand; we absorbed every word of it. It was shocking for me and for all of us. There had been nothing like this in the doctor book. I had never imagined anything like this. It was at once repulsive and ugly, yet attractive. Every word of it was impressed on my mind; the images, the sensations it evoked took root.

"I bet it's one of those men wrote it. You know, those men that you see . . ." said one of the girls.

I had seen the men too, standing behind trees and wagging something in front of them. Always we ran when we saw one, and were never followed. We didn't know what they were doing or what they wanted.

"Now I believe what you told me, Willie," Marcelle said. We discussed what to do with the letter. It couldn't just be thrown away for someone else to read. Finally we tore it up in little bits and put it in the nearest trash can. That letter I am sure marked an irrevocable step for the children who read it. It marked the end of innocence and with it the end of freedom, of carefree enjoyment of the park. From now on some unknown menace lurked in every corner.

To help out Mother, our Aunt Anna used to take one of us children each year in Bristol for the summer vacation, never both together because we fought so. How dull were the summer months in the years that it was

Ora's turn! I would go down on the street to play with Ethel or Marcelle ...a game of jacks sitting on the dirty curb or listlessly doing our embroidery on the stoop. The humid, bad-smelling air weighed on us like a blanket. It was too hot to walk to the tent in Claremont Park, or even to sit in the nickelodeon—and it cost a whole nickel, too.

My sixth-year vacation had been little more than one long homesickness for my mother. The summer I was eight I broke my arm. On the quiet street of modest homes where the Squires lived were also two fine big homes with vast lawns, trees, and flowers. Here two leading families lived: the Pecks, who were bankers, and the Ingrahams, owners of a clock factory. The playmates of Mary Peck and Dudley Ingraham included Marion Stevenson, Geraldine Barnes, and some other children of workers, and me, waif from a Bronx slum. One evening we were romping over the newly mown lawn, the damp cuttings clinging to our shoes. I tried to run down a steep sloping stone terrace. Then I was on the ground, a sharp pain, my left forearm bent in the middle; I saw the children far away racing toward the Pecks' house. Next I was in the arms of the gardener, who carried me home. How heroically I bore the pain of setting the bones without anesthesia. "A brave little girl," the doctor called me. The next day the Ingrahams' carriage with two beautiful horses and a coachman came to take me out driving. And the Pecks invited me to dinner in their lovely dignified mansion, with the maid cutting my meat for me since my arm was in a sling.

And then at age ten, again my turn in fairyland. I remembered it all: Fall Mountain blue in the distance, the walk up the hill beside Aunt Anna on the familiar street with its lawns and trees, its lovely houses, above all the beautiful quiet that enveloped one so soothingly. . . . The pansies and sweet alyssum in the flower bed were the same, so too the Virginia creeper draped over the basement door. . . .

Uncle Fred, a big lanky bald man with metal-rimmed glasses sliding down on his long nose, got up from his rocking chair in the dining room.

"Hi, Skeezicks!" he exclaimed, bending down to poke me in the ribs, his voice assuming the high falsetto with which people address a pet dog. "She's grown. Looks kinda peaked, don't she?"

"I'm taking her around to Doctor Humphrey first thing in the morning," replied Aunt Anna. Every visit began like this; the doctor would give me a bitter tonic and tell Aunt Anna to fatten me up.

Here I had a bedroom all to myself with the sweet-smelling air coming in through green shutters, mingling with the bathroom odors of Orris root powder and Absorbine Junior that pervaded the top floor. The caroling of robins awoke me in the morning, katydids and crickets soothed me at night. Here was a home where you had cake or pie every single day, home-

made ice cream for Sunday dinner, and shortcake for Sunday supper—
strawberry, raspberry, or peach according to the season. The huge quick-
biscuit crust, hot from the oven, was split and buttered, the chilled sweetened fruit loaded upon it, topped with ladles of whipped cream. Despite
the abundant meals, I still made sneak raids on the pantry when Aunt
Anna was busy upstairs. Just a spoonful of brown sugar out of the jar, a
few walnut meats quickly snatched from the tin box, a sliver of layer cake
(surely she wouldn't notice that little). Hunger was not the motivation
here, nor was it merely the temptation of sweets, but rather the lure of
doing the forbidden.

On the next street lived the little Stone girls. Up the back way climbing a stone wall under basswood trees, then through an orchard murmur-
ous with wasps and bees, where the close warm air smelled of fresh and
rotted fruit, then the berry patch, brambly to slip through, the clothes-
lines, and finally here was Marjorie Stone running to meet me. My own
age, olive-skinned, curly-haired, and dark-eyed, this child was always
aquiver with suppressed excitement.

"Oh, Wilhelmine!" she greeted me joyfully. "Now you're here we
can play Indians again. Oh, we'll have such fun!" We slipped back at
once into our comradeship of two years ago. With her sedate older sister
Marion and a couple of small boys we acted out endless stories. We were
slave children pursued by bloodhounds like Little Eva. We were Indians,
our prairie was the street or the big field next to the Congregational
Church across the way, we fought whites with tomahawks, attacked, took
refuge in our tepees under the porch. Feverishly excited we threw ourselves into these imaginary events. At last, hungry, sweating, and dirty,
hoarse with screaming, we would troop into the kitchen for cookies and
milk. The Stones, rich in my eyes, had a comfortable big house, always
orderly and clean, with carpets, glossy furniture, and pictures. The children had a playroom upstairs for rainy days. Never did I divulge the poverty of my own home.

At the other end of the block of townhouses lived Geraldine Barnes,
nearly three years older than I yet still willing to accept me as a companion. She had ripe red lips and a wealth of curly, golden-brown hair. Sometimes we went up to her room. She showed me a lovely fan wrapped in
tissue paper.

"It comes from Italy. Dudley Ingraham brought it back for me. Have
you got a fellow, Wilhelmine?"

"Yes, his name is Robert."

"Has your mother told you about M yet?"

Remembering the doctor book, I nodded assent.

"Mine is due tomorrow. Oh, it'll come dripping down." Her chin rested in her hand as she leaned on the arm of her chair, her full brown eyes were dreamy and shadowed. "Do you know, Wilhelmine?" she said, suddenly somber. "I think this is an *awful* world."

One Sunday afternoon I made a visit to Grandma Buch . . . a long walk to the shabby outskirts of town, where the streets were not paved and a railroad ran beyond meadows. At last a big house with a white birch tree in front, a broad lawn bordered by flower beds, a group of people laughing and talking in the back. Unable to make up my mind to face these strangers, I walked up and down playing with my braids. At last, overcoming my shyness, I crossed the lawn.

"Why, it's Minnie!" exclaimed Grandma, a small, plain-looking, gray-haired woman who came up warmly to kiss and hug me.

"We just finished the ice cream, but I'll give you a cookie," said Grandma. So I had missed the ice cream! A feeling of inadequacy, a vague indefinable, unwelcome feeling that something was wrong with me dimmed the enjoyment of this cheerful family gathering.

In the morning I helped Grandma care for her flowers, learning their unfamiliar names: calendula, foxglove, Sweet William, gladioli, dahlias, roses, and many more. In the afternoon my Aunt Lillie Newport took me downtown for an ice cream soda at the drugstore where her husband Bert worked. She had a sweet, gentle voice and didn't holler so much as the others; she was blonde and blue-eyed with shiny white teeth and a big nose like Papa's. That day Aunt Emma, who was a singer, came back from a trip. She was brown-eyed, buxom, very lively and bossy. Now the house was all bustle and loud talk. She told racy, funny stories, making us laugh. The parlor, ordinarily a dark room with shutters closed so the furniture wouldn't fade, was opened up; Aunt Emma placed her two trunks full of clothes in there and called me in to see her fancy wardrobe. She went about the house humming scales or talking; sometimes she would sit at the piano and play or lie in the hammock in the back yard. She ordered what she wanted for supper, never helping to make it. At night, since Aunt Emma had the spare room, I slept on a pallet in Grandma's room, a delightful novelty. There was such a hubbub for the couple of days she stayed that it was a relief when she left.

At the Squires' Sunday mornings were given over to churchgoing. Uncle Fred, like Papa, never went to church. Aunt Anna and I walked there in our Sunday finery: I in a new straw hat with flowers and patent leather shoes with straps that had to be fastened with a button hook, all of which she had bought me; she in a feathered hat over her pompadour and a dress that closely hugged her corseted bosom and flowed out behind.

"Always turn your toes out when you walk, Wilhelmine," she instructed me; obediently I adopted this uncomfortable gait. "You'll see Mr. Sessions, the richest man in this town. He donated us the church. I go to sew for the Sessions one week every spring. They treat me like one of the family; they're not stuck up at all! They have such thick carpets, your feet sink into them, and a set of china that cost five hundred dollars. You know their house with the big white columns and the landscaping in front." The Methodist Episcopal Church was much grander than our little church at home. Somewhat overawed I sat in the pew until Aunt Anna whispered, "There he comes," and I craned my neck to watch a fat little man with a round belly strutting down the central aisle. A kewpie doll was what the great Mr. Sessions looked like to me, but not a word of this would I breathe.

Sunday afternoons I would read Aunt Anna's little book on our branch of the Tuttle family. They weren't all farmers; doctors, teachers, and lawyers were among them. I enjoyed the women's names: Patience, Prudence, and Loyalty. Thankful Doolittle, who lived back in the late 1600's, was my favorite. Because one of the ancestors named Smith had fought in the Revolutionary War, Aunt Anna was a member of the local DAR chapter. Once we went to an old cemetery where her organization was restoring the stones. They bore gloomy inscriptions dated back in the 1700's such as:

> As you are now so once was I.
> As I am now so you will be.
> Prepare for death and follow me.

Many little children and babies lay buried there with their parents, and it seemed as though every man had at least two wives, some three or four. The women had to work hard, and had so many children one right after the other. We couldn't have any idea of the hardships they put up with in those days.

Here on the hill where the Squires lived people were all of English origin, and no doubt many had ancestors lying beneath those stones. But the town was filling up with foreigners called "Polacks" and resented by the original Bristolites. They worked in the clock factories and in the New Departure, Mr. Sessions' firm, and lived in the shabby section of town beyond the railroad. Aunt Anna had a Polish woman named Helen come once a week to do the washing. We got up early to prepare to heat the water in the copper boiler and set out the tubs, readying everything for Helen.

But first Mrs. Bross, the lady in the adjoining row house, came over. Her straight dark hair was gathered in a knot at the back, falling in stray locks around her face. Her invalid husband was in a wheelchair and rarely seen. Standing on the steps that led down into the kitchen, arms akimbo, she asked, "Are you going to say anything this time?" The particular sort of smile on her face I understood—Helen was going to have a baby. Seating myself in a low chair in the corner of the dining room out of sight from the kitchen, I began busily to sew a doll's dress.

"Something's got to be done. I think I'll just put it to her very plain," said Aunt Anna. "Now see here, Helen, I don't know what people do where *you* come from, but in this country a woman's got to be *married* before she has children. Now how would that do?"

"That's plain enough. But do you believe she *cares*? And what if the man *won't*? How many has she got already?"

"She said she had two when I hired her. This'll be three. A different father for each one, I presume."

"She's gettin' fatter *an' fatter*". . . . With this both women broke into laughter and then, suddenly lowering their voices, talked in whispers.

Once in a while I would recall home with a letter from Mamma, dutifully answered. And then at last all the sunny, fun-filled weeks had run their course and once more I was on the New York–New Haven and Hartford headed south this time. Every turn of the wheels was robbing me of the flowers and birds, the quiet, the shortcakes, the Indian games, all the delightful things that had been mine. After a while, however, I began to long to see Mother again, to hear her gentle voice. Perhaps even Ora might be a little glad to see me, and I knew Papa would.

Back in our flat, Mother told me to lie down a while before supper. Like a dark cloud, reality overwhelmed me now: Bristol was despairingly far away; the vacation really was gone; here I was back in this dreary flat, my ears assailed with nothing but noise from outside. Yes, back with the bedbugs, the roaches, the kerosene smell, the worries, the skimpy meals. I could see Mamma had cleaned up for my homecoming—bless her heart! —still, it was all so much worse than I remembered. Poor Mamma, how wan and tired she looked, how slow her step as she plodded about the kitchen. In the midst of my depressing thoughts I was beginning to doze off when suddenly Mamma was beside me. "Peggy, why don't you run down and play with the girls before supper," she said. "They'll be glad to see you." I could hear their clear young voices ringing above the street noises.

> A tisket, a tasket,
> A green and yellow basket.
> I wrote a letter to my love
> And on the way I dropped it.
> Dropped it, dropped it. . . .

Eagerly I ran down. Though the girls didn't notice my Connecticut accent, my suntan or my new dress, I knew by their smiles as they hugged me they were glad I was back. So I joined heartily in singing "London Bridge is falling down," walking under the raised arms in my turn. Quickly the old excitement, the old rapture of the street came back. Yes, I was home again—here was my place, here I belonged, and here I was glad to be.

Soon after that Papa lost his job and despite an assiduous search found nothing. So there we were back again in the old slump. Talk of "hard times" was going around; we only knew our own little corner of the world, our street, our building, our flat which continuously deteriorated. The new cheap rug we had bought in better times was now threadbare. The oilcloth for the dining room table was completely worn out, and having no money for a new one, we now spread newspapers over the table for meals. Butter was out of the question; we bought the cheaper margarine, which was white tasteless stuff.

Once we couldn't pay the gas bill; the company shut off our gas. Mamma swore she'd never use gas again, she'd show them! So in the twentieth century in one of the world's largest cities we went back to kerosene. Some old lamps, relics of the Forestville days, were brought up from the cellar. The light was not bad but the lamps were messy to fill, the wicks had to be trimmed. We cooked our meals with a wood fire in the kitchen range. Later on, when we could, we bought a kerosene stove for the summer. Papa was generally sitting around the house in shirtsleeves; coming home from a fruitless search, he would say, "I feel disgusted and discouraged." Mamma was working furiously all day on the collars, Ora and I helping after school. The Dolls were affected also by lack of work. Mrs. Doll, always pale and thin, had become sickly and was coughing; people were saying she had consumption.

Once Mother sent me after school to Weisman's grocery, where we had credit. How much we owed I didn't know; in any case I had no money. I asked for a loaf of bread, a pound of beans, a can of Karo syrup. Mrs. Weisman looked angry, and as she got what I wanted from the shelves with quick jerky movements and put the things in a bag, she gave me what I thought was a terrible scolding.

"You've got to begin to pay something on your bill," she screamed. "My God, I can't go on like this forever. There's nobody in the store has run up a bill like this. You have got to try to pay something."

I stood there as though taking a whipping and left quietly with my package, feeling as though I would like to shrink into nothing, to disappear altogether. As I went out the door, I heard Mr. Weisman, who perhaps had noticed my stricken face, remonstrating with his wife.

Walking home, struggling not to cry, I made up my mind I wouldn't tell Mother . . . to what good? Composing my face, I went home as to a haven. Often, in spite of the poverty and fighting at home, it was a refuge from the greater cruelties of the world outside.

Once more we had to resort to begging letters to Aunt Anna; once more Mother had to put her pride in her pocket and borrow from Mrs. Buchsbaum. One of these occasions remains indelibly with me; it was, in fact, in certain aspects a turning point. It was a fall evening, already dark—I was eleven years old. Standing by the kitchen window I watched Mamma down below crossing the street on her humiliating errand. Looking up toward the night sky over the building opposite, fervently I sent my prayers—those same old prayers—heavenward: "Oh, please, God, please help us! Please make her give Mamma the money. . . ." In the midst of my pleas, something happened. Suddenly I knew I was just *wishing*, wishing very hard for what I couldn't do for myself. The futility of my prayers, the emptiness of those skies overwhelmed me. It was not yet the complete loss of faith; no, God was still there, but unattainable in some remote region of space; cruel, implacable in his unfair decisions, glacial in his indifference to the earnest beseeching of a little girl here below. No, there was no help in Heaven. I would pray no more. Whatever happened would be due to our own efforts, or perhaps just to luck. That was all there was.

As my sister grew into adolescence, she became more and more unmanageable. So far, the strife and fighting between us might have been considered normal. But now Ora was becoming entirely uncooperative; when we were so poor, hardly eating enough, she was loudly demanding clothes, even piano lessons. Her rejection of me was taking on a real hostility. She resisted all Mamma's attempts to control her and Mamma, at her wit's end, would threaten to have her put in a reform school. Ora was in puberty now, her body was developing noticeably and for her that situation involved feelings of shame. When the summer vacation began again, Ora, refusing to go out, moped in the house. She wanted Mamma to buy her a Ferris waist, a special garment for young girls to control the developing figure.

When Aunt Anna arrived for her annual visit, the truth came out, not through open frank discussion but by innuendos, with Ora sulking, Mamma furtive and troubled. At last Nellie spelled it out: "She's ashamed of . . . of what's coming on her in front——"

"Why!" exclaimed Aunt Anna, "Most women want that, they're proud of it. Do you know when I make dresses for flat-chested women they have me put padding in to make them look fuller?" At any rate, the three of them went downtown; the Ferris waist was procured; Ora could go out again. In fact, as it was her turn for the vacation in Bristol, soon afterward she left with Aunt Anna and we had a peaceful interval.

The next year Ora graduated from grade school; it was a hot June day, in spite of which the principal ordered the doors kept shut till the last minute, the children having to stand in the street exposed to the sun. Ora came home really sick, feverish and vomiting. After that she never could stand sun exposure.

For my last year I went to a new school around the corner where the farm used to be. Though I was in a class of girls, boys were about. Girls less shy than I would go up to them and get acquainted. Then one afternoon on the street a small boy ran up beside me and tugged my arm. "Murray wants to see you. He's waiting for you on the corner at Wendover." I stopped. I knew this Murray by sight; he was one of the big boys, and popular. Did he really mean me? I wanted so much tó go. And I didn't go. I walked home alone, regretting that I hadn't gone.

That winter during Christmas vacation a boy cousin from Syracuse visited the Buchsbaum girls. Cyril Cash—what a beautiful name—and how I loved his crisp, curly auburn hair, his eyes of the same color, his freckles, his voice. "Aw, don't hit a fellow *too* hard," he said when I threw a snowball at him. He seemed to like to be near me as we all played together in the lot. Then suddenly one day he was gone and I knew in my heart I would never see him again.

I was growing fast, Mother was always letting down my hems. One day as I was going down the stairs in my middy blouse and pleated skirt, one of the neighbors on a landing said to another, "Willie's growing up." Oh, how tall, how proud I felt as I straightened up in the joy of growing. And the end of the term brought a real triumph: I rated highest in the graduating class; I would be the valedictorian and get a gold medal. Here at last was some reward for Mother's toil and self-denial. The teachers made a fuss over me, kept me after school to brief me on my valedictory address. I was the youngest in the class, the others were thirteen, fourteen, even fifteen. I was still a child, somewhat round-shouldered, flat-chested, and thin, though tall for my age. And when the time came, for reasons I am unable to fathom, Papa went on a tear, one of the worst ever. So we faced our great day with heavy hearts and Mother went alone to see me graduate. I saw her from the platform, but it was all unreal: I was aware of a silvery voice that was my own, of my new white dress trimmed with lace Mother had made, of my long hair flooding down my back, of the ranks of faces all concentrated on me. My address began characteristically with a quotation of poetry:

> Heaven is not reached in a single bound
> But we build the ladder by which we rise. . . .

This episode in a way epitomized my life and myself that far. I had never striven to be first in the class, had indeed never thought of such a thing. Without great effort I had excelled in the subjects I liked, satisfied in my weak areas (chiefly arithmetic and handwriting) to be just passable.

On the verge of going to high school I decided to take my first name Vera, which involved getting rid of the name Wilhelmine and the nicknames Minnie, Peggy, Willie, and Punkin. Since there was little response, I was obliged to carry on a real campaign for weeks, refusing to respond to anything but Vera. Finally I had my way, the old names were heard no more. And then, to my surprise, I missed the nicknames, there was a feeling of real loss. Did I perhaps have an inkling of the affection from many people that had gone into those old pet names? Or was it perhaps my childhood itself upon which I had thus so unthinkingly and so rudely slammed the door? Whatever it was, I could not turn back, I could only go forward now as best I might.

2

Triumph and Disaster

With my sister already in Hunter High, and with my mother determined for us to train as teachers in Hunter College, I had no choice. Secretly I had longed to go to coeducational Morris High in the Bronx where a few girls in my class were going, though most of them got working papers and started their working life at fourteen or fifteen.

I couldn't even mention Morris High: by a quiet, persistent propaganda my mother had created an atmosphere that precluded certain subjects; boys especially were taboo. Papa's idea of sending me to Cooper Union Art School, my talent for drawing having always been rated exceptional, was simply suppressed in the same way.

Hunter High offered the beginnings of a good academic education, which stressed the humanities rather than science, although we did have some introduction to botany, zoology, and physics. Not merely for a year or two but throughout the four years, we had daily Latin and French, and something of art history, not to mention English. I liked Latin but French was fascinating. I would take French books from the library when I knew less than a quarter of the words and could just vaguely follow the story. The languages created a certain bond between my sister and me: we'd practice them together. Attending Hunter also let us see more of the city, since, having no building of its own, the school held classes in public schools in various parts of New York. We didn't really mind having no gymnasium, lunchroom, library, auditorium, or laboratory, for in spite of these shortcomings Hunter was stimulating.

Strange to say, when the boys were no longer around they were not missed. Quickly I found my place among the twenty or twenty-five girls of my class, all a little older than I and most, judging by their clothes and manners, from a more affluent social class. Among the few poor girls was

Pauline Horwitt, who soon became my closest friend. She was intelligent, alert, lively, and communicative. A comparative newcomer, born in Russia of Jewish parents, she had struggled with her family as they went from the lower East Side to an apartment in the Bronx around 149th Street. With me Pauline could improve her English and in spite of the barbaric backwardness of my home, could learn something of American ways. For me, contact with the more emotional, communicative Horwitt family would open up a new horizon beyond the narrow, repressed Presbyterianism of my own home.

Pauline, not in the least shy as I was, also linked us up with the lovely Beatrice Piccirilli, the center of a group of genteel, well-dressed Catholic girls. Beatrice—Bice to us—was beautiful without vanity, intelligent though not studious, gentle, gracious, and kind. No wonder she was unanimously elected class president, while I was quite glad and content to be chosen vice president. Thus we continued throughout the four years.

With Pauline's help the great mystery of the public library was soon solved. At last I found myself in that Mecca of books, shelves full of many I had wanted to read and many never yet heard of—all mine now! Charles Dickens, George Eliot, Sir Walter Scott, Nathaniel Hawthorne, James Fenimore Cooper, Edgar Allan Poe, Victor Hugo . . . all these treasures and more I could possess at last.

Now the old days of play in the streets were no more. Some of the girls were getting too old: my sister a high school sophomore, Nellie Buchsbaum in a secretarial course, her sister Ethel apprenticed to the bookbinding trade, and Marcelle Doll nursing her mother. But this was not all. A mystifying turn of events of a year earlier had given my sister and me a taste of social injustice of a very personal sort. A girl named Maude Geach started it. Her family had moved into the neighborhood two years before. She was a black-haired, brown-eyed girl about my age; her parents were English and served as janitors in a building around the corner. Maude and I used to play in a little enclosed courtyard, a quiet, cool place behind their ground-floor flat. Now one day, when I went outside as usual after school, Maude came around the corner. I ran up, greeting her. She stopped, looking at me coldly. "I can't play with you, Wilhelmine. My mother said I'm not allowed to play with you any more." She turned and ran away. What had I done? What had happened? I was absolutely dismayed.

A sort of boycott was organized in the street against Ora and me, for what reason we had no idea. Marcelle did not participate nor did the Buchsbaum girls. Ethel said once, "They seem to have a grudge against you and Ora around here." I couldn't explain. A grayness had settled over

the street and within my heart. At any rate the street now became just a
passage between those two wholly unconnected parts of my life: school
and home.

My father's joblessness continuing, our poverty became a thing to be
borne like some secret disgrace, certainly impossible to confide to those
well-to-do girls at school. Often my interest in the classes enabled me to
forget for a time the gnawing of my empty stomach, my breakfast of just
a slice of bread being long gone. Come lunchtime, the girls would spread
ample packages of lunch out on top of their desks. Big fat sandwiches of
roast beef, ham, or peanut butter, stalks of celery, a tomato or pickle, even
a hard-boiled egg, and a piece of cake or a cookie wrapped in waxed paper;
finally a piece of fruit.

I would hide my tiny package in my lap under the desk as I un-
wrapped it so that they wouldn't see how little I had. As slowly as possible I would munch my sandwich of two thin slices of white bread with
apple jelly or Karo corn syrup between. Sometimes there would be two
sandwiches, generally only one; sometimes an apple, sometimes not.
That was all.

Truly, I ate my bread in bitterness and humiliation, ashamed of my
poverty, smarting at every exposure of it. Sometimes it seemed to me I
was crying inside, my food flavored by those unseen tears. There was
never enough to fill my stomach. No one said anything. Pauline was
poor too, but her father could work steadily as a rabbi in a slaughterhouse
and she had a bigger lunch than mine. Sometimes after eating, the girls
would go out for an ice cream soda, or would bring back Hershey bars.
When they offered me a piece, out of pity or politeness perhaps, I would
eat it gratefully like some dog snatching a fallen morsel.

While I had never been talkative, I now became taciturn, withdrawn.
One of the girls said to me once, "We were talking about you—everyone
thinks you're so smart, Vera. You're so wonderful in French, and oh, they
wouldn't want to be you. . . ." I felt the first part of this remark was made
just in order to add the last part. And perhaps I didn't want to be me
either, that part of me that had to listen to such disparaging remarks.

Coming home at four o'clock—oh so hungry!—I would cut myself a
slice of bread in the kitchen. Mother, sewing at the dining room table,
would give a quiet, quick look, the meaning of which I well understood.
She was hungry too, but she wouldn't take a slice; the loaf had to be
stretched as long as possible. The slice did not, in any case, relieve the
permanent gnawing inside me. Feeling very tired, I would sit down by
the window with a book to try to lose myself in a story. But often food
fantasies took control. The foods I most craved were not the good, solid
things like beef stew, pork chops, or baked beans. It was sweets I most
longed for, daydreaming of the Third Avenue bakery and candy store,

imagining myself devouring the chocolate layer cakes, coconut cakes, the jelly rolls and charlotte russes; or, again, the candies—chocolate cream drops, walnut creams, fudge, and caramels. . . . Daydreams fill no empty stomach. They can, however, momentarily produce a hollow and very transient sort of delight.

For two whole years my father had not a stroke of work. How we survived is hard to tell. I believe our mother would literally rather have died than have asked for charity, the only public recourse in those days. She persevered; her daughters must not be taken out of school. We lived, as the Spanish say, by the grace of God: hungry, sick from hunger, borrowing, using every possible means we could find.

Little by little we pawned what few things we had of value: a gold brooch, a wedding present from Aunt Anna; Grandfather Buch's Civil War musket; some good pieces of Grandmother Crawford's silverware. At last the wedding ring, a thick, solid gold band, was all that was left. Mother pleaded; she hated to give it up. And Father argued to convince her: it was all they had, we couldn't all starve, he would try hard to redeem it. When the time came, there was nothing to redeem it with. Mother wept quietly for a few days. And then one day there appeared on her finger another, fancier ring with stones. I wanted to ask where it came from, but she looked so grim it was not possible to approach her.

We seemed to have reached absolute rock bottom. One day Mamma had no money at all to buy supper with, not one cent. She looked in the cupboard; it was bare.

She sent me over to Mrs. Bell, the lady from whom she got the collars. "Just say, 'Mamma wants to know can she lend me a dollar on the bundle—I'll have it finished soon.'" Mrs. Bell lived near by on Third Avenue in an interior flat where only the front room was light. She let me into the gas-lit dining room, a cavernous room stacked with boxes and bundles. She was a big tall woman with what seemed to me a stern look.

"Why, no, I can't do anything like that," she snapped without hesitation. "I don't get paid anything myself till the bundles are finished. And I have to spend carfare and time taking them downtown. No, just bring me the bundle when it's done and you'll get your money."

As I went down the stairs, I wanted so badly to cry. Should I have begged, told her we were hungry, didn't have money for food? I also had my pride. And she looked so hard and businesslike. Everything seemed so final. I forced back my tears, wiping my eyes on my sleeve.

Mamma looked again in the cupboard, found a bit of flour in the bottom of a bag. "There's something called salt-rising bread," she said. "I'll see if I can remember how to make it."

The little loaf nicely browned was placed on a plate in the middle of the table. Papa, coming home exhausted from fruitless tramping, stalked without a word through the flat to sit down by the front window, letting his head sink into his hands in a familiar attitude of despair. The three of us ate our small meal in silence.

In the midst of the prevailing gloom, I felt a certain excitement. We seemed to have reached the very end: beyond . . . darkness. Were we actually going to starve to death? And what would that be like? And what would Mrs. Bell say when she heard about our deaths? And the girls at school?

Finally, as a last resort, Mother got a job as a machine operator in the factory that gave out the work to Mrs. Bell. I believe her wage was $5 a week to start. How empty the flat was now in the afternoon! Loneliness lurked in every corner. I would do the marketing, make the beds and tidy up, have the potatoes on to boil and the table set when Mamma would come home, tired but full of stories of what the boss had said and what the forelady had said and what she herself had said. Apparently she enjoyed this brief interlude away from the home.

About this time a letter came from Bristol announcing that Grandmother Buch had died of a leaking heart valve. Her loss cut me deeply; I had really loved this kindly, earthy little old lady of sixty-two, to me all bound up with her flowers, the vegetables she grew in her garden, plum jelly on my bread, and so many other wholesome considerate things. She was someone who would always be there.

But the letter also contained Grandmother's legacy to Papa—a check for $50. When Papa saw it he broke into a terrible rage, directed this time not at us but at those stinkers his brothers and sisters. Tony was the worst, the one who never married, stayed at home to be waited on by his poor mother, worked on her to turn her against John. No, for him the furniture factory at age twelve; all his wages went into paying for that house in Bristol. If there was any partiality shown *he* should have got more, or at any rate the house should be shared equally by all. Papa stormed: send them back their goddamn stinking crumb, he would choke on it, send it back to that rat Tony. While we all had nothing but sympathy for Papa in this crisis, Mother refused to send the $50 back.

Soon afterward came some clothes of Grandma's, some materials, laces, and ribbons. A big crate later held an organ, a mandolin, and a guitar, all made by Uncle Ed. Were these guilt offerings? We set up the organ in the parlor; I played it sometimes since I could read notes. The mandolin fell to me, Ora had the guitar. We already had a zither, and making music, however amateurishly, was a solace at times.

At last, at long last, the tide turned: Papa got a job again. Loaded with debts, our resources drained, our health impaired, we could at last resume something like normal living. In fact, never again did we fall quite so low as that time. Sometime later, by dint of buying new tools and practicing at home with lettering books, John worked his way into another trade: wood engraving. In limited use in those days for the production of theater posters, it was as seasonal as carving; but having now two strings to his bow, Father could do better. The new trade had its hazards: in doing something called "heavy routing" Papa sustained a rupture and had to wear a truss. It was during these years that I was moved from my chair bed and from then on slept with Mamma in the big bed, Papa being relegated to the chairs in the front room and later to a canvas cot set up at night in the dining room. At that age I had no inkling of what this change implied in the relationship between my parents.

One Saturday in springtime, Mamma, Ora, and I were in the dining room with the windows open. Suddenly we found a moth on the window sill, a lovely large moth. We carried it over to the table to admire it as it walked about exploring. It had feelers with branches like ferns and a wingspread of five inches. Its soft brown, lavender, and yellow wings were glossy as though it were newly hatched. Whence did it come, from what fairer world than this, how had it found its way to this shabby, grubby room in the slum? How we loved this moth! And then, and then—yes, I killed it. It would be such a splendid "specimen." I was taking zoology at the time; we were studying insects; in my collection were some beetles and a small monarch butterfly fastened with pins in a box. Yes, I killed our moth. I put it on a piece of cardboard, daubed its head with formaldehyde, and stuck a pin through its body. It struggled for a while, its wings flapping up and down, until at last the lovely wings were still.

Science . . . it was all done in the name of science. Today I find no forgiveness for this deed. Oh, the many selves that rise to confront one . . . how we would like to repudiate them, and the fact that we hesitated, committed the act with reluctance, is no atonement. It was done, and done by me. That could not be changed.

The Dolls had now moved around the corner on Washington Avenue. Mrs. Doll lay all day in a hammock. When I would visit, it was hard to see her shrunken and so pale. I didn't know what to say, but her face would light up as she held my hand. And Marcelle would stand quietly by the hammock, pale and thin too. Mother had told me Mrs. Doll had said that she hated to die leaving Marcelle alone with those two brutes, her father and her brother. Now of all the old tenants in our building, only we and the Rooneys remained. Mr. Rooney had gone through the years unchanged, but Mrs. Rooney had long since abandoned her vociferous struggle to keep her stoop clean and clear of kids. She and Mother were fast friends.

I spent all my spare time now with Pauline. Her home, a poor home too, was much barer and cleaner than ours. The board floors, scrubbed and gray, were uncovered. On the green painted walls no pictures hung. There were none of the oddments, calendars, souvenirs, crocheted doilies and such which, added to Mamma's sewing, were a constant clutter in our flat. The Horwitts had a minimum of furniture, and in the bedroom some hooks on the walls held a few clothes.

But their flat was always full of people. In a corner of the parlor, beside a big bookcase full of ancient volumes, Pauline's father, with a long beard and a skullcap on his head, would sometimes be bent over a book on a table. Her mother was always there either cooking or bringing someone coffee. Besides Pauline there was an older brother studying to be a doctor; Anna, a nurse; and two younger children still at home. Another older sister, Rebecca, was practicing dentistry and had her own apartment. Married sister Edith lived in Far Rockaway. All these people were so full of vitality and warmth, so good-humored and talkative, the apartment brimmed with life. I, quiet as usual, observed and liked them all.

Whenever of a Friday afternoon Pauline and I would be out somewhere after school, she would leave abruptly to run home. The whole family had to be home by sundown for the beginning of Sabbath, Pauline a little earlier to scrub all the floors by hand on her knees. She used to tell how the family clustered around the dinner table, with the house very clean and with candles lighted—what a feeling of peace and closeness, what a happy glow they would experience.

I managed to keep from bringing Pauline to my home as long as possible, but at last she came. She ran around in her usual uninhibited way, poking into everything, including Mamma's sewing. Mamma said afterward this girl was too "forward"—a real stigma of disapproval in our world. Eventually she got used to Pauline and liked her. Similarly, Pauline told me later her parents said at first, "Why can't you have a Jewish friend? This Christian girl will find a boy for herself, then she'll forget all about you." As the years passed without this dire prophecy coming true, I believe the family became really fond of me.

As themes for our English classes, Pauline used to write stories she remembered from Russia, old fairy stories such as "How the Bear Lost His Tail." She would tell of the dreadful pogroms against the Jews. Big sister Rebecca, a woman of ready sympathy, had been a member of a secret revolutionary organization opposed to the czar; they had to sign their names in blood when they joined. Sister Edith sang Russian songs in a rich, vibrant voice; these songs were charged with longing, with regret and poignant feeling like nothing I had ever heard. One was about the Golden Steppes, another an old Russian prisoners' song beginning, *Sol-*

nzye zachodit y nachodit—The sun rises and sets. These songs moved me deeply.

For the first time I was being initiated into the life of the foreign-born in our country, which until now I had seen only from the native point of view, from my father's rantings against the Italians, the complaints and slurs in Bristol against the Polacks, most of all the invasion of our own neighborhood and its deterioration. Now I discovered in myself a fund of sympathy that went out readily to a group that had experienced real oppression.

Once Pauline and I went on a sort of rescue mission to the lower East Side to fetch two little girls whose mother was sick in the hospital. At last I saw the inside of one of those grim old buildings glimpsed from the L on childhood outings. This family of three lived in two rooms: the kitchen, a large bare room with a cook stove, a table, and three chairs; and the other room, holding just a big bed. The children were ready with their little bundle and we took them uptown, placing them with relatives. The next day Pauline told me Masha, the older one, had liked me very much. "But how can such a nice girl be a *Goy?*" she had asked. I was learning there were other points of view than mine.

In due course Pauline's sister Rebecca gave birth to a baby, which opened up new opportunity for us both. In exchange for our minding the baby while she tended patients, Becky gave us Russian lessons. With delight I learned the new alphabet, mastered without difficulty the strange sounds, the clusters of consonants and vowels nonexistent in any language I had met so far. Becky gave me paper books intended for Russian children, one a primer with pictures and big letters, the other fairy stories, one of which I remember particularly, *Zolotaya Ribka*, "The Golden Fish."

As we grew up together, Pauline and I explored and criticized our religious beliefs. This was complicated for me by the role of Jesus Christ. In my early years I had admired the courageous Christian missionaries who carried the word of the Savior over the earth. Eventually when I was about thirteen came a realization: many millions of people had lived and died never hearing one word about the man born to be their savior. The crying injustice of this fate overwhelmed me. The unfairness of God I had experienced in my own life, but in such a fundamental question as this, and on so massive a scale . . . ? My Sunday school teacher could only tell me we cannot expect to understand all of God's mysteries, we must have faith notwithstanding.

For Pauline the beginnings of disbelief came when she first heard or saw the English translation of the synagogue ritual: how sonorous in Hebrew, how mysterious it had sounded, how it had inspired her as she sat beside her mother in the gallery! Reduced to English, it became so

stage in a resplendent emerald green gown and walk about, voluptuously swaying her hips as she sang:

> Has anybody here seen Kelly?
> His hair is red, his eyes are blue,
> He is Irish through and through,
> Kelly with the green necktie!

As substitute romances, girls had crushes on their teachers. Pauline's crush was an English teacher, a spinster who loved Greek so much she gave a voluntary course in ancient Greek after school hours, which we of course took. She advised once in confidence: "Get married, Pauline, by all means, get married." My own romantic object was Mlle. Charvet, a rather swarthy Meridionale who was an outstanding French teacher.

One episode of high school days totally out of character for me was nevertheless revealing. Our math teacher, Miss Kromak, was a thin, flat-chested, bony-faced woman who used to wear mannish flannel shirt-waists. Since math was my *bête noire*, perhaps my lack of enthusiasm for the subject leaked over onto Miss Kromak; while she was writing algebraic formulae on the board I used to pass around unflattering but life-like sketches of her. One day when Miss Kromak was absent no substitute was sent. A holiday atmosphere of freedom and restlessness prevailed. Then one of the girls suddenly jumped up shouting "Let's fix her, girls!" Running to the blackboard, she began marking it up with chalk. A few others quickly joined in, throwing the things off Miss Kromak's desk. Without hesitation I entered into the fray, running, shouting, and tossing things about. I climbed up on one of the desks and with another girl took down everything that was on top of the corner closet—books, boxes of chalk, blackboard erasers, etc.—and spread them around the room. As I was engaged in this disorderly conduct, Agnes Mackin, she of the luxuriant blond curls and pretty dresses, said to me reproachfully, "You don't look like what you are, Vera." I enjoyed the whole escapade tremendously. Of my own accord I would not have initiated such a prank, yet I threw myself into it completely. The excitement and release of it linked up with the old days of play on the street, the adventurous follow-master, the Indian games with Marjorie Stone in Bristol, the wild joy of election night fires, all that was stimulating in my street life. Something that had become buried in me came to life, though the episode was an isolated one.

In the later high school years, with the cooperation of Pauline and her family, I found a better way to earn money than sewing: teaching English to foreigners. My pupils were Russian Jewish women, dentists, friends of sister Rebecca. One I remember especially, a friendly, dumpy, shiny-faced woman, Anushka Gottlieb, who used to serve tea in glasses with raspberry jam. Another had two big growing sons named Vasha and Abrasha, who bowed deeply from the waist whenever I came in. My teaching continued off and on, whenever a pupil would turn up, for years, and led to an increasing group of Russian friends with whom I maintained contact for a long time.

Sometime during this period Mrs. Doll died. The funeral was held in the dining room of their flat where the hammock used to be. Now she lay in her coffin on top of a table, her sharp bony features scarcely recognizable. Marcelle, all in black and very sad, was like a shadow beside her mother. The rooms were crowded with people. The perfume of the flowers was overpowering. It was my first funeral and I believe I cried. It was all a dream: Mrs. Doll had been so long a-dying that it didn't seem so very different for her to be laid away under the ground.

Later Marcelle came to see us, greatly changed. She looked a little less thin, sad as ever, but lovely as she had not been before. Her face was a perfect oval, her skin was olive-colored, and her heavy eyelashes shadowed gray eyes that had a new light in them. She told us she was engaged now (she was just sixteen) and would marry her cousin Marcel, an athletic-looking young man whom we had seen a few times. Later on we heard that she was married and had gone to live in some other part of the city. So this first friend passed forever out of my life.

Hunter High School had no graduation exercises because we went directly into Hunter College. We did, however, have a little party at school, and a committee gave an appropriate nickname to every girl. Mine was "Half-sister to the Sphinx." Naturally, I couldn't welcome a name like that. I suppose, after all, Full Stomach can never understand Empty Stomach. Empty may have the compensation of thinking that as the world is now constituted probably the majority of human beings are in his boat, giving him a better insight into life, a poor consolation at best.

By slow degrees I was growing up. The summer I was sixteen, a half-year before the graduation, Mamma, Ora, and I together went to Bristol for a vacation. We girls would go out for long walks, outside the town through the farm country, sometimes climbing Fall Mountain. One Sunday all of us including Aunt Anna and Uncle Fred went to Lake Compounce. As we were coming down the hill, we passed two boys standing beside the path. One of them smiled at me, I smiled back, and as our eyes met I had a wonderful new feeling. I loitered behind the others and the boy and I smiled again. I kept looking back to prolong this lovely feeling. It was a revelation; I seemed to sense what love was all about and why people went so crazy over each other.

After that there were no more boys, and education was to occupy the chief place in my life for some years longer.

The old Hunter College building at 67th and Lexington, red-bricked and ivy-covered in the midst of its lawns, became my second home for the next four years. At one end of the old building was a big auditorium with galleries known as the chapel. The old rooms overflowed with young women and the halls echoed with their clear youthful voices. To me, the college was a romantic place, a place for the living if not the fulfillment of dreams.

A dream indeed it was, a four-year-long dream. College was one world; home and all I knew from my childhood was another world; there was no link between the two. Equally disconnected from the world at large was our Hunter education. Then with the great conflict of World War I approaching, our courses even in history were irrelevant, so much oriented to the past that we had no basis for understanding either the causes or the significance of this global war. Political awareness was completely lacking. It is possible that some socialists may have been clustered in an economics major. If they were around, one heard nothing from them.

History courses led always to disappointment. The long array of kings, of presidents or emperors or pharaohs, their dates of birth and death, the terms of their reigns to be memorized, their battles and their wars . . . dates were erected like a grille separating me from what I really wanted to know: how did people live in the past? Of this only a little paragraph here and there could be found. A cluster of subjects prepared those who expected to teach, which included most of us: pedagogy, psychology, history of education. Of the first of these not one solitary item can I recall. Psychology in those naive pre-Freudian days was a comparatively simple matter. Novelists and dramatists were the chief psychologists then (they were also the sociologists), and they didn't do such a bad job.

Our one year of science offered the alternatives of chemistry, biology, or geology. My choice was the history of the earth. I enjoyed especially being shown a diagram of a cross-section of rocks and giving an interpretation of what had happened there. Immense convulsions, titanic shifts of rock layers, earthquakes, volcanic overflows from the fiery inner core, vast inland seas appearing and disappearing, mountain ranges tossed up and slowly eroded: here was drama on a colossal scale.

Physical education was conspicuous by its absence; like the high school, the college didn't have a gymnasium. The sole indicator of any body-awareness was a compulsory course for freshmen in physiology and hygiene. Elocution was another required course and was held in the big empty chapel. Projecting our voices with the diaphragm muscles, we had to make ourselves heard all the way to the back where the teacher stood.

> An Austrian Army awfully arrayed
> Boldly by battery besieged Belgrade.
> Cossacks commanding cannonading come
> Dealing destruction's devastating doom . . .

and so on through the alphabet. This voice training actually was to stand me in good stead in the undreamed-of future.

French, in which I majored, was organized by Professor Bargy, department head, according to a unique system since adopted by many colleges throughout the United States. Students of all years were under the same program, moving from one period of literature to another, term by term. Joint lectures brought out the historical background of literary works being taken in class, with occasional dramatic performances by the students (I took part in some of them). Only French was spoken; three of our teachers were graduates of the highly rated Ecole Normale Supérieure of Paris. The French method of *explication de texte* was adhered to: each student in turn had to sit in the teacher's place and give in French an explanation of a page or two from a book being studied.

In a French composition course Professor Bargy himself gave us training in thinking that we got nowhere else. He was a short, wiry man of about forty-five with a full black beard and roving eyes. His remarks were incisive.

M. Jean Ducros, a shy young Frenchman and a dedicated teacher, gave us a noncredit French–Latin class based on Lucretius' *De Rerum Naturae.*

I had made up my mind to study art and had registered for a watercolor class. In the rear of the big studio a kindly, middle-aged woman of ample figure put me to work on a still life. "Use plenty of water" was her only direction. Wallowing in water and color for an hour brought no result but frustration. Ask the teacher for help? Not me. I simply dropped out. I did, however, take all the excellent art history courses the college offered.

With pride I recall marching in a woman's suffrage parade. It may have been in 1915. I didn't belong to the movement; probably the suffragettes appealed to students to join the march. With a number of classmates I waited in a side street to enter, then at last marched down Fifth Avenue, exultant to be part of such an inspiring, forward-looking movement.

When Professor Blanche Colton Williams came to criticize the first batch of papers turned in for her short story course, she read mine to the class. "Every once in a while," she said, "a student turns up whose work stands out from the general run of stories written by amateurs. The manner of telling this little story holds one; you feel as though you want to continue reading it. That is to a certain degree a test. You can write, Miss Buch."

Hadn't I always wanted to write, scribbling little stories as a child, always getting praise in school for my compositions? Now this teacher's estimation confirmed a hitherto undefined urge, encouraged a resolve in the back of my mind that a writer was what I wanted to be, not a teacher.

Our little circle from high school went into the French department together. Soon Bice and her friends received bids from a sorority. Pauline and I, left out, didn't mind too much. We were here for an education, and side by side we went on. Our circle of friends broadened. With us in the French classes was a blonde, fuzzy-haired, blue-eyed girl named Tehilla Hirschensohn. Invited to spend a weekend at her home in Hoboken, I found an intellectual family of Palestinian Jews, Hebrew their native language. The father was a rabbi, two older sisters were graduates of the Sorbonne, a brother was studying engineering, and Tamar, older than Tehilla, was also in the French department at Hunter. A young French teacher, Dolores Toledano, became a close friend, as well as witty, sophisticated Ida Greenhauser.

Though my sister was in college too, we rarely came in contact. Her major was Latin, her minor science. Professor Helen Tanzer, head of the Ancient Languages department was probably Ora's crush, and Ora was much dominated by this woman, not to her own good as it turned out. One of my sister's friends was mine too: Rose Kantor, a Russian Jewish girl who looked as Japanese as anyone could, the little epicanthic eyes, the small flat features, the coarse straight black hair. Rose was an orphan; though she had an uncle and aunt (Dyadya and Tyetya) in New York, she lived an entirely independent life in a rented room. Her wardrobe consisted of a skirt and one blouse, which she would wash out every night and iron in the morning. She was an ebullient, talkative person, uninhibited and tactless. Under her influence I started going to the Sunday afternoon concerts in Carnegie Hall, sitting in the top gallery.

Afternoons after classes we girls, proud to be New Yorkers, would stroll down Fifth Avenue enjoying the store windows and the galleries. Saturdays we used to spend in the big reference room of the central public library at 42nd Street and Fifth Avenue. A few tables away a young man used to sit, rather small, dark-skinned, with black hair, dark eyes, and an aquiline nose. I was quickly attracted and imagined I was in love with this person. What outlet did we have after all for our developing womanly feelings?

One time Ida Greenhauser and I remained after classes in a room in the old college. As we talked of all sorts of things we felt more and more drawn to each other, until spontaneously in a moment of tenderness we embraced. It was a revelation that we could feel so strongly. A few of the girls including Bice had young men friends, but for most of us the college might as well have been a nunnery. Still, we were not rebellious about this or any other question. Marriage was something for the far-away future.

Since I had dropped out of church and Sunday school, my opportunities for social life were confined to the college. Once the Alliance Française gave a party in a hotel for students. I made myself a new dress for the occasion. Recently, when I had given an *explication de texte*, M. Ducros had said, "Vous parlez couramment et avec beaucoup de charme" ("You speak fluently and very charmingly"); Pauline thought this meant I could be attractive to a man. I might dance with M. Ducros—but I didn't know how to dance! Sure enough, when we tried it, after a few awkward moments of my treading on his toes and he on mine, embarrassed he said, "Mais il me semble que nous ne dansons pas de la même manière" ("It seems to me we are not dancing in the same way"). All my latent inferiority overwhelmed me. Seventeen years old and never did and never would know how to act socially. How could I ever face M. Ducros in class? And why hadn't I let Papa see my new dress? He had asked to as I was leaving and rudely I had answered I didn't have time....

Pauline couldn't wait to get out and become a teacher in order to help her family. I wanted to help mine too but never quite faced the fact of becoming a teacher. Teachers seemed for the most part drab creatures confined to a dull routine. Beyond graduation lay a blank in my mind.

The dichotomy of my life of school and home continued. It was like a set of cards printed on both sides: the one in cheerful colors in designs for the most part decipherable, the other somber, of murky intricate patterns often beyond my power to interpret. Though our poverty was less than it had been—we were eating enough now—it was still out of the question for us to quit the slum. The blight of Papa's "mad" spells continued. Now he used to rave about how he had been a slave to females all his life: "the good mother, the good wife ... *and* the good daughters." Always there resulted the same shock, the same sick feeling reaching to the pit of my stomach, the dread and the aftermath of depression.

I would try to analyze the various cross-currents of the strife, the anger and fighting, the bitterness that underlay it all. Papa was not understandable because the hatred and resentment that he spewed out when mad contradicted his usual behavior. At times he showed tenderness for Mamma. That she did not like him was plain enough, although she would take his part if any injustice were involved. Ora and I never got along. Try to be nice to her, she would take advantage of you; try to be tough, she could out-tough you any time. Ora, as a matter of fact, didn't get along with anyone. Rose told me she was losing all her friends. She dominated Mamma by sheer noise and persistence in getting what she wanted. Between Ora and Papa there was more and more antagonism. Only Mamma and I got along pretty well. Papa and I got along but had no closeness. It was all beyond my grasp. Unsolvable contradictions, all of our lives. . . .

Once we were sitting at the dining room table after supper, my mother, my father, and I. Here we were, still in this same shabby room with the streaked engravings of the deer and Mamma's Ladies' Aid picture on the faded dirty wallpaper, the old crash and roar of the L trains coming through the open windows. Papa was in shirt-sleeves, Mamma in a faded cotton dress. How careworn they looked, though not old, their faces lined, their hands heavy with toil. Torn with love and pity at the same time, I thought what hope have I ever to get out of this trap, how can I ever rise higher than they? As a matter of fact I was to get out of that slum sooner than I knew, by means completely unforeseen. But before that, a few more turns of the wheel. . . .

It was during my upper sophomore term that something rewarding happened. A contest was held for all French students of the United States and Canada, run by the *Société Nationale des Professeurs Français*, offering twelve prizes. There was a translation from English to French (*version*) and an original composition in French on the subject of some book recently read. Mine was on Alphonse Daudet's *Jack*. With so many prizes, I hoped I might win one. I was really quite unprepared for what happened. Three first prizes were mine; as I had been judged first in both *version* and composition, the first honor prize was mine also. This was really unprecedented. In the separate contest for seniors Tamar Hirschensohn won a trip to Paris and a course at the Sorbonne! Of the twelve prizes nine went to Hunter students. Pauline had a second prize; so did Ida Greenhauser, Katherine Kümmerle, and Ethel Lifschitz. When our awards were presented to us in a chapel assembly of the full college, the president said as he handed me my prizes: "Miss Buch looks perfectly satisfied." There was a big silver gilt (*vermeil*) medal, a big French dictionary, and a book, *Alsace Française*.

It was good that I had this one taste of success. For me there was to be no more achievement for a long time to come—a very different fate awaited me. Even then, though I did not know it, my life was already locked into a declining plane that before long would lead to complete collapse.

Now my friends were preparing to go to Paris. Besides Tamar, the senior prizewinner, Pauline was going and also Katherine Kümmerle, Ida Greenhauser, and Pearl Epstein as well as Dolores, who went abroad every summer with her mother. They all bought themselves chic new suits and hats; all they talked of now was Paris. Pauline asked, "Can't your aunt advance you the money?" Her sister Becky was staking her. I knew it was out of the question. I made myself a new spring suit, but it didn't have the fit and the style of theirs. I felt lonely and left out.

What was more, I wasn't feeling well at all that spring. I had been tired for so long I had forgotten what it was like not to be tired. The other girls would complain about my lack of pep as though it were some defect of character. Now I was getting to feel weak also and at times feverish. Some menstrual difficulties developed, and at last, after some prodding, I got Mamma to take me to a doctor. We found a woman, Dr. Nancy Jennison, tall, thin, with graying hair and a young face, gracious in manner. She gave me a thorough physical examination, something I never before in my life had had. "I can't find the spot in her lungs, but I know it's there," she said after she had gone over every inch of my chest with her stethoscope. There was the loss of weight, the fatigue and weakness, the telltale afternoon temperature. Now for the first time I heard the word *tuberculosis* applied to myself. She recommended complete bed rest for the summer. "And she must eat," she cautioned Mother. "Get all the food and milk into her you can. We've got to build up her resistance. Then we'll see."

So my friends went off to Europe and I went to bed. I spent the days lying in Ora's bed. Mother would bring me my meals, a plentiful breakfast, for lunch a big steak or the equivalent, potatoes and vegetables twice a day. Luckily Papa was working, we could afford this. Though all this good food should have been a treat for one undernourished so long, my appetite had absolutely and completely disappeared. Food was tasteless. I simply forced down all those meals. A strange thing, this loss of appetite when everything depended on food. It is as though the organism had already given up its struggle against the invaders, only the will, the intelligence forced it to continue to fight. And what was this strange blank in my mind about my future, when all the others were so full of plans? Was it perhaps the sick lungs sending messages too obscure for the brain to interpret, telling it there would be no future? During that summer World War I broke out. Exciting letters would come from my friends, aliens in a country at war, who were having novel experiences. Everything seemed remote from my sickbed.

Near the end of the summer Mother and I went for a two-week vacation to a farm in the Catskills. Except for going to Bristol, this was the first vacation we ever had. Here we were out in the open country with fragrant fields, pine woods, and hills in the background. We could see the stars at night and hear the crickets and whippoorwills. At first I could only sit on the porch; later I went for short walks.

A young man at the boarding house looked nice. How did one get acquainted with a young man? There must be some magic formula, some special things to say, which I didn't know. We were not the only guests. Among the others was Hannah Wylie—around sixty-five, vigorous and stocky, a little masculine in appearance. "Nana Wylie," as everyone called her, was the center of every gathering. She told stories, she made jokes, she laughed and made other people laugh. She was different from anyone I had ever known—versatile, sophisticated, rather cynical in some respects—and had traveled a little in Europe. She fascinated me. We went for short walks in the woods together. She loved trees, as I did, and we would stop while she patted a sturdy trunk, exclaiming on the strength, the durability. An attraction grew between us.

So this was my first love affair, my introduction to the love life. At night I would slip out of the room Mother and I shared, hoping she was asleep. She never said anything. There was a great poignancy in my feelings as I climbed the stairs to those clandestine night rendezvous with a glimpse through the landing window of the great star-spangled sky, an impression of the soft night sounds of the woods outside. For long afterward a whiff of the perfume she used would bring it all back. Her story was of an unhappy marriage. "He was a brute. Once I happened to stand behind him at the table with a knife in my hand. I wanted to kill him. Any jury would have let me go scot free." He used to have rages at regular intervals; she called this "his menstrual period." In the stifling narrowness of a small Pennsylvania town she had made her home a center for theatrical troupes that came through in the winter; she loved the stage people. She had had three children, had lost a little girl. To give some excuse for the affection between us, she told my mother I resembled this lost daughter. She said men and women were alike to her as far as sexual relations were concerned. Her theory was that personality was the real attracting force between people, not sex. What did I know, novice that I was?

Our two weeks over, Mother and I went back to New York. Dr. Jennison examined me again. I had gained a little weight, felt a little better. I told her how I wanted to finish college and get my degree. Though dubious she finally consented provided I follow a strict regime: bed every night at 9 P.M., as little study as possible, good meals.

My life now had a new center: an apartment opposite Morningside Park where Mrs. Wylie lived with her unmarried sister, who was rarely there. There I would run after school, often staying for supper. She took me out to concerts, treated me to the opera—to the whole Ring Cycle, Wagner being a favorite of hers. The nine o'clock bedtime was often ignored.

Actually my horizons were greatly broadened by this friendship: I met new people and acquired a little worldly wisdom. It was during this year, too, that I took up Italian with an elderly Italian man whom I met in Morningside Park. So good was my pronunciation, he refused to believe I was a beginner. With old-fashioned courtliness, he would bow deeply and kiss my hand on arrival and departure.

During this time, my junior year, my health deteriorated. I was losing weight again. Once Papa took hold of my wrist saying, "Your hands are like bird claws." My voice developed a constant huskiness. I had begun a singing course the previous spring, not with illusions that I had a voice, but simply for some contact with music. The teacher said my voice had a natural sweet quality. But now I could barely speak, much less sing. She urged me to go to a doctor; I soon dropped out of her class.

My sister had graduated the previous June. Not having taken any pedagogical courses, she was not qualified to teach. Miss Tanzer, the head of the library, took her on as an assistant. Mother told her that her first month's wages would be hers but after that she must contribute half her pay to the household. Ora had to leave home early; from the time she got up in the morning until she left was one continuous shriek. Mamma would stand ready at the kitchen door, in one hand a glass of water, in the other a clothes brush. While Miss Ora downed the water, Mamma brushed her coat. Never a thank-you either. When at last the door closed behind her, a blessed peace descended. Once when Ora was on the L platform with a couple of her friends Papa came up there. She wouldn't greet him, she turned away. We learned of this when Papa came home and exploded. Mamma and I were wholeheartedly with him that time as Mamma tried to make her daughter understand what a shameful thing she had done.

The college was dreary now with Professor Bargy and the other two male teachers gone to war. After a few months I received a letter from France, from a little town in the Gars Department. The father of Jean Ducros wrote that his son had been killed by a bullet in the head.

At last this long difficult year came to an end. Most of my friends graduated then; I was to continue for the full four years, which meant one more term. During the vacation I got a job in a little school downtown for about six weeks, the Jane Tricha English–Greek School. The students were mostly young Greeks. One of them wanted me to go to Coney Island with him Sunday. When I refused, I heard him muttering under his breath "Snob." I couldn't tell him I needed to rest on Sundays or that, never having been out with a young man, I was afraid.

The last term in college I went through "on a wing and a prayer." Often I was obliged to cut classes in order to go home early and rest. One night when I went to bed something came up in my mouth. It tasted like blood. I swallowed it, but more kept coming up until my mouth was full. I got up and ran to the kitchen to spit it out in the sink—bright red, frothy blood. A trail of red spots was on the kitchen floor. Papa, sitting by the dining room table, looked astonished but didn't say anything. The next day Mamma telephoned Dr. Jennison, but she was out on a confinement case so we went to a Russian doctor around the corner. After some questions he took my skinny wrist between two fingers: "My dear leetle girl," he said, "do you theenk you should be so theen? Rest a week and come back." I rested a while, but I didn't go back.

One day in December someone came from the college library to tell me my sister had been taken very sick, had vomited, was feverish, and had gone home in a taxicab. I hurried home at once. Mother had called in a neighborhood doctor. My sister had pneumonia; she was seriously ill and would have to be watched around the clock. I took the night shift.

Staying up all night was a novel situation, something I had never done before. After a time the street noises would die down, leaving only the occasional roar of an L train. We seemed to be alone in the world, we two, with my light in the parlor, Ora in her alcove bedroom, the black night outside. There was not much to do for her: an occasional drink of water, a cold compress on her forehead, her medicine on time. I entertained myself and kept awake by reading and reciting poetry—French, English, German, even Latin.

Then one night came a sudden new voice from the bed, a quiet gentle voice saying, "I won't have any Christmas present for you this year, Peggy." I rushed in to tell my sister that didn't matter at all, all that mattered was for her to get well. That little remark was a revelation—it seemed to tell me that underneath all her meanness and fighting she did have a little love for me after all. I cherished that remark, trying to keep it with me even when she reverted to her usual ways.

Finally came a change. She had been quiet but all at once she was talking in a loud, garbled way: something about her blanket. Her forehead was hot. I tried to reassure her, her blanket was right here, she was all right. She looked wild, her face flushed, her hair all awry, her eyes glittering. Now she was trying to get out of bed; someone was tying her blanket around the post in the hall. I struggled till I got her flat on the bed and sat down on top of her, pinning down her arms. We remained so until she quieted down. Later she seemed to be sleeping. I felt her forehead; it was cool and dry. She had passed the crisis and would get well.

Now at last as the end of my last term at Hunter approached, I made an effort to face my situation. I was graduating. I would have that degree. I would have to get a job as a teacher. I didn't feel *able* to go out and look, much less to work at an energy-draining job like teaching. I had been ill and tired for so long that the condition had come to be second nature. How could I tell Mamma I couldn't teach when this had been the dream for which she had worked and sacrificed for so long? Feeling I must in some way gain time, put off the conclusive step, I wrote my aunt in Bristol asking for a loan of $100 so that I could register for a course at Columbia. With the money I registered for a philosophy course. Ever since I had liberated myself I had always wanted to know the meaning of man's life on earth, our destiny, the meaning of history, of my own life. Perhaps in a philosophy course the enigma of life would be solved. But I never got to go to that course.

At last graduation came. In spite of a rather depressed general mood, there was some solid satisfaction in receiving that diploma. On the whole I had done pretty well. Though my cutting of classes the last term had lowered my grades somewhat, I was an honor student and had won a prize of $50 for greatest progress in French. There had been much inspiration, many rewarding friendships, many happy hours in that old building.

But when the great moment was over, when I went home with my diploma, I experienced a complete let-down. Now I knew that I was very sick; there was no ignoring it any more; this was all now that had to be faced. Hardly able to walk out on the street any more, I went again with Mamma to Dr. Jennison, whom I hadn't seen since the previous fall. When she heard about the hemorrhages, she wanted to know why she hadn't been notified. I would have to go to a sanatorium.

I left her office relieved. The situation was out of my hands now. No longer would I have to drag myself around half-dead trying to perform like a normal person; no longer did I have to worry about becoming a teacher. . . . After some inquiries Dr. Jennison found there would be a vacancy in Stony Wold Sanatorium in the Adirondacks, but not until April. There were examinations, forms to fill out, interviews. For the two-month waiting period I sat all day in our front room wrapped in blankets with the windows open.

It was during this interval that a letter came from Claudine Gray, acting head of the French department, asking me to come down to teach a class in the Model School. I knew what this meant; I was being considered for the college staff. I had to write Miss Gray that I was ill and couldn't possibly teach.

At last to be able to rest. . . . For the most part I felt at peace. Once in a while the awareness would come over me like a cold shower: I have tuberculosis; people die of this. I would think of my friends hearing of my death. Now they would see that having no pep wasn't my fault; they shouldn't have blamed me. And poor Mother! And I would repeat to myself John Keats's words:

> Still wouldst thou sing, and I have ears in vain,
> To thy high requiem become a sod.

Dr. Jennison took up with my mother the financial arrangements. Because the sanatorium was subsidized by private endowment, the fee was just five dollars a week. Even this could be covered by one of the ladies' auxiliaries. My mother at once rejected that notion. Not while she was able to push a needle, no, she would earn the money, her daughter didn't have to accept charity. It was a girls' sanatorium, only girls would be there she told me reassuringly. Of course, I thought, but actually I don't believe I minded too much this time. I didn't have the energy to think of finding a lover. To get well was my only goal. The doctor had said it would take six months at least. Surely in that length of time I could be cured.

3

A Very Special Club

A SPRAWLING L-SHAPED BUILDING, A SNOW-COVERED LAWN SLOPING DOWN TO the shores of Lake Kushaqua opposite the high reaches of Whiteface Mountain, and all about the great Adirondack woods: this was Stony Wold.

Here, after fifteen years as a student, in the boarding-school atmosphere of this hospital I had to adjust to a new identity as "patient." Never could we forget the hospital: the white-clad nurses with their trays of thermometers, the disinfectant odor, a whole ward of bed patients on the second floor of the main wing, the examinations, the sputum cup that we kept always with us. In that pre-antibiotic period, rest, fresh air, and food to build up the patient's natural resistance were the chief treatment at a time when TB was the number one killer.

Except for Dr. Lent, the head physician, two male assistant doctors, a couple of handymen, and the keeper of the commissary, the place abounded with females, chiefly between the ages of eighteen and thirty. It was rumored that the doctors and perhaps the nurses too were TBs— who else would take a job in such a remote, isolated place? The superintendent, a plump, elderly little woman, inhabited an office on the second floor and was rarely seen.

Because the first day of acclimatization had to be spent indoors, I sat alone nearly all day in the big lounge with its many tables and chairs, its wide windows. The tiny railroad station was opposite, beyond it the head doctor's cottage, and close by a little chapel. The snow fell quietly outside on a landscape already white. From the chapel came chimes every quarter hour.

Starting the cure in the afternoon of the second day, wrapped up in an ankle-length fur coat which had been issued me, a woolen horse blanket Mother had provided, and calf-high, sheepskin-lined boots bought at the commissary, I found myself one in a long row of young women similarly tucked and bundled up in canvas reclining chairs, drinking in the pure Adirondack air. A row of beds was there too for those sleeping out.

Evenings, we gathered either in the lounge or around the fireplace in the library, getting acquainted, reading, or writing letters. Generally two or three of the bed patients would be allowed down for an hour. One of them was going to have pneumothorax: a new surgical technique still experimental. A portion of rib was cut out, and the bad lung was collapsed. Later, if healed, it could be inflated again. This patient, languid, pale, wraith-like with lustrous dark eyes in a delicately-featured face, reminded me of some night-blooming lily coming out only for an hour.

Mornings at seven o'clock chattering young women gathered in the washroom. Sponging our chests daily with cold water was supposed to strengthen us. As I stood in a booth at the wash basin, stripped to the waist, the dark red curtains drawn behind me, the light overhead threw a shocking image in the mirror. Every rib could be counted on my skinny chest. (I only weighed one hundred pounds.) At these moments I would feel overwhelmed . . . What would become of me? On all sides I was hearing of chronic cases who went from one sanatorium to another, always hoping to be cured. One heard too of the other institutions in the state. With a cottage system, Trudeau at Saranac Lake in the Adirondacks was the best, but it was an expensive place. At Raybrook was the state institution, which accommodated both sexes, like Trudeau. In any "san" not one of the bed patients ever died, simply because the institution didn't want a stain on its records, or the inconvenience either: those who got worse were either sent home or transferred to another hospital.

New friendships awaited me here in Stony Wold. Curing next to me was Hansi Weismeyer, a German woman who spoke English poorly, but with what German I could muster we got along. Short and buxom, twenty-eight years old, with clear gray eyes, white teeth, and glossy brown hair, she was lively and talkative, laughed a lot. In Germany she had been married to a man older than herself, and she had a two-year-old child. She had already been in several sanatoria in Germany and Switzerland. She had a good voice and some training in singing, but TB had put an end to her ambition to be an actress. When her husband died, Hansi had come to America; her little daughter was boarding now with strangers in Brooklyn.

At the table with me in the dining room were three Jewish girls who roomed together, Lottie Kantor, Marie Fantusz, and Bertha Eisenstein. We were all about the same age. Only eighteen, Lottie was a really sick girl and often had to stay in bed. She was slender, languid, with almond-shaped brown eyes, ivory-tinted skin, and black hair. Marie, of Hungarian descent, had something of the gypsy in her aquiline nose, small mouth, and heavy-lidded brown eyes. She looked so sad sometimes: was she thinking of her father, who had died last year of the same disease? Bertha Eisenstein, an orphan, had been raised by an aunt. In Bertha there was something warm and motherly: she was the one who tried most to make me feel at home in the "san," who took care of Lottie too when Lottie had to stay in bed. The girls' speech was more frank than any I was accustomed to, a difference I suppose between working girls and students.

In the milk line three times a day I used to see a tall, graceful young woman in a big white Shaker sweater and yellow silk knitted cap: Dorothy Ottoson, a secretary from Brooklyn. Three years older than I, she was engaged to be married. Her gentle voice, her intelligence, and her sympathetic ways attracted me. When she later told me of her family life, how her father had ferocious drunken spells and became so violent that her mother with her two girls had to sit out at night on the back steps for safety, I could then tell her of Papa's rages.

As I slowly improved, in the second month I was allowed a ten-minute walk daily and later still was assigned the dusting of a bed patient's room. Many of the patients were discontented and homesick. They couldn't stand the quiet, the isolation, the monotony. For me to have the sky, the woods, the mountains, to see the sunrise in the morning, to go to bed with the big trees only a few feet away, to hear at night the gentle chiming of the chapel bells—with all this and my new friends I was content. Home seemed far away. I had no perspective beyond the sanatorium, which I hoped would send me home well. There was time for reading and above all for daydreaming.

Spring came slowly to the Adirondacks. At last the snowdrifts settled down; patches of bare earth appeared; buds were swelling. All during the month of April the ice broke up on the lake; gradually swirls of dark water would appear as with loud cracking sounds the ice would split apart until at last the water was free with only a few floes remaining. We shed our fur coats, our horse blankets, our boots. In May came the delicate veil of green over the trees; spring flowers bloomed near the lake. Later we took our chairs out on the lawn to enjoy the sun. It was almost like a vacation now to be at Stony Wold.

Sensitive Dorothy Ottoson shared my enthusiasm for nature. She was deeply religious. When I told her I didn't believe anymore, she found my atheism hard to accept. Finally she concluded that since I loved nature, and since God is in nature, I really was religious though I didn't know it.

After all, how can the true believer admit that people can be good without the faith to which he attributes all that is good in himself?

We were barely aware that Europe was involved in World War I. We had no newspapers; there was no commercial radio yet. For the most part Stony Wold went on its own very special way quite undisturbed in the midst of the woods.

After six months it appeared I was to remain for the full year. I was glad. It was not my decision; as a matter of fact few patients left after six months. Although I had made much improvement, the disease still gave evidence of activity, and after the half-hour walk I was now allowed, I was ready to get back into my chair and rest.

The faces in the dining room changed: Lottie Kantor had been sent to Seaview on Staten Island, where she was now a bed patient. Two new-comers became my friends. Miss Fiano was an Italian woman of good education who had the broad nose and lips of an African; she was tall, with a light brown complexion and fuzzy hair. She had a low-pitched but rather cacophonous voice and spoke in outbursts.

When Miss Fiano was admitted, I happened to be in the head nurse's office. As nurse Horton handed the new patient the usual issue of towels and sputum cup, "Put her in 7," she said to another nurse, who led the new patient away. Then turning to me, she added with a wink, "We'll keep 'em all together." What did she mean? Her remark lingered in my mind, an unsolved puzzle until suddenly one day the reason was clear.

The lower floor of the wing where Miss Fiano was taken was less de-sirable than the upper. It was darkened by a hedge row or fence, the maintenance was not so good, there was noise from the diet kitchen. Be-sides my three Jewish friends there (another Jewish girl had taken Lottie's place), I can remember a Greek woman, a Swede who had been a servant, and a raw-boned, rough-speaking hillbilly from Kentucky. So this was really a segregation scheme. "We'll keep 'em all together,"—the foreign born, the badly educated, the poor! I myself, poor as Job's turkey but hav-ing a college education and native origin, rated a better place. I had to wonder if this was the reason Lottie Kantor was never made a bed pa-tient, which would have given her better care.

Miss Fiano wanted to become a writer and spoke fluent English, French, and Italian. She used to quote Dante's sonorous lines in her native tongue. Never for one moment did she think of herself as anything but an Italian. How could I tell her that here she was a Negro, a subject for dis-crimination, for aversion? It is possible that without me she would have been isolated (needless to say, at that time there were no Negro patients there). I could at least be a sort of buffer for her. We were congenial and often sat in the library talking of an evening. Voluble and gregarious, she would really have suffered had she found herself shunned and alone.

Later on a person came who was to have a decisive influence in my life. Bob Van Patten, a native of Buffalo, New York, and a telegraph operator, was a thin, wiry little woman of thirty-five; with a rather birdlike appearance, she had dark hair, a clear-cut profile, and snapping brown eyes behind big horned-rimmed glasses. She was separated from her husband and had a daughter of fifteen in a convent in New York City. A well-to-do aunt gave Bob a home. (She probably had some other first name, but I knew her only as Bob.) Bob was a Socialist, a member of the Party. Her views were imparted to me bit by bit in passing as we talked of many things. She found in me a responsive listener. It was as though all my life I had waited to hear this. Since college days, with the prop of religion removed, I had merely drifted in an existentialist manner. But now the broken pieces of my life began to fit together in an understandable pattern. Now at last I began to acquire a new basic philosophy as well as the possibility of a new way of living. There was a pattern in human destiny. My father was no longer an unlucky fellow who worked in a seasonal trade; he was a member of the working class and of a union too, though a small one of wood engravers. I became aware of society—of social forces— and especially of the class struggle as the prime mover of history.

Those I had thought of as the idle rich, the Rockefellers, the Morgans, the Vanderbilts, the DuPonts, upon whom I had looked with envy mixed with contempt, I now saw as members of the capitalist class, the minority who owned the means of production. The workers sold their labor power and produced surplus value, source of the capitalist's profit. The workers received enough wages in compensation just to keep them alive and to reproduce their kind so that the capitalists might continue to have workers to exploit. A rudimentary picture and one acquired gradually; still, my conception of society was clearer than it had been before.

"First of all we must get well!" Bob would say as we sat in the lounge of an evening or walked along the road in the woods during an exercise period. "Just wait till we're back in New York. I'll see that you get some real education. As a college graduate, you could do a lot in the movement."

Bob had common sense (good judgment based on contact with real life). She was a realistic, plainspoken person. Often she lamented her lack of sex life. She had had a lover or two after breaking up with her husband. "What I need, what everyone needs," she would say, "is good, regular sexual intercourse." Seeing me shocked or embarrassed, she would lay her hand on mine in a protective, big-sisterly sort of way. "Oh Vera," she would say with a smile bringing out dimples in her flat pale cheeks, "you're so young, so inexperienced." My immaturity was a thorn in the flesh. What did I know, bookworm that I had always been? My one experience of sex was something I couldn't talk about. Of what Bob meant I knew nothing.

Although my life was now completely absorbed in the san as though I had been there always, frequent letters kept me in touch with home and friends. My college mates were fulfilling their lives: Pauline, Tehilla, Ethel Lifschitz, and others were teaching French. Ida and Pearl were secretaries in a French import firm; Beatrice, who had got married upon graduation, had a baby now; Rose Kantor was now Rose Entenberg. And I . . . laid away on a shelf, waiting, dreaming instead of living. If I wanted to be a writer, why didn't I use this leisure to write? When I thought of writing, always I was confronted by how little I knew of life. There were moments of bitterness, but there were moments of fun and relaxation too in what the san offered: boat rides on Lake Kushaqua in summer, sleigh rides through the woods in winter; parties now and then; interludes on Friday afternoons, when we would bathe and then sit around the fireplace, drying our hair.

In late August and September the Adirondack woods were aflame; the maples, oaks, and birches all scarlet, russet, and gold against the deep constant green of the pines, hemlocks, firs, and spruces. Once out walking alone, I broke rules to investigate a certain valley that branched off from the road to which we were restricted. There among the tall evergreens and oaks, on the valley floor and covered with moss lay supine rotted trunks, giants of a past age. I had to climb and pick my way cautiously among them; actually it was a dangerous thing to do. I called the place The Valley of the Dead.

In September, too, the snow began to fall, brief flurries at first. The green slope of Whiteface whitened, the lake was freezing, by mid-November the winter blanket was well established and soon the snowplow had to go through to clear the road. The air was crisp, cold, dry, and perfumed with balsam. We would breathe deeply as we lay again tucked up in fur coats and blankets on our chairs. Actually it was snowing almost every day. Rarely were there windy storms; it was mostly a gentle, constant drifting down of flakes. There was a certain mesmerism in this continuously, quietly falling snow. Blended with it was the sound of the chimes, muffled somewhat by the snow. Regularly, day and night, every quarter hour the little tunes were repeated, sad, monotonous, and meaningless like some voice of fate. There were times when I felt I had always been and always would be there in the snow.

Among the few inhabitants of the region was a man known only as the Hermit. He lived somewhere in the woods, a big burly character bundled in ragged clothes and so dirty and hairy one could hardly know what he really looked like. Once seeing him disappear into the woods, Bob and I had noted the location. We decided to explore that trail another afternoon. It must have been early in the winter for the snow was not yet too deep; it was trampled down over the path, which led us on and on among the thick ranks of the tall trees. We walked a long time without a sign of a hut or any place a man might live, nothing but the serried tree trunks. It was beginning to snow and we felt chilly. Finally we turned back and reached the san so worn out we realized we were not yet fit for high adventure.

I was a veteran now of the place. Most of my friends had left. Dorothy was in Brooklyn preparing to get married. Hansi was there too with her little girl. Marie Fantusz was now a patient in a sanatorium at Bedford Hills, near New York City, where Bertha Eisenstein had a job in the office.

With December began the real winter cold. From 10° to 20° above by day to 10° to 20° below at night was the normal range. Sometimes in the intervals between snows the sun would come out bringing with it glimpses of deep cobalt sky and a blinding glare from the prevailing whiteness. The porches were now draped with a long fringe of icicles. Sleeping out of doors became heroic. My porch was glass-enclosed, but on the big main porch they slept in the open. I had a bunny suit with feet my mother had made for me of some woolly gray material—underneath it underwear and sometimes a sweater. For warming our beds we had a big crockery jar called a "pig," which was filled with hot water. In January it was colder. At night occasionally a loud booming sound resounded in the woods; it was the rocks cracking from the frost.

At last came one night when it was 45° below. There was not much sleeping that night though we did remain in our beds. We were warned not to touch a doorknob or other metal out of doors with bare hands; the skin would be torn off. I went to bed on the porch with six layers of clothing on, several woolen blankets, my fur coat on top, and pig and hot water bottle next to my body. One's breath froze into ice on eyelashes, brows, and any other facial hair.

As the signs of spring began to appear, the end of my term was drawing near. I had gained twenty-five pounds. I had got back my rosy cheeks, Mother's gift to both her girls, and I seemed to feel well. In my final exam, an x-ray (the first they had taken) revealed that not only was the involvement in my right lung more extensive than they had believed, there was also a small spot in the upper left lung. I was discharged as an arrested case, with the advice to continue resting for at least another year.

Returning home after a year's absence was a mixed experience. There were improvements in the environment; in myself perhaps greater changes than I realized had occurred. At last, at long last, with Ora's contribution and Father's better-paid, more steady work in the wood-engraving trade they had left the slum. I returned to a pleasant ground-floor flat in a clean, quiet neighborhood north of Crotona Park. The sanatorium had informed my mother I must have a separate room, so I had a little alcove bedroom off the parlor just big enough to hold a narrow bed they had bought for me, a chair, and a little old commode.

The first evening, as we were sitting reunited at supper, Papa asked for a glass of milk. Mamma said there wasn't enough. After a year in a sanatorium I was a very milk-conscious person. I went to the refrigerator and brought him a glassful. The one fair-sized bedroom of the apartment was occupied now by Mamma and Ora sleeping together in the big bed. Papa had his usual camp cot put up in the dining room. I was beginning to see, as I had not been able to before, the position of this man, the breadwinner, as a sort of second-class citizen in the house. Mamma had written me that John had made a big scene when she had told him they must move. How to account for this?

I had always loved my folks: in absence they were never long out of my mind. There had been frequent letters. When Mamma had written that Papa felt jealous that I only wrote to her I sent him a letter. In his reply were the words "I think the world of you." Actually this was the only verbal expression of love I had ever received from my father; still, there had been a certain communion at times, and I had seen his loyal efforts to find work, his satisfaction and generosity when he did have a job. Once he had bought me an enormous box of pastel crayons, costing much more than he could afford. Yes, I believed Papa loved me. And how could I doubt Mother's love when she had toiled late at night all through that year to earn the five dollars weekly she had to pay for me? Still, returning home I felt like an outsider. Even that first evening Mamma worked as usual on her collars as though nothing had happened. Was it just lack of communication among us? There was something negative, a lack of warmth never really expressed but felt. Finally, some time later, this something came out more overtly.

The ceiling in the bathroom had cracked and weakened. Complaints to the landlord brought no results. One morning, as I stood before the wash basin, suddenly the whole thing came down on me. Besides the shock of the crash, I received numerous bruises, cuts, and scratches on my head, shoulders, and arms. And what did Mamma have to say? It happened that Ora had just taken a bath. Mamma's reaction was and remained: "What would have happened if the ceiling had come down on *her?*" I was hurt and to a certain degree alienated by this misplaced sympathy.

Ora was still working in the Hunter College library and in the evenings studying for a master's degree in geology at New York University. Sundays she would go out on field trips with a group and bring back rock specimens. We could sometimes exchange a few words about some interesting rock formation; otherwise the old hostility continued unabated. She lost no opportunity to warn Mamma how dangerous it was to have me around with my TB germs. As I had no cough nor sputum at the time, her fears were exaggerated. Had she managed to affect Mother during my absence? Perhaps they all felt a grown-up daughter should be contributing to the income. But the doctors in the san had said to rest another year. The freshness I felt while in the Adirondacks soon evaporated; once more I was tired, weak; when the warm weather came I would sit for hours on a park bench. Of course I helped around the house as I had always done. And I did make one attempt to earn money.

With Dolores Toledano I undertook the translation of a typical French novel that was currently a best-seller in France: *Ariane, Jeune Fille Russe.* It was the story of a love relationship between a Russian girl and an older man. The crux of the story was the virginity of the girl, still a vital matter in France at that time. At any rate, while the book was readable enough, it failed to interest publishers here.

While in the sanatorium I had pictured my friends as leading successful, fulfilled lives. ("They have everything, I have nothing.") Actually seeing them now was disillusioning. Pauline and I went a few times to visit the new Rose Kantor, married now to a women's wear salesman. Marriage had effected a remarkable change in Rose. Always having been avid for culture and having filled her spare time with concerts and art exhibits as well as flirtations, she had now settled down into the most assiduous housekeeping. She would be found on her knees scrubbing the kitchen floor with a piece of yellow soap, a big brush, and a huge pail of water, or cleaning windows, or dusting an already clean living room. She cooked copious meals with a big pot of soup, meat, vegetables, always a dish of prunes, cake, and fruit. When her husband came home she would greet him noisily, often with complaints or with a rough reproach that he was late. We could see Ralph, a gentle, retiring soul, withdraw from her. Rose was pregnant: did this account for the change? Pauline and I remonstrated with Rose, who replied disdainfully, "Oh, I know how to handle him!" Of what use three and a half years of college to produce such a result?

Disappointing too was a visit to Beatrice, now Mrs. Miletti, installed in a cozy apartment with her baby daughter. The child had a crust over its scalp which the mother said was a milk crust, it would disappear in time. Bice wore now permanently the look of sadness and resignation that had sometimes in passing shadowed her lovely face as a girl. Later Pauline's sister Anna, the nurse, told me that Bice's husband had "bad blood," a euphemism in those days for V.D. Later still, Bice's baby died, and then she went to the hospital to be, as she said, "all made over." She eventually bore three robust boys, but never ceased to lament the lost little daughter.

Once I went downtown to have lunch at the Hotel George with Ida Greenhauser, with whom I had been quite close in college. While teaching in Philadelphia, she became involved with a married man. They met once in a while in the very hotel where we sat.

There was no political life now, no talk of socialism, a subject foreign to the people I knew. Bob, still in the sanatorium, was no letter writer. However, when the newspapers came out with huge headlines of the Russian Revolution, of the fall of the czar, the flight of the royal family, and all the stirring events of the summer of 1917, I could feel that even far away and remote as it all was, here was something I was involved in too.

At this time the chief solace in my uneasy existence was my TB friends. Really, we all belonged to a club now, a rather strange club in which membership fell to one automatically, the length of our participation being beyond our control. Once I went out to the sanatorium in Bedford Hills, where I found Marie Fantusz still in a curing chair and Bertha Eisenstein a stenographer in the office. Our reunion was a joyful one. As this sanatorium admitted both sexes, Marie had found a lover, a tall, sallow-faced, dark-haired young man, a patient who worked part-time as a helper in the x-ray room. She had met him there a few times after work. "He uses a condom. He needs the biggest size," she confided proudly, adding: "Oh, Vera, it *hurts*. But I mustn't think of it, it makes me want it, and it isn't good for me." Another young woman staying there, Ida Psakis, a chronic case who despite her youth had spent years in various sanatoria, was added to our circle.

Soon after that a letter from Bertha informed me of the death of Lottie Kantor at Seaview. Lottie had never made any progress in fighting the disease; for her, as for many others, it had been a steady decline, a complete wasting away of the body, a "consumption" of the lungs to the end.

Later on in the fall both Marie and Ida returned to their homes, which happened to be in the Bronx not far from mine.

Soon Marie married her Jo; they moved out to a small town in New Jersey, where with the help of parents and friends they set up a little variety store. I visited them once. It was pathetic, with Jo going out to canvass since the store brought in little. Marie was coughing still: the "cure" of two years hadn't helped her much. Sitting at the back of the store as we waited for the customers that did not appear, Marie enlightened me on marriage. "He can't wait for my menstruation to be over, but I make him wait. It's not always good. You have to feel very warm, Vera; otherwise it's no good." And she encouraged me, though I uttered no word of complaint, indeed told little of myself: "Don't worry Vera, you'll find someone . . . with those red cheeks, those blue eyes. . . ."

It was with Ida Psakis, the person then closest to me, that I spent my best hours. I would go several times a week to her home, not far from mine. She was on a complete rest schedule, and she used to lie dressed on her narrow bed next to the window while I sat in a little straight chair beside her. The only other furniture was a battered dresser. From the air-shaft window we could glimpse a section of sky. Here we roamed over many things, books we had read, people we had known, things we had experienced. She had a young male friend whom she called Munya, a doctor at Bedford Sanatorium who spoke Russian. Wistfully she would say: "He'd never want to marry *me*," not needing to tell me why. She had a vivacious face that expressed her every thought and feeling. With a well-rounded body, chubby, rosy cheeks, clear gray eyes, and shining brown hair, she showed no hint of illness. Only a slight blueness around the eyes, a constant huskiness of voice, an infrequent cough, and easy fatigue betrayed her membership in the club. With all our handicaps we had one supreme advantage: youth, which gave us the confidence of a better life some day, someplace, somewhere. . . .

With the spring, as Marie's condition worsened, she gave up her brave attempt to make a living and came home to her mother. Without a word being said it was understood she came home to die. One day as I went up their stairs I met her husband coming down. He was a tall, lanky, awkward man of about twenty-five, with a long nose, full lips and a pale, pimply complexion. Eagerly, half-crying, he began to talk. "They blame me," he said. "They don't know how I used to go out in the woods when I had a hemorrhage, not to frighten Marie. Well, we both have it. Can I help it? She wanted to get married."

Marie never left her bed now. She was yellow-pale in the morning, her eyes enormous in her thin face, her black hair clinging with sweat to her temples. Her body made a small elevation like a child's under the blankets.

In the afternoon there would be red spots on her cheeks, sometimes on one cheek only. Her coughing was frequent; she kept a sanitary sputum box with her. I remember how I used to see her mother outside the door, her face pinched with anxiety, and how she would force a smile and a brisk tone as she came in. "Well, what can I make you for lunch, my darling?" And Marie would answer, "A steak big like that, Mamma," both of them knowing there was no appetite at all, nor any steak, and that a little soup and a cracker would be all Marie would be able to get down.

As for me, it appeared I wasn't getting any better. I had discontinued my monthly checkups with the doctor because they didn't seem to help. Then I heard that some of the old Stony Wold patients were "curing" in Caldwell, New Jersey, a place reputed to have a good climate. In the spring Mother and I went out to look the place over. We found a house to rent at the edge of town. I borrowed $100 from Pauline's sister Becky. Papa and Ora would have to commute from the city. It was all arranged without participation by either of them, not unusual in our always divided family.

Mamma had responded loyally when she saw this move was needed for my health, and we both delighted in the new place. With only a few other houses on Mountain Avenue, which branched out from the main road, with low hills and fields surrounding us on three sides, on the other a small wood separating us from the town, we had at last something long dreamed of, a home in the country. We had unlimited fresh air and sunlight, seven big rooms, a porch, and a spacious yard. We bought a porch hammock so that I could sleep out of doors when the weather got warmer.

The first day after we were settled, seeing Papa coming up the road in the evening and thinking how tired he must be after his long day, I went to greet him at the door. Even this simple amenity was not customary with us: his face lit up in surprise and pleasure. He lost no time in making a garden in the big lot behind the home. Before long Dorothy Ottoson Chapman came out to board with us, her husband Harry coming out weekends. Perhaps Dorothy was glad to get away from home. As much as she loved Harry, she could not be content in a crowded flat with a jealous mother-in-law who nagged her. And after a month of commuting, Ora found a furnished room in the city and also visited us weekends. Her occupation was never disclosed; always she went her own peculiar way.

Soon after our retreat to Caldwell I received a not unexpected letter from Mrs. Fantusz informing me of her daughter's death. Marie had been failing rapidly and even before I left had lost control of her bodily functions. "I'm wearing diapers, I've gone back to babyhood," she had said, keeping up her cheerful front. And the day I said goodbye, "You're deserting me." Yes, I had deserted her. Just to see a friendly face every day is a link with the world one is being pushed out of. I never knew what to say to her those last days ... what after all can one say as one goes on, neither whole nor fulfilled, yet still going on, to the friend who has come to the end of the road?

In a feeble way in those days I tried to write. I recall one story about a man from another world transferred by some natural catastrophe to earth. Adapting well and learning to like the ways of this planet, he could still never forget the beloved woman left behind, nor the beautiful light of the star called Lente, which had lighted his former home. Dorothy loved that one.

One night, as autumn came on, we were awakened by a sound of church bells ringing, peal after peal. I thought I heard voices chanting. It was November 11, 1918. In the morning we learned it was the armistice of World War I. Wanting to be closer to this great event, I took the bus into New York, thinking there would be a parade. I arrived at Fifth Avenue to find the streets strewn with ticker tape, papers, and refuse of all sorts, but empty.

At last I was again in touch with Bob Van Patten, now back from the sanatorium. She was staying with her aunt in New York and working part-time as a waitress. She was eager to have me come to the city. Then in January came an excited letter: Aunt Flo would be away for a few weeks. Bob could put me up. Come, Vera, come! Since I had a little money on hand, there were no obstacles. Mamma offered no objections, thought I knew she would be lonely because Dorothy had gone back to Brooklyn.

Aunt Flo's apartment was a well-furnished one in a good upper West Side neighborhood. I was to have the aunt's bedroom; Bob had her own little room off the kitchen. And there was good old Bob, still thin, still pale, a little tired, but vibrant and happy to see me. "It's all ours," she said, spreading a hand to indicate the apartment. "Aunt Flo's all right. We get along fine when we don't see each other. She could never see socialism in a thousand years. But it helps me out. Vera, did you ever try to work and support yourself and a child too? When I got TB Aunt Flo took Agnes, put her in a convent. I don't want my child raised in a convent, but what can I do? I'll see to it she gets over all that stuff when she gets out. I couldn't go back to telegraphy," she said. "That was what got me. They advised me when I left the san to find something easier. Oh, Vera, it's so good to see you, and we need you in our branch." Her face became serious. "We've got a situation on our hands. We're an opposition, we need more members on our side. They call us the 'Silk Stocking' local, but don't be fooled. That's just the neighborhood. We have plenty of worker members. I'll bring you around to the meeting Thursday."

As we were doing up the dishes after our first meal, Bob suddenly stopped, her brown eyes dreamy behind the horn-rimmed glasses. "Vera," she said, "you wouldn't believe it. I'm in love." No schoolgirl could have been quivering more with a first passion. "You're going to meet him Thursday. Kay Hansen. Isn't that a terrific name? Oh, but maybe he shouldn't see you—what chance would I have?" The improbability of this made me laugh.

When we arrived, the meeting of the Socialist Party branch had already started. The chairman up front was speaking to a big crowded hall. Bob and I slipped into chairs along the side wall. The membership, chiefly men but with a sprinkling of women, appeared to be composed of some manual workers, with a number of professionals and small business-men. I felt at home there even though it was the first political meeting I had ever attended. Most of the people were no different from those of my old Bronx neighborhood: my own father could have been one of them.

On the opposite wall through the haze of tobacco smoke I could see two large framed portraits. The hirsute gentleman with the broad brow and the intelligent eyes I knew; next to Karl Marx was a lean wiry, very American personality with the burning eyes of a zealot. "Eugene Debs," said Bob, following my gaze. "He's sentenced to jail for war resistance. That's Kay Hansen," she whispered later, nodding and smiling a greeting to a very tall, pale blond man who slouched into a chair among the ranks. A cigarette drooping from his lips, his keen, cold, half-closed eyes never ceased to stray over the audience.

During the brief intermission after the business meeting, we went over to meet him. "Welcome, Vee," he said warmly, extending a friendly hand. "I know all about you. This is nothing. Just wait, you'll see how our dear Socialist comrades get along with each other." He spoke rapidly in that slurring, garbling accent with which the Danes disguise all languages including their own.

Now, as the members returned to their seats, all conversations stopped and there was tense concentration as the meeting turned into a debate. It was not a question of some issue of transient interest but rather the fundamental program and direction of the Party which was at stake. The Old Guard, the majority, stood pat for gradualism, for change through education and through the ballot, for parliamentarianism, for reform of the capitalist system. To the Left Wing, which was inspired by the Russian Revolution and which took the Bolsheviks as its model, such a course had become intolerable; it could lead only to a blind alley of complete futility. They were for revolution, for direct action; only the armed revolt of the masses could overthrow the capitalist system, making an end to it once and for all and clearing the ground for socialism.

Voices grew louder and louder. Many people were on their feet at once talking and shaking their fists, while others stood up to shout "point of order" or "Keep order, Comrade Chairman." With sharp blows of the gavel the chairman would achieve a momentary lull.

When at last the meeting adjourned, we joined Hansen and a few other comrades in the still arguing throng. They were going to stop somewhere for coffee, but Bob said, "No, we'd better leave now. I'm not going to have you get sick again," with an anxious look at me. She couldn't wait to know what I thought of Kay Hansen. Could I tell her my impression of his dissipation, his unhealthiness? "Looks very interesting," I said noncommittally, but this was also true.

Daytimes, while Bob was at work, I would get up late and after a leisurely breakfast would take the subway downtown to 14th Street, destination the Rand School. In those days this center of New York socialism bubbled with activity. I would eat in the cafeteria, overhearing arguments like those in the branch, would loiter in the bookstore, picking up newspapers and pamphlets by Karl Marx and Friedrich Engels. I bought and studied *Robert's Rules of Order* in order to participate intelligently in meetings. Probably in these days I also saw my other friends Nana Wylie, Pauline, Dolores, Rose, and the Russians. But my thoughts were concentrated on the Revolution, of which I now felt myself a part.

I turned in an application to join the branch, and in due course was summoned downtown to Party headquarters for an interview. Comrade Julius Gerber, a small dark man with a Jewish accent, looked me over cautiously as he questioned me. I played innocent, for which role I surely needed little pretense, admitted I didn't know much but was eager to be a good socialist. Since my connection with the Left Wing comrades in the branch was known, my application was rejected.

In a hall on the lower East Side large mass meetings called by the Left Wing were taking place. Bob and I, with Kay Hansen and the few adherents from the Silk Stocking local, were eager participants. English was only one of the languages spoken there; Russian was prevalent; German, Yiddish, Hungarian, and others were sometimes resorted to. The various language federations of the foreign-born were the very backbone of this movement. Of Americans of the old stock like Bob and myself few indeed were to be seen. Most of the audience were working men, with only a sprinkling of women.

A big muscular, middle-aged Irishman, Jim Larkin by name, leader of Irish dock workers, frequently roused the audience with his speeches, hurled out as powerful challenges. Also frequently on the platform was Jay Lovestone, a graduate of City College and a social worker. An intellectual and an animated speaker, Lovestone had neither the power nor the earthiness of Larkin, who told ribald stories and appealed directly to the workers. More proletarian was Benjamin Gitlow of the Retail Clerks Union (affiliated with the Amalgamated Clothing Workers). "Gitlow never talks about anything but his union," someone said, and it was true. Whatever Gitlow started with, he would wind up on the subject of the union. He was large and ponderous and spoke with force and directness. Nicholas Hourwich spoke excitedly, sometimes in Russian and sometimes in English, and often one could hardly tell the difference. A short man with reddish hair and glasses, he showed big square teeth when he talked. Occasionally Rose Pastor Stokes was on the platform. Originally from my old Bronx neighborhood, she had married a Socialist millionaire but had remained true to her origins. Another prominent participant was Eamonn MacAlpine, a young Irishman, who was editor of *Revolutionary Age* in Boston. Occasionally Ed Lindgren spoke too. He appeared to be a worker in some trade; he was a small, compact, dark-haired man. At the door, behind a table, checking entrances was Maximilian Cohen, a dentist and one of the leaders. Once when his companion questioned my admittance, Comrade Cohen said with assurance, "That comrade is all right." How proud I felt at this display of confidence by someone in authority!

The liveliness, the fervor, the ebullience of those meetings in 1919 can hardly be re-created or imagined now. In that period the ongoing Russian Revolution was lifting us all on its mighty flood. What we were experiencing was the birth of a movement aimed toward the same goal. The atmosphere was free and easy, everything appeared spontaneous. While the speaking went on, and it was practically continuous, clots of leaders would be talking at the side of the platform or along the wall below; from the audience came frequent applause and laughter. Even those speakers who were not particularly effective had a message to deliver. Everything was high-keyed and optimistic.

I remember one evening in a small room with a number of people, perhaps an anteroom to the meeting hall. It was in a Socialist Party headquarters (a branch known as "the Irish") on West 29th Street, near Broadway. Some leaders were there, among them a large, handsome, brown-eyed man in a tweed overcoat. This was John Reed, well-known as a news correspondent, poet, and author of *Ten Days That Shook the World*. Someone who had actually been there, who had participated in the Russian Revolution! I wanted no more potent inspiration than to bask in his aura.

The word was being passed around that evening that henceforth no one would be admitted to the meetings who didn't carry a Party card. So I had to leave, and the problem of how to get me into the Party seemed urgent to my friends. It was actually solved easily. Since I had a residence in New Jersey, I went over to the headquarters in Newark, apparently a quiet backwater not yet touched by the dissention. There, without obstacle or delay, I was given the card.

Evenings were often spent in Kay Hansen's apartment. He lived in a tenement in a poor upper West Side neighborhood in the vicinity of 110th Street. One had to climb to the fifth floor to reach the modest five-room home. With Hansen lived a little dark Hungarian never called anything but Rudy who attended the branch meetings. Rudy was the wife. He liked to cook and clean, so Hansen informed us. "I go out to make the living. I'm a printer. Rudy, he likes to be around the kitchen, so I let him stay here." Off the living room a small second bedroom was converted into a den with drapery-covered couches. This room was never entered; it had a rather mysterious Oriental appearance. Its possible uses intrigued us much.

The living room walls were covered from top to bottom with well-filled bookshelves. Our host informed us, "Some people buy books to have something fancy to show. My books are plain, second-hand mostly, but I read them all."

Besides ourselves there would always be several other people present, some of them comrades from the branch. Newcomers were potential converts. As the discussions ranged over many subjects, a consistent point of view new to me developed: a materialist approach, which attributed opinions, attitudes, and policies to the material circumstances of the person or group involved. It was a little shocking at first, for my early religious and later college training had stressed ideas as the sources of actions and conduct. Still, prepared by the hard facts of my poor home and my illness, I easily became convinced of this more realistic point of view.

"These well-dressed people you saw in the branch—" Kay said, "lawyers, small businessmen—they have a stake in the society. They don't care how long it takes to get socialism. Let it be a hundred years, all right with them. The worker is low-paid, he gets laid off, can't pay his rent, his children are hungry. The belly squeezes. He has nothing to lose. We think according to our material circumstances."

Religion was mocked along with all the institutions of society: churches, schools, colleges, the press, the government, even marriage came under the ban. What were they all but instruments of the capitalist class to keep the people enslaved? Once I brought Pauline around, feeling it my duty to convert her. She didn't say much, and left rolling her eyes in dismay and shock at all this radicalism. There was no subtlety in our arguments; we drew no fine distinctions. Capitalism had to be destroyed; the proletariat would be the agent of this task, we ourselves but the feeble representatives of its power. The basic distinction between reform and revolution was a recurrent theme. We made scathing attacks on anyone who disagreed with us.

Kay Hansen grew in stature with each encounter. Here was a man who had never been to college, yet he knew so much more than I. His was not merely worldly knowledge, in which I saw myself as a babe in the woods, but book knowledge too. He seemed completely without illusions, without the slightest trace of romantic feeling, cynical yet with much enthusiasm for the Revolution. In his tall, well-proportioned frame, so languid as he slouched in a door, in his quick movements there was a certain grace. He spoke always rapidly and animatedly. In spite of a sallow, unhealthy look, his well-modeled features were still handsome. Before long—it might have been expected though I had no such thought at the beginning—before long there were two of us in love with Kay Hansen.

And then in the midst of all this intellectual stimulation, this daily excitement, the anticipated blow fell: a letter from Florida telling Bob Aunt Flo was coming back. So I packed my little bag, severed myself from this attractive group of new friends, and went back to Caldwell.

Back to the snow-covered fields, to the quiet, to the glimpses of ice-blue sky behind the fleeting storm clouds of February, to the cheeping of birds in the winter sunshine, to my mother's gentle companionship. But it was not the same, nothing would ever be the same again. I myself had changed, and fundamentally. Now, instead of poetry and novels, there was a pile of pamphlets and newspapers to mull over and absorb. There was a medley of memories to sort out, to dwell upon, an ideology to clarify. I was content. I had had a taste of life and found it more intoxicating and fulfilling than I could have hoped. But I was tired, I needed the quiet and rest. My shuttling between New York and the country would continue for a long time, but I knew I would find the means to go back to stay.

When spring came, we rented two rooms to the Entenbergs—Rose, Ralph, who commuted, and their baby. Barbara Jean, the infant, was left in her carriage on the front porch and gave me welcome experience in baby care while Rose upstairs engaged in her customary scrubbings and elaborate cookery on a kerosene stove we had installed.

Every Sunday friends would come from New York: the Chapmans, Pauline, Rose's uncle and aunt, Dr. and Mrs. Kantor (known always as Dyadya and Tyetya). My sister would come weekends too, but she kept to herself. I don't find her picture in any of the numerous snapshots of those weekend groups.

Then one Sunday, after some hesitation, I invited Bob Van Patten, Kay Hansen, and Rudy. Though I never expected them to be enthusiastically received, I was unprepared for the complete rejection that ensued. From Mamma: "Better stick to *bees*, they'll do you more good than *Bolshevism*." (I had experimented in beekeeping.) And Papa: "Those people [meaning the Left Wingers in the printing trade like Kay Hansen] done us a lot of harm in my line." But most devastating was the judgment handed down by Rose Entenberg, now securely ensconced behind a husband with a good job. "I am *shocked* that you should have given a moment's attention to such a person." She quoted Ralph, "I could have brought out plenty of fellows. I thought they wouldn't be good enough for her." She rattled on, elaborating, but I listened no more. A leaden weight had fallen in my chest; I felt bruised and wanted to cry. It was days before I could control myself enough to analyze the situation calmly.

It was clear they thought that I was considering Kay Hansen as a prospective husband. This was not the case. I didn't want marriage, I wanted love, the all-enveloping experience. I knew that Kay Hansen was no ideal person; nor for that matter did I have an ideal at that time. They saw him only superficially; I was able to understand his human qualities —the broadmindedness and tolerance, the keen penetration, the humor underneath the ravages that society had caused. So I reasoned myself into some self-respect once more: inexperienced and naive I was, but a complete fool, no!

Always planning now how to get back to New York, I had bought a Pitman's shorthand manual, which I studied. To help me in my dream of becoming a writer, Nana Wylie had got me a second-hand Smith typewriter, of antique vintage; it should have been in a museum. On this clumsy machine I practiced typing, but in my ignorance, not realizing there is a system to this skill, I didn't learn to use the right fingers. It was hit or miss from the beginning.

Then in the fall an ad appeared in the Caldwell paper for female help in a straw hat factory. Having run a foot-powered sewing machine since I was fifteen, I was not entirely unskilled and was taken on as a learner. Handling the rough wet sennit straw scraped my hands: they became sore, then blistered, later on calloused. As I became accustomed to the work, I was considered a good operator, then one of the best, able to turn the straw skillfully to make the center with which the hat is started.

With my education why did I become a factory hand? Even though it was now two years since I had left the sanatorium, health still had to

Vera, probably seven years old

Caldwell, New Jersey. Seated left to right: John Casper Buch, Vera,
Dorothy Chapman, Rose Entenberg. Standing: Nellie Buch, Harry Chapman

be a primary consideration. My only training had been as a French teacher, but teaching was an occupation one entered permanently. My jobs had to be short-range. I could only feel my way along. Besides, I had by this time reached the conviction that it would be good if all students had experience in the outside world before they committed themselves to the schoolroom for life. Still it was not this theory I was carrying out in the straw hat factory. In addition to my own situational needs there was a scarcely formulated urge, even a certain excitement felt, to get a job in that little place. One thing had been made very clear from what Bob said, from my reading, and from the meetings: the Revolution was in the hands of the proletariat. Teachers were all right; they could play a role if they would side with the workers; but it was the person at the machine, producing surplus value, whose position was strategic. So in my own modest way I was preparing myself to be a revolutionary.

When I had saved up enough money (keeping what I earned, since Papa was working and it didn't seem necessary to contribute at home), I felt ready to leave. How I dreaded to tell Mamma! Was it the old childish reluctance to confess some misdemeanor? I knew she would neither object nor argue. Just as she refrained from comment in the old days when Papa was on the rampage, now she stoically bore her pain. I knew she had nobody but me, but I wanted to live and had to leave. When I told her at the last minute, her silence made me feel like an executioner.

4

I Begin To Live at Last

WITH THE HELP OF MY LEFT WING FRIENDS I ESTABLISHED A DOMICILE: a tiny furnished bedroom with a young Swedish couple, members of our group, who had a flat in the building adjacent to Kay Hansen's. Now to get a job.

A newspaper ad for a straw hat operator in a Newark factory was worth a try. It was a large plant. The forelady, believing me experienced, left me sitting in front of a machine with a bundle of straw and a finished hat as a model. To my dismay, I found immediately that the machine was different from the one in Caldwell, the straw was a narrow braid, not wide like the sennit; it was handled dry, not soaked. I struggled, but in vain. Humiliated, I left without a word.

Next I tried for a secretarial position. "A college girl is what I want," the man said optimistically. But then the test: he dictated a letter; not remembering some Pitman symbols, I used longhand. Nervously I muddled through the typing. "You made a lot of mistakes," the boss hurled angrily after me as I made for the door. Soon, however, I did get a job as stenographer and translator with the French American Banking Company (Frenambank) located in the Wall Street financial district.

Now for the first time in my life I was independent: living alone and supporting myself. To have my own key, to come and go unrestricted, to eat in restaurants, to travel downtown in the morning anonymous among the crowds; it was all exhilarating at first, and there was about this period a delicious whiff of freedom. The job was a congenial one, my associates all helpful, friendly people, and the Wall Street environment stimulating. What was wrong was my own poor technical preparation. The translations they assigned me I could handle, but as a stenographer and typist I was no more than an amateur. To me at that time any job was only a means to sustain myself. Revolution was my real interest. My ineptness for the job troubled my Presbyterian conscience, but really I lived only for the evenings. Here I quickly picked up the threads of last winter's beginnings.

Great political upheavals had taken place in the meantime: the frenzied debates on fundamental issues in the silk stocking local and throughout the country had been carried to their inevitable conclusions. Mass expulsions had taken place; large sections of the membership now found themselves outside the Socialist Party. The split was a vertical one, first convulsing, then cleaving the Party in two, separating the Left Wing, the revolutionists, from the stand-patters, the gradualists, the reformists. The entire state memberships of Michigan and Massachusetts had been expelled. (See Appendix A.)

On February 16, 1919, the New York Left Wing had held a convention and drafted a program that called for "the organization of workingmen's councils as instruments for the seizure of power and proletarian dictatorship, control of industry by industrial unions, repudiation of national debts (with provision to safeguard small investors), expropriation of banks, of railways and large trust-organizations of capital, socialization of foreign trade."*

In September the Left Wing held a national convention in Chicago. There was a difference of opinion over whether the expelled elements should fight to get back into the Party or split and form a new party. When some of the Left Wingers tried to attend the Socialist Party convention being held at the same time, they were met at the door by police waiting to evict them. One group split then to form a Communist Party. The Russian Federation dominated this group, which was composed chiefly of the foreign federations. Here were the foreign-born industrial workers, many of Communist inclination. The leaders of this group were Louis Fraina, C. E. Ruthenberg, secretary of the Cleveland local of the Socialist Party, Isaac Ferguson, former secretary to a Chicago millionaire Socialist, John Ballam of Massachusetts, Dr. Maximilian Cohen, and Bertram Wolfe.

Another group formed the Communist Labor Party, composed of

---

*Benjamin Gitlow, I Confess (New York: Dutton, 1940). For a history of the Left Wing see Irving Howe and Lewis Coser, The American Communist Party: A Critical History (New York: Frederick Praeger, 1962). Briefly, Communist evolution in the U.S. is as follows: In 1919 the Communist Party (CP) and the Communist Labor Party (CLP) were formed; they went underground after the Palmer raids. In 1922 they were ordered by the Comintern to unite and become legal. The Workers Party formed early in 1922. In December of that year it was renamed the Workers (Communist) Party. From 1929 on it was called the Communist Party.

more Americanized elements and headed by John Reed, Benjamin Gitlow, and some men from the Midwest, among them Alfred Wagenknecht, former state secretary of the Socialist Party in Ohio, L. Katterfeld, a Kansas farmer, and James P. Cannon, an adherent of the IWW and editor of a Socialist paper in Kansas City. Still another split occurred in the Michigan group, a faction of which established the Proletarian Party.

Our group was faced with a choice: the Communist Party centered in New York or the Communist Labor Party based in the Midwest. The Proletarian Party we did not consider, having no information about it. Bob Van Patten had delayed joining until I came; now, meeting with the group in Hansen's flat, we carefully went over the published statements of both parties. Was some principled difference concealed in the wording of "a mass party" as contrasted with "party of the masses"? Feeling that "Communist Labor Party" might imply some dilution of the program, we chose to go the whole route with the "Communist Party."*

The newly formed Communist Party had a headquarters where one could go to join; no branches were yet organized, nor do I recall any Party mass meetings of this period. I recall sending in a burning revolutionary article under the name of John Lawrence to one of the Left Wing papers. Its contents? Probably just a rehash of something read. The year before I had done some writing, had a story of a Jewish Sabbath printed in the *New York Call*, and I have in my files an acceptance slip signed by Floyd Dell, a then popular Leftish writer and editor of the *New Masses*. "Your little story . . ."; perhaps it was that one about a tramp on a park bench in Union Square inspired by spring. To write was always in the back of my mind.

Since the Left Wing endorsed the Industrial Workers of the World (the official Socialist Party supporting the American Federation of Labor), we joined the IWW, proudly carried the red card, and went once a week to the "Wobbly" headquarters on the waterfront. This local's membership was composed mainly of seamen, who dropped in once in a while when their ships docked in that port; there was also a sprinkling of members from various trades in the city, plus a few office workers. Only wage workers could become members. It was always a lively place with a comradely atmosphere. "Fellow Worker" was their salutation, never "Comrade," which to them was tainted with the contempt they felt for all

---

*It is likely there was a difference not revealed in the statements: the Communist Labor Party may have desired to orient more toward the American working class; its leaders included more Americans. Above all, it sought to avoid domination by the Russian Federation. In the end, during the underground (ca. 1922), the Communist International (i.e., Russia) forced the fusion of the two groups.

political parties. We collected and read their literature, sang their songs, absorbed something of their tradition and history.

We could not agree with the IWW's ignoring of the State (which certainly never ignored them but rather punished them heavily). In their much simplified concept of society, industrial unionism alone would be the vehicle of the Revolution. "To build the new society within the shell of the old" was one of their slogans. "Pie-card artists" meant office-based leaders. They had a limit of one year that any member could be a leader in an office; he then had to return to his shop, mine, or ship.

We liked their militancy, their forthright statement of the class struggle. "The working class and the employing class have nothing in common." So began their preamble. Their members had a record of militant mass struggles in the Western Federation of Miners, in Paterson, New Jersey, with the silk workers, among the migratory agricultural workers in the West, and in many other places. Their war resistance had resulted in ninety-five convictions and long jail sentences.

With great gusto we would sing:

> Oh, why don't you work like other men do?
> How the hell can I work when there's no work to do?
> Hallelujah, I'm a bum, hallelujah, bum again.
> Hallelujah, give us a hand-out, to revive us again . . .

and the lusty song of the trials of Casey Jones, who "pushed the S. P. freight."

> Casey Jones got a job in Heaven,
> Casey Jones was doin' mighty fine.
> Casey Jones went scabbin' on the angels
> Just like he did to workers on the S. P. line.

The frequent gatherings at Hansen's place were not merely a substitute for branch meetings, they were now a magnet for my newly aroused feelings. I merely had to go over the roof from my own room, to which I would repair for a brief rest after work and dinner. Now to the intellectual interest were added the fast-beating heart, the delicious turmoil of the blood, the moodiness, in fact all the well-known symptoms of that sickness known as being in love.

Bob and I were sharing an experience shadowed by an element of something strange. Hansen was always friendly, glad to see us, eager to talk of our common interest. Missing was the special bond, the contact, the lingering hand clasp or look, the electric communication one associated with a man. "He treats us like two other fellows," Bob summarized. We brought in Nana Wylie, so much more experienced than either of us, who without being a political person sympathized with the Left Wing and out of temperament liked to see herself as a revolutionist. As for our host, her verdict on Hansen was, "I think the man is impotent."

As the weeks went by, the mystery of Kay Hansen gradually cleared up. There was the Friday night matter: somehow or other we knew that people came to his apartment Friday nights, yet we were never invited. Kay would refuse to go anywhere on Fridays. Bob went once to investigate. She was met by Rudy. A hum of male voices came from within as he told her through the cracked door that Kay was busy, couldn't see her. Finally, there was the time Bob and I were talking with a man, a waiter who used to frequent the gatherings at Hansen's, and he got to discussing Kay Hansen. "Don't you know what Hansen is?" and answered his own question by illustrating with a gesture of fingers in his mouth. Although the conclusion had gradually been forming in our minds, still there was a shock about this.

Formerly, I had known a homosexual pair, friends of Nana Wylie's. We had visited them once in the old days in a little house they had brought in Mariners' Harbor, Staten Island, sparsely furnished with American antiques and lighted by candles. An artistic pair, they ran a tiny restaurant on Great Jones Street in Greenwich Village. One was an older man of about forty; the other, in his early twenties, was a hermaphrodite. I remember the older man said to me once, "In those days, if Arthur had left me, I'd have died." This I could understand; this was love. But these Friday evenings . . . that bedraped, close, oriental-looking room of couches . . . what mass orgies, what promiscuity did it shelter? This we could only vaguely picture: more than anything else it seemed disgusting. Still my feelings were all absorbed now in this baffling, throttling, never-to-be-realized desire. It helped that there were two of us, Bob and I who understood each other so well and could at least commiserate now as we realized the hopelessness of our situation.

Once that winter I spent an evening with my old friends the Auerbachs, who had also been expelled from the Socialist Party and were marking time. Rissie, a dressmaker, was always occupied with her union, the International Ladies Garment Workers Union. She was a highly nervous and talkative woman, thin, tall, and wiry with bushy black hair and sparkling brown eyes behind glasses. Her husband was an inconspicuous quiet little man. A Russian man was also present. As we left, he invited me to go to the theater with him.

Saturday afternoon it was snowing as I went to my date bundled up in my shabby winter coat. I must have arrived quite bedraggled, for my young man displayed a certain look of disappointment. I had thought that with some conversation perhaps out of this vague gray blot might emerge a personality. But as we sat in the balcony, losing no time when the lights went out, he moved close, panting, put his arm around me, and tried to fondle me. Not merely was I unaccustomed to the ways of men, I had no feeling whatever for this one and I drew away. There were no more dates from that quarter.

However, I did go to the theater and ballet sometimes. I remember a play of John Barrymore's, "The Jest," where Pauline and I had seats in the first row right under the stage, so close we could see the powder rising in clouds when Barrymore thumped his chest. I saw also performances by Pavlova, that exquisite doll, and Isadora Duncan, whom I admired as much for the personal freedom of her life as for her great contribution to the art of dancing and choreography.

Somewhere in this period Bob and I attended a mass meeting held possibly by the IWW on the subject of defense of Soviet Russia, a popular topic in those days. The chief speaker was the well-known IWW leader Bill Haywood, then out on bail facing a sentence of twenty years for war resistance. The hall was small and we were close to the men on the platform. Haywood was a burly, strong-looking man, middle-aged and somewhat bald, and apparently had lost the sight of one eye. His speech was simple and very direct, his manner calm; he nevertheless conveyed an extraordinary impression of power. I could see how he had been able to sway masses in the Western Federation of Miners and the IWW.

There could not have been a greater contrast to him than the chairman and other speaker, Robert Minor. An artist whose cartoons were featured in radical papers, he had also gone to Russia in 1918 as a correspondent of the *New York World*, the *Philadelphia Public Ledger*, and Max Eastman's *Liberator*. He was an anarchist. Now, as he spoke, Minor's whole body was in motion every minute. He gyrated, he gesticulated, he grimaced. The black arches of his eyebrows rose and fell as his forehead wrinkled and unwrinkled. His eyes bulged, his mouth was stretched to its fullest, showing all his teeth as he shouted. Quickly he became hoarse. What he said was actually more or less like Haywood's speech, but how different the effect! Minor affected the audience in inverse proportion to the violence of his bodily and facial contortions. Minor is a good cartoonist, I thought; why can't he confine himself to that?

We had now entered a period of reprisals from the United States government. All this revolutionary ferment was bound to provoke counterattacks. In New York beginning in November 1918, meetings for defense of the Soviet Union were forbidden. On June 21, 1919, the Lusk Committee appointed by the state legislature raided the Left Wing headquarters on West 29th Street. A national convention of the Left Wing with one hundred delegates and all the leaders was being held. Even though the meetings shifted from one hall to another in an attempt at secrecy, the "dicks" broke in. Other centers and newspaper offices were raided at that time by returned soldiers stirred up against "the Reds."

In late January 1920, through the intervention of U.S. Attorney General A. Mitchell Palmer, radical headquarters in many cities were raided, with mass arrests, chiefly of the foreign-born. Ellis Island was crowded with thousands of deportees. The Communist Party and Communist Labor Party headquarters, the IWW hall, offices of foreign radical papers—none escaped.*

If our little group was not directly involved in these raids, it was just by chance, since we went frequently to the IWW headquarters. We soon heard an account of the events from people we knew. A large group of cops had burst in. All the women in the hall were sent out, and the men were lined up against the wall. The police then brutally assaulted them with clubs and blackjacks, leaving them helpless. The cops then smashed the typewriter and mimeograph machine, threw the literature all over the floor, and finally arrested a number of the bleeding, injured men. All the groups suffered losses from the raids, not merely through deportation, but by the dropping out of members who were not prepared to face the harassment.

Not long afterward Bob and I did something that was probably foolhardy. We went to visit the Communist Party headquarters (perhaps on East Broadway): we wanted to break through the isolation in which we found ourselves. Breathlessly we climbed the stairs. The door was ajar. We advanced cautiously, braced for cops. We found the office empty, the desks and floor strewn with papers, some chairs overturned, everything apparently remaining as it had been left by the raid. What had become of the Party, of the comrades, the leaders we had depended on? We felt quite desolate.

Before long the IWW local rented a new headquarters, a smaller, less congenial place, a little store on one of those innumerable lower East Side streets. We went there sometimes to mull over the raids and the current situation with the loyal fellow workers who still came around.

During this winter I would go out to Caldwell weekends but no longer to the big house on Mountain Avenue, which had been given up as too expensive. Only Nellie was home now most of the time. They had moved to a small, cozy garret apartment in the center of Caldwell (still

*F. P. Cook, *The American Struggle* (New York: Doubleday, 1974), pp. 156-57.

"country" to New Yorkers like us). Mamma was feeling abandoned. Plaintively she said once, "Some day I'm going to go away and never come back." Whenever I returned I would slip back into the old patterns of childhood, the inability to communicate. The old barrier I was never able to break through was still there. The original move to the country had been made for me, for the sake of my health. Still, Mamma had liked it there on Mountain Avenue, and Papa at least had enjoyed his gardening. Ora wasn't seen much any more. It was clear our family was breaking up. In spite of this Nellie and John were talking now of buying a home in the country. The old dream that had tantalized us in the slum on 171st Street seemed now realizable. They had saved up some money and were actually looking at ads in the paper.

All this time I had been working at Frenambank, always feeling ambivalent and making little progress since I did nothing systematically to improve myself. That the job continued seemed a good sign until one day as I was coming down the little spiral staircase from the women's room, the bookkeeper at my side said, "Maybe I'd better tell you, Vera, you're on the temporary payroll here."

At once my self-confidence tottered in feelings of failure, of inadequacy. Actually my situation was salvaged by a stroke of luck. I spent an evening with my Russian friends in the home of some people named Kramer. The Auerbachs and a few others were there. Some of them spoke little or no English including the hostess, who was addressed always as "Vera Dorevna." Although my Russian was not adequate for full conversation, I could follow a little and I loved the sound of the language. Mr. Kramer told of his place of work with the Central Committee of the Russian Cooperative Unions (Centrosoyus), which had recently established an office in New York, actually the first base of the Soviets in this country. They were looking for trade, but they also did publicity. They needed an English-speaking person in the publicity office. Would I be interested in such a job? Would I be interested! Hope flared big and bright.

I applied the very next day. A kindly, genial, typical American liberal woman in charge of the publicity office apologized for the small salary (actually the same as I was getting at Frenambank: $25 a week). There would be only a little stenography; I was to assist her generally in her work. After a little questioning and no test, the job was mine. Miss Stevens took me to meet Dr. Sherman, the head of the organization. "Miss Buch has commanded more salary," she explained, "but she wants to help in our work." "Such a place is just where I would want to work," I added truthfully, and with a handclasp and a few murmured words in a heavily accented English, Dr. Sherman welcomed me into the fold. So ended my brief inglorious career in banking. I gave a few days notice, then with happy smiles I bade my associates at Frenambank goodbye.

My new boss was teaching herself to type; my limited knowledge of the skill was adequate to get her started, and as I was not nervous about that, I did well enough. There was also some filing and checking of newspapers and magazines for items related to the Soviets. In the cozy little two-room office a small plump Russian woman who knew very little English also worked; when she wasn't typing on a Russian typewriter she was making long personal telephone calls in Russian. "Sloushayou," (I listen) she would say when answering a call, and when making one, "Anushka doma?" (Is Annette home?). It appeared Russian lessons were being given me as a bonus.

I hadn't been there long when I went to the Auerbachs one evening. A newcomer was present, a dark, keen-eyed young man named Mord Wilgus. I told him about the difficulties Bob and I were having and about our visit to the deserted Communist Party headquarters. The Auerbachs hadn't joined the new party, but Mord Wilgus had; he was the person I needed; the party had gone underground, he said: he would connect us.

Next Bob received a visitor who told her where to go for a meeting. We went one winter evening to a rundown tenement building in a poor lower East Side neighborhood. Six or eight people were gathered in a shabby living room all silently ogling us. The leader of the little group, the one who had contacted Bob, asked what our national affiliation was. We couldn't admit to being anything but American. He spoke English well though with a slight accent; most of the others spoke brokenly; it was clearly a foreign-born group. The leader explained that the underground party was functioning only through these little private meetings, and our work right now was leaflet distribution. We were to be very careful never to mention to any nonmember where we met or in fact anything concerning the organization. It seemed to us the people looked at us suspiciously, nobody said much, and the atmosphere was anything but congenial.

We were each given a batch of leaflets in a paper bag and were assigned a block on which to distribute them. Since it was not far away, we went immediately. Furtively we walked through the chilly dark streets always on the alert for the cop that wasn't there. Hastily we would climb the steps, duck into the dark hallways, quickly fold up the leaflets, and stuff them into the letter boxes. The content of the leaflet was "left" enough to satisfy the most insurgent. It called for nothing less than general strikes leading to armed insurrection for the overthrow of the capitalist system. We felt very brave and conspiratorial. This is what the

Russian revolutionists did, we told each other. Still there was something unreal about the whole thing.

The next meeting place was never announced ahead of time; each time the leader would come to Bob's home to inform her; there was a different living room each time and the day of the week was different, but the same group of uncommunicative, suspicious people met us. We wondered sometimes if this were not a trap; if we weren't about to be caught red-handed with those incriminating leaflets. Then after a few weeks, the young man didn't come anymore. What had happened? We tried going to one of the meeting places, but none of the members were there. We were simply disconnected. There was nothing we could do about it. In all likelihood our American background in itself aroused distrust, so rare were the native Americans in the movement at that time. (In fact, Mord Wilgus confirmed this later.) Disappointed and baffled, we fell back upon the meetings at Hansen's which remained the same. Although he had signed up for the new party, Kay Hansen didn't join the underground. He ridiculed the leaflets we were giving out; they were nonsense. In this country it was hard enough even to get a worker to join a union, armed insurrection was nowhere in sight, so he said. Was our leader turning Right Wing on us?

That spring was actually a turning point in my life much more than I realized then. When I arrived for work one morning, Miss Stevens told me Dr. Sherman wanted to see me. Feeling sure my inadequacies had been discovered, I went bracing myself for the blow. Nothing of the sort—I was in fact offered a new job as secretary to Dr. Sherman himself. I told him my stenography was not very good. "That doesn't matter. You can at least correct my mistakes in English, can't you?" I admitted I could do that. I was overwhelmed by the offer, and told Dr. Sherman I had to think it over.

What-might-have-been is always a futile line of thought, whether applied to personal or to social history. We may, however, and should indeed carefully examine our choices. Why didn't I jump to accept his offer? The salary would probably have been much more than what I was getting, the environment congenial.

In the first place, I wasn't a stenographer and only a marginal typist. My health was still too poor to allow me to practice evenings to improve myself. My situation was complicated, though probably not exceptionally so since any reality overlaps or holds within itself a number of other realities. I had neither wanted nor planned to be a secretary. I never wanted to be a teacher either. A writer was what I had always dreamed of being. But I also wanted most of all to be a revolutionist. The severance with the underground group left Bob and me isolated: there was no telling how long it would be till we could make contact again. So that outlet seemed to be closed.

These considerations, however, didn't get to the bottom of the matter. The health issue could not be ignored. That winter I had developed a cough. Whether it was simply a cold or a return of TB I didn't know since I had foresworn doctors.

And last of all was the strong orientation to nature which was part of my American heritage. Only a couple of weeks earlier Mamma and I had gone out one Sunday to look at a place near Dover, New Jersey. It would really be a home of our own in the country. (In Caldwell we had only rented.) The price was reasonable and Mamma had paid a deposit. I was at that time victim of an illusion, based on a story I had read about Theodore Roosevelt, who as a youth had passed through an infection with TB and by rugged outdoor life had built up a robust physique. This might be my chance to do likewise. I also thought I might be able to do some writing. So I went into Dr. Sherman's office the next morning to tell him I regretted I couldn't accept his offer; my parents were moving out to New Jersey and I would go with them.

Had I no inkling that day of early spring when I went with Mother to look at the new place, saw its isolation, the mile-long walk to the bus stop to Dover and as much in the other direction to the Denville DL&W station, of what sort of trap I was getting into? In refusing that job at Centrosoyus I had really cut myself off. Still, I hoped for a new life. Actually I reckoned without my host, in this case myself. I was so recently emerged from the pupa stage, my wings having given only a few feeble flutters. I still felt very young. Life seemed to stretch out endlessly, invitingly ahead. I could afford this year, or two years, I told myself. That I would remain there four years with each one becoming more and more entangled in a situation which from the start had no suitability for me— of this I had no intimation. If I had any misgivings, I consoled myself with the thought that for my mother and father it seemed to be a fulfillment. Alas, for them too in the long run it became a trap; for my sister even more so.

Of course, I realized a young woman with a college education would be a rarity here. Soon the word spread that there was a new girl in the neighborhood with short hair. Various young males came around to have a look at the novelty. Meanwhile I was not forgetting I was a revolutionary. Armed with a package of leaflets I had saved from the underground, under cover of darkness one night, feeling very daring and Russian, I went around pushing them into all the letter boxes within walking distance. Comments from the neighbors ensued: "Oh, they were *rank* red," and "Whoever could have done such a thing?" Did anyone suspect me? I doubt it. The Bolshevist scare stirred up by the Palmer raids had touched even this remote community, and possibly some fear was aroused. But since nothing further occurred, it soon quieted down.

At first Papa commuted to his job in New York, leaving before we were up in the morning as he had always done, and returning late and tired. His working hours were fewer; still, since he worked standing, it meant ten hours on his feet. Later on he rented a room in New York but at the start, with Ora coming out weekends, we were something of a family again. We got acquainted with the neighbors and became part of the community.

It was in the early days of that first April, with its short flashes of sunlight, its cold blue sky between swiftly passing white clouds, its snow patches lingering in the shadows mottling the wet black earth, its young green shoots on the berry bushes, its joyous caroling of birds in the surrounding maples, that I had a visit from a young man. Mord Wilgus came out from New York to see me. I had met him only two or three times before, always briefly and with other people around. Now he stayed a few hours, which we spent walking about the place and discussing the interests we had in common: socialism, the Palmer raids, the new party and whatever news he had of its development. I liked this young man. There was no question of his congeniality, and it was clear he liked me. The few hours passed all too swiftly. And what did I do then, when he was leaving and I was walking him down to the bus stop?

It is sometimes hard to face oneself even after the lapse of so many years. What impulse of misguided coquetry, what feeling of inferiority led me to think I must maneuver, must in some way build up an image of myself other than the simple inexperienced young woman I was? When Mord said something about another date, I answered—yes, idiot that I was—that "maybe Kay would be jealous." Completely unfounded in fact, from whence came this stupid, uncalled-for, unmeant rebuff? At any rate it ended that beginning friendship, and indeed I deserved no better.

Now in my twenties, as I made belated contact with the young people living in the scattered farmhouses thereabouts, I was able to have the social life involving the other sex that I should have had at sixteen. There were parties, hayrides, and buggy rides in the moonlight. In those days of the early 1920's an automobile was still a novelty in isolated communities. The postman delivered in a horse-drawn buggy. One family in the neighborhood had a radio; Mamma and I sometimes of an evening listened with them using earphones. There were also, at least during the summer, visits by New York friends, with picnics in surrounding resort areas. Dorothy Chapman came out again to board during the summer; Harry came out weekends.

With all the open air and sunshine and the quiet relaxed environment, my cough soon dried up. I built up some strength. I also found a swimming place in the Rockaway River, which ran nearby; the depth was no more than hip-high, but I did learn to swim and to float on the rapid current.

Involvement in an inappropriate love affair with a man much younger than myself was something that seemed more important then than it was, nor shall I dwell upon it. Nature will have its way, and if no suitable objects are present, one will make do with unsuitable. The deep involvement I experienced at the time was evidently something characteristic of me. My faithful friend Pauline would occasionally urge me to drop it all, come to New York, and get a job. It took a few more turns of the wheel, and I had to be really desperate before I could heed her sensible advice.

With the spring of 1922 came an economic depression matching some of those previous periods which had had such dire effects on our family. Now Papa, who had been doing pretty well, was once more home without work. Ora soon joined us out there where fresh air was more plentiful than food. It was too early to start a garden though we did scrounge around for tender young dock greens and watercress, which grew along the banks of the icy river.

Now I bestirred myself, went down to Dover, and got a job as a looper in a large silk-stocking factory on the outskirts of the town. This job, low-paid though far from unskilled, I could have kept. The foot of the full-fashioned silk stocking was knit on one machine, then transferred to another, the looper's job being to slip all the tiny meshes one by one onto a little circle of needles, itself in motion. Because the eyestrain was great, I had constant headaches. There was back strain also, and so I quit the job. I did, however, write a poem called "Looping Silk Stockings," which was published first in the *Daily Worker*, later in a book called *Revolutionary Anthology* edited by Marcus Graham.

Soon afterward I obtained another job in a shirt factory located on Dover's Main Street. With the experience of the straw hat factory behind me, I needed only a little assistance to learn cuff-setting. I worked with a will, walking the mile to and from the bus stop. When Saturday came, remembering how Papa used to return on payday unloading big packages of food, I rushed to the market and returned well-laden. Now for the first time in my life I experienced that unique, primary satisfaction of providing food for one's family. Before the astonished eyes of those three who were mine I unloaded the contents of two big bags.

I worked for a while in the shirt factory, saving as much as I could for another attempt in New York, this time with the intent of helping my family. In New York I put up in a working girls' home on the lower East Side where one slept in a dormitory for a dollar a night. I answered ads for a governess and for a cottage mother in an orphanage. The governess job I could have had but it was out of town and I didn't want to be isolated. For the cottage mother position I was rejected for being too young. Actually I was twenty-five but I always looked like a big kid in those days. Encouraged by Bob, I even tried to be a waitress but that didn't work out either. Finally, at the end of my money, I had to return to the country.

The final period of my stay there was one of collapse from both a mental and a moral point of view. My inappropriate love affair finally terminated. I saw the years passing, empty, my life a cul-de-sac. A strange feeling developed that I was no longer myself. The self had taken its departure, was located somewhere far away, beyond my reach. I felt an unbearable melancholy that gave way at times to fits of bitter weeping.

From this sad situation I was rescued by my dear old Pauline, who had borne patiently with all my vagaries. She loaned me money to buy a decent winter coat and get a start in New York. During the years since I had graduated a surfeit of teachers had developed in the city. Long lists of licensed teachers awaited appointment while the board hired substitutes at a lower rate of pay. The examination in French was not given for years, and finally for men only. I passed the substitute exam and got a job in Julia Richman High, where Pauline taught, replacing a teacher away on sabbatical leave.

I was conscientious about this job, and I did at the start make a fine impression on the head of my department. Weekends I could bring home favorable reports to Mamma, for which shreds, belated as they were, she was proud and happy. At last one of her girls was attaining her goal. I had rented a small furnished room one block away from the school. Having my evenings free, I soon made contact with my old Left Wing associates.

The Party, having recently emerged from its underground phase (in 1922), was now the Workers Party. I visited the headquarters, but found little activity. Soon I joined the Harlem English branch, which met on a street north of Central Park. The first meeting was amazing and disillusioning. Although English was the official language, the majority of the members were Jews along with a few Poles, Russians, Italians, and some others. Only a few were articulate in English. The chairman was a tall, blond young man named Yampolsky, perhaps a needle-trades worker. Among the members was a buxom, talkative mature woman of about thirty-five, a teacher named Juliet Stuart Poyntz, whom I got to know

well later on. Since other members had told me she was a Central Execu·
tive Committee member, I looked upon her with some respect. She
seemed a well-poised, self-assured person. There were some needle-trades
workers, a dentist or two, a few miscellaneous skilled and service workers.
It was not a large group; some thirty-five or forty generally attended.

The chief subject of discussion here was not the principles of Communism, as it had been in 1919. The Workers Communist Party was now
apparently divided into two factions, one led nationally by Charles E.
Ruthenberg, general secretary of the Party, the other by William Z.
Foster, national chairman. Upon what principled platforms these groups
rested never became clear in the Harlem English branch. The comrades
would refer to events or activities of which I had no knowledge. The question of the Labor Party appeared to be a bone of particular contention. I
knew there had been a Farmer–Labor Party headed by Robert La Follette of Wisconsin. The involvement of Communists in this movement
could not be divined. Sometimes the name of Ludwig Lore came up; it
appeared Juliet Poyntz was under a stigma for having been associated with
him and she would have to defend herself. I used to hear of Lore in the
old days as a respected leader, though I had never met him. Just what was
wrong with him now I couldn't make out.

The arguments would wax hot, noisy, and bitter. Accusations and
counteraccusations were hurled, faces became flushed, fists were clenched,
voices were loud and angry. In vain would the chairman pound with his
gavel and shout for order. It appeared the Foster faction prided itself on
being proletarian, and on having a monopoly on this distinction, for they
were always denouncing the others as petit-bourgeois and intellectual (a
term uttered with scathing contempt). However, one could infer nothing
from this since the other side made the same accusations. Insults were
flung about freely; such terms as "opportunist," "careerist," "Right
Winger" filled the air. Once there was a fistfight.

To the uninitiated onlooker the scene was complete bedlam: to make
any sense of the turmoil of words was impossible. Nevertheless, I had a
deep conviction that the road to Communism was the only one for me.
If this was it, stony, harsh, and repellent though it might be, I had to
follow it. In addition I rationalized: the present scene is surely not the
whole picture; this insanity may be merely local or temporary. If a
struggle is going on, surely the better, more rational elements will prevail in the end. My reasoning, my optimism were the merest guesses of
an amateur, having no basis in reality. They did, however, keep me coming to the branch meetings and did assure me an experience, traumatic at
times, yet of incomparable value in the long run.

Besides the Harlem English branch, there was a small Party fraction in the Teachers Union, at that time a beginning organization. The fraction included a stenography teacher at Julia Richman named Bert Miller, who became for a while a friend; Ray Ragozzin, a member of the Party since its inception who prided herself greatly upon having been through the whole underground as well as having for a time shared the life of C. E. Ruthenberg; a young couple named Benjamin; Bertram D. Wolfe, a Party leader who was a teacher but who showed up only rarely in the fraction; and a bald, studious man named Bosse. There may have been a few others. We concerned ourselves mainly with getting members for the union.

The pressure to take sides with one fraction or the other was great. Since I had no principled basis for choice, I went along with the teachers fraction who were Ruthenbergites. Bob Van Patten was also in this group. My old friend Rissie Auerbach, on the other hand, as a needle-trades worker was a committed Fosterite.

My life at this time was neither easy nor carefree. My wage of $5 a day was adequate for daily expenses but I owed Pauline $50, and then her sister unexpectedly asked that I return the $100 she had loaned when we moved to Caldwell and which I, alas, had forgotten. I wasn't used to a monthly paycheck—nor to any paycheck for that matter, fresh from the country as I was. Invariably the last few days of the month I ate only bread and cheese in my room for supper.

I was moody in those days. While at times I could take satisfaction in the activities that were now mine, I was still so lacking in self-confidence that the least setback would throw me into depression. Such was the case when my teaching came under criticism. Miss Hyde, a big ungainly, gray-haired, rather sloppy woman with the face of a suspicious little owl ruled as head of my department. As usual I had made an excellent impression at the beginning (a pretty face, a trim figure will do a lot for a girl, even with females, as one learns too late after time has traced its lamentable arabesques upon the one, blurred the seductive outlines of the other). I could speak French well and had a firm knowledge of the language.

Miss Hyde had looked into my room briefly a couple of times. A more extensive visit was to be expected and in due course befell. The subject of the lesson that day was some aspect of French grammar (perhaps the agreement of the past participle), and I spent the period at the blackboard. Miss Hyde sat in the rear. Getting up as the bell rang, she commented curtly to the class, "It's too bad this excellent lesson didn't receive all the attention it deserved." To me privately when the girls had left she said tartly, "I saw some novels being read, a crossword puzzle being done. Attention was poor."

When out of my crushed pride I gave a verbatim report to Pauline, "Oh, Vera," she exclaimed, "go to Miss Hyde, go at once. Tell her you'll try hard to correct your faults. She may not keep you." If I didn't go to Miss Hyde it was not because of pride but because of a sheer and utter lack of confidence. For me the ax had already fallen: my job was gone; I had slipped back into that dark phase from which I had been so recently rescued. The truth of the matter was that while I was well trained in my subject, I had only a meager sense of the classroom discipline I might have absorbed years ago in one term of practice teaching at Hunter. I was inexperienced at an age when I should have had several years of work behind me. As the end of the term was approaching, I looked for another job.

Pauline was smiling these days; there was a quickly kindled light in her blue eyes. She was enjoying her teaching and anticipating the time spent with a young man who had come into her life, a cultured European named Kozma. Pauline was completely in love with him. Uninhibited as always, her face glowed with adoration in her idol's presence. She had bought a car so that they could go about weekends, and sister Edith in Rockaway was doing everything possible to smooth the way.

The summer vacation brought an event which was to me the most important, the most exciting and stimulating of my life so far. A Party convention was to be held in Chicago and I was going! The comrades of the teachers' fraction, Bob Van Patten, and I were hitchhiking out.

The whole teachers' fraction except Bert Miller, who was going by train, left New York as a group but soon we had to separate, Bob and I remaining together. The pickups in the main were safe and friendly. The constantly changing scene, the little towns, the hills of Pennsylvania, the unending cornfields of Indiana, all this kaleidoscopic jumble of our native land Bob and I were seeing for the first time. At last, in the late afternoon of the second day at the edge of a great sun-gilded plain, the smoky spread of the steel mills . . . Gary, then at long last Chicago, my first glimpse of a great industrial city.

My anticipations of the Party convention were not disappointed. Even though the sessions were often noisy and at times chaotic, and the dissensions in the Party came out openly, still on the whole I could feel I belonged to a live, active organization with a principled base. I saw and heard all the chief leaders, besides the many delegates from the whole country and onlookers like myself. The Workers Party had its national headquarters in its own building at 1113 West Washington Boulevard. On August 21, 1925, opening day of the convention, we found people milling about everywhere. The seating of the delegates alone took several days because a number of delegations and individuals were contested.

Heated debates took place. Often the sessions were interrupted or post-poned while caucuses met for hours.

During these intervals Bob and I went out to see Chicago. The splen-did lakefront was the principal esthetic asset of the city; we admired the many boulevards with their center aisles of trees and the numerous large parks. Much of the city on the other hand was drab, immense, sprawling, and ugly.

At last the proceedings got underway. From the start it appeared there had been recent Comintern decisions condemning the factionalism and power struggles of the American Party. The shop-nucleus form of organi-zation of the Party was the one recommended and stressed. The Labor Party came up too in discussion. Here there seemed to be room for dif-ference of opinion. As a means of rallying the masses in America it was clearly a policy to be considered. On the other hand, there was a danger of sidetracking the agitation for Communism, which was the principal goal. On August 26, following a report on the Party press, a tremendous demonstration for unity took place with long continued cheering and sing-ing of the "International." Spontaneous as the display appeared, it must surely have been agreed to by the factions.

The high point of the convention, however, occurred on the following day when a cablegram was received from the Comintern awarding the Party to Ruthenberg, whose group was designated as being more loyal to it. The majority (the Foster group) was instructed not to suppress the Ruthenberg group. The Foster group was accused of ultra-factional me-chanical methods. It seems Foster was bitterly opposed to the decision. This did not appear openly, but I got some briefing on the inner caucus developments from Bert Miller, who was close to the leaders of the Ruthenberg group.

Present at all meetings was a quiet, inconspicuous little man known as P. Green, the Comintern representative. Green used diplomacy in the situation, working on James P. Cannon, who was with the Foster group but showed signs of independence, which Green encouraged. Cannon persuaded William F. Dunne from Minneapolis, another Fosterite, to side with him. Together the two men put pressure on Foster to accept the Comintern decision. The Central Committee was to be divided equally between the two factions, with P. Green always present and sup-porting the Ruthenberg group. Such was the Communist International decision, which Foster unwillingly had to follow.*

For my part, I was pleased that my team had won. Ruthenberg made a much better impression than Foster did: he seemed more mature, more

---

*For a full account of the convention see the *Daily Worker*, August 21-28, 1925.

mellow and stable, and more detached from the petty power struggle. He was personally a rather handsome man of about forty, tall, slender, blonde, with blue eyes and a rather hawklike face. Foster on the other hand seemed overwrought, easily provoked, and contentious.

A note of sadness was struck at the very end by the death of William F. Dunne's seven-year-old son, who was killed by an auto. Many of the comrades went to the funeral. I didn't go, but I felt myself one with these many people rallying to share the grief of a member.

Back in New York it took me at least a week to settle into the rather hectic routine of a job in a newly opened school in the Bronx, the James Monroe High. I had a new furnished room near the school with a kind, friendly Hungarian Jewish couple. When I left every Friday afternoon to go out to Dover, my good landlady would insist on my sitting down first in her kitchen to eat a big plateful of chicken soup full of homemade noodles, to build up my strength for the journey.

In discussing the convention reports the Harlem English branch pulled together a bit better than usual, even abandoning, at least for a while, the factional strife. Because the convention had given me a deeper understanding of the Party, I could follow the agenda better.

In October, with the Party entering the election campaign, the branch decided to hold a street meeting. With a half-dozen others I volunteered to participate. Arriving on time on the appointed evening, I found the street empty, the building closed. It was already getting dark. After a little while just one more comrade showed up, a young Negro from Jamaica named George Padmore. We decided to hold the meeting by ourselves. Rousting up the janitor, we got the stepladder and literature out of the basement and proceeded over to Lenox Avenue, where our meeting attracted some fifteen or twenty people. I was the chairman, Padmore the speaker. Sharing satisfaction in this modest achievement, we got better acquainted as we returned the materials to the headquarters. George was restless. He didn't like this country; he was dissatisfied with the Party. I agreed with him although the convention with its new line had given me a ray of hope. The evening was a unique one, for Padmore soon disappeared from the scene, apparently seeking greener pastures elsewhere, and it was long till I would see him again.

5

Passaic: Achievement
and Betrayal

FOR ME THE HISTORIC PASSAIC STRIKE BEGAN ONE EVENING IN DECEMBER
1925, as I was westward bound from New York on a train of the Erie Railroad. This time I was not headed for Caldwell or Dover, but for Passaic,
one of the many small industrial towns of northern New Jersey. As we
jogged over the Jersey Meadows, a vast, barren, swampy tract, little inhabited and bisected by the Hackensack River, all of it now smothered in
evening mist, I was feeling a certain trepidation.

When a couple of weeks earlier Bert Miller, industrial organizer for
the Party district, had told me of some organization work among New
Jersey textile workers being conducted by a young Harvard graduate,
Albert Weisbord, "This is just what the Party should be doing," I
said. Still, when he had informed me that I was scheduled to speak to
some women textile workers in Passaic I was hesitant. "I've never in my
life spoken in public. What will I say to them?" . . . my old characteristic of resisting something I really wanted very much to do.

Albert Weisbord met me at the station. As we walked down Main
Avenue, with just a quick appraising glance at me, he plunged at once
into an exposition of what seemed to be his dominating interest. He
talked fast, a sort of machine-gun fire. Though he appeared tired, as if
from lack of sleep, he was nonetheless vigorous and his concentration was
intense.

"The chief task of the Party is to organize the unorganized, the millions of unskilled, badly exploited workers whom the AFL leaves untouched. There's no use expecting the Party leaders to undertake this

100

work. In fact, not merely will they themselves not start it, they'll resist to the limit anyone who does. Oh yes, the Central Committee passed a resolution in December to organize the unorganized, but as far as they are concerned it remains on paper. A small group of comrades have already begun work in New England among the cotton workers. I left there to start something here in this important center for wool and worsted, as well as silk weaving and dyeing. Have been working as a silk weaver in Paterson, but I've had to quit that. I'm now leading a strike of four hundred workers in the Hillcrest, a silk mill in west New York."

A sort of boyish grin broke his intense seriousness. There was a gleam of pride in his eyes and at the same time a note of self-deprecation in his voice. He paused and for just a minute he appeared young and unsure of himself.

"Our real objective is right here in Passaic. It's the biggest woolen and worsted center in the entire country, not less than fifteen thousand workers, about half of them women. Children work too, nine, ten hours a day. Average wage about twenty dollars a week, skilled workers maybe twenty-five for a full week. And last October the bosses put over a ten percent wage cut in some mills. Think of that, on wages already so low and the work speeded up at the same time.

"The time is ripe now for organizing more than ever before. You know there are many nationalities here: the Poles are the biggest group, but there are many Italians and Hungarians too, as well as Slavs and Germans. The Germans are chiefly foremen. At the turn of the century, when the heaviest immigration was taking place, workers were sent here directly from Ellis Island with tags around their necks like cattle. The bosses kept the nationalities separate at work so they couldn't communicate. It's different now, some have learned English, and their children, born here, are now at work in the mills. Through them we can reach the older workers.

"I've been getting help from the various Communist-dominated language federations here in Passaic, the Italian, Polish, and especially the Hungarian. They publish papers and have meeting halls and many of the workers belong to them. Without the federations I'd never make first base here, alone as I am.

"The mills are mostly German-owned, heavily capitalized, real giant corporations. Botany Worsted Mill has assets of twenty-eight million dollars net and makes profits of over six million a year. They had to organize a holding company in 1922, Botany Consolidated, to hide their enormous profits of twenty percent net. They've bought up the Garfield Worsted Company, a smaller place. Forstmann-Huffmann has a net worth of eleven million and powerful German connections. In 1922 New Jersey

Worsted was able to buy up the Gera Mills, which were making profits of fifty-three percent a year. And then there's the dyeing industry—silk dyeing—we have that here too. The United Piece Dye Works of Lodi is one of the biggest.*

"The textile workers have had their strikes. Passaic had one in 1919, won the forty-eight-hour week and a seventeen percent increase in wages, but the union they formed soon died out. In 1922 the OBU (One Big Union) was active in Massachusetts but they've never been able to win a union, only a few skilled workers in craft groups looking out for their own interests. Oh, these textile barons——" he broke off vehemently as we climbed the broad staircase to his office at 743 Main Avenue, "We'll teach them a lesson yet!"

In the little office some workingmen were playing checkers in one corner, while in another a slim, dark-eyed youth softly drew a tune out of a harmonica.

"Miss Smith, this is Mike Elasik. Meet Miss Smith from New York," Weisbord introduced me to the harmonica player. Leona Smith was the name I had taken following Miller's advice not to use my own name. "Nobody here yet? Well, I suppose it's too hard for women to get out at night. We'll give them another ten minutes." And then later, when nobody else came, "Mike is going to show you the mills. I'll have a few words with these fellows here."

Mike Elasik and I crossed the railroad tracks, at once entering the mill section of the town. Relieved, yet at the same time disappointed that the women hadn't come, I felt at ease with this direct, polite, soft-spoken young man as we walked through the almost empty, poorly lighted streets. The dingy, two- or three-storied frame buildings were dark, and complete silence prevailed as though everyone were already asleep.

Soon we came to a bridge over a river. Here a raw wind swept down the valley. I shivered in my winter coat; young Elasik with only a light jacket over his sweater paid no attention. The city behind us cast a faint glow over the sky; the water shimmered vaguely. Here the mills were all around us near and far, up and down the river.

"Forstmann-Huffmann, big rich company," said Mike, pointing to a huge structure not far away, lighted by floodlights on the lawn in front. "They have other big mills in Garfield," pointing in another direction. "Here is Botany Worsted Mill. I work here. Father, Mother also. Mother works on night shift. Sister works in Dundee, little silk mill in Clifton."

It appeared to be a big complex of buildings of different sizes, some

*For full details on the mills, see Paul Murphy, D. Klassen, and K. Hall, *The Passaic Strike of 1926* (Belmont, Calif.: Wadsworth Press, 1974).

lighted, some dark. In one immense building windows were all alight. The whole structure throbbed with life, looms crashed and wheels whirred, all blending in an incessant pounding rhythm, like some giant heart, permeating the winter night.

When we parted that evening, Organizer Weisbord asked me almost pleadingly, "You'll come again, Miss Smith?"

"I'm not a public speaker. But I'm very interested in your work. If you can find something for me, I'd like to help."

"I've been considering the idea of an English class. That's badly needed. It would help to bring the workers together. Could you do that?"

"I used to earn my pocket money through high school and college teaching English to foreigners. Yes, I could do that."

"So you'll be here next week? Come earlier. We'll have supper together."

All week I mulled over the impressions of this unique evening. The term "Harvard graduate," which was about all Bert Miller had given me, had conjured up someone tall, blond, athletic, handsome, and suave, a combination Greek god and present-day football hero. Organizer Weisbord fulfilled none of these expectations. He looked shabby in a worn overcoat and funny little tweed hat. He wore glasses. His nose was shiny, his eyelids red, as though from lack of sleep, with the beginning of a stye on one eye. He had bombarded me with a lot of figures that I found hard to absorb. However, he had impressed me, not merely with the magnitude and importance of the job he was undertaking, but with his own intellectual power as well as his total dedication. And he seemed to be all alone to carry out a great task. There was something somber in this first impression—or was it perhaps the dreary mill town itself which cast its shadow over him?

And the lives of the people of that town? I knew my father's and mother's lives, the poverty of my own childhood, but these mills, this brutal exploitation of thousands of human being so badly overworked and underpaid, in every way deprived, this I could only try to imagine.

I could hardly wait for the week to pass.

Now I found myself opposite Organizer Weisbord at a little table in a Chinese restaurant. Here for the first time we faced each other as two individuals. With his hat off, I saw his dark hair was thinning on top. His stye had cleared up, but the lids were still red. His head was a fine one, of the square Russian type. Sensitivity was expressed in his full, flexible lips, keenness in the glance of his brown eyes. There was a suggestion of suppressed passion in his heavy eyelids and in the softness of his voice.

We talked chiefly of our backgrounds. What I said had to be in words pushed in edgewise whenever there might be a pause in his almost unceasing flow of speech. I told him a little of my home life, my Puritan background, my long struggle with TB. When he heard I had joined the Communist Party among the first, had been briefly in the underground and also in the IWW, I could see some hint of respect from him.

He spoke of what he called his petit-bourgeois family, his father a small manufacturer. "I tried to organize my father's workers once. He didn't like that." Here came another of those sudden transforming grins. He had broken with them all except his more tolerant mother, whom he saw occasionally. His interest in socialism had begun in his boyhood when the family was poor and Albert used to sell newspapers. His older sisters' young men were Socialists, who apparently had had more influence on Albert than on the girls.

While a history student at the City College of New York, he had been an active member of a Socialist Party branch in Brooklyn and taught classes in the Rand School. He wrote a paper on the role of unofficial schools in the USA, really a defense of the Rand School, which was under attack from the Lusk Committee. Then the Socialist Party co-opted him into becoming director of the YPSL (Young People's Socialist League). When he went to Harvard, he supplemented his partial scholarship by working first in a cafeteria, then at a soda fountain. Because of its chicanery, law had never appealed to him as a profession; however, he wanted to understand the law as a product of social forces, and ultimately to use it to help in organizing workers. At that time there was a wave of strikes, and during summer vacations he spoke to mine and railroad strikers in Utica, New York, in Terre Haute, Indiana, and elsewhere.

In 1922 after a national tour the convention of the YPSL elected him national secretary, which placed him also on the National Executive Board of the Party.

It was his intensive reading and pondering the works of Lenin that were available then, especially *State and Revolution*, that had drawn him to the Workers (Communist) Party (WCP), which he considered to be more representative of the workers than the Socialist Party (SP). In addition he found the Communist International thesis on Bolshevization, on testing of leadership, and on shop nuclei especially convincing. After long deliberation, upon graduating from Harvard in 1924, he tendered his resignation from the SP to the National Executive Committee and joined the WCP.

"To get someone prominent in the Socialist Party was decidedly a catch for the WCP. Right away I was offered the opportunity to go to Chicago to their national office. My answer was, 'How do you know I'm a Communist? Do you mean to say you would place an untested person at once in leadership? How do you know I've broken from my petit-bourgeois background?' No, I declined. Instead, I remained in New England to begin work there.

"It was then that we began the formation of the United Front Committees of Textile Workers. I was the most active factor. John Ballam was in it, but as Party district organizer his chief interest was in factional fighting. We also had Fred Beal in Lawrence, who had worked in cotton mills, and a dentist named Nicholson. We spoke at mill gates. That was when, seeing the gap between the college youth that I was and the workers, I realized I had to become one of them. Really to know their problems I had to learn the trade.

"So I went to Woonsocket, Rhode Island, and canvassed for Watkins Emulsified Coconut Oil. I went down the Blackstone valley from Woonsocket to Central Falls and Providence. At last in one village I met the wife of a mill superintendent whose husband put me on as a learner in charge of an Englishman, who taught me to run the automatic Draper loom. When that mill closed down for lack of work, I went to Central Falls and, claiming to be a cotton weaver, got a job on the night shift in a silk mill. A German woman, a weaver, taught me to weave silk."

When I told him of my disappointment, having succeeded after years of isolation in rejoining the Party, of the dead-rot atmosphere of the headquarters downtown, of the constant factional wrangling in the Harlem English branch, of that one street meeting in Harlem held by George Padmore and myself, he exploded.

"Oh, those bastards!" he exclaimed hotly. "You see how they drive good people away from the Party. I have to fight tooth and nail; they block every constructive proposal. . . . But at least you didn't leave. . . ."

He paused to give me a sort of tentatively probing look, as though he were seeing me for the first time. "And you came out here. . . . Do you know," he added wistfully, "I hardly dared believe you'd come again? Well, we'll have to run. I have a meeting scheduled," looking at his watch. Our chop suey, rice, and tea had long since been consumed. Jumping up abruptly, he walked quickly toward the cashier's desk. On the way he threw casually over his shoulder, "I was married once; she left me after three months."

That evening revealed new facets of this man who the week before had appeared not much more than a personified idea. During our talk over the dinner table an individual of some stature with already a significant history had emerged. Now in the headquarters, with little jokes and smiles he got the dozen or so men out of their overcoats and seated. They were of varying ages and ethnic groups, but they were one in a responding confidence in their organizer, who spoke in a tender, almost fatherly way, although barely twenty-five he was actually younger than most of them.

It was this quality of empathy that won me over. For the first time I began to think I might love, perhaps already did love, this young man.

He introduced me as the English teacher; I was to come out once a week. As I sat in at that meeting, and as Weisbord explained the aims and methods of the United Front Committee of Textile Workers, which these mill workers had joined, I had a very satisfying feeling of belonging to this progressive enterprise. The immediate purpose of the Committee was to organize a union here in Passaic and in the contiguous towns of Garfield, Clifton, and Wallington, where the mills were located and the workers lived. It would also try to bring about the eventual amalgamation of the several small ineffective unions that already existed elsewhere.

Meanwhile at school there were continuing difficulties and vexations. Besides the drain of energy the job demanded, every morning one's letter box was stuffed with notices of records to be turned in. Rarely did we leave before 4:00 P.M.

The building of the James Monroe High School in the North Bronx was barely completed; some classes had to be held in the auditorium and workmen were still about. It was a coeducational school and an atmosphere of hysteria pervaded it. Every change of class found a mob of excited babbling youth rushing confusedly about to locate their next classroom. In my old job in a comparatively sedate atmosphere I had been criticized for lack of discipline; here teachers much more experienced than I were having trouble. The quiet of the teachers' restroom was jarred by tales of how impossible the kids were. The teachers, chiefly women middle-aged and single, displayed an antagonism toward the children that shocked me. I really liked the kids and deplored any inability to control them. At Christmas the presents on my desk were cheering evidence that some of them at least liked me too. Because my job was for the term only, I looked around for another position. The only one I could find was in a junior high with longer hours and less pay.

The weekly trips out to Dover to see my family continued, but there was no more noodle soup; I had changed my room in order to be nearer the Party headquarters downtown. My new room was in a widow's small apartment. One evening, coming home late, as I crossed the living room in the dark, I heard from the widow's bedroom a sympathetic utterance: "Never mind, Miss Buch, some day Mr. Right will turn up!" Did I really show my loneliness, my frustration so patently?

After a few trips out to Passaic for the English class, events there came to a head. I arrived one evening to find the headquarters spilling over with people all talking at once. Organizer Weisbord, elated, could only slip me a few words.

"It's possible a strike may break out. In that event I could use you in the office. Will you come?"

I told him I was committed to finish my term at school, but after that I'd consider it. It was clear there would be no English class that night. A man active for the union in Botany Worsted Mill had been fired; people here tonight would elect a committee of three to protest to the company.

The committee of three met on January 21, Thursday, with a vice president of Botany. His answer was that any union people caught would be fired. All those who had joined the United Front Committee met in a hall on Monday, January 25, to elect a committee of forty-five to tackle the mill management again, this time not to ask for reinstatement but to present the following demands:

1. Abolition of the 10 percent wage cut in effect since October,
2. Time and a half for overtime,
3. No discrimination against union people.

In the meantime the interview was rehearsed and its outcomes analyzed so that the committee, as well as all union people in the plant, were prepared for the critical moment. At a prearranged time all committee members left their machines and in regular order got together; the workers in the departments, alerted, stopped work to await the outcome. As expected, the committee was summarily ejected and told to go out the front gate. There stood Passaic Chief of Police Zober waiting with a contingent of officers. Pushing the police aside, the committee members ran back into the mill and went from one department to another throughout the big building shouting "Strike! Strike!" The workers left their machines, poured by the thousands out of the front gate, and the strike was on. I learned all this through Bert Miller, with whom Weisbord kept in touch.

Soon I was free to make my decision, which was in a way already determined. The only deterrent factor was what seemed to be my own inadequacy, or lack of suitability, for such work. The people who stood out in Party activities seemed to be naturally aggressive, talkative, and outgoing. I with my Puritan New England background was shy, reserved, and quiet. My education, my immersion in literature, poetry, and art, were all wrong as preparation for a labor organizer. Still, it seemed as though I got along well with the workers in the English class. And when I had told Comrade Weisbord frankly of my limited clerical skills, he had said that didn't matter at all.

Actually for the first time I was making a choice in a wholehearted manner, doing what I most wanted to do, and at the same time following my deepest convictions. That the pay was minimal meant nothing; there would be enough for a room and food. What more could I want?

Losing no time, I notified the Board of Education I couldn't accept their splendid offer of a junior high position, made a flying trip out to the country to deposit some surplus belongings, then a visit to the Party headquarters, where I was taking a course in Marx's *Capital*, Volume I, with Comrade Mandel, one of the local leaders, and this I really regretted giving up. Comrade Mandel congratulated me on becoming an "activist." "The Party needs more like you." The others were full of admiration. Finally, my little suitcase in hand I arrived at 743 Main Avenue.

Organizer Weisbord briefly introduced me to the crowd of strikers. I found him quite changed; his serious ascetic mien had given way to a beaming, smiling one.

"At last some help," he exclaimed. "I've been really swamped. Let's hope there'll be others."

A room had been engaged for me with some Party members named Bogorad who owned a big house not far from the office. It was in the good half of town, west of the tracks with broad streets, lawns, and trees, where less than ten percent of the people lived.

Though my tasks in the office were never really defined, there was much to do: applications, union cards, and relief cards to fill out, and occasional typing.

A few days later one other helper was sent out by the Party District, Jack Bryan, whom Comrade Miller had found hanging around meetings. He had seemed eager to come. He was a tall, lanky, red-haired, shabbily dressed man of about thirty-five, talkative and usually in need of a shave. He was assigned as captain to one of the picket stations. Bryan was prompt on the job, shouted a lot to the pickets. He had a lingo that reminded me of the old IWW crowd on the waterfront. He used to hang around the headquarters every evening. It was not long before he made a remark that aroused suspicion. When I went one morning to the picket station, I found him hoarse with shouting; his face and hands were red and chapped. As he paused for a cup of coffee, he sat down beside me on a bench. "Smith," he said, "I think you ought to have more authority around here. You're a capable girl. They don't seem to appreciate you." More authority was one thing I surely did not crave; I was satisfied with my position. When I reported this statement to Albert he listened gravely.

Organizer Weisbord was now a veritable dynamo working from morning to night, speaking to committees, to mass meetings, to individual strikers, to newspaper reporters. He had long planned this event; now that it was coming to pass he never had a moment's hesitation or doubt. His energy, determination, and confidence were communicated to everyone around him.

The strikers were not just passive pawns to be pushed at his will. For months now a good number of them (a thousand people in the Botany) had been signing up with the United Front Committee. They had been listening to the leader's analyses of their situation in all its phases, so that they understood the background, the purposes, and the strategy of this strike. Now the fact of having decided to quit work and actually take this venturous step had inspired courage and decisiveness in people who not long before had been merely sullen and helplessly resentful. Coming out, the strong brought the weak with them, educating them. Leader and strikers were firmly united.

There was a picket station, usually a rented vacant store, near each striking mill with a captain in charge, and coffee and sandwiches were handed out. It was winter and there was snow in the streets. When people came in bundled in overcoats and scarves, they brought a breath of cold air with them.

A strike committee had been organized at the very beginning increasing in size as other mills came out. It met daily to plan the strategy for a rapid extension of the strike to those mills which had cut wages, in stages that would not swamp the office and create confusion. One by one the mills were brought out by picket lines of the workers already on strike. On Wednesday, January 27, the Garfield Worsted Mill; on January 30 the Passaic Worsted Spinning Mill; and the next week, on February 6, the big Gera Mill, followed by the New Jersey Spinning Company. Now, with a permit obtained from a surprised chief of police, a great parade of all these strikers marched past an amazed city population.

Since the activity still allowed occasional moments for personal contact, the friendship between the organizer and me grew rapidly. We went out together for meals, generally to the Chinese place, where the food was cheap and good. We got to know each other better. The attraction that had probably been there from the first was fed by the intimate glances and touches snatched in brief lulls in the strike activity. Then one evening, it happened there was no one in the headquarters but Jack Bryan.

"Look here, Jack," said Albert, somewhat embarrassed, "Smith and I would like to . . . well, we'd like to have the place to ourselves just this once . . . you don't mind? Take the evening off."

Bryan left in astonishment. I had been reading a big book on the textile industry that Albert had borrowed from the library. Sitting close together we thumbed through it, looking at the pictures. Then, after our first kiss, he said, "Do you know I don't even know your real name? What is your name, Leona?"

When I told him, he repeated it thoughtfully, "Vera Buch. I can't call you that. We have to be careful always." Again, quietly, as though he were practicing the name, he said, "Vera."

Though I had very much desired the kisses, I wondered, is it the same thing again, just fooling around? And I remained reserved.

One morning he said I was to act as his secretary at the daily mass meeting; a newspaper had misquoted something; he couldn't have that. So now for a few days there I was, right up on the platform in Neubauer's Hall taking notes, overlooking the audience. The organizer's language was simple and direct, the words hurled out in a powerful vibrant voice that penetrated every corner of the hall. As he talked, he gestured and walked back and forth. My note-taking continued only for a few days until he concluded the newspapers had learned their lesson and wouldn't try any more stunts.

They were always lively, rousing meetings. The stress was on extension of the strike; the coming out of each mill in turn was hailed with cheers as a great victory. Always the low wages, speed-up, and bad conditions were the focus, and always the emphasis was on winning the strike. The strikers were not there to prove someone's sociological theory. They were literally fighting for their lives, which were being shortened by the exploitation. Solidarity, sticking together in the union, was to be the means of winning. Because of their own powerful organizations the employers could act together to cut wages and to introduce speed-up methods. If they remained divided and unorganized, the workers could never be anything but helpless. "The United Front of the Workers against the United Front of the Bosses" was one of our principal slogans.

The next step in extending the strike—a great one—was to tackle one of the strongest employers, the Forstmann-Huffmann Company, which owned three mills in the vicinity. The workers in F–H had not yet received wage cuts; they were on the "hunger treatment," that is, they were working part time, a situation which, as they had learned by experience, often preceded wage cuts. With their spirits broken, the workers would not resist the cuts when they came. Forstmann-Huffmann had a company union called "The Assembly," the chief purpose of which was to keep the workers obedient to the company. This did not prevent a good number of people from the largest F–H mill, which employed four thousand, from joining the United Front Committee.

So now in the third week of the strike careful preparations were made. First, the original modest demands were expanded and strengthened. The new demands, which were mailed out on February 4 to six of the largest mills, were:

1. Not only the abolition of the wage cut but a 10 percent increase over the old wage scale,
2. Return of the money taken from the workers by wage cuts since the time the last cuts were given,
3. Time and a half for overtime,
4. A forty-four hour week,
5. Decent sanitary working conditions,
6. No discrimination against union workers,
7. Recognition of the union.

Whereas at first the wage cuts had appeared to be the principal objective, now the fight for a union was coming to the fore. The workers had learned by experience that without a recognized union there would be no guarantee of maintaining any concessions won.

To reach the biggest of the F–H mills, located in nearby Garfield, it was necessary to cross the Ackerman Avenue bridge over the Passaic River. Having been briefed to expect trouble, the workers braced themselves. The strongest forces had been mobilized; the entire strike committee headed the march. Newspapers from the whole metropolitan area had been notified so that reporters and cameramen were ready at the bridge. This was on February 9. When the unarmed picket line reached the bridge, it was met by a large body of police who pushed the line back, trampling men, women, and children, and clubbing them mercilessly.

Many of the casualties came into the office that day with bleeding head wounds, or limping, or holding an arm or shoulder bruised by the clubs. At the mass meeting that evening one of the most severely beaten strikers was up on the platform. When he took off his shirt to expose to the audience his broad upper back, completely covered with black and blue marks, a shudder and a groan went through the ranks. Some wept. The town, the New York area, and the entire country were horrified when the pictures were released showing the police wielding their clubs on defenseless strikers.

This brutal assault at the Ackerman Avenue bridge resulted in a more determined effort of the workers not to give in. The strike committee resolved to have another picket line try again the next day. Police and officials, unnerved by the publication of the pictures, weakened. The next day the line went through to the plant and large numbers of the workers there, prepared by those within who had already joined the United Front Committee, poured out of the gates, the skilled workers, spinners, and weavers leading the way. The F–H mill worked a few more days with reduced forces and a picket line outside. Then the employers, alleging that the remaining workers were "in fear of their lives," closed down that mill. The F–H management may possibly have intended to flood the strike with workers not yet under the union influence who had not voluntarily walked out.

Here Albert ventured a rather daring tactic. He knew that sooner or later the Protestant employers would use the Jewish question to try to influence the mainly Catholic workers. Since the commissioner of public safety in charge of the police, Abram Preiskel, was also a Jew, Weisbord made it a point to denounce Preiskel "as one Jew to another." This prevented the potential anti-Semitic line that the employers could have taken.

Then he countered the "foreign agitator" and "un-American Communist" attacks by exposing the fact that the owners of the Botany Mill and others had been declared "enemy aliens" during World War I, with their property sequestered under trust.

Now fully alerted, the mill owners mobilized their forces, but in the meantime the situation at 743 Main Avenue had drastically changed. At last, with the great extension of the strike and the resultant publicity, the Party was jostled out of its sluggishness and resistance; real forces were sent out to Passaic. From an obscure struggle we became a nationally known event and were flooded with helpers from New York and elsewhere. No lack of speakers now. Labor leaders and liberals of all stripes came out.

A real staff was quickly built up. The newcomers sent out from New York, all young, were members either of the Party or of the Young People's Communist League (YCL). Some would be working with the ethnic groups in Passaic. Emil Gardos, a studious, gentle, young Hungarian with curly blond hair and glasses, was on the editorial staff of *Uj Elore*, the paper of the Hungarian Federation. He spoke in Hungarian at the mass meetings, always beginning his speech with the words *"Munkas starshim,"* which apparently meant "fellow workers." The Italian Federation sent Joe Magliacano and Tom DeFazio. Both spent most of their time in Lodi, where many Italians worked in the dye plant.

Lena Chernenko from the Amalgamated Clothing Workers had had experience in the strikes of her union. She was a young woman in her late twenties, distinguished by her courage, energy, and militant determination. She was, according to Albert, a "confirmed Fosterite." Here in Passaic, however, there was no time for factionalism. As picket captain, Lena had to get up at four o'clock in the bitter morning chill to see that the picket lines were organized and directed around the Gera Mill, where many women worked. Since organizers were not spared the policemen's clubs, she had many a bruise.

In charge of all picket stations was a tall, lanky youth of nineteen, Jack Rubenstein, a rather emotional fellow with a soft-lipped, pimply, very young face. A graduate of Brookwood Labor College, he was at his first strike. He threw himself enthusiastically into all the scrimmages with the police and was often arrested and beaten up while in jail.

A little later two youths were sent out by the YCL to work among the striking youth and strikers' children. Clarence Miller, a big, tall fellow with sandy red hair and glasses was a college graduate and a member of the League Central Committee. Miriam Silverfarb was a curly-haired, vivacious little person, college-bred also, from a middle-class family. She became active among the children and organized them in Pioneer groups, teaching them songs and mobilizing them to support the strike. Later Sophie Melvin and Martha Stone came to help her.

To enlarge our headquarters we rented a series of rooms, including a large office overlooking the street. Here was soon ensconced Alfred Wagenknecht (commonly known as "Wag") from the Workers International Relief. He was an energetic, businesslike individual. He promptly built up a network of relief contacts, sent out streams of publicity, organized conferences and meetings. He declined to speak at strike meetings. "I'm just here for the relief," he would say, rubbing his hands together briskly, "only for the relief."

With funds coming in from this office we could organize our strikers' relief on a sound basis. Single strikers got $5 weekly, a couple $6, family heads from $7 to $10, depending on the number of children. A great help was the donation of several truckloads daily of freshly baked rye bread from the Paterson Bakers' Cooperative.

The participation of the liberals and socialists continued throughout the strike. Roger Baldwin, then head of the American Civil Liberties Union, came out to speak and also enlisted his organization to help handle the numerous cases of arrested strikers and staff.*

An occasional visitor was an Italian named Coco, who was in the Party but also had anarchist connections. He had long hair and wore a bow tie. Coco spoke in Italian at the meetings in Lodi. Once in a while we also saw a man named George Ashkenudze, who looked like a businessman and whose role was a little mysterious.†

---

*Norman Thomas, prominent socialist leader, came out a number of times. Others who put in appearances were John Haynes Holmes, a well-known liberal clergyman; Forrest Bailey of the ACLU; Alfred Baker Lewis of the Rand School; the Reverend Edward Chaffee of the Labor Temple; Frieda Kirchway, editor of *The Nation*; and Arthur Garfield Hays of the ACLU.

†Both Coco and Ashkenudze were certainly Russian G.P.U. (secret police) agents. Later, during the Spanish Civil War, Coco shepherded a group of American volun-

Carlo Tresca, a well-known anarchist, came out once or twice. We saw much of Elizabeth Gurley Flynn, who was also among the anarchists. She had participated in the New England textile strikes of 1912 and 1919 and was a warm, vibrant person and a powerful speaker. Albert set himself the task of winning her over for the Party. Eventually he succeeded.

Two women liberals made a contribution in publicity. Margaret Larkin came to live in Passaic, staying at the Bogorads', where I lived. Mary Heaton Vorse, a writer and journalist, came out often to get material for articles in support of the strike, and later she wrote a pamphlet. Both women helped issue a weekly *Textile Strike Bulletin*, containing articles by Weisbord and other staff members, as well as correspondence from strikers.

Of the WCP leaders, Foster never came at all, nor any leaders of his faction, nor Lovestone, Ruthenberg, and James P. Cannon. Their non-appearance seemed to support Albert's contention that they were indifferent, if not hostile, toward the strike. The exception was Benjamin Gitlow of the Amalgamated Clothing Workers, who had come out to speak before the strike broke out. He was at that time a member of the Central Executive Committee (with voice but no vote). Later on the leaders made him the head of a CEC textile committee. Seated in Chicago, this committee dealt with the Passaic strike, but as anyone who has participated in a strike knows, such activity cannot be directed from afar.

Other individuals not so welcome soon appeared: the men from the Department of Justice. They would hang around like the police on the outskirts at the mass meetings, and every morning we would have to pass a line-up of them in the hall, all eyeing us with that hard, cold, scrutinizing look with which the "dick" memorizes the appearance of a suspect, in order to spot him or her the next time.

The strike committee, now much larger, met every day at nine in the morning. The committee had been formed so as to give representation: first, to all mills on strike; second, to all important crafts in the mill; third, to men, women, and youth; and last, to the principal ethnic groups. Thus it was a truly composite body.

The chairman of the committee was twenty-one-year-old Gus Deak, of Hungarian descent, clean-cut, alert, and articulate. He had worked for seven years in the finishing department of the Botany, where the temperature was 110°, running a machine that dried and pressed wet material. Gus had started at ten cents an hour and worked up to fifty cents, but the work was not steady.

---

teers across the ocean, a very confidential position. Ashkenudze, a member of the Russian Federation, played no role in the strike. He was merely there.

From Botany also was Eli Keller, a Jewish loom fixer. As the most skilled of all textile workers, the loom fixers were mostly English or Scotch and they generally remained aloof from the unskilled. Not Eli Keller; he mingled freely with everyone. Another Botany worker was Ellen Dawson, a Scotch weaver. Panerisi was a stocky, baldish little Italian from "Forsamanna-Huffamanna," as he always said.

Outstanding was a short, broad, powerful-looking Czech woman, Ma Brezniak from the Gera Mill. She worked on "heavy drawing," pulling the warps into the frames. "Takes good strong woman to do that," she would say with pride. She was a real pillar of strength, understanding everything so readily, spreading the word to the women, a tiger on the picket line.

A good number of youths were on the committee too: Mike Elasik, from the office, was dependable. Chester Grabinsky of the Polish group had been in the vanguard pulling out the Botany Mill and he continued to be very active.

The meetings were disciplined, following a strict order of business. Weisbord's report came first, giving the new developments of the strike, its daily tactics, and what could be divined of the employers' intentions. Then came public relations, the reactions of the local population and the general public. The relief office made an occasional report, then the strikers told of their picket lines, and of any rumors being circulated. Tasks were assigned and plans laid for the immediate period. Discussion was lively and included all the members.

In the midst of it all, one day during a brief, quiet interval in the office, Albert drew me over to the window and as we stood close said in a businesslike way, "Smith, I want to live with you on a permanent basis. I believe you have the qualities I want in a partner. You have courage, intelligence, and the desire to be a Bolshevik. You'll be my Krupskaya. You will go with me from one strike to another. This is just the beginning. When we have the textile industry organized, we'll move on to steel, and so on, building the Party. You can never have children, not even a home. But you'll be always by my side, fighting with me, helping me. . . ."

Just then someone interrupted and I went back to work. In this brief snatched interval we had come to an understanding. For hours afterward his words swirled in my mind, like froth on deep water, one phrase and another repeating itself as though I hadn't understood, but I had. Had he really said those all-important words "on a permanent basis"? Yes, he had. The word LOVE, so essential to me, had never once been uttered by him, nor had he ever expressed any sort of opinion concerning me nor, for that matter, had I of him. Now, however, he had put into words what must have been to him the highest praise. I realized I had just received a proposal. That we couldn't be legally married was clear enough and to me meant little, though I foresaw difficulties with my family. I could never have a home, he had said, but I was certain I could show him I knew how to make a home of any place, however small, however poor. And no children. Well, I had always hoped to have a child sometime. Clearly the present was not the time. To me it was simply being deferred like so many other things. But now at last it seemed my years of loneliness and futility were ended. Now I could really love my man without reservation; now I experienced not merely the joy and elation of being in love, but with it a deeply felt satisfaction never known before.

Always so sure of himself, Albert was ready with a definition of what he wanted in a wife. I had no such prepared formula. As I thought it over, however, I could tell myself I wanted someone better than I, someone I could look up to. Having more formal education than I, Albert knew vastly more in the fields of history and social sciences, a necessary background for our work. My education appeared useless by comparison, but I was willing to learn. As an organizer he had extraordinary ability, knew the facts concerning the mills as well as the workers' lives, applied maximum energy and thoroughness in executing policies. He was also something of a "born leader," with the necessary charisma, the urge to lead and to teach others. A circumstance that contributed to his success in Passaic was that quite early in his life his orientation and his purpose had been defined, and he had already had several years' experience in pursuing his aims. Not unimportant, too, was the fact that he was a textile worker; he could approach the workers as one of them.

As for me, I had had little control over my life so far and now it seemed I was being swept into his orbit, my place to be by his side. But his ideals were, after all, mine too; I had made this choice years before I had met him.

I never said "yes" for I had not been asked a question. Everything was understood between us from then on. In the background of our romance was the harmonica playing of our gentle friend Mike Elasik. In the early days, in the few idle moments in the evening, Albert liked to sing, "Ah moon of my delight that knows no wane." One song, "Oh how I miss you tonight, miss you when lights are low," became our theme song. Returning from occasional trips to New York, we enjoyed such intimacy as we could achieve sitting on the back seat of the bus. And then that night when he climbed up the back porch at the Bogorads'. . . . Every bit of it was interwoven with the strike in which we were both completely involved.

Despite the onslaughts of the police, our strike tactics of gradual extension and absorption of new forces had been successful so far. Our forces were now close to sixteen thousand strikers. Organizer Weisbord seemed to have something of a military sense and had done some reading on military tactics. Like a general, he saw that we had now reached a lull in which the employers would surely stage some new offensive. For this we had not long to wait.

The sixth week of the strike was one that the workers will never forget. The frantic bosses were determined to stop the onward march of the workers. On Monday police mounted on horses and motorcycles appeared. "Terror Week" had started, such a terror that filled all the newspapers with horrifying tales and pictures. Men, women, and children were mercilessly beaten and ridden down. Tear-gas bombs were thrown and it being winter streams of icy water were played on them. The police were really frothing at the mouth. Drunk and mad with hate they beat down all indiscriminately, including even the reporters and photographers of the New York and other newspapers whose heads and cameras were smashed . . . the picket lines stood firm . . . where the lines were clubbed, the workers would sullenly retreat, only to begin again.*

The workers, stunned and bruised, were by no means crushed by this attack. Their chief reaction was one of rage. That the employers were their enemies, their life in the mill had already taught them; now they saw also the state forces of law and order lined up with the mill owners to break their strike. The workers clenched their fists and resolved to fight harder.

Public reaction to these fresh outrages was intense. We had publicized the extremely low wages, the new wage cuts inflicted, the long hours, the speed-up, the night work of women (illegal at that time in New Jersey), the high death rate of babies and young children in the mill towns, the illiteracy of the workers (Passaic's illiteracy rate was among the three highest in the nation), and the employers' resistance to efforts of the Board of Education to teach the workers English.†

In the wake of public indignation some of the more decent men on the Passaic police force, disgusted with what they were called upon to do,

---

*Albert Weisbord, *Passaic*. For a fuller account see the *New York Times*, March 3, 1926.

†See M. Siegel, "The Passaic Textile Strike of 1926," Ph.D. diss., Columbia Univ., 1952, pp. 100-106.

resigned, their places being filled by thugs picked up from the Bowery of New York. The strike had become a scandal.

Although the police managed to stop the picketing for a little while, public pressure eventually forced the police chief in Garfield, as well as Preiskel and Zober in Passaic, to retreat; and the daily lines were resumed.

Our principal strategy upon which success depended was to extend the strike to bring in the silk mill workers and dye workers of Paterson and vicinity. Wages in silk were low, even for the few unionized silk workers in Paterson. In the dye works the pay was even lower, the hours longer, the work conditions extremely unhealthy. Dye workers were subjected to great heat, steam, and fumes from poisonous chemicals. Men had to slave sixty or seventy hours a week to earn only $20 to $25. The dye industry had a strategic importance also: if it were tied up, no broad silk whatever could reach the market.

Our immediate objective was the big United Piece Dye Works of Lodi, three miles away from Passaic. Capitalized at ten million dollars, they had several other plants. Many Italians were among UP's three thousand employees as well as a few hundred Negroes (the only black workers in the area at that time). Our organizers were active in Lodi.

At last we felt certain a base had been laid for calling out the workers of that mill. Our headquarters was in a ferment of preparation; all work was done by strikers and staff. I served on a committee with Miriam Silverfarb and perhaps Wag's secretary to make up slogans for the picket signs. Besides "The Union Will Win" and "United Front of the Workers Against the United Front of the Bosses," we had titles with more bite, such as "You Bosses, You Murderers! 50% More Children Die in Passaic," "Bosses Keep Us Ignorant! Passaic One of 3 Cities Highest in Illiteracy," "Millions for the Bosses, $15 a Week for Us," and "Down with Cossack Police Brutality!"

The important day arrived, a springlike day; it was March 9. We had to cross an open stretch of meadow, a couple of miles wide. Patches of snow lingered on the black, plashy ground. Since this was outside the Passaic city limits, our lines were not molested. At the head of the parade marched the full strike committee, then Organizer Weisbord with me beside him, followed by the mass of strikers. We had six thousand people on that line.

Oh, the pride, the exultation, the joy of that march under the broad open sky! The ranks, four abreast, stretched out ahead and behind us as far as the eye could reach, holding aloft their colorful signs, singing and chanting. "Solidarity Forever" was the song they sang most. Its tune was that of the "Battle Hymn of the Republic"; its new words had been written for them by their leader.

The workers learned their lesson now
As everyone can see.
The workers know their bosses are
Their greatest enemy.
We'll fight and fight until we win
Our final victory
Through One Big Solid Union.

Solidarity forever,
Solidarity forever,
Solidarity forever,
For the Union makes us strong.

The men all stick together
And the boys are fighting fine.
The women and the girls are all right
On the picket line.
No scabs, no threats can stop us
As we all march out on time
In One Big Solid Union.

When we neared the mill, no sooner were we in sight than the workers inside pushed the doors wide open and, rushing out tumultuously, marched with the paraders to a nearby hall for a triumphant mass meeting.

As a next step we called out the Dundee Textile Mill in Clifton, which manufactured broad silk and employed three hundred workers. We carried on work meanwhile in Paterson. Then occurred a walk-out of fifty workers of the large National Silk Dyeing Company of East Paterson, four miles away from Passaic. While they were asking for a picket line to pull out the others, two hundred more people spontaneously walked out.

On March 15, three hundred pickets headed by Jack Rubinstein, many of them sent from Passaic, marched on the mill of the National. Sheriff Nimmo of Bergen County was on hand with well-armed deputies to break up the line. Rubinstein was arrested and sentenced to ninety days in jail. The next day five other pickets were arrested and sentenced to fines or prison terms, but all were soon bailed out.*

We could not spare the forces from Passaic, where we had our hands full with the many mills on strike in that vicinity. Due to lack of support

---

*See Siegel, p. 197, citing the *New York Times*.

by the Party and to the violent attacks by the police, the East Paterson situation flattened out.

In the midst of all the turmoil and work that Albert and I shared, our personal relationship had moved ahead. We were living together now as man and wife. A young Party member of the town, Bailin and his wife rented us a bedroom in their small apartment near the office. A far from ideal setting for the beginning of love. The Spartan furniture of the little bedroom I didn't mind, but the haste, the fortuitous character of our few moments of leisure, above all the lack of privacy inhibited me. There were just two bedrooms, which opened off of the kitchen, the common room. The Bailins were friendly, cooperative people, their crib-sized little daughter Claruchka was charming, but closing our door didn't give me any feeling of being alone with Albert. (Nor did sleeping with a revolver between our pillows contribute to relaxation.)

As the strike had taken a difficult turn since the latest attacks of the employers, Albert had a bodyguard now, a stalwart Hungarian of impressive muscular frame. Mat Haidu would arrive promptly at eight each morning to escort us to the office. I chuckle still as I recall the procession going down toward Main Avenue each day: Haidu first, broad-shouldered, erect, Albert striding close behind, his overcoat flapping, last myself, always outpaced.

Organizer Weisbord was regarded by the workers not merely with respect but with warm affection; the women fairly worshipped him. They would cut out a picture of him from the paper and paste it on a piece of cardboard. Decorated with a bit of ribbon or an artificial flower, it hung like an icon in their homes. He was their little Jesus. He did nothing to stimulate this personal cult. "The workers appreciate correct Marxist tactics as well as courage, honesty, and loyalty"—so he explained his popularity.

Though I was affected by the prevailing hero-worship, still life with Albert was not without its disturbing incidents, jostling me out of my love dream. One morning I was as usual working in the office; Margaret Larkin was also present. Earlier a short meeting of those responsible for the clerical tasks had decided that I should handle the relief applications. Albert came in and, seeing me at work, came over to look at the cards. "What are you doing?" he asked abruptly. "I'm in charge of the relief; these are the cards," I answered. He broke out in sudden rage. "You are not in charge of anything here," he shouted. "I am the only one in charge; hereafter you'll do only what I tell you!" and he strode out of the room.

His eyes flashing as he glowered as though in hate, the whiplike sharpness of his voice, the suddenness of the attack broke me down completely.

I actually cried. I had been so happy in my work, I had so gladly put in long hours on tedious clerical tasks. Only the other day Theresa, one of the pickets from the Gera Mill, had said as she stood near me in the office, "Smith is always working and always smiling." This was indeed the picture of myself those days. And now all this congenial little world crumbled around me. Later Albert came in, casual but snapping his finger joints, a sign of nervousness in him, and walked over to my table.

"What's the matter?" he asked. I couldn't speak. "Silly girl," he said as though talking to a child, "you're just too sensitive."

A few days later, having somewhat recovered my equilibrium, I realized what a gulf of insecurity still existed in me. Later on he proffered an explanation: It seemed that Wagenknecht, the representative of the WIR, a Communist-controlled mass organization, refused to make detailed reports on receipt of funds either to the strike committee, to Weisbord, or to anyone. Albert had to suspect that Wag was siphoning off money from the relief to Foster, Wag's factional leader. It worried Albert that he didn't have complete control over the situation for which as organizer he was responsible. What this had to do with poor little me was not clear; however, I could see he had cause for nervousness. But I didn't get used to his outbreaks of rage, each time they broke me down.

Very much on Albert's mind was his relationship with the Party leaders. From the first day he had sensed that they didn't support him. Ruthenberg had endorsed the policy of organization of the unorganized, but he was in the Party center of Chicago at that time and couldn't participate in the day-to-day conduct of the strike. To Foster, organizing the unorganized was just dual unionism; it was IWWism. Cannon and Dunne, worse still, believed the employers would never settle with Communists, so the workers could never win under our leadership. Lovestone and Weinstone had no clear position. They refused to come out against the organization of the unorganized but neither would they help.

A crisis had occurred when on the eve of the strike the District Industrial Committee had called Albert to New York to tell him there was no money to continue the Passaic work. They gave him peremptory instructions to issue no more membership books or stamps and to turn over all members to the AFL.

"That I would never have done," said Albert. "Luckily, just then the strike broke out."

Always after his weekly sessions with the Party Committee he would unburden himself of a lot of expletives. Since the meetings never began before twelve o'clock at night, he often got no sleep at all those nights. It is possible, even likely, that the Russian situation underlay what seemed to us to be irrational proposals by the Party. From 1920 on, the Russian

Revolution was deflected from its goals of 1917. Having failed to spread the revolution in Europe and harassed by invasions and internal difficulties, the Russians retreated into a purely nationalist position. The Comintern became solely an apparatus by which Russia could obtain recognition in the capitalist world and expand its own industries. To this end was sacrificed support for the workers in other countries. The Communist Party of the U.S.A. had to make clear to its government that there would be no militant strikes, no challenges to capitalism.*

Now a change took place in my own status in the strike. One day I went to visit the soup kitchen for the strikers' children, run by the Council of Workingclass Housewives, a group of Jewish women, residents of Passaic, most of them members of the Workers (Communist) Party. They were giving hours of their time daily, canvassing stores to get donations of food, and preparing a hearty soup or stew which with bread and milk provided one good meal a day for the strikers' children. It occurred to me this work should be done by the women strikers. I reported the idea to Albert, who concurred and made arrangements for me to contact the women at the picket station. Although my little speech was amateurish enough, the women responded at once, a good number coming out to a meeting to get the work organized. Within a few days, the striking women had a new kitchen operating, following the methods of the original one; later several others were established, including one in Lodi and one in Wallington. They were located in empty stores in sections where the workers lived. It looked as though the women had only been waiting for a chance to apply their creative energies; it took just a little push and a minimum of direction to get them started.

In the meantime the women were organized into groups that met weekly. We called them Working Women's Councils. They were chiefly to support the strike but also educational. The wife of Robert Dunn, a New York liberal, came out to talk to the Slavic women on problems of maternity and child care. Ukrainian by birth, she knew several Slavonic languages and was an intellectual with a warm friendly approach.

No longer was I in the office most of the day; now going freely about the mill town, I experienced the grubby daylight realities of those streets I had glimpsed silent and deserted that first night. I became a familiar figure to large numbers of women, mostly textile workers on strike, few housewives being here. I could see they liked me and had confidence in me. Albert listened in on one of my talks. "You're too gentle," he counseled. "Remember, Leona, these people have been ground down very

---

*Albert Weisbord, *Passaic Reviewed* (San Francisco: Germinal Press, 1976).

much. Try to picture the effects of years of the oppression by their bosses. It takes a lot of guts to stand up and fight as they are doing. We can't build up their courage by soft talk. You have to holler more, be more emphatic." This good advice I tried to apply.

The women carried three jobs: mill worker, houseworker, and mother. Often they worked in the mill up to the last day of a pregnancy. Inability to give proper care to their children was the greatest worry and sorrow of the younger women. Sometimes an old woman in the neighborhood would care for many young children, or else older children would have to give up school to stay home with the younger ones. Often the women preferred to work the night shift so they could give the family some care during the day. So much work with so little sleep would often result in illness for the mother, sometimes a complete breakdown.

When the parents grew older and had a child or two at work, the load became lighter. Some families even owned their own homes at this stage.

Since I wanted the councils to survive after I left, I trained the women to run their own meetings. I insisted that each one had to take her turn at being chairwoman. Many would hesitate, object; these workworn women, mothers of families would even cry. I insisted, "If you can't speak English, do it in Polish, or Italian, or whatever." With gentle urging and with the help of Mrs. Brezniak, I got them to make that effort, each and every one. And as a matter of fact, when I had news of these organizations a few years later, they had turned into mutual help organizations—not exactly their original purpose, but survive they did.

The groups were affiliated with a center in New York called the United Council of Workingclass Housewives. Its secretary and founder was Kate Gitlow, mother of Benjamin Gitlow. She came out at least once a week to speak to the women's meetings. The lines in her face recorded the hard struggle of a poor immigrant woman to raise a family in the new world. She was a person of great determination, patience, and persistence. Her face had sometimes a look of strain, and it may have been difficult at her age to be so active, but she never uttered a complaint. She seemed to have a high opinion of me and offered great praise for what I was doing. Perhaps she changed her mind later on in June when the women netted $500 for the strike by a picnic and I, as secretary trying ineptly to balance the accounts, came out short on the income side!

Later, when summer came the soup kitchens were given up as the women took the children out daily to an open-air playground that the strike committee maintained. Sandwiches and milk were now prepared and distributed by the women.

Around the beginning of May, the Relief Department felt the need of a small fund-raising pamphlet emphasizing the miserable conditions of the mill workers. As I had written a few stories on the strike for the *Daily Worker* and for the *Textile Strike Bulletin*, I was assigned to pull together some of the wealth of statistics available into a small pamphlet, *The Textile Strike of 1926.*

When it was edited, printed, and piled up on a table in the office, Albert came over to where I was sitting, put his hand on my shoulder, and said with pride in his voice, "That's our Smith, no task too small, no task too great." This was, I thought, a public admission of our relationship, which probably everyone knew anyway.

The strike activity meanwhile was incessant. We sent a letter to the Associated Silk Workers in Paterson urging them to strike in a joint organization drive with us. Officials of their organization replied that the workers didn't want to be organized at that time. United Front Committee organizers, giving what time they could in Paterson, reported that the unorganized silk workers there who were working long hours for low wages and felt a solidarity with the Passaic strike were really amenable to a strike movement. But now, thanks to this decision by the officials of the Associated, we were frustrated in the strategy on which we had staked so much. (See Appendix B.) Still, we made what efforts we could to further our organization drive.

The strikers sent a delegation to Washington to see President Calvin Coolidge, who was found too busy watching Charleston dance performers. Secretary of Labor Davis told the delegates to go back to work. Their answer was: "Yes, when we get decent wages and a union."

On March 25 Weisbord sent a letter to William Green, AFL President, stressing the imperative need to organize the textile workers, the importance of the present struggle in Passaic, and the need for unity of all existing labor organizations in the textile industry.

William Green replied on March 29, stating that the United Textile Workers of the AFL was the sole recognized union of textile workers. "We know nothing of the United Front Committee of Textile Workers organization which you explain you represent. It has no standing with the American Federation of Labor. For that reason it cannot be recognized by the American Federation of Labor."* To cap this, Hilfers, AFL representative for New Jersey, gave out a statement that the strike was lost due to the bad season.

At the height of this period of rebuffs a successful labor conference was called in Passaic to mobilize support and money for the relief. Mean-

---

*For full text see Murphy, Klassen, and Hall.

while clergymen and other professional people were offering to mediate. Even while Weisbord was engrossed in extending the strike he issued the statement that the union was open for negotiations at any time.

Efforts toward settlement, some of them well-intentioned, others not, came from a variety of quarters but were at this time inconclusive.* Typical was a committee of four appointed by Governor Moore to mediate between mill owners and strikers. When the Forstmann-Huffmann Company rejected this committee, Governor Moore gave up. Since Moore had implied that Weisbord did not represent them, five thousand strikers meeting in Wallington voted to retain Weisbord as leader.

With the defeat in Paterson and in East Paterson, we had now reached the end of the first period of the strike, the period of success, of expansion, of what seemed to be brilliant achievement. The march on Lodi was the last of such victories. Now we could pull out no more mills, but only doggedly hang on to what we had. From then on we were on the defensive against the mill owners' unremitting attacks.

Vicious clubbings of the picket lines continued. At this point a New York bus company actually ran daily sightseeing buses out to Passaic with a sign "See the Police Clubbings in Passaic." The American Civil Liberties Union had Chief of Police Zober of Passaic and some of his forces arrested and charged with atrocious assault in no less than one hundred cases. Judge Davidson countered this move by refusing to issue warrants of arrest or to entertain charges against any officer during the strike. Now the police closed down Neubauer's Hall in Passaic, which forced the strikers to meet in Garfield. The mill owners wanted the militia brought in, but there was enough opposition of workers and others throughout the state to prevent this move.

Then came the arrest of Weisbord and almost the entire strike leadership. Albert had anticipated this step since Forstmann-Huffmann had announced their mill would be reopened April 12, supposedly at the request of their company union. On Saturday, April 10, Albert was in the office dictating a statement for the press: "Understanding how the bosses manipulate the law and the police for their own purposes, the workers will know this reign of terror is a sign of weakness in the mill owners.... This is the last desperate move of the bosses to break the strike...."

It was just at this point that seven plainclothesmen entered the office to arrest him and twenty-four others, all of whom were held in jail until Monday, then arraigned on charges of having advocated violence in a speech on April 8, also for having attended a meeting under Communist

---

*See Weisbord, *Passaic*, pp. 34-36.

auspices on October 30, 1925, and one on February 9, 1926, advocating hostility to the government, in violation of a New Jersey law of 1902. Bail was set at $100,000 for all, $25,000 for Weisbord alone.

On the same day in Garfield, where the main Forstmann-Huffmann plant was located, Mayor Burke went to the county seat at Hackensack and requested Bergen County authorities to assign special officers to Garfield to be on duty on Monday the 12th. On that day Sheriff Nimmo of East Paterson appeared in Garfield with seventy Bergen County deputies. A long line was moving on the mill, in front of which was a young active striker, Nancy Sandowski, later popularized as "Joan of Arc" by the Party. Sheriff Nimmo ordered the line to disperse. He then produced and read the "riot act" and gave one hour for dispersal.

At once the deputies attacked the line. There were many arrests and Nimmo ordered everybody indoors. Esther Lowell, a New York liberal, was arrested, charged with disorderly conduct, and held on $1,500 bail, Robert Dunn on $10,000 bail. The deputies furnished for Nimmo by the mill owners were paid for by them in open defiance of the law.* At this time Sheriff Morgan was called into Passaic with armed deputies to put a stop to the mass picket lines there.

In the evening following the arrests those of us left of the staff—a few women—went into New York to obtain whatever counsel and help we could at the Party headquarters. I was unable to sleep at all that night imagining Albert attacked and beaten in jail. A few days later I went out to see him in the county jail at Paterson. He had on a sort of striped pajama suit, looked pale and heroic. He told me the first night he had been held alone in a jail cell in Passaic, which had a window on the street. Jack Bryan, "our" picket captain, had stood outside making jeering remarks. As this confirmed our earlier suspicions of Bryan's disloyalty he was forced to leave.

On April 17 Weisbord appeared in the court of Oyer and Terminer in Paterson on a writ of habeas corpus. Bainbridge Colby, former secretary of state under President Wilson, argued on his behalf against excessive bail and succeeded in getting the case nol-prossed.

In the raid most of our papers had been seized. An interesting corollary here was that among the papers was a big stack of leaflets addressed to the rubber workers of Passaic. We had been planning to organize them in extension of our own strike. But with the added difficulties of the arrests this plan too had to be dropped.

Organized labor in New York City, rallying now to the defense of the strike, established a United Front Committee consisting of numerous

---

*See Siegel for details of the foregoing account.

organizations of various shades of opinion of which the International Labor Defense was a part.* This Committee raised $250,000 as a bail fund. At last after eleven days Weisbord and the other arrested Passaic strike leaders were released from jail.

I remember participating in a picket line at that time in front of the Forstmann-Huffmann mill, one of the last we were able to hold. It was a very large line, police and deputies were everywhere, and so were prominent liberals from New York: Norman Thomas, for example, marched and was arrested as a test case.

I was walking with a contingent of the women and was singing loudly. Nimmo himself came up alongside, evidently recognized me, and said, "Cut that out. No singing!" I might have defied him with the result of another arrest. Not seeing any contribution to our cause in this I stopped my singing.

The liberals of the ACLU were active meanwhile in contesting the "riot act" in Garfield, and on April 30 they obtained an injunction allowing the use of a hall in Garfield that Sheriff Nimmo had ordered closed.

From Washington Senators Edwards (Democrat) and Edge (Republican) spread rumors that Weisbord was in the pay of Soviet Russia, that the strikers were Bolsheviks who wanted to overthrow the whole capitalist system.

From Paterson there was New Jersey Secretary of Labor McBride swearing that the sanitary conditions inside the mills were excellent. Actually, in some of the mills there were no toilets, just an open trough; there were no seats anywhere; air was overheated and full of dust. Secretary McBride claimed wages were the highest in the world.

To cap it all, the Forstmann-Huffmann Company secured the most drastic temporary restraining order (injunction) in New Jersey legal history. Not merely picketing was forbidden. No one was allowed even to talk about the strike or contribute money to it. Since this injunction was enforced by the presence of seven hundred armed men who did not hesitate to use their weapons, it carried weight. A reign of terror prevailed. Professor Felix Frankfurter of the Harvard law school helped prepare a brief contesting the Forstmann-Huffman injunction, which was read at a hearing on April 26.† Finally, on June 1, the injunction was dissolved.

Under all of these maneuvers by the employers, the strike, now already five months old, still remained strong. It is true a certain crumbling around the periphery was beginning. I remember Lena Chernenko worrying about the scabs going into the Gera Mill. Lena, gray-pale and grim-

---

*For details of this committee see Murphy, Klassen and Hall, pp. 34-35.
†See Siegel.

faced now from her regime of the four A.M. alarm clock, never free of
bruises from the policemen's clubs, hung on to her harsh assignment with
a will of iron.

The pressure on the organizers was enormous, and the job was pretty
nearly a fulltime one, seven days a week. Still, there would be an occasional rare moment of relaxation. So it was one Sunday afternoon following a mass meeting, when a small group was in the office. It included
Elizabeth Gurley Flynn, Coco and his companion Anne Washington
Creighton, as well as Albert and myself. Flynn suggested we all go in to
New York and drink a glass of wine at her place. She said my eyes sparkled
at the suggestion and perhaps they did. At any rate, the five of us went
in to New York, stopping first at the one-room apartment of Coco and
Creighton. They got out a bottle of wine and we tried to fix our minds on
lighter matters than usual. I remember Coco saying he never could fall
asleep except with his head on a woman's bosom. After a while we went
over to Flynn's place, not far away. She had rented a huge basement, one
big room that served for everything. Albert told funny stories. Like the
one about the house-painter who was traveling from Minsk to Pinsk, or
was it the old favorite "the bewildered fart"? While I laughed with the
others, I really felt like a fish out of water. I had never been used to dally-
ing; I was always so serious. Finally Albert and I left to return to Passaic,
there where duty lay and more than that, our absorbing interest in life,
the strike. I was glad to get back.

With mass picketing impossible, new tactics were devised by the strike
committee. Mass groups walked about the neighborhoods or stood at
corners to protect the small picket lines of eight people, which were permitted. Later block committees enabled the strikers to meet in small
closed groups. We found a hall in Wallington for our meetings and forced
Sheriffs Nimmo and Morgan to retire from the field. A bigger than ever
national relief campaign was carried on, and large funds coming in helped
to sustain the strikers both physically and morally.

As was inevitable with such a long strike, the whole population of
Passaic and surrounding towns eventually became involved, their loyalties
polarized. Storekeepers, doctors, and lawyers felt the pinch from the start,
and many sided with the strikers. In the churches too there were two
Passaics. The mill owners and well-to-do people were Protestant. Among
them the Reverend Talbott stood out in defense of the mill owners.

The Catholic priests, shepherds of the strikers, knew too well the
sufferings of their flocks to take a hostile position; perhaps though, they
feared they would lose many of the sheep to Communist agitators. So, in
a sincere effort to end the strike, they formed a Catholic Mediation Com-

mittee, which succeeded for a time in making some contact with the mill owners.

A citizens' committee of the Elks and Lions clubs lined up by the Chamber of Commerce and backed by the considerable office staff of the mills launched attacks against Weisbord as a Communist. In opposition a Catholic group called the Associated Societies and Parishes of Passaic and Vicinity held a parade of twenty thousand in defense of the strike.

Gradually Forstmann-Huffmann, the wealthiest firm, took over the leadership of the mill owners and held Botany and the weaker firms in line. F–H was intransigent in their anti-union stand. By publicly using Weisbord as a scapegoat, they were able to undermine all mediation efforts.

Certain external developments at this point played into the employers' hands. The Paterson silk industry entered a temporary slump, thus defusing the workers' militancy as well as providing a few scabs for the woolen mills. The woolen trade was also dull, the mills actually having huge stocks on hand, a fact of which we could have had no knowledge at the start. Then, 40,000 members of the International Ladies' Garment Workers Union in New York went on strike, thus restricting the market for woolens.

Now, to add to our difficulties, the AFL leadership, which so far had followed a hands-off, no-help policy toward our strike, came out openly against it. On July 1 William Green in the name of the AFL Executive Council broadcasted a hostile statement. "The leaders of the United Front Committee are prominently identified with the Communistic movement in the United States. . . . The membership of organized labor should not contribute funds to be used for the purpose of advancing the cause of a dual organization or to pay the salaries of Communist leaders who are seeking the destruction of the American Federation of Labor and the substitution of a communistic organization. . . ."* The New Jersey representative capped this statement by announcing that the strike was lost and all should return to work.

In spite of obstacles, during this very trying period the block committees and fifty district committees intensified their educational work, and the union actually strengthened and increased its forces locally.

The hostile statements of the AFL leadership provoked protests from the ranks: the Seattle *Union Record* and *Labor Age* denounced the leadership for its reactionary stand; in many cities, in central labor unions, local

---

*Given in full in Murphy, Klassen, and Hall, p. 137.

unions, and even district bodies, funds continued to be voted for Passaic strike relief.

During this third and last period of the strike the employers' tactics reached their lowest level. They took as scabs children just out of school from other localities. They brought in hundreds of professional strike-breakers who knew nothing of textile work and who were recruited by agencies all over the country. They did no work but merely harassed the strikers. They roamed the city in gangs, fully armed, shooting and stab-bing strikers, beating up union organizers, and exploding bombs. The ground work was being laid for a lynching citizens' vigilante committee to drive out the Communists.

Progress was made meanwhile toward settlement. Senator William Borah pushed the Senate to conduct a hearing on the strike through its Committee on Education and Labor.

At the same time, with the help of the American Civil Liberties Union the Lauck Committee was set up. Jett Lauck, a well-known economist, had worked for the United Mine Workers Union and for the United Auto Workers. Several attorneys of the ACLU were also on the com-mittee, some of whom testified on behalf of the strikers at the Senate hearing.

The pressure by the Lauck Committee finally yielded results. At last the UTW agreed to admit the Passaic textile strikers, but with the condi-tion that Weisbord get out. They were now prepared to negotiate with the employers.

On July 31, upon Weisbord's return from Washington, where he had gone to meet with Senator Borah, a huge mass meeting of the strikers endorsed the Lauck Committee, giving it power 1) to represent them in settling the strike through Senator Borah or any other mediation agency, 2) to conduct a special election by secret ballot to establish a union local with officers and committees to deal with representatives of the mills, and 3) to arrange with the United Textile Workers for the admission of said union.*

It was here that the role of the Workers (Communist) Party became crucial. When the cry "Remove Weisbord," raised by the mill owners, was taken up by the leadership of the AFL, the Party leaders were only too glad to align themselves on this side. They announced they had re-ceived word through secret channels that the mill owners had consented to negotiate with the strikers once in the AFL if Albert Weisbord were withdrawn. This was just a ruse, but Albert gave his word to comply,

---

*Mary Heaton Vorse, The Passaic Textile Strike (Passaic, N.J.: General Relief Committee of Textile Strikers, 1927), p. 94.

though he had resisted their decision and did not vote for their motion.*

Accordingly, on August 13 Weisbord sent an official statement to Jett Lauck that he would withdraw upon issuance of a charter to the Passaic local of the United Textile Workers.†

Now the mill owners revealed what they really had in mind. On August 19 Charles F. H. Johnson, vice president of Botany Worsted Mill, announced to his employees gathered in the mill yard that the company would have nothing to do with the new union sponsored by the American Federation of Labor claiming to represent those no longer employed at the mills, in other words the strikers.‡

On August 20 Julius Forstmann, president of the Forstmann-Huffmann Company, told his employees he would deal with them only through the representative assembly, in other words, the company union.‡

Now the matter of Weisbord's withdrawal was taken up with the strike committee. It had to be put that the leader had "decided" to take this step in the workers' interests. (Part of the staff were to leave with him.) With deep regret, yet hoping he might return some time, the committee organized a send-off.

On September 2 at Belmont Park, Garfield, an open-air meeting was held attended by ten thousand strikers. The United Textile Workers was represented by Henry Hunt of the Lauck Committee, who presented the union charter for local 1603 to Gustav Deak, chairman of the new local.

Weisbord then made his public farewell. He stated he had no interests apart from those of the workers. The union was the real issue, not Weisbord. To prove this he would withdraw but the union could never withdraw. Tremendous enthusiasm prevailed. The workers presented Weisbord with a gold watch and other tokens. With cheers, songs, and moving expressions of appreciation of loyalty, the workers bade their leaders farewell.

A few people were selected to remain to keep contact with the workers. I was one of them; others were Lena Chernenko, Miriam Silverfarb, Clarence Miller, Emil Gardos, and Joe Magliacano. The relief office remained open as funds continued to come in.

And now it was all over: the great meetings, the parades, the eloquent speeches, the cheers and singing, the terror, the turmoil, the constant daily effort, the travail and the glory of our strike—all gone now. The

---

*See Albert Weisbord, "Critical Moments in Textile Strikes," *Class Struggle* (Greenwood Editions), vol. 1, p. 5.

†*New York Times*, August 14, 1926.

‡*New York Times*, August 20, 1926.

‡*New York Times*, August 21, 1926.

headquarters returned to the subdued quiet that had preceded the strike. Our small staff would gather forlornly for consultation and mutual commiseration. We were all tired and some were ill. I had the most awful cold imaginable. Lena was not well at all; later when a doctor diagnosed beginning TB, she was released to go to California, where she had relatives.

Now in New York, Albert wrote a pamphlet on the strike: *Passaic, The Story of a Struggle Against Starvation Wages and for the Right to Organize Told by Albert Weisbord*, which was widely distributed and well received. After that Albert left for a nationwide speaking tour to spread the story of our strike.

Those of us who remained were in an anomalous position. We could not represent the United Front Committee, which could not be in competition once the UTW took over the organized workers. Nor could we have anything to do with this takeover.

Like the strikers, we could only wait. And wait we did, day after day. No word, no sign of anyone. Meanwhile, we had to meet with the strikers, not in strike committee, not in mass meeting, but in their separate groups —I with the women, Miriam Silverfarb with the children, Clarence Miller with the youth, the others with the block groups. It would be hard to find a more difficult assignment than this one. We had to summon all our courage and wit to find something to say to the people. We knew their plight, how they would have to listen to the jibes of the scabs along with everything else. As the empty days passed, doubt and distrust increased on the faces before us. Meetings were becoming smaller. We knew some were going back to work but were powerless to prevent them.

One morning I went to Wallington to visit a woman who had been active in the council there. She had just returned from her night shift in the mill. Pale and fatigued, barefooted, she was mopping the kitchen floor. I sat down, though she didn't ask me to. I told her my story: we must build the union on the job, stick together, and try again later. She was not hostile, nor was she friendly; she actually didn't pay too much attention to me. I left feeling completely supernumerary.

It was heartening in that period to be with Mrs. Brezniak, who remained stalwart and stable. No need to propagandize her; she grasped the situation; she could bear the disappointment and the pain of it without breaking down. She helped to encourage the others.

We were in those days too close to the defeat, too much involved in its difficulties and its trauma to have a philosophic perspective of the whole. This came only much later.

At last we heard from Thomas McMahon, President of the United Textile Workers. On September 11 he came to town for a parade of fifteen thousand men, women, and children culminating in an open-air meeting. Middle-aged, baldish, and paunchy, McMahon seemed to glower as he spoke; if he conveyed anything of himself it appeared as only hatred for these people who had resisted their employers for eight long months. McMahon urged them to repudiate the influence of their old leaders and follow the policies of the United Textile Workers: no more abuse of employers and heckling on the street, no more militancy.

During this brief speech the workers stood patiently, stolid, unresponsive. How different from what we had been accustomed to; from those meetings so full of drama, of challenge, where so many vital things were taken up. And how different this person from the dedicated young man who had thrown himself so passionately, so completely, into the workers' struggle! This meeting was a short one. The workers, dismissed, quickly disappeared.

And after that—more waiting. McMahon had come, he had spoken, he had left. There was no open activity, no union headquarters established, no cards issued, no representative seen, no meeting with the strikers, no open negotiations with the employers. With all the difficulties, a solid core of perhaps six thousand strikers still held firm. Some picketing went on. Only later could we learn what was happening behind the scenes.

On September 13 at a convention of the UTW the new local 1603 was set up. The Passaic strike was barely mentioned, and only through pressure by the delegates was Gus Deak able to get the floor to tell of the union officials' total neglect of the strike. It seems the UTW was taking these workers into its fold on the following conditions:

1. That Weisbord and all associated with him be eliminated;
2. That the UTW would assume no financial obligation in relief funds;
3. That no work was promised: "Our entrance is not a question of hours and wages. It is purely and simply a matter of recognition of the union. You must learn to work with the 'scabs,' those who are now working inside."*

Finally, on October 11, after listening to the pleas of Rabbi Stephen S. Wise, the AFL belatedly adopted a resolution calling on organized labor to assist the Passaic strikers. A local mediation committee was set up including the mayor, three clergymen, and a judge to cooperate with the UTW officials. At last, on Armistice Day, November 11, 1926, it was announced that agreement had been reached with the Passaic Worsted

---

*John B. MacPherson, "The Passaic Textile Strike of 1926-27," *Bulletin of the National Association of Wool Manufacturers*, Boston, Jan. 1928.

Spinning Company, signed by the president of the mill and by Vice President Starr of the UTW. This agreement, in which the workers had no part, was accepted unanimously by the strikers of that mill. The workers were given the right to organize in a "legitimate" union; collective bargaining and nondiscrimination in hiring were promised.*

It was not until December 13, almost eleven months after its start, that the strike in Botany Worsted Mill and its subsidiary, Garfield Worsted Mill, was settled. On that day the Botany strikers met in the Ukrainian Hall in Passaic and ratified an agreement between Charles F. Johnson, vice president of the company and Thomas McMahon, international president of the UTW.

The settlement was substantially the same as that of the Passaic Worsted Spinning Company. At last now the picketing of the Botany Mill was discontinued.

Forstmann-Huffmann would go no farther than an oral agreement by Forstmann that the workers might join an outside organization if they wished, and with this, on February 14, those strikers voted to end their strike. On the 16th the strikes of Gera Mill and New Jersey Worsted Mill ended with the workers accepting a plan that gave them the right to affiliate with the AFL and assured them of no discrimination. On the 18th came the settlement in Dundee. It was not till February 28, 1927, that the strikers of the United Piece Dye Works in Lodi voted to end their long struggle on the sole oral promise of the employer not to discriminate.†

Employers' promises are not reliable, as experience had previously shown, and the union in the whole area rapidly dwindled.

Now the employers dealt their last blows. A new series of bomb explosions startled the town, followed by wholesale arrests of strikers. The ACLU and the International Labor Defense tried to defend these people, but the UTW did nothing to help them.‡

While the Passaic strike was not successful in the narrow sense of winning its demands, it did, however, succeed in stopping the wave of wage cuts that employers were trying to extend throughout the textile industry. No boss wanted to see the kind of volcanic eruption in his mill that had broken out in Passaic.

Despite the fine organization of that strike, we had to see the Passaic

---

*For full details see *Textile Worker* (UTW), November 1926. See also MacPherson, ibid.

†For all of above see Murphy, Klassen, and Hall, pp. 56-57.

‡See the pamphlet "Prisoners of the Passaic Strike: Joint Committee for Passaic Defense" (established by the ACLU and the ILD). See also Siegel, p. 262.

struggle go into history as one more unsuccessful attempt to organize the textile workers.

Historically, the Passaic strike marked the beginning of a new period in labor history: a period of mass strikes, of renewed militancy in the organization of the unorganized unskilled workers, which would culminate a decade later in the formation of the Congress of Industrial Organizations. Bursting forth on a labor scene that had become stagnant, it gave continuity to the struggle for mass industrial unions begun by Debs in the railway strike, then in the steel strikes of the 1890s, and later by the IWW in the early 1900s.

The Passaic strike is significant too as the first attempt of Communists to lead a workers' industrial struggle. It demonstrated what massive labor support the Party could build up through its subsidiary organizations for defense and for relief, not to speak of the Language Federations, which were so strategic at the start of the strike. The estimated million dollars raised for relief was a testimonial to this labor backing. The fine support of the liberals was in part due to the fortunate circumstance that Passaic was situated only a half hour away from the country's principal liberal center.

While we were not able to influence the Party leadership as we had hoped to do, many members, especially the youth, were inspired both to initiate and to participate in labor struggles elsewhere. We were defeated by forces beyond our control, by historical forces of superior strength. Only a rank opportunist would say that the strike should not have been undertaken because it did not win its demands. Only through such struggles could the workers as a whole emerge from the sort of wage slavery Passaic typified.

For me this strike, my first venture into what we called mass work, was a great step forward. Irrevocably far behind now lay my old life of the classroom and the library, of poetry, literature, and art. For the first time I began really to know the society in which I lived, more than that, actively to try to change it.

Through the work among the women, I developed more confidence in myself. I identified so much with them that it was never difficult to speak to them; I was one of them. Outside of the women's sphere, however, I remained diffident. Whenever male Party comrades were discussing questions, I could never speak out. I remember the Polish organizer once saying to me: "Vera, if only you could be all you are now, and at the same time be more—Well, speak out more, be tougher, be an agitator!"

A platform speaker was what I secretly longed to be more than anything else. Only once in the strike did it happen. I spoke at the one women's mass meeting, held in one of the halls with only women present.

Even as I spoke I realized I was too genteel, too literary. Rebecca Grecht spoke after me. Her manner of speaking was as refined as mine, but she was much more a "politician" than I would ever be. She stressed the fact that she had been born in Poland, a strong point with that audience. Still, I was sure my sincerity and real love for the women were appreciated.

Perhaps I grew in strength and stature during the period after the leader's withdrawal. To realize the seeming vanity of one's efforts, to taste the bitterness of defeat, indeed really to drink it to the dregs, yet still to remain at one's post is a chastening experience which in the long run may leave one more disciplined and more realistic.

That I met my husband in that strike was so much bound up with the event as to seem inevitable, like destiny. Henceforth my life was to be something shared. I could go forward with a partner by my side. For a long time to come, however, he was to play a dominant role.

6

Just Good Soldiers

AT LAST, WHEN ALBERT RETURNED FROM HIS TOUR, WE COULD TAKE UP OUR relationship where we had left off in August when he had been forced to leave the strike. I recall as background a large furnished room in Brooklyn in one of those dignified old brownstone houses with a bay window overlooking a quiet street.

The tour had provided a close-up view of the Party organization; the units were fewer and smaller than he had supposed. On the other hand, everywhere he found the membership, especially the youth, inspired by Passaic, confirming his belief that the Party could be pushed onto a correct path, and a new leadership created, through mass work.

In California a well-to-do liberal woman, Kate Crane-Gartz, donated generously to the strike fund and then handed Albert $500 for himself. "Of course I turned it all over to the Party." We were so poor then, I in my baseness thought he might have kept the gift for us, but I kept quiet.

Barely were we established when in December came another separation: Albert was sent to Mexico as an envoy for the Workers (Communist) Party, bearing a gift of $1,000 from the Profintern (Red International of Trade Unions) to the Mexican trade unions, which were to be set up with this money.

Carrying it all in gold pieces in his pockets in the quiet capital Mexico City was at that time, Albert could walk unconcerned through the streets. He came back enthusiastic, bringing photographs of himself with Mexican trade union leaders, including David Siquieros. Oh, the sorry tricks of history! Could we then know that eighteen years later this same Siquieros would engineer and lead an unsuccessful attempt on the life of Trotsky, who was then to be in exile in Mexico? Though Siquieros is

ranked by the Mexicans among their leading muralists, I cannot look at
his pictures now.

We were for the moment unattached to any unit of the Party, though
such attachment was required. Albert never had unit membership in
New York. As for me, not for anything would I return to the sordid
wrangling of the Harlem English branch. Nor did I feel any urge to resume the old classes at Party headquarters.

There was still the teachers' fraction—but I was no longer a teacher.
Once in Passaic Mary Heaton Vorse had told me she had learned from
one of the detectives that the Department of Justice knew all about me:
my real name, and the school where I had worked—a fact not too disturbing since I had never really wanted to teach. All my former activities appeared so trivial, so futile. Now, having leisure, I read what was available
of Lenin, Marx, Engels, and others, acquiring a better basis of theory.

We saw ourselves now as committed revolutionists. Since Albert had
been made an alternate on the Central Committee, it was understood he
would be assigned to some post and in the interval he was receiving a
stipend. It was about this time that a pronouncement came from the C.I.
condemning the factionalism of the American Party as unprincipled and
forbidding the holding of any factional meetings. The decision seemed
to make little difference in practice, at any rate in New York. I attended
some of the faction meetings, though never as an enthusiast. I was for
the Party, not a faction. To adhere mechanically to some official position
not thoroughly understood or agreed with, or to support X or Y simply as
a factional member with no better basis went against the grain with me.

I chuckle whenever I recall one of those meetings. A communique
had been received from Moscow regarding a Swiss comrade named Hum-
boldt Droz, who was being expelled or removed from his post and denounced as a "pusillanimous opportunist." Every single leading comrade present (except Albert), like puppets pulled by invisible wires, took
the floor to support the factional position and to denounce the man—
of whom they had in all likelihood never heard before—each and every
one in his speech using that expression (did they understand it any more
than I did?) of "pusillanimous opportunist!"

During this period we maintained few contacts outside the Party. Of
my old friends of the 1919 days Nana Wylie had died, Kay Hansen had
dropped completely out of sight, and my good friend Bob Van Patten, as
well as my Russian friends, the Auerbachs, the Kramers, and others, I
saw only at infrequent general party meetings. A few times I met with
my old college friends Pauline, Dolores, and some others. Of all I had
done in that eventful year, what seemed to impress these women most
was that I had "captured" a prominent person as a husband. Albert was

now indeed well-known. In the wake of all the strike publicity, *The Nation* had just chosen him "Young man of the year who has done the most for his country."

"How did you do it?" queried Dolores, to which I must have answered in my usual blunt way, "I didn't do anything. Albert seemed to think I was the sort of wife he wanted." ". . . to think that *you* should be able to get the most talked-of man! . . ." She sounded incredulous. It was as though some poor worm had suddenly leaped up and caught a butterfly.

As a matter of fact, had Albert been "successful" at the start, I would have most likely been intimidated. I found him obscure, poor, unappreciated, alone. The first link between us had been the very difficulty of his position and his need of help. At any rate, neither of us now could feel much at home with people who were to us just "bourgeois."

The restricted orbit of the Party actually never seemed narrow to us since our interests encompassed the entire world. Far from viewing ourselves as an isolated little group, we rather believed the Party to be as the center, reaching out to influence the society around it. And what was our objective? Succinctly it may be stated as a cooperative rather than an exploitative society. The root of all the evils of this world—poverty, war, racism, turmoil of all sorts—we saw in the productive system where a few owned the means of production, the many toiling for wages, the few reaping the profits, the state upholding this system. We wanted the toilers and other productive workers not merely to control but to own the factories, mines, ships, railroads, etc., sharing the fruits of their cooperative labor. For exploiters there would be no place.

Actually not much was ever said about this society of the future; we were too busy trying through our activities to prepare for the revolution that would make its creation possible. At any rate, by this time we were aware of a necessary preparatory period, a big step forward from the old Left Wing days of 1919, when armed only with a basic distinction between reform and revolution, and fired by the flames of the Russian Revolution, the comrades were ready at once to go out and man the nonexistent barricades.

We read the *Inprecor* (International Press Correspondence, a bulletin put out in Moscow) faithfully, talked with comrades at the headquarters, knew all the rumors and gossip, took part in activities as they came up. We knew Ben Gold, leader of the fur workers, who had been much affected by the Passaic strike, and some of the devoted women leaders in the International Ladies Garment Workers Union such as Rose Wortis. Once I stayed up all night in a Left Wing sit-in in the headquarters of Local 22 of the ILGWU. In the usual tobacco-saturated atmosphere many young people waited, braced for an attack to take over the headquarters (from the Right Wing, thugs, or police), which never occurred. There was much talking and singing of militant songs in English, Russian, and Yiddish.

As far as I can recall, my life with Albert in those days was in the main a happy one. We accepted the fact of frequent separations as part of the revolutionist's life, trying to make the most of the interludes we might have together. To be mobile, to run about hither and yon carrying out Party assignments: wasn't that what the Russians had always done?

A little later, however, our relationship was really put to a test. First, a meeting of women comrades chaired by Kate Gitlow was held at Party headquarters, with Comrade Ruthenberg as principal speaker. After his speech various women, including myself, took the floor. I described the work in Passaic, emphasizing the building of the Party through mass work. Soon afterward the word got around that the Party would establish a department of Woman's Work, under some pressure from the C.I., no doubt; then Mrs. Gitlow told me I was being considered for the post, finally that it was definitely offered me. Because the Party center was then in Chicago, I would have to go there.

This prospective move precipitated a major crisis in my personal life. Strangely enough, at the start I was not aware of a conflict. Pleased to have won some recognition, I resolved to live up to the demands of the new post. The course was clear: the Party came first. Perhaps I was supposing that Albert would go to Chicago too, or it may be I didn't consider his side of the question at all.

At any rate, I was all ready to leave when I found myself confronted with a rebellious husband. Albert described the dire fate that would be mine were I to leave him. I would have to stay up till 3 A.M. every night in meetings, breathing in tobacco smoke—oh, I would surely break down, my lungs couldn't stand that, I would get TB again. Maybe Ruthenberg had his eye on me. I didn't know what chicanery, what opportunism those bastards the Party leaders were capable of. I would be just a pawn in the factional struggle. Maybe they really did want to keep us apart. I would go from one man to another as a bed partner—and what antagonisms I would stir up among the women!

I did not see myself as the poor rag I was being portrayed, but as I listened I found myself weakening. What had at first appeared firm and clear in my mind became clouded. If this fine, brilliant young man wanted so much to keep me, how could I leave him? Though I had had no intention of leaving him, he seemed to see it that way.

And I yielded.

I yielded not on the basis of a decision between love and duty, but rather of being won over by a very earnest pleading. I not merely gave up something I wanted very much; I acted against my conscience. In humiliation I went to invent an excuse for renouncing the post—Albert tried to console me, just wait till he got a place, he'd find something for me. I would have a wonderful life as his partner. Hadn't my work in Passaic been worthwhile? Nevertheless, this renunciation left me with a certain loss of self-respect, a feeling of damaged integrity.

Nothing was solved; rather, a conflict was brought to light, the basis of which was there from the beginning and would remain covertly, erupting now and then in futile inconclusive rebellions. I remember writing a letter to Albert around that time in which I said: ". . . with you I'll always be just a child under your tutelage."

As to the merits of Albert's arguments, I could not see that the women in the Party who held posts were any more faction-manipulated than the men. As things worked out, it is possible I might not have got the post after all, since Ruthenberg died prematurely soon after that (in March 1927). Lovestone, who took over his position, might not have wanted to carry out his policy. At any rate, speculations as to what might have been are always futile.

Once during this period I went with a delegation of women militants to Washington to protest something or other. Was it in the Senate, the House, or in some committee room? The Washington newspaper reported my getting up to shout something from the gallery where we were sitting.

Our leader was Juliet Stuart Poyntz, whom I had known in the Harlem English branch, one of the few women acknowledged as a leader in the Party. Poyntz, always an energetic, vibrant, cheerful person, appeared to enjoy the Washington adventure to the fullest. We stayed overnight in a hotel, and were all as merry as schoolgirls. Poyntz was then doing "women's work" in New York, setting up an educational department for the ILGWU. Although she was warm and friendly with the women garment workers, still her cultivated voice, her sophistication, her correct English, her good clothes, plus a something not easily defined, set her apart. She had a fine education, was a graduate of Barnard and of the London School of Economics, and she earned a living teaching a course in history at Columbia University Extension School.

While I joined in the laughter and jokes, the occasion, like all the Party work, was a serious one to me. At one point I sensed a certain reaction in Comrade Poyntz, a passing look she gave me. This look I had seen in Chicago in 1925, when for the first time I met Party leaders; it had reappeared in New York whenever the Passaic staff had gone in. Was it pity, was it contempt, or perhaps a sort of reluctant respect? It seemed to be a reaction to my naiveté, my seriousness, my enthusiasm. Just a quick look, subtle, disturbing, it seemed to put me on some different plane from themselves, as thought they were aware of something important that I didn't know.

The May Day parade held in lower New York that spring was a large turbulent demonstration full of songs, banners, and enthusiasm. Marching in the ranks, I felt heroic and revolutionary. It is unlikely that at the time I attempted any analysis of the uplift, the exultant mood that was mine.

With Calvin Coolidge in the White House the country was nearing the end of a boom cycle. The large stocks the woolen mills in Passaic had on hand testified to a glut accumulated during a period of boom. As a matter of fact the U.S.A. was just two and a half years ahead of the catastrophic stock-market crash and run on the banks, which in 1929 was to initiate the worst depression in its history. Still, that May Day of 1927 the mood of the country was optimistic. Inspired by the parade, I felt so sure our Party was growing. The Passaic strike probably had netted some small gains in membership. Those marchers represented almost the total New York membership plus a good number of worker sympathizers from the needle trades. That in relationship to the country at large we were still no more than a sect was for the moment forgotten. In the subjective mood of that day the path to the revolution appeared as a broad clear avenue leading directly upward. Of course there would be setbacks, reversals; we might have to go to prison sometimes; but in some not too distant future all obstacles would be overcome to the ultimate triumph of the Revolution. Of this I was certain . . . Ah, yes, it was all long ago, a very long time ago. . . .

That spring our one-week vacation at Lake George in upper New York State—we called it our honeymoon—was a joyous interlude. The limpid waters of the lake, so clear one could see to the very bottom over the edge of the boat, the big bedroom with the straw matting on the floor, and that special odor of a country house where a touch of mustiness combines with the breath of growing vegetation outside, above all, the big woods which surrounded us—all was sheer delight.

My husband was his usual self: buoyant, radiating energy, and talking from morning to night. Though all his ideas were interesting, the fact of being always just a listener was beginning to pall. In Passaic Albert the leader had been everybody's teacher; I, as a novice, was content to learn. Now at last having leisure and being together for more than a night at a time I felt a certain frustration. Didn't I also have something to give? Once as we walked in the woods where I was so much at home, the unending flow of words became irksome. This was not the place or the time for the laws of social change. I wanted to share my joy in nature with him.

I interrupted: "Please don't talk, just listen a minute to the birds, to the stirring of the leaves, to the beautiful quiet."

Irritated impatience was his first reaction, but he did listen as I talked of the strength and power of those lofty trunks, with now and then a fallen log decaying below in the endless intertwining cycle of life and death. The soft carpet of leaves and pine needles under our feet, the flickering of filtered sunlight on the rich brown and black of the trunks, the intense green of young leaves ... With all this beauty for the eyes, a web of blended sounds permeated the silence, bird calls and trillings, insect shrillings, the soughing of the wind among the leaves. I showed him the delicacy of the blossoms almost hidden under our feet: anemones, violets of several kinds, spring beauties, wild geraniums, hepatica, bloodroot, and Jack-in-the-pulpit. And how sweet and penetrating were the woodsy scents! ... Albert did listen and perhaps for the first time began to make contact with nature. I was realizing with a shock I had taken for a husband a man who didn't know an oriole from a blackbird, an oak from a sycamore. Albert was a city person, his life had been confined to the intellectual, nature had played no part. After all, not such a serious matter, nor one that need come between us.

There was an incident also of a horse. As we walked along the path, believing ourselves completely alone, suddenly ahead in a clearing appeared without warning a white horse—all white, mane and tail, all vibrant with life. Giving us a flashing glance through its full mane, it cantered away, in a moment disappearing. A certain mystery about this horse, the suddenness and unaccountability of its brief appearance, its beauty, moved us, and we long remembered it as part of our honeymoon.

I discovered other facets of Albert's complex personality: his love and knowledge of music I had glimpsed, but now I realized he could hum whole passages of symphonies. Chess was a favorite hobby—he could play it blindfolded and seized every opportunity for a game. But what of the big experience we had just passed through, the Passaic strike? Not yet could we assimilate and objectively analyze its lessons; the trauma of the disappointment had been too great. If we referred to it, it would be only to recall some of its happier aspects.

At last came an assignment as assistant district organizer in Philadelphia. The D.O. there, Alex Bail, Albert saw as a firm factional man probably advised by the leaders to keep him in line. The assignment from that point of view was rather galling; still he went eager to get back to work. As it developed, Bail showed an appreciation of Albert's work in Passaic, and Albert himself made a special effort toward smooth relations, so the two got along well enough.

As for me, I was there without great enthusiasm, seeing my position now only as somebody's wife, as a sort of appendage, a tail wagged by a dog. No, much as I loved my husband, this was not the life I wanted.

In general the situation of women in the Party—and of wives in particular—was an ignominious one. Few were just housewives minding the children. Many who held no posts contributed a devoted activity. If they were married, they were considered to be mere echoes of their husbands in any question of opinion. This simply reflected women's position in the society at large—but in the Party we felt we could expect more. Weren't we all fighting for a better world? Hadn't Engels, Bebel, and others in the socialist and Communist movements written on equality for women? We could only be resentful to find such bourgeois attitudes in our ranks. No matter what the women's contribution, it was taken for granted.

I remember a meeting of Party activists in New York at that time, in which some special questions were being discussed. In the hall outside the closed door stood about a dozen women, some among us holding important posts in the needle trades, all activists having no interest outside the Party. We had been excluded as women, for no other reason. As one man went in, before the door closed we heard him say, "There's a bunch of wives outside."

When the leaders, under pressure from the C.I., set up a department of "Woman's Work," they felt that everything was taken care of. Women's liberation was not an issue in that period in America. That women in the various European socialist movements of the early and middle nineteenth century already were dealing with the woman question, were even organizing their own groups and putting out their own papers, we Americans were unaware. The great complexity of the problem, involving as it does age-long prejudices and practices carried down from long before capitalism, and its very personal aspects of sex and family relations, intertwined with the economic and political ones, was not yet appreciated. If a man felt sorry for women it was enough to rate him their champion.

I recall little of Philadelphia in those days except that the Party headquarters was located on Spring Garden Street. Here was the center of our life for the coming few months. In the long run the interlude was interesting enough. Albert did all he could to involve me in work. Gradually I got acquainted with the local people. Miners from the anthracite works were about.

At that time, two campaigns were going on. The defense of Sacco and Vanzetti was now reaching its culmination. Much has been written about the case. It had been back in 1922 in South Braintree, Massachusetts, that two humble men, Italian by birth, one a fish peddler, the other a skilled worker in a shoe factory, were indicted for a murder that occurred during a payroll holdup. No evidence was ever brought out connecting the two prisoners with the crime. The obvious reason for their indictment in that period following the Palmer raids was that they were avowed anarchists, and in a modest way also activists.*

Albert, at that time still in the Socialist Party, had been on the original defense committee in Boston and had kept up with the developments of the case. The Communists were a small element in a defense which included anarchists and liberals as well as Socialists. The controversy was so widespread that Nicolo Sacco and Bartolomeo Vanzetti became household words. They were indeed internationally known. And now in August 1927 the final desperate appeal to the governor of Massachusetts for a stay of execution was taking place. A mass meeting was being called for August 23. I went around door to door with a team distributing handbills, talking to housewives.

At nightfall people began coming to the open public square. There was no platform, there were no speakers, it was something like a Quaker meeting. A signal was to be given: if the reprieve should be granted, a celebration would then take place; if not, the meeting would be a death vigil. People kept coming, singly and in groups until thousands stood quietly waiting. At last a bell began to toll. A sort of hushed murmur ran through the crowd—we knew the last appeal had been denied. A man named Alvin Fuller, governor of Massachusetts, had remained adamant to the end. The two victims were being led to their final agony. We gave them the tribute of our presence there, of our swallowed tears, of our resolve to devote ourselves more totally to creating a society where such outrages would no longer be.

The second campaign in those days was the united front with the Chinese residents of the city in support of Chiang Kai-shek. Then in the summer of 1927, this man's betrayal of the Chinese revolution was already an accomplished fact. People often ask, "What, you actually supported that old buzzard, that imperalist agent, that killer of hundreds of thousands of Chinese people?" For those coming later it is easy enough simply to denounce after reading what had taken place. We were far removed from Chinese events: we depended on the *Daily Worker* and *Inprecorr* for our briefing. Earl Browder was at that time in China as a Communist agent. His reports, when they did come, contained no de-

---

*See F. P. Cook, *The American Struggle* (New York: Doubleday, 1974), pp. 53-188.

nunciation of Chiang Kai-shek. Trotsky had warned that the Communists must remain independent, must not put themselves at the mercy of that leader as they were doing. But we followed the Party line. Often we must say: from the closed womb of the future comes no warning cry: we advance stumblingly, learning only through the shocks of experience.

In Philadelphia the alliance with Chiang Kai-shek as the symbol of a democratic revolution was then at its enthusiastic height. There was a parade and a banquet to which Albert was invited to feast on such delicacies (little known in those days) as bird's-nest soup and hundred-year-old eggs. So much for Chiang Kai-shek.

As the Philadelphia district included the anthracite coal region, Albert arranged for us to make several trips there and for me to stay a few days with a miner's family. We visited a mine village near Wilkes-Barre with the Vratarics. They were South Slavs; the man had worked for some years in the soft coal, had been blacklisted there as a radical, and was precariously hanging on here in the anthracite.

One Sunday morning I was taken to visit a slope mine. We—a miner and I—simply walked into a hole in the ground. The rotting timbers, the close earthy smell, the ceiling so oppressively low made me anxious, though of course I said nothing as the miner told me how they often had to walk a mile underground to reach their work.

It was a hot summer, I recall. The mountains were hidden all day in a white haze. At the end of the rambling, unpaved village street, lined by the miners' shacks, the coal-crushing breakers ten stories high reared their crazy, blackened structure. The nearby culm heap—the children's desolate playground—cut off the horizon. At the end of the street was what they called a "house," a cottage better than the others where the single miners flocked at night for a drink and an hour of lustful oblivion after their day in the dark underground. The miners talked much of unemployment that summer as they sat sweltering on the front steps after work.

All day the breakers crushing the coal roared rhythmically like the sea, and when they ceased at night, it was as though the pulse of the village had stopped.

It was in the fall of 1927, just when we were getting used to Philadelphia, that a real assignment came: district organizer in Detroit. Here was a windfall: to be at the heart of what was then the most modern and rapidly becoming the most important of United States industries. To be surrounded by giant factories filled with many thousands of workers! Albert was at once a war-horse smelling battle.

He would have liked to plunge immediately into organizing the auto industry, but, since he was here primarily in a political role, it was first necessary to take over the old office on Grand River Avenue, to install more efficient procedures, and above all to win political adherents. The previous incumbent had been a Fosterite, and some comrades held back at first, but were won over—as much as factionalists can be won over—by the new organizer's unbounded energy, optimism, and eagerness to work. Of course there were comrades of the former opposition, now the Lovestone faction, who cooperated from the start.

We stayed at first with the Schmies family, two comrades who owned a little house. Home ownership, like car ownership was encouraged by the Ford Company in order to anchor the worker to his job through debts. John Schmies, an auto worker who now gave his time to the Party, was a tall, thin man with a shock of thick black graying hair and a pale kindly face behind glasses. A German from the slums of Hamburg, he spoke with a heavy accent in a bumbling voice like a great bee. His young wife Hedi of Hungarian origin had grown up in the sugar beet fields of Michigan. Often she would tell of the wretched unsanitary barracks in which the families had to live, of the constant underfeeding, of how she went to work in the fields at age six. There was no escaping the penalty for such a deprived beginning. Pale and thin, she tired easily; she was a sickly woman.

By this time the C.I. had sent out its epoch-making instructions to reorganize the Party on a factory nucleus basis. Slow in coming, this step was an essential distinction from the Socialist or Social Democratic parties, out of which the Communist parties had emerged. As legal vote-seeking parties participating in the government, the European parties were organized on a territorial basis; the Russian Party under the Czar was an exception. This new structure would enable the Party directly to reach the workers in industry, who were to be the backbone of the revolution. Such nuclei were, of course, underground and took the greatest precautions to protect their members from discovery and consequent blacklisting.

Here in Detroit, where there was a basis for applying the new method, already a few Communist shop nuclei based on departments in auto plants were functioning. Still, there were many workers in plants where membership was not yet sufficient for a nucleus, and these comrades met with others, non-auto workers and housewives, at the district headquarters. So now we had meetings that included men with drawn, grim faces who came in so exhausted by the day's toil on drill, punch press or assembly line that they had to struggle to keep awake. They would refuse to remain later than ten o'clock.

As soon as Albert had finished his research on the auto industry, we went for a tour of the city. There were plants there at that time that are no longer in existence: Briggs Body, distinguished for particularly unsanitary dangerous conditions and super-exploitation, as well as Hudson, Fisher Body, Dodge, Chrysler, General Motors, and Ford's Highland Park plant. We visited Hamtramck, an auto workers' suburb, at that time overwhelmingly Polish, and finally Ford's new River Rouge plant. To see this giant complex spread out on the open prairie under the immensity of sky with human beings by the thousands swarming like ants in the distance was enormously impressive.

Whereas Passaic as a town had been something of a stagnant backwater, Detroit was all alive and growing, an exciting place to live. The Ford Company prided itself on innovation; Ford's eight-hour day was advertised far and wide as a symbol of progress. Those who daily poured by the thousands into Ford's plants well knew, however, that Ford got more out of them in eight hours than other employers did in nine. The ferocious speed-up plus improved mechanical processes were the backbone of the advanced technology.

At the start I spent most of my time in the office helping out with typing, filing, addressing, etc. Often in the evening I used to sit in the big lounge where local comrades were accustomed to gather. Like most workers' headquarters, it was a big plain bare room, with a worn linoleum on the floor, wooden settees and chairs, tables with literature spread out, pictures of Marx and Lenin, and some posters on the walls. From my favorite place on a settee facing the door, I would see people coming down the hall before they could see me. John Suma, an activist who came nearly every day displayed rather odd behavior. As he approached the door, he would straighten up as though bracing himself for something distasteful. Every day I would see him go through this routine.

Then one day, as I was typing in the office at a table next to Albert's desk, Suma was standing behind us talking. Suddenly I noted a false note in his voice, an out-of-place mocking tone. Glancing up at him I saw the same expression on his face. These observations I reported to Albert, who heard them gravely. Suma, it developed, was already under suspicion. He was a ready volunteer for work, but especially for such tasks as mailing which would put him in possession of names and addresses. Having been a Fosterite with the previous administration, he at once had switched his allegiance when the new organizer arrived. He was chronically unemployed, had contracted lead poisoning at work, and went to Chicago sometimes for treatment—so he said. He shifted his rooming house frequently. It all added up to a suspected employers' agent, such spies and provocateurs being common in the big industries, and many were the men deprived of employment by the report of a spy.

A careful watch was kept on John Suma. Ultimately, comrades who checked his room once while he was at the headquarters found a letter addressed to him from a private detective agency in Chicago. Albert opened the letter: it was an inquiry as to why Suma's weekly report had not been received. Without delay, Suma was expelled. A group of able-bodied comrades went to his room to administer justice and left him fit for a hospital. No compunction was shown; everyone here knew what firings, what blacklisting, what harassment and difficulty for the auto workers in finding work lay in the wake of a stoolie.

An important phase of party work was the issuing and circulating of factory newspapers for the auto workers. These papers, small in format, were both propaganda sheets and information bulletins: they printed letters from workers or their wives reporting on home conditions as well as oppressive conditions in the shops and any new developments there. The need for a union was constantly stressed. *The Ford Worker* was sold openly on the streets outside the Highland Park plant, the others quietly distributed inside the auto factories. Albert had me put in charge as editor of these papers. My tasks were to collect material, write an article or two, prepare copy, take it to the printer, and proofread.

I could now become a member of an organizing committee that was actively working for the unionization of the auto plants. It consisted of representatives of shop committees, or of party nuclei, of individuals in plants where no such group existed, and also of men auto workers too from the Mechanics Educational Society, a Socialist-oriented group that published a paper. I believe I was the only woman on the committee. We tried holding a mass meeting, but attendance was so small—chiefly stool pigeons, we felt—that such open tactics were deferred in favor of quiet work through personal contacts and the circulation of the papers. We did, however, conduct small department strikes wherever a shop committee had sufficient strength and a pressing issue arose.

Because it would be of advantage to work in an auto plant, we decided I should try for a job. Given my lack of robustness, I doubted whether I could hold up on the assembly line. An ad of a small parts manufacturer suggested lighter work. Being able-bodied and English-speaking, I got the job easily. No experience was required. As I crossed the big dirty room, cluttered with hand trucks, into which one entered directly from the street, I received my first introduction to the auto industry. A man white and dazed, supported by two others, was being led out, extending in front of him a crushed, bleeding right hand.

I was taken by a foreman to the rear into a small entirely closed room. Around the walls were ranged six or eight booths, in front of which women stood working. "Now this is it," the foreman said. "It ain't hard —just stick this on the rack," picking up one of a stack of small metal frames. "Now here's your spray gun—just press this, don't spray too thick, one coat is enough. The trick is to aim just right—don't waste paint sprayin' the air. There's a blower back there sucks in the spray."

He left me to adjust to my new job of spraying windshield frames. The gun seemed heavy to me, though it actually wasn't. Back strain would be my chief difficulty. The air of the room was close, warm, reeking with a chemical odor. A light job for the auto industry, it nevertheless had its hazards. I soon discovered the blower was not effective in sucking in the spray, which circled slowly upward, settling on the face, hands, hair, and shoulders of the sprayer. Breathing its probably noxious particles was unavoidable. Before one emission of spray mist could be absorbed, it would be succeeded by the next one—a dirty, unhealthy job. . . .

At the end of the day, the women would rush to the washroom for a twenty- to thirty-minute clean-up period. We had to bring our own cold cream and tissues. There wasn't much opportunity to get acquainted. The women complained constantly of the filthy, lousy job. The factory provided no place whatever to eat a home lunch, so we hurried to the nearest slop-joint to gulp down a sandwich, chili, or a frank in our half-hour break.

I had not been long on that job when there came an interruption, a favorable one, to our routine. Albert had been chosen to go to Moscow as a delegate to the Profintern Congress, which would open in Moscow on March 10, 1928. This privilege was for him in a sense a reward and recognition for his work in Passaic, for faction leaders a chance to display their trade-union man. After a little delay in procuring a passport, in a flurry of eager excitement and anticipation he was gone.

Soon afterward I began to develop a sore throat. Whether it was the irritation of the fumes or going out in the winter cold after sweating in the close hot room, I knew a sore throat for me signaled an oncoming chest cold or bronchitis. I couldn't afford to get sick now that I was dependent on my own earnings. So after only a few weeks I quit that job.

I found one somewhat lighter, but in its own way just as unhealthy. It had the further disadvantage that I worked alone in a little room where some small metal parts had to be soaked in cold water, then removed by me. Having my hands in cold water all day and being on my feet too was too much for me. I caught cold, my throat worsened, and before the week was over I went home with fever.

I was renting a bedroom with two congenial young Jewish comrades, the Winikurs. The husband Aaron was an auto worker, the wife Edith was staying home to care for their one child. She lived in daily dread of pregnancy. She was sure she broke all records as the world's most easily impregnable female. Nothing was of any avail. Contraceptives? She had tried them, they didn't work on her. "I just need one drop," she would say, "just one tiny little drop," indicating with two fingers this infinitesimal amount. "Right away I get pregnant. We can't afford another child. I should get a job to help out. I can't with taking care of this one." Only recently, when she had become pregnant, one of the Party physicians had performed an abortion on her right here on the kitchen table—and it was not the first time. Shuddering, I wondered whether I should ever have to undergo such a barbarous thing.

It was Comrade Winikur who took care of me when I went home sick that day; got me a doctor, gave me my medicine and drinks of water, all with the gentleness of a mother. As I was recuperating sitting around headquarters, the district had a visit from Ella Reeve Bloor, known as Mother Bloor, a Fosterite who was considered a popular leader. After raising a family of children, products of two marriages, she had joined the Socialist Party and become an activist, even full-time organizer.*

Comrade Schmies, who was taking Albert's place, informed me casually of this visit, handing me a leaflet from the coal fields in Pennsylvania where a strike was in progress. It appeared Bloor expected to have a meeting here. "You take care of this, yes, Vera?" Schmies said. "The other women will help you." A small hall was rented and a leaflet circulated.

When the evening came, a group of women Party members and a few others were gathered. Mother Bloor arrived late, swept down the aisle accompanied by several other people. She was getting on in her sixties; wrinkled, gray-haired, and haggard, she fully looked her age. After glancing around the hall she turned to me crestfallen. "Why is the meeting so small?" she queried, apparently disappointed almost to tears. "I sat up all night on a train to get here." She sniffed at smelling salts as I led her to the platform.

A big case was made of this meeting by the Fosterites. According to them, the small attendance showed how little the district under Lovestonite leadership appreciated the women's work or the struggle in the coal fields. Bloor had evidently expected a great hall filled with thousands. Although her talk had been effective and direct, stressing the hardships of the miner's life and of the women bereaved by mine disasters, still she was no great orator. Actually I had seen the meeting as something chiefly

---

*See Ella Reeve Bloor, *We Are Many* (New York; International Publishers, 1940).

for the Party. Had I made a mistake, missed an opportunity to reach the masses, failed in an assignment? With a gnawing sense of insufficiency and failure, I missed Albert more than ever. He would have been a buffer in the Bloor meeting affair or at least have shared the responsibility. He might have seen in it a way to reach nonparty workers and women, something I had overlooked. Schmies merely shrugged his shoulders; to him it was just something for the women, hence a trifling matter.

At the headquarters the day after the meeting Mother Bloor told me how she had always struggled as a woman to be independent. She stressed this point so much I felt she was really advising me. Actually I was as independent then, at least in a material way, as I ever had been. Was I not supporting myself, living alone? Perhaps Bloor sensed something of my lack of inner self-sufficiency.

After an absence of two months, with only a couple of letters from Albert, word came that he was being recalled from Moscow. A strike had broken out in the cotton mills of New Bedford, Massachusetts. Who could take charge of it but Weisbord, leader of Passaic? He must rush back, and shortly after that news I was informed I had been selected by the Central Committee to spend some time in the Pennsylvania coal fields now out in general strike. Specifically I was to work with the ladies auxiliaries of the United Mine Workers Union.

So already the Detroit chapter, for me just beginning, was at an end. My work there had seemed to be of value, and my inclination is always to stay with an accepted task. The comrades gave me credit for an improvement in the factory papers. Albert too was well liked in Detroit. Somewhat confused and frustrated I still had no thought of objecting. The discipline of the Party I knew was necessary and I was glad to be entrusted with a responsible post. So consoling myself I went gladly to the new assignment.

7

A Place for Me

Comrade Abraham Jakira, the D.O. and a supporter of the Lovestone
faction, a man whom I knew only by reputation, had been in the movement since its inception. Notable in the Russian Federation in New York,
he was prominent in the Underground, in fact a leader of the Goose
Caucus. Jakira was modest and friendly and welcomed me.

The movement I was about to attach myself to already had a history,
he explained. It was in 1922 that a Progressive Committee was first organized among the union miners. The general strike of that year in the
soft-coal fields had netted the miners little. The program of the Progres-
sives was: to organize the unorganized, to restore democracy in the union,
to support a Farmer–Labor party, and to attain government ownership
of the mines. It was in 1923 that the Committee began attacking the
union president, John L. Lewis, for being on the employers' side. Lewis
fought back with expulsions and suspensions.

"By 1926 the coal industry was in a bad way, the union also. After the
overdevelopment of the industry during wartime inflation, when a lot of
little mines with small-time owners appeared, the coal mining industry
slumped. Unemployment set in. Many bosses are moving to the nonunion
South. The Pittsburgh Coal Company, one of the big ones, has gone open
shop. This present strike has lasted a year already. The Anthracite Union
members are working, and about half the soft-coal, unorganized, are
working too.

"Now the employers are taking advantage of the strike to reorganize
the industry, to consolidate, and they're eliminating some of the small
inefficient mines. They're beginning to mechanize also. John L. Lewis has
not tried to deal with the reduction of employment that results. With all

this, the membership of the United Mine Workers in West Virginia, Missouri, Oklahoma, and Kansas has fallen drastically. The Lewis leadership can't handle the situation. We are trying with a militant spirit to revive the union. In the elections in the latter part of 1926 John L. Lewis got 173,000 votes; John Brophy, our candidate—he is chairman of the Save the Union Committee—had well over 60,000. That gives you an idea of the lineup.

"This policy of fighting the Lewis machine, which is well entrenched, is, of course, in line with the Comintern principle of no dual unions but support of the AFL. Our Committee has a genuine following; it's a minority, but no mere paper organization." Comrade Jakira then showed me a list of the mine camps where either the local was loyal to us, or there was at least a nucleus. It looked like a considerable list to me.

"You'll be working with the ladies' auxiliaries. You'll copy this list of the contacts you'll have to see. I suggest you go right out to the camps. You don't have to notify them. They're always there."

I went next to the office of the Workers International Relief, where I found Alfred Wagenknecht, who knew me from Passaic and greeted me as "Smith." Since this miners' strike was not in any way spectacular and had received little publicity, the money brought in by the WIR campaign was much less than in Passaic, he said. Various miners were sometimes around, among them Pat Toohey, Tony Minerich, and George Papçun, members of the Young Communist League whom I had known in Philadelphia.

Magliacano, the former Italian organizer of Passaic, was also on the staff as well as Rebecca Grecht from New York and others. It was only later on that I realized that I had been sent because Comrade Grecht was there. She was a Fosterite; there was always this rivalry, with each faction insisting on having its comrades in any given situation. Wagenknecht gave me a railroad schedule, some minimal information on how to get around, and a week's pay in advance.

As I went out daily to one camp or another, or sometimes covering two in a day, my grasp of the situation increased. The camps were generally isolated, located in out-of-the-way valleys—the Monongahela Valley, the Shenandoah Valley, the Allegheny Valley. There wasn't much there: the mine tipple, the breakers, the culm heap, the commissary, the church, the school, the union hall, and the "patch," or group of company-owned shacks that housed the miners' families. The miners' homes had electricity but no gas in most of the camps.

While in the anthracite region there were a number of silk-throwing mills that employed a miner's wife and daughters, here there was nothing for them. The girls could go into Pittsburgh for a sleep-in servant job, or travel by bus to a nearby town to work in a store or laundry. Mothers were at home caring for numerous children. And for the sons, alas, for the grown lads, what was there for them at age fourteen or fifteen but to follow Dad's footsteps down into the black, menacing tunnels?

The homes in the patch generally had no running water; one hand-worked pump had to serve all. What this meant in winter can only be imagined. The women had to haul water by the pailful, not merely for cooking and personal use and washing the clothes (the miners' clothes were always soot-impregnated), but when the mine was working they had to fill the washtub daily with hot water heated on a coal- or wood-burning cook stove for their husbands' baths after work. The shacks ran from fair to dilapidated in condition. Squalor was everywhere.

Food was scarce wherever I went. Once in a miner's home the children were playing around a littered table. As I talked with the wife, a crust of bread near the edge of the table was jostled to the floor. The mother got up, picked up the bread, and after wiping it carefully on her apron replaced it on the table.

The lack of food was a problem for me too. There was no way to have the midday meal or snack to which I was accustomed. There was no restaurant, nor could I have gone to one when the people weren't eating. I'd take along a candy bar in my purse to gobble as I got off the train. Then, arriving back in Pittsburgh at eight or nine o'clock in the evening famished, I would eat a hearty meal accompanied by guilt-thoughts of the miners' empty stomachs. Eventually this unwholesome regime brought on a stubborn indigestion. One thing in this assignment fascinated me—the steel mills strung along the river, especially when I would return after dark and see them all aglow against the black sky.

Generally when the miners were called out on strike the walkout was complete. In one mine in the Pittsburgh area the workers had lagged in coming out. The nearby mining camp of Renton, a large one and solidly for the Save the Union Committee, forming a mass picket line of men, women, and children, had marched several miles to pull out the other mine. Once everyone was out, the mine was at a standstill and there was no need of picketing. In a union like the UMW all efforts at negotiations, as well as any other activity concerning the strike, had to be left to the officials. The members merely waited, receiving some minimal cash and food benefits.

In such a situation there wasn't too much an organizer could do. Generally the women would have a meeting arranged for me. I would give a short talk on the general conditions that faced them, stressing the failure of John L. Lewis to get the strike settled or to solve any of the union's problems and the necessity of building up our committee and our morale.

Then we would take up individual problems, which generally centered on relief, or on some person who was weakening, or perhaps on some rumor. A rumor was about, which unfortunately had a basis in fact, that agents of John L. Lewis were paying families $5 if the man would return to work. This couldn't happen in a Save-the-Union camp.

I learned after I had been there some time that the union contract was of overwhelming importance. Miners who had generations of union-ism behind them were very contract-conscious. Without the UMW they saw little prospect of a contract, and this was really what held them to the union despite the failure of John L. Lewis.

A rumor that Negro strikebreakers were being brought in from the South I saw confirmed. One evening, looking out of my bus as it stopped to let off a passenger, I saw standing beside the road half a dozen black men with soot-blackened clothing and lamps still clipped to their caps. Their shoulders, in fact their entire bodies drooped in fatigue. Never have I seen men more dejected, more forlorn than these. Strikebreakers here did not come in with awareness of the situation. The company would send a truck into the hill country in the South, promising good pay and a steady job. It was quite possible these men had never worked in a mine before.

The dangerous, unhealthy nature of the miner's work, the isolation of the camps, the stark poverty of the environment, all these factors tended to build a certain type of character. In men who take their lives into their hands every time they go to work, courage is a basic quality. Devotion to the union is another essential in a life that offers little in the way of dis-traction, entertainment, or uplift. The church may have some devotees, chiefly among the women, but the union wins the miners' loyalty. They are independent, upright, and brave people, realistic in their thinking, open and friendly, and generous though their resources are few.

Once I happened to make contact with a man from a John L. Lewis camp that was out on strike. The man arranged a meeting for me and I went out one Sunday. There in a grove of trees on a grassy slope some twelve or fifteen people were waiting. The church was nearby; beyond, over a hill I could see the patch and the mine buildings. I hadn't gone far in my talk when someone released among the little group several large dogs. The animals were brought out on leashes. When let go, they leaped about barking. While the people scattered, I held my ground. I am not afraid of dogs; in fact I like them. I couldn't picture an organizer turning tail and running. The dogs made no attempt to molest anybody, but my meeting had melted away. If I try it again, I thought, they'll have something worse cooked up, so I didn't tackle the Lewis camps any more.

Comrade Rebecca Grecht, a good-looking, red-haired young woman, lively and articulate, was a member of the Millinery Workers Union, though she didn't appear to be a worker. I had met her briefly in Passaic.

An attempt I made to get acquainted with Rebecca Grecht didn't get me very far.

"I've been going out every day to visit with the women. I'm doing women's work, you know," I began.

"So I see," she answered. "In my opinion, you're not going about it in the right way." Then she proceeded to set me straight: I should arrange a series of meetings, get a car to take me around, and cover several in a day. I sensed a factional approach; whatever I did, it wouldn't be approved of by Comrade Grecht. And she didn't convince me. I preferred my own method of patient, individual contact.

Grecht's assignment was a political one: to build the Party in the coal fields. Tours were arranged for her, leaflets put out. The meetings were well attended, stacks of applications for membership in the Communist Party were signed. As the tours continued, how the *Daily Worker* celebrated the remarkable success in the coal fields of Comrade Grecht!

Later the picture began to look somewhat different. One day, after Grecht had left, Comrade Jakira went out to assemble his new members, talk to them, organize them in party groups. Later I happened to find Jakira sitting at his desk with stacks of cards in piles before him. "Look at that," he said with more animation than usual. "Hundreds of names—new Party members! Yes, but where are they? In some places only three or four people showed up when I went to the camps; in others no one at all!"

It took some time to assess that these results were general. But why? One possibility was that the miners' English was not adequate. The smooth college-bred talk of Grecht may have flowed over them like so much water. Also, since the meeting was held in the union hall, it may have appeared to be something for the union's benefit. A miner is ready to die for his union; how could he refuse to sign a little card held out by an attractive, smiling young woman? At any rate, for whatever reason, it was clear that a speaking tour was not the way to build the Party. I remained convinced that steady, persistent personal contact in the field, where Party members were active, was the best means.

What was really missing in our situation was a leader—a coordinator of the various activities. Here we were, four or five organizers running around independently of each other, with no long-range plan, sometimes perhaps acting at cross-purposes, or at any rate not supplementing each other's work or carrying out a common objective.

Jakira's job was district organizer of the Party; he could not appear to be directing the Save the Union Committee, which was a mass organization. Wagenknecht, also a Party member, was head of the WIR. I had been sent there by the Party Central Committee and submitted monthly reports to it, yet I was involved also with the ladies auxiliaries of the UMW, and through them was trying to help build the Save the Union Committee. Such contradictions were always present in the Party's mass work.

All members of the Party involved in the work here got together once a week in a hired (neutral) hall for what was called a "fraction meeting." A Central Committee representative met with us, who was none other than William Z. Foster. This was the only opportunity I had to meet at close range the well-known leader.

Foster was a big man with a physique that might have been powerful but had deteriorated into flabbiness. He appeared to be about fifty, with a strong-featured, lined face, thinning grayish hair, and tired eyes. There was a beaten look about him that I didn't know how to account for. He appeared to feel put out at having to come down here from New York every week. Never was there a spark of enthusiasm or even of animation. He would report whatever there was of news from the Central Committee, and he would listen to reports from the field. Foster could not be the coordinator we needed, as that would have meant being constantly in the field; still he might have given more help than he did.

As for my own role in these fraction meetings, I was still backward, still too inhibited to speak out. The order of business consisted chiefly of reports, but there was also some discussion, and any comrade having a criticism was expected to bring it up. Once there was a question of a leaflet that had been passed out. I thought the wording was poor and I had a better one. As I was trying to work up my courage to speak, Comrade Foster came out with the very same idea. Had I spoken first, my stature would have been greatly increased in Party circles; but I was still confined to the traditional role of women, which was, like children, to be "seen but not heard."

After a time I was sent to East Lansing in eastern Ohio, Sub-District 6 of the UMW. This was actually a loyal John L. Lewis district, but we had a small outpost of the SUC there. Because the mine there was at the outskirts of town, it was not so isolated as some others. Here I stayed with a miner's family, the Gwynns. Maw Gwynn was the strongest personality I had yet met among the stalwart mine people. She was rugged like the Cumberland hills she came from, raw-boned and vigorous, with a deep voice like a man's—a real soldier of a woman. Pappy was older than his wife and a little bent, but still a strong man. Their two grown sons were tall and handsome.

"Before I took up with the union," Maw Gwynn narrated as we sat in the big kitchen (which, as usual, was also dining and living room), "I had done raised my boys and I had time on my hands then. I never did nothin' but stick in the house and sew on patchwork quilts. We made us a little money that way. I never went out nowheres, you just couldn't git me away from them patches, and, my lands, I was sick all the time. I was always for the union but never got right out to fight in it like I done in this strike. It was when they put my two boys in jail, that was what done it." She then described the picket line of fifty women that went to St. Clairsville to pull out the mine there. They were all arrested, lined up, and marched in the rain over a mile to the jail, where they were herded into three dirty cells. They had to wring the water out of their clothes and sleep on the iron floor with only one cotton blanket each. The food was so bad they told the jailer to feed it to the pigs.

"I'm the only American woman in this place that ain't stickin' with John L. Lewis," she continued. "They talk about Hunkies, but believe me, it's the Hunkies is doin' the fightin' in this strike, and I stick with them." I heard her once talking to a group of the Lewis women, her gray hair disheveled, her sunburnt forehead wrinkled: "You poor miserable low-lived things, do you mean to tell me you've signed over to John L. Lewis after he's robbed you and sucked the lifeblood out of you all these years? Just because he promised you a dollar a week more for relief, and you didn't even get the dollar. I've seen the time in this strike when we didn't have a crumb of food in the house for four days, and did John L. Lewis help us? Don't you ever come near me with any of your dirty yellow dog papers,"* she yelled, shaking a powerful fist in their faces. "If you do, I'll smash your face in so you'll never see again." No wonder she was feared by the Lewis people in town as much as she was respected by the Save the Union people.

Food was scarce in the Gwynns' home. For supper just a dish of red beans cooked on the range with a wood fire. For breakfast there was a cup of brown liquid called coffee, which had at least the virtue of being hot; for lunch a piece of cornbread and more of the coffee. Thinking to contribute something to the scanty rations, I went down to the commissary the second day. Here I found the storekeeper at his counter with rows of empty shelves behind him. "No Ma'm," he said, "I ain't got a thing. I'm done cleaned out. I done gave credit to the miners just as long as I could till I hadn't a cent to my name to restock with. No, Ma'm, you won't find much to eat round these parts."

Down the road from the Gwynns' on a billboard outside the union

---

*The "yellow dog" contract was one made between Lewis and the employers without worker participation or knowledge.

hall was posted a large notice of a coming district 6 meeting of the UMW called by the district organizer. I had the privilege of attending this unbelievable meeting. Maw Gwynn and I and the other women of the auxiliary took seats along the wall at the back. Several armed guards were posted at a few points around the hall. There were also ushers in the aisles. The union members filed in quietly and sat expectant in their chairs. The atmosphere was tense, not a word of conversation was heard, and no time was lost before the chairman got up to introduce the organizer, who said that this meeting was called by the UMW to give a report of the organization. There would be no discussion. The report was a short routine one having nothing to do with the strike. As the organizer sat down, a miner in the ranks rose to his feet. Before he could say a word an usher was behind him, seized him by the shoulders, and pushed him roughly back into his chair. Already the chairman was calling the meeting adjourned.

All present got up and filed out without a word. Outside the crowd burst into a hubbub. The meeting had exposed the autocratic methods, the lack of democracy, and the UMW's failure to end the strike. It was grist for the Save-the-Union mill and many arguments broke out before the meeting we held later. Here in East Lansing our meetings were attended by men and women together because the forces were small.

It was after my return to Pittsburgh in late August that something significant occurred: an important fraction meeting was held with all comrades active in the field called in, even from other states.

It was a much larger meeting than usual. Juliet Poyntz was there; she was doing defense work now. There were plenty of cases. Pat Toohey and Chairman John Brophy had been arrested at a Renton meeting in March. Tony Minerich in eastern Ohio had been convicted of violating a federal injunction against picketing and was out on bail. Grecht, arrested in Burgettstown, was charged with sedition.* All these people were present, as well as John Watt from Springfield, Illinois, a leader of the Progressive miners in his state.

Comrade Foster as usual gave the report. A drastic change had been made by the C.I. in trade union policy. Until now Party members had tried to work with the AFL even when it failed to cooperate, as it had in Passaic. Now the decision was to form new unions affiliated with the Profintern. Here in the coal fields the Save the Union Committee was to transform itself into the National Miners' Union. This policy was to be carried out completely and without delay.

The decision must have been previously known to some of the people

---

*See *Labor Defender*, April 1928.

present. Comrade Jakira gave his usual mousy but unqualified assent.
Juliet Poyntz also supported the ruling. To the people who, like myself,
were active in the field this was nothing less than a bombshell. What? To
go out and recant? To suddenly and without warning tell people to leave
the union, the union of their fathers, of their grandfathers? And to start
a new union with the comparatively slim forces we had? There was resistance from all of us including, I believe, the only miners present—Watt,
Toohey, Minerich, and Papçun. There were a good number of rank and
file Party members in the camps but they, it seemed, were not called to
the meeting. Foster was adamant; it was a C.I. decision, it was not to be
argued but applied.

I had a meeting scheduled for the following evening. Instead of
spending the day in the field as I would normally have done, I sat around
the office discussing the new turn with those present. We had to admit
the UMW leadership was rotten to the core, the union machine controlled. Elections were rigged. Still, the miners hated the idea of working
without a contract; there was little chance their employers would negotiate with a small new organization. Had there been more time at least to
prepare, we would have had more chance to win them over.

At any rate, when the time came, I had to face my meeting. It was
perhaps in Avila, or possibly Charleroi; I am not sure. The mine was on
the outskirts of a town where there were typical business streets with
stores, banks, a few churches and schools, as well as some good houses
for the business people. I was met at the bus stop by Tonnelli,* husband
of one of the women. As we went toward the union hall, he talked about
his wife. She was pregnant and had no appetite. He was going to buy a
steak for her. This last statement stuck in my mind; how could a striker
have the money to buy a steak?

The attendance at the meeting was good, including around sixty
women as well as a few men, Tonnelli among them. The meeting was
opened and the minutes read; then came my turn. It goes without saying
I could make no mention of the C.I. Party. I recapitulated the crimes
of the UMW, described the meeting in East Lansing, brought up the
total inactivity of the officials in this strike, the inadequate relief, and
so on. The leaders of the Save the Union Committee, I stated, had decided it was time to take a new step. To get rid of a machine so firmly
entrenched was not possible. We had to make a new turn and under
honest militant leadership build up the SUC as an independent union.

The women listened unsmiling with complete attention. When I sat
down again in the front row, Tonnelli jumped to his feet and began to

---

*An assumed name.

shout. He launched into a violent attack against the leadership of the Save the Union Committee in Pittsburgh: they were traitors, strikebreakers, union smashers, crooks—every one of them. Wagenknecht, he said, was so crooked he could hide behind a corkscrew.

"And you, Vera Buch," he yelled facing me glaring, "You got a nerve coming here and talking like that. Throw her out." Turning to the women, "Throw her out, throw them all out, crooks, bastards, traitors."

When he sat down the meeting burst into an excited babble of talk. The principal ethnic group here was South Slav, either Slovene or Croatian, and the language they spoke was known in the coal fields as Granich. There must have been some other nationalities present, such as Italian and Hungarian; at any rate I heard no English. There was not a word I could understand. Tonnelli jumped up again and stood glowering at me.

My position didn't look very good. At the least, I thought, the state troopers, the coal and iron police, the men on horseback (I had seen two as we came to the hall) hearing the noise would come in and break up the meeting. Unable to think of anything I could do, I sat quietly, my heart beating fast and my palms damp, wishing I could make myself invisible. At last they quieted down and the meeting was adjourned. When I said goodbye to those near me, their response was not really hostile yet not friendly either. I went alone to the bus stop. Normally some of the women would have walked there with me, but I was glad enough to find myself still intact on the bus bound for Pittsburgh.

Of course I reported to Jakira in the morning. It was only a few days afterward that Tonnelli turned violent in the union hall, shot three men, and escaped into the hills. I had had a narrow escape.

A little later the Pittsburgh chapter also was closed. Since the New Bedford strike had reached a point where Albert's presence was no longer necessary, he was relieved of his post. The Central Committee withdrew me from my work also and I was to join Albert in New York. While I experienced the usual pull of loyalty toward the miners, that last meeting had indicated such great difficulties ahead that I was not too sorry to leave.

The summer in the coal fields had done me good physically. I had gone about despite the weather in days of simmering heat when the green hills were hidden behind a white haze, in rainy days sloshing through puddles and mud. Except for the indigestion I have mentioned, I was really feeling fit. I had even taken on a little of the miners' speech, would say "hell" and "Goddamn" once in a while.

In other respects too I had come a long way. Here in the coal fields I was completely independent, with little support from the comrades. Confronted with difficult situations at times, it seemed to me I handled them probably as well as anyone else. What is more, my conceptions of mass work and of leadership had been greatly clarified both in the work in Detroit and here in Pittsburgh. In the auto workers' organizing committee there had been no leaders in the usual sense, no paid organizers, no speechmaking. Though the Party gave some orientation to its own members, the actual work was done by rank and file auto workers. As for leadership, that situation did not require a personality with a powerful mass-appeal; nor did the work among the miners. Intelligent understanding of the aims of the work, acquaintance with the workers' conditions, combined with courage and determination—these were the essentials. No longer did I feel myself unfit because I was different from the people I saw playing leading roles. I had learned that the revolution, as well as a strike, is above all a collective activity in which the resources of many must be pooled. There would always be a place for me.

A furnished room in New York was the setting for a happy reunion as Albert and I took up where we had left off. Already Detroit seemed far behind. Albert had much to tell about his trip to the Profintern Congress. (For details of the trip, see Appendix C.)

The Russian Party was found to be deeply torn with factional struggle since Lenin's death, or in fact since the attempted assassination that had paralyzed him. We had heard vague rumors of Trotsky's so-called defection, but we knew little of him since his works were not available in America. To us, he had remained one of the heroes of the revolution, the chairman of the Petrograd Soviet in 1905, the leader and organizer of the Red Army, always mentioned in the same breath with Lenin. Cannon had lined up as a supporter of Trotsky, while the Fosterites were backing Stalin. This name was just beginning to be heard in the U.S., but he apparently was already in a strong position in Russia. Conditions in Russia were not good; there were unemployment and food shortages. Large numbers of homeless children, the *byezpryjorny*, were also a problem.

What Albert had observed and learned in Russia could only have a very disturbing effect on us. While we both were dissatisfied with the American Party leadership, still our confidence in the Russian Party and in the Comintern had remained. Now the Russian Party was seen as unstable and in crisis; maneuvers for power were sapping its strength, as in America. One thing was clear: from now on the divisions of the American Party would be but reflections of those in Russia. We were a tail wagged by that giant bear; any independence was out of the question. Our relation with the Comintern was a question we could not solve. Albert was convinced he knew little of what was really going on internationally. We agreed that all we could do was to plunge into mass work and proceed along those lines until the situation cleared.

The Congress was to last for another month, and Albert was chagrined when the telegram came instructing him to hurry back to New Bedford. "What about all their Fosters, their Dunnes, their Gitlows, all their great trade union leaders—why weren't they called in? No, it had to be Weisbord." So like a good soldier he had obeyed, had rushed on an express train from Moscow to Paris, gone two days and a half with practically no sleep, then with difficulty obtained a berth on the *Leviathan*. Then from New York directly to New Bedford.

A general walkout of skilled workers in the cotton mills had occurred there. The local leaders were two men with socialist leanings named Batty and Binns. Our policy was to extend the strike to nearby Fall River, where 28,000 cotton workers had also got a wage cut of 10 percent. More important, we wanted to pull out all the unskilled in New Bedford and at the same time to form one union including everybody. As leader of the Passaic strike, Albert was welcomed by the unskilled workers, but the leaders remained aloof, considering the Communists intruders. The strike there was of a different character than the one in Passaic. Loom fixers, spinners, and weavers, practically all of British origin, were already organized in small craft locals affiliated with the Amalgamated Textile Workers.

Fred Beal, who had been in the United Front committees in Lawrence, Massachusetts, was there with another man named William Murdoch. These two carried the load as the principal strike leaders. Coco, the Italian organizer, a confirmed Fosterite, came in also with his companion, Anne Washington Creighton. So did Eli Keller and Ellen Dawson from Passaic. Helpers for youth work were sent in from Boston.

It was a sorry and familiar story: lack of support from the Party, the leaders too busy in Moscow, relief and defense campaigns poor, no real national effort. The leaders made a ruling that the strikers could get relief only from New England and a few other cities. The defense policy of the ILD under Cannon's leadership was a disgrace. The ILD rep in the field made a deal with the prosecution for Murdoch to accept two months imprisonment, Beal one month, instead of longer terms (but they were not guilty of the charges). This at the height of the strike! Cannon upheld this, refused to appeal. The militancy of the workers was wonderful: they took a terrible beating; police and militia were brought in, even from towns outside; one thousand strikers were arrested. Well, we did the best we could. The bosses took back half of the 10 percent cut, which benefited the unskilled as well as the skilled.

At last we got to discuss the Comintern decision on the formation of new Communist-led unions. Had Albert spoken on the question in the Congress? No, Gitlow vetoed that in the caucus meetings. The Party leaders all saw Albert as a newcomer, an upstart; they hated him for the opposition he had given them in Passaic, were jealous of his role there and no doubt also for his attainments, his better education.

Albert advocated the Comintern policy on the new unions; his own bitter personal experience as well as the general situation had convinced him. My experience in the coal fields made me doubtful. The situation was different in textiles; there had been ample demonstration of the futility of trying to work through the AFL and small independent unions. A new union in textiles was the order of the day; in fact, Albert was assigned to organize it. With all his doubts as to what help he would get from the Party in its present troubled situation, he still looked forward to this work. There seemed to be a good basis for the new union in Massachusetts, New Jersey, New York, and Pennsylvania. He would have to tour the area. Success would depend on how the new policy was carried out.

As for me, I had decided that I wanted to go to the Lenin School in Moscow. Perhaps I wanted a better background in theory; perhaps I wanted simply to visit the Soviet Union. On Albert's advice I went to the national office, where I was received by Jack Stachel, who handled much of National Secretary Lovestone's routine work. Comrade Stachel was a short, wiry man, abrupt in his movements and speech, his voice harsh and grating. He was neither cheerful nor friendly. Unsmiling, he said, "I'll take care of it, Comrade Buch."

Apparently my request fell into some bottomless pit, for there was never the least response to it.

For a brief interval we were happy to be together again and comparatively free from care. We had found a rather charming, unusual nook facing Gramercy Park, a small private park in the vicinity of 23rd and Lexington. We rented a tiny furnished apartment on the top floor of one of those dignified old buildings surrounding the park. Really no more than a room and an alcove, it had a window overlooking the park below and the sun came in. I recovered something of my old love of New York of college days, finding time to take walks, though most of my time was as usual spent at headquarters near Union Square.

It was with this pleasant temporary home as a setting that I should have had one of the best experiences of my life. Every woman knows how it is ... the first few days with just a suspicion, then the multiplying days ... a week ... two weeks, the signs increasing. Yes, it was pretty certain without an examination; I was pregnant.

Life must be hard indeed and her lot pretty desperate if a woman cannot feel wonder and joy when this happens to her for the first time. I was no exception. I would get up in the morning feeling unusually well and buoyant. After a few minutes it would come over me with a rush ... the baby! I would indulge myself in tender, foolish imaginings of myself as a mother. Even though ten years had elapsed since the sanatorium, I had always seen myself as something salvaged from the scrap heap. It was all the more wonderful that I should be able to conceive. Yes, I too, even I had my moment of joy.

Albert had made it clear from the start there were to be no children. The logic of this was plain enough. The inconvenience would be great if we wanted to be active revolutionists, which we did. Probably for me it would mean the end of activity, at least for a time. After a few weeks when we finally faced the situation squarely, for him there were no two ways about it; I had to have an abortion. "Why don't you get an examination?" he prodded me. At last I forced myself to act.

Some trick of memory brought back Dr. Jennison of the old TB days. It would be easier to talk to a woman. It was the same waiting room, uncluttered, artistic, and she was the same gracious person, her hair a little grayer. Obviously she didn't remember me, but the old charming smile was forthcoming, wrinkling up a youthful face. She jotted down some facts on a card, calling me "little lady" as she had done ten years before. "Now you just go behind that screen and get those panties off." With icy hands I prepared. The pregnancy was confirmed; she estimated that it was at least two months. Briskly she went to her desk and started to write on her pad.

With effort I said, "But I don't want to go on with it. I want to have an abortion."

"Why, whatever put that into your head? Nonsense. Of course you want the baby."

I blurted the truth or a semblance of the truth, "I can't. It's not convenient. I'm not married." Whatever illusion had prompted me to this uncalled-for confidence was quickly dispelled. The doctor gasped, her smile vanished; one could fairly see her nose turn up.

"I can't get mixed up with anything like that." She fluttered her hands as though she were dropping hot potatoes.

"All I want is to find out where I can have it done," I persisted in my misery.

"No, I can't have anything to do with it," she repeated in a hard voice of finality. "No respectable doctor is going to risk her license in a thing like that." And with this she got up and opened the door.

Next a Party physician: he too confirmed the pregnancy. Though sympathetic, he too didn't have anything to do with abortion. He tried to encourage me. "Wouldn't you like to raise a nice little pioneer for the Party?" The last thing I wanted to do! Had he warned me of the dangers, which he must have known, the outcome might have been different.

Finally, after more delays I went to Albert's brother-in-law, a doctor in Brooklyn. He called up a colleague. "I'm sending you a friend of mine. She has a little trouble with her breast. Tell Albert he should go with you," he added to me.

But Albert didn't want to go. Was he reluctant to appear as the author of a baby? "My responsibility is to provide the money, that is all," he said.

As I sat in Dr. Epstein's waiting room, the glass-enclosed porch of a private house in the Bronx, the last illusion of freedom of will left me. I seemed to have entered a chute which would carry me inevitably down . . . . down to the bottom. A woman came out now; pale and walking gingerly, she left. Nobody uttered a word. At last my turn came. A youngish man in a not-too-clean white coat sat behind a desk. His unsmiling manner indicated that dispatch was necessary here; no wasting of time on amenities. After a few perfunctory questions he said, "I can fix you up in two weeks from Monday at ten. My fee is one hundred dollars. You'll have to put down the money before I can touch you." When I agreed, he said he would have to examine me.

After confirming the pregnancy he stuffed my vagina with a lot of gauze strips, saying, "You let that stay in a week. Sometimes it's enough to induce an abortion."

"How shall I know?" I stupidly asked.

"Oh, you'll know all right." And hopes were raised that perhaps I'd have it easily that way. At home I wondered: is this man even a doctor? I didn't recall seeing any framed diploma. The place didn't look too clean. His speech was uncultured.

The week passed and I pulled the gauze out. Then after a ten-day wait until the man could fit me into his crowded schedule, I went alone again for the operation. When I first entered the office, "Doctor" Epstein made a phone call, telling someone to come over for an "anesthesia." For a brief interval I experienced relief, but soon when another man came, they got me on the table and set to work. It was clear there would be no anesthetic.

"Every time I make a move toward her, she thinks her last hour has come," said Dr. Epstein to his colleague. "Relax, now, slide down here. Relax, Mrs. Weisbord."

Was it possible to relax under torture? The minute the instrument commenced its work, I cringed. My whole body rigid, an icy sweat on my skin, I clutched the gown over my chest. "Put your hands down at your sides. Now, breathe through your mouth. Relax, I can't do a thing if you're going to stay stiff like that."

His voice rattled on, chatting with his assistant. "Say, why don't you come over to the stable with me this afternoon. I've got my eye on a peach of a filly. You ought to get out in the park more. Nothing like riding to keep a man fit. Relax, Mrs. Weisbord, slide down. Isn't she the limit?" Sweating from every pore, I gripped the sides of the table, as the fierce grinding pain went on without a minute's respite.

The doctor continued to chat with his friend. "Oh, say, do you know Engelberg took that case? I mean the kid, fifteen years old and five months along. The mother offered me a thousand bucks, but not me. Liberty means something in my sweet life. The mother bawled, but the kid was like brass. It was just natural she said. Well, Engelberg takes it, the damn fool. He no sooner gets her on the table and her temperature shoots up to a hundred and four. Now she's home with a day and night nurse. I wouldn't be in his shoes."

It must end sometime . . . I have to bear it . . . it can't last forever. . . . The instruments were making a little clanking sound as the doctor's voice, flat and unfeeling, ran on. At last they withdrew the instruments. They fussed for a while with some cotton and gauze. "You can get down now, Mrs. Weisbord. Say, you look a little pooped. Drink this." He handed me something in a glass.

Then he showed me into a little narrow darkened room containing a leather couch on which I had left my clothes. "Now, you just lay down here for a half hour. Just relax and keep quiet." I couldn't straighten out my knees, which remained bent in the position of the operating table. My body was cold as ice, but the pain was over.

After a week's rest at a comrade's house I went home for a time. I had written Mother I had had an attack of grippe and needed a rest. I had been seeing little of my folks, though we had exchanged occasional letters.

Alone in that quiet place where I could walk on the earth with sky above, trees and open spaces about me, healing could take place. Nature took me to her bosom, mother of all, undiscouraged in her vigor, conquering all deaths and disasters in the eternal sequence of birth and death. My sorrow too was part, just an infinitesimal part, of this universal travail and rebirth. I could feel myself part too of womankind, bearing our special sufferings, our own unique wrongs.

There are wounds that never heal; let us not fool ourselves, decades later a pin prick will set them bleeding under the scar. I had been hurt as much morally as physically. Something very strong and primitive in me had been violated; there was also a feeling of maiming indescribable except by that word. Behind it all was resentment at what seemed to be Albert's callousness. Why had he refused to go there with me? Is it possible to love and feel no concern for the loved one? My pain had been beyond anything he could conceive of, yet he had—or so it seemed—gone through it all unscathed, untouched.

It is true he was very busy during this time in the textile work which I would have been helping with had I not been ill. The call was sent out for a convention to organize the new textile union. Albert then had to go on a series of tours for the necessary personal contacts. With fewer illusions than in Passaic two years ago, yet still with all his old vigor and confidence, he not only made most of the technical arrangements, but he found time also for extensive research.

The convention to organize the National Textile Workers Union was big and enthusiastic. It was held in Manhattan Lyceum, New York City, on September 28, 1928. Several hundred delegates were present, with a good representation by trades, particularly of the unskilled from New England cotton centers, silk and dye workers from Paterson and vicinity, woolen workers from Passaic and Lawrence, Mass., some women and girls from the silk-throwing mills in the anthracite, full-fashioned hosiery workers from Philadelphia, a few carpet workers from Connecticut and some from the Bigelow Mills in upper New York State, and knit goods workers from New York City and Brooklyn. An executive board was elected with Jim Reid of Providence, Rhode Island, as president and Albert Weisbord as national secretary.

Albert's three-hour-long report recapitulated the work already done in Passaic, New Bedford, and elsewhere and presented the results of his research. The next strategic move of the union must be to the South, the great refuge of union-fleeing employers, stronghold as well of the cotton industry for several generations, and a festering sore of some of the country's worst conditions and lowest pay.

During the 1920's the industrial shift to the South meant that while in 1921 the cotton goods output of the Southern mills was 54 percent of the national total, with 44 percent of the dollar value, in 1927 the share of the South had increased to 67 percent of the yardage, with 56 percent of the dollar value. Gaston County, North Carolina, was the center of the cotton industry. Gastonia, the county seat, had more looms and particularly more spindles within a range of one hundred miles than any other Southern city. Although most of the mills in that locale were spinning mills that employed just a few hundred workers, there was one really large mill, the Loray, a branch of the Manville-Jenckes Company of Rhode Island, located right outside Gastonia with over two thousand people making coarse cotton cloth for automobile tires.

In 1927 and 1928 the Southern mill owners had been introducing the speed-up (called stretch-out in the South) already prevalent in New

England. The Gastonia Chamber of Commerce in a bulletin put out in 1928 stated that cotton mill wages in Gastonia ranged from eighteen cents to thirty cents an hour for skilled workers, that children from fourteen to eighteen could only work eleven hours, that females under sixteen were not allowed to work at night. They failed to state that children were working as much as sixty-six hours for less than five dollars weekly pay. Employers' advertisements luring other manufacturers to move or to invest in the South always stressed the "docility" of the labor force. We who had seen other "docile" textile workers fight for eight months were not fooled by such propaganda.

One thing must not be forgotten: the background of slavery, which has left its impress deeply on our society. Even the "docile" slave, with hatred in his heart enduring his hopeless lot, broke out at times in rebellion. Poor white people, restrained from competition with slave labor, were forced to scrape a living from small plots of the poorest land. Whether owners or tenants, the whole family, including the children, had to toil from dawn to dark to achieve bare survival in a country impoverished by the Civil War. Thousands escaping the draft during the war, and others later squeezed out of eastern North Carolina by the growth of large plantations, fled to the mountains to wrest a living from tiny steep patches of poor soil. Isolation and the absence of any law fostered illusions of freedom, together with an independent, individualistic way of thinking and acting. Here was the frontier influence that has also strongly affected our society.

Later, lured into the mills by the possibility of "cash money" in their hands each week, first the poor Piedmont farmers, and later the mountaineers were the chief source of the cotton textile labor force. Although the industrialization of the South had already begun bringing steel mills, paper mills, chemicals, and furniture mills to other sections, in this particular region there was still little but textiles, thus increasing the employers' control. The workers there were in a real bind. Generations of them were accustomed to long hours of work, to women and children working, to substandard living. Now on top of all this the employers were introducing Northern methods to get more labor from them.

Albert wanted me to help and felt I would be best used as an organizer in the union work (and in any case there was no money for office help). Nothing would be more helpful in preparing for this task than to actually work myself for a time in the trade in order to know the workers' problems. There was an industry in New York which overlapped with the textile, namely the knit goods. In the making of woolen sweaters and bathing suits the material was in most cases knitted on the premises in a separate department of the shop so that the industry could be classified as either textile or garment. Women workers (the majority in this trade) were most numerous among the low-paid Merrow operators. Since I had held two factory jobs operating a power machine on straw hats and on shirts, we thought I might possibly be able to work into this occupation.

Using the assumed name Anna Miller, I answered an ad. I was set down in front of a Merrow machine, one used generally only on knitted or very heavy materials, which in one operation sews a seam, binds it, and cuts off the surplus material. As it differs both in construction and operation from the ordinary Singer machine I was used to, a few minutes convinced the boss as well as me that I couldn't run that machine. He put me on the trimming table, snipping off threads. During the lunch hour I told some of the operators I wanted to learn the machine, and one of them helped me, showing me how to thread it. So after a week I found a new job, saying I was experienced. There followed a few weeks of grueling apprenticeship. My work would be sent back for errors, constantly at first, then less. The real difficulty was that the machine was incredibly fast. Soon there started in a certain spot on my left scapula the size of a dime, a most intense pain, unremitting all the nine-hour day.

Then, all of a sudden, one morning just as all the operators had sat down to work, there came marching down the aisle a group of women yelling, "Strike! Get up, girls. Join us!" How wonderful, a strike! was all I could think as I rushed to join them, and I was right up front, yelling with the rest. Most of the operators didn't get up, their eyes remained glued to their machines, and it wasn't long before the boss, bulgy-eyed and furious, came tearing out of the office.

Some of us including myself tried to speak, but he could yell louder than we. "What the hell do you think you're doin'? You think it's so easy to get a job? Girls are walkin' the streets right now. You got a fine job here. You got the best job in the city," he screamed. "Nobody gets pay like you get ... And you," he turned to me glaring, "what do *you* want ... workin' here a coupla days and you talk about strike. Get back to your machines, all of you, and don't let me hear another word out of you."

The leaders tried again to speak; he shoved us away and reluctantly we went back to our places. The women told me in the lunch hour that I shouldn't have spoken up, I was too new here; they seemed resentful; and sure enough, two days later I was fired.

A few months after the textile convention the newspapers carried reports of a wave of wage cuts in the South and of many spontaneous strikes breaking out in textile mills in both North and South Carolina, Tennessee, and Georgia. So at last the "docile" ones had reached the limit of their endurance. Albert concluded the time was ripe and that Gaston County, North Carolina, was the place for us to start. Accordingly, in January of 1929 Fred Beal, who had been a leader in the New Bedford strike of last summer was sent down to live in the territory in order to contact the mill workers and establish a local. Albert was to give him the ten dollars a week he himself was receiving from the union. Beal rented a room in Charlotte twenty miles from Gastonia and began the work.

On March 30 came a phone call from Charlotte that a union member in the Loray Mill had been fired; then on April 1 word came that a strike had been voted and eighteen hundred people had walked out of Loray Mill. So now our second big venture in the textile industry was under way.

8

On Strike in Loray

WEARY AND RUMPLED, HUDDLED IN THE COACH SEAT WHERE I HAD SPENT THE
night, I peered bleary-eyed at the Piedmont landscape speeding by in the
gray predawn. Soon the rising sun reached with long golden fingers across
the low green hills sparkling with orchards in bloom. This was the fifth of
April, 1929. My destination was Gastonia, North Carolina. Already I had
glimpsed an occasional mill village, the landscape was dotted with them.
Right here in the Piedmont was the biggest yarn center in the South.
"Matchboxes on stilts" came to my mind as I watched the mill cottages
pass, flimsy structures all, elevated on posts, some painted white, others
shabbily unpainted, dilapidated.

My heart was beating faster as I thought that here I would have to be
one of the principal organizers, a leader. In fact, Albert had said he was
sending me to "stiffen up" Beal, to "straighten him out." I would have to
be right up on the platform making speeches to rouse the workers, no
more shrinking in the background. Albert, our secretary, would be guid-
ing us from New York.

When a big roadside sign sped by, "Gaston County, Combed Yarn
Center of the South," I was all excitement. Here it is now with Ellen
Dawson, whom I hadn't seen since Passaic, running down the platform.
We got into a taxi. Ellen was a small, wiry, somewhat elfish young woman
in the middle twenties, with shining black cropped hair, twinkling little
brown eyes, and a Scotch accent. She had been a weaver in the Botany
Mill in Passaic, a member of the strike committee there and on the staff
also in the New Bedford strike. She was now a vice president of the
NTWU.

Already we had reached Loray Village, just outside Gastonia. There
loomed the mill, a huge long rectangular building, five stories high, of

173

dull red brick with tall narrow windows, fortresslike as most textile mills were. It sat on a slight eminence so that it dominated the scene. Behind it and around it were the many mill workers' cottages. The mill stood silent now, closed by the strike.

"The troopers came yesterday," said Ellen indicating the many young men in khaki walking about or lounging on the grass. Some, shouldering guns, were lined up on guard duty against the wall of the mill. The tents of the state militia were set up on the lawn off to one side. There were also a few men on horseback. The sight of the guns produced certain qualms in me that I quickly suppressed. "They'll be here, better get used to them," I told myself.

We went down a poorly paved street. Opposite the mill, on the other side of the street was a row of nondescript, low buildings. "That'll be our relief store," Ellen said as we passed a brick building somewhat better than the others.

Now at last our headquarters, a tiny unpainted shack set between two small cottages and in the doorway Fred Beal, grinning broadly, waiting to greet us. I met him for the first time: he was rather stout, of medium height, in his early thirties, with reddish-blond hair and very blue eyes with pale lashes standing out against his sunburn. The first impression was one of naiveté, honesty, and friendliness. I could see he would be a good contact man. His high pitched soft voice had a certain feminine quality.

Here again I had missed the beginning of the strike; the great outpouring of thousands of cheering, joyful people released temporarily from slavery. The event was, however, still young and that special exhilaration that accompanies the successful opening of a strike was still to be felt here in Loray. It was in Ellen Dawson's smile, in her voice, her gestures, it was in Beal too, it was in the freshness of the morning and the vitalizing power of the hot sun, in the suggestion of danger of the troopers. Soon it was in me too, making my step lighter, wiping out the fatigue of a night sitting up on the train, eliminating all remnants of self-doubt so that I could gladly assume my responsibilities.

After Fred had introduced me to a few strikers, we withdrew with Ellen into a tiny cubicle of an office.

"This place used to be a post office," said Beal as we sat down at a table at the back of which stood a row of pigeon holes for sorting letters, now occupied by filing cards. The table was littered with newspapers, letters, and cards.

Had Albert sent any money? was Fred's first question. He had not. I had used my last paycheck from the knit goods job for railroad fare, only a few dollars remaining. We lacked money, it seemed. We had two other mills on strike besides the Loray, a little mill in Pineville, some ten miles out of Charlotte, and in nearby Bessemer City the American Mill, which had come out spontaneously. George Pershing from the Young Communist League, who had come down at the end of March, was staying there to organize that strike.

"I phoned your husband this morning," said Beal. "He bawled me out. Albert was fit to be tied. You know, a few Negroes were there in Bessemer City when we called all the strikers to a meeting. This is the South. Workers don't like Negroes here. The whites insisted there had to be a rope put up to keep the races separate. Well, it was the workers who wanted it; they don't understand much about white chauvinism down here." This was one of the points on which I was supposed to "straighten out" Beal. I let the matter wait in order to get more information.

One very pressing need now was the organization of the relief. Workers as poor as these, always in debt at the mill commissary—and surely no credit would be extended to strikers—could not hold out many days without help. We were lucky to have been able to rent this poor place as headquarters, and a really nice big store for the relief.

Now Beal took from the desk a copy of the Gastonia *Daily Gazette*, on the front page of which in livid red and black was a cartoon depicting a devil with horns; this was our union invading this peaceful Southern community.

"You'll die laughing," Beal said. "We can't wait to see these cartoons every day. They had one of me yesterday. We're not popular around here. Some workers in the town sympathize with the strike, they know the conditions. And, of course, there are a lot of mills; their workers come around to our meetings, too. But actual helpers—you can count them on one hand.

"There's lawyer Tom Jimison in Charlotte, one of these Southern liberals—you know, a pretty good guy. Then there's a Party member in Charlotte, this Jewish man named Cohen. He's like a member at large, has a junk business, owns a house in Charlotte. He'll do anything we want him to do. Well, there's one more, a cotton mill worker in Charlotte named Grier. He used to take me to Pineville when I was visiting the workers nights. Then finally I met a millhand who had a brother working in Loray. All during March I came here every evening and concentrated on building the local here."

As for money, a few dollars collected in dues before the strike had enabled them to rent this shack and put a deposit on the relief store. We'd have to get more soon.

A pile of leaflets lay on the desk outlining the strike demands. This Albert had briefed me on in New York; the demands had been worked out via letter and telephone between himself and Beal after consultation with the workers.

A minimum weekly wage of $20
A forty-hour, five-day working week
Better sanitary conditions
No more hank-clocks
No more piecework
Repair of company houses
Addition of screens and tubs
Cheaper rents and lights
Recognition of the union

"You can realize how drastic these demands are if you compare them with the actual conditions: the wage cut meant that people who had been earning eighteen dollars a week were down to thirteen. As for the hours, they work sixty-six a week for the day shift, sixty for the night. The workers went with these demands to Superintendent J. A. Baugh. He said we wanted the whole plant. Well, of course we didn't expect them to be accepted. And then all the local mill owners met in Gastonia and raised a fund of two hundred and fifty thousand dollars to fight the strike. That was their answer. So I put out a leaflet giving our demands. I have the use of a mimeograph down in Charlotte and we distributed it in Gastonia, along with other leaflets on children working eleven hours for less than five dollars a week, and women working twelve hours all night."

Now the shuffling of feet outside reminded Beal it was time for the strike committee meeting. We went out to find the stuffy room filled with lean, gaunt men and youths in overalls and women and girls in faded cotton dresses. They sat down on some old chairs and on a few rough benches while other strikers stood about. The hall was not large, perhaps fifteen by thirty-five feet. There was another door at the right near the back. It was all of weathered gray boards, with a strip of fresh lumber here and there indicating a repair.

The meeting was called to order by the strike committee chairman, Roy Stroud. Beal gave his report, then presented me. I brought the greetings of the national organization and told them that in a day or two there would be a representative of the Workers International Relief, the organization that had raised nearly a million dollars for the Passaic strike, here in Gastonia to set up a relief station for them. A whoop of joy greeted this announcement.

Next there was talk of the troopers: an incident of two days before was reviewed for my benefit. A big mass of workers was picketing the mill when the troopers came and forced them to retreat. One of the pickets, a little woman named Bertha Tompkins, was called on to speak.

"They was pushin' at me," she said. "I done tole them, I kin walk, you don't need to push me. That law pushed me again and I had a stick in my hand and I hit him on the head. Then y'all knows what they did, four of 'em took hold of me and dragged me into that wagon and they done put me in a cell in the jail. They let me out later. I've got four little children an' I work three nights a week for four dollars. I'm on strike and I'm goin' to go right on strikin'. They cain't stop me." Mrs. Tompkins' thin face was flushed, her eyes shining, her hair somewhat awry. Enthusiasm and responsive shouts greeted her story. There were more reports and at last the meeting closed in a spirit of optimism.

After a hasty but welcome meal at a little restaurant nearby, Beal, Dawson, and I went on a tour of Loray Village. The mill owned all the land down to the street that ran past it. In back of the mill was something of a hill. Here and beyond the farther end of the big building were straggling, unpaved streets lined with cottages rented by the mill to its workers, little one-story shacks elevated on brick piles or wooden posts some three feet high. All were of the most minimal construction. The houses contained generally three or four rooms; a few may have had five. The rent was twenty-five cents per room, so Beal said. Many of the cottages held two families or even more; this was generally the case where there were many small children to support.

In front of the mill on the sloping lawn were on one side an office building, on the other a commissary, with a walk between them leading up to the mill's front door. Close to the mill was a large frame building known as the dormitory, which was a rooming house for single mill workers. On the other side of Franklin Street was what was known as "free land." A few streets there were lined with other cottages also inhabited by mill workers. All this constituted Loray, poor, shabby, squalid, a typical mill village. This was to be my home, as well as the setting for the unfolding drama of the Loray strike.

A quiet interval followed in which I could rest and at the same time try to get a clearer picture of the situation. Back in the little office, Beal described his first days in Loray.

"I used to come here in the evenings. It was dark then and I could get by more easily. I made a point of staying a whole evening with each family so as to get to know them. Did they really want a union? In Charlotte I felt sure they did, especially after I organized that mill in Pineville. But this big mill, the Loray? I found out they did want a union, and badly. They were disappointed once in 1919 when the UTW sent a couple of organizers in here. They organized a local, even had a strike, but as soon as the going got rough those guys took the money and skipped. That's what I've got to live down. But the workers have shown their confidence in me."

"How many members did you have when the strike started?"

"Well, you see, we tried to keep it small, just a little secret local, so's not to provoke the employers. It was a regular local with a secretary-treasurer—that was Will Truet. Will is quiet, but he gets things done. He found this shack, did the repairs, and helped make the benches too. But then they fired Truet. We called another meeting in a cottage. Some meeting that was, more like a revival. They were signing up so fast we couldn't keep up with them. 'If they fire us, we'll strike the whole plant'; that's what they were saying.

"So then we held an open meeting right out in back of the mill. That was Saturday, March thirtieth. Albert sent down Ellen Dawson after I called the national office and hollered for help. So she spoke too. They had some preachers there tried to tell the workers I was a Communist, not to listen to me. The women began talking about their bad conditions, their night work and stretch-out. The preachers soon shut up.

"Monday, April first, we had a meeting out in back here by the tracks and took a strike vote. I declared a strike in the Manville-Jenckes Company. Then they fired a whole bunch, and the strike was on. We went into Gastonia and paraded down Main Street with signs, singing *Solidarity*. Well, it's near three o'clock," he broke off, looking at his watch. "Time for the meeting. The speaking is what they call it here."

Between the row of buildings and the railroad tracks was a big open lot, a sort of grassy meadow sloping down to meet the embankment of the Southern Pacific tracks, a natural amphitheater which we found now crowded with strikers—men, women, and children. A rough platform had been erected behind the shack.

The sun shone already hot, the lean upturned faces were browned. A striker was chairman, I was the first speaker. I spoke of the great need for a union as the only way to better the wretched conditions, worse even than in the textile mills of the North. I stressed the miserable living conditions, the "matchboxes on stilts" in which they had to live, the inhuman long hours that drained their strength, the complete lack of human dignity in their lives, the presence of the state troopers as proof that the state was supporting the mill owners; this was the first maneuver in retaliation for the strike—we wouldn't let them scare us.

At one point a sort of strange whoop came up from the audience, a momentary loud cry: something quite new to me and rather disconcerting. But at the end Beal told me that was their rebel yell, a real Southern thing; it was their way of applause and showed they liked me. Beal, in his turn, drew laughter by holding up the *Gazette* with its cartoon. He had an easy familiar way of speaking, and his popularity among the workers was very apparent. A preacher-man also spoke, a mill worker on strike like the others, distinguished from them by a black suit complete with vest and hat. Ellen Dawson spoke briefly. Join the union, build the union, keep the strike strong, was an ever-recurring theme which each of us put in his or her own way. Before the meeting was over George Pershing (a nephew of General Pershing of World War I fame) arrived from Bessemer City. Young, tall, and handsome as he was, I noticed the admiring glances of women and girls while he was on the platform.

For all of us staff members except Beal the South was a completely new experience. We often had to ask people to repeat what they said, and from their point of view, our speech (mine: New Yorkese with a touch of Connecticut; Beal's: broad Massachusetts; Ellen Dawson's: crisply Scotch) was equally strange. Coming from beyond the North Carolina limits we were all foreigners.

The meeting over, I mingled for a while with the crowd of strikers, close to them, smelling their sweat and my own there in the full sunlight. We shook hands, I listened to their stories of the mill and of their life in Loray Village. What stories I heard that day, poured out as though they'd been long held in restraint, waiting for a sympathetic ear! For a moment each man or woman became individualized, detached from the crowd, though there was a uniformity in their poor clothes, in their common look of toil and age, even though some were not old at all. I noted also what poor teeth they had; a dentist was probably unknown here.

"They got a thing now they call a hank-clock. I say it's an invention of the devil. It measures the yarn you're spinnin'. They tells you how much you got to spin, but you cain't make it. Nobody kin make it."

"We used to git five, ten minutes off from work now and then. That way you could bear the mill. Now they keeps you a-runnin' every bit of them eleven hours. Hit just ain't possible for a human bein' to do what they're askin'."

"I wuz a weaver an' we had a lot of other women in the weave room. We run six to eight sides then. Now they's askin' you to run ten, twelve looms. All the women are havin' to quit weavin'. They can't bear it."

"My husband's home sick with the pelagry. He cain't work no more. I makes only twelve dollars a week spinnin' since the cut. I made sixteen before. We's got four children, all too small to work. Six people cain't live no way on twelve dollars."

"Manville-Jenckes won't hire a man who has a wife without the both of 'em workin'. If the woman's about to have a baby and cain't keep up with the work, or if she has a very young baby, they fires the husband too."

"Ma'm, you might think workin' twelve hours at night, we'd have time off to eat a bite. No'm, we don't have no time off. What we do is spell each other, we let one woman sit down on the floor and eat a bit o' biscuit or whatever that we bring wrapped in a li'l ol' scrap o' paper and the next one watches that woman's sides besides her own. When we say we works twelve hours a night, we means we works twelve hours."

After a while my mind became confused, faces and stories blurred together in fatigue and dizziness. I was glad when at last I could go inside and sit down. The men and youths remained to linger a while inside the shack, the women probably going home to cook beans or do other housework.

The workers here had a diversion: snuff chewing, dipping, and spitting. It seemed to be nearly universal and was pursued now as they lolled about and told jokes. A man would hold his lower lip open with the fingers of one hand, with the other stuffing into his mouth a big wad of snuff taken from a bag generally kept in his pocket. This wad would be shifted from one cheek to the other as it was chewed. Dippin' consisted of dipping a stick into the bag of snuff and then chewing on the stick. Women also indulged in this habit. The spitting was something less informal: they actually had spitting contests to see who could project the emission of brown juice the farthest. Six feet, I believe, was about average. The bare wall of the shack was already plastered with many proofs of mastery of the Southern art of snuff-spittin'.

Later some of the women came back, and there was to be ballad singing. Beal said they sometimes held another speaking if enough people came around. As for me, I had had about enough this long eventful day. I was tired out and left to go with Ellen Dawson to Gastonia, where I was to share her hotel room.

The next day the morning train brought a welcome addition to our staff in the person of Amy Schechter, representing the WIR, with money to set up and maintain a relief station. She opened a bank account and paid the rent due on the store. A fine big sign was already posted outside above the door.

The new relief headquarters was a large roomy place, equipped with counters and shelves and a tiny office partitioned in one corner in back. Some benches and a few chairs had been brought over from the other place. Now we held our first relief meeting with a group of strikers, chiefly women.

Schechter sat on a chair facing the row of women in their worn cotton dresses, holding a little pad and trying to get a list of the food items needed. Cabbage, oatmeal, and cornmeal were rejected. When they mentioned meat, I put in, "But then we'd have to have a refrigerator," but they all said, no, they didn't need one. In this climate? No, they never needed a refrigerator for their meat. It was only later that I realized the only meat these people had was salt pork—no chops, steaks, roasts, or soup meat, just fat sowbelly. Finally the list was complete: flour, rice, red beans, "meat," and canned milk for babies. Then Amy went into Gastonia to shop with Bertha Crawford, who had been assigned to help her, and Red Hendricks, a striker who had a car.

Meanwhile, in the office of the old shack we prepared temporary relief cards with the union stamp and the name of the head of the family, so that before evening, when the food was unpacked and on the shelves, we could make a first issue to the most needy people, to the great relief and encouragement of them all.

We three women, Amy Schechter, Ellen Dawson, and I, were sharing one hotel room in Gastonia, paid for by Dawson—not too comfortable sleeping three in a bed. Whether our illegal comings and going were noticed we didn't know: we would slip in and go up by the stairway. Ellen had carried up my little suitcase the first night; Amy hadn't brought anything but her purse; she said she could buy clean underwear as she needed it. The room had a bath, which enabled us to wash our hair and our clothes as well as ourselves.

Now a word about Amy Schechter. On first impression she appeared odd. Although her thin aquiline face showed strength, she was somewhat sloppy, her clothes askew; her reddish-brown hair wound up in a knot in back looked uncombed. Her speech had a slight English accent, she talked fast and incoherently; she had some nervous twitchings of the face and shoulder. From her uncertainty it didn't look as though she had experience in this kind of work. Perhaps she had been sent because the Fosterites had insisted on having one of theirs in the situation.

Eventually, when I got to know Schechter well, I valued her highly. That she had guts and really wanted to be in Gastonia were points in her favor. Her little personal peculiarities didn't matter, though for the strikers the first impression wasn't too good. As they couldn't pronounce her name, they referred to her as "that woman." But Amy worked hard, and her inborn kindliness and her dedication won their confidence.

Meanwhile, that day I used some of my spare time to look over the newspapers in the office. From the Charlotte *Observer* I got full details of the troops sent in. There were five small companies of different categories, totaling two hundred men. Adjutant General J. Van Metts of the North Carolina National Guard had come to Gastonia to supervise the installment of the troops with Captain Dolley of Gastonia in charge locally. Beal had told me that Captain Dolley had gone into the mill several times and personally dragged out people he thought were in sympathy with the union. The troops included a howitzer company from Gastonia, an infantry company from Shelby, foot troops and cavalry from Lincolnton, and two companies, one of engineers and one of infantry, from Charlotte.

General Van Metts was quoted as saying he "was advised the strikers were in a mean humor this afternoon, they were throwing rocks and creating other disturbances, they had completely overrun the city and county officers, Northern inciters are among the workers."* Governor Gardner had said he called out the troops following an urgent report from the county sheriff and the mayor of Gastonia.

The Gastonia *Gazette* of the day before stated that "before the troops arrived yesterday, the mob was rampant at or near the Loray Mill in all of its seething hideousness, ready to kill, ready to destroy property. The troops arrived—and all became quiet and the mob dispersed." The pictures in the paper showed the crowd of paraders in Gastonia and a huge group in front of the Loray, with signs, "To Hell with the Hank-Clock!" "The International Will Feed You," "No Union Man Will Starve," and "Solidarity Forever."

Ellen Dawson had told me the troops were called in following a picketing incident the second day. There was really a fine turnout of strikers, but a fight broke out with the police when they stretched a rope in front of the entrance to prevent the workers from reaching the mill. The rope was cut; they put up a cable. A tug of war followed, which the strikers won. That was really the excuse for bringing in the militia.

According to the Charlotte *Observer*, on the second day of the strike no less than eleven circulars were distributed in the town and among the strikers by the employers, agitating against the union.

> Our Religion, Our Morale, Our Common Decency, Our Government and the very foundations of Modern Civilization, all that we are now and all that we plan for our children IS IN DANGER. Communism will destroy the efforts of Christians of 2,000 years. Do we want it? Will we have it? NO! It must GO from the Southland.

On April 3, 4, and 5 the *Gazette* ran full-page ads allegedly "paid for by citizens." One was headed: RED RUSSIANISM LIFTS ITS GORY HANDS RIGHT HERE IN GASTONIA.

---

*Charlotte *Observer*, April 4, 1929.

Another account in the paper disturbed me. It seems George Pershing had come down there not for the union, but for the YCL. And there he was right on the front page in the Charlotte *Observer* of April 3 proclaiming through the intermediary of a reporter his intention of building groups of the YCL here in Gastonia and later in the entire South, their aim the abolishment of capitalism. COMMUNIST LEADER BARES PLOT—OUST CAPITAL IN SOUTHLAND, BOLSHEVIKS CRY. So screamed the headline—a foolish, rash beginning, not in the least helpful to our strike. We were there to build a union and to help the textile workers win their strike. We were fighting only one small section of the capitalist class, namely the employers owning the mills we had on strike.

True, the strike involved confrontation of the workers not merely with their employers, whom in fact they never saw, but with the state apparatus; police, sheriffs, judges, as well as forces beyond the law hired by the employers, such as sheriff's deputies and thugs. The workers would gain experience in the class struggle, they would learn to organize as a group employed in the same mill or in nearby mills, they would come to understand what was their class position in society, to maneuver and to fight within the limits of this given situation. All this was a far cry from an attempt to oust capitalism. Such a reckless speech would only provide the employers with a wedge that they would surely drive deeper. Beal told me he had had to persuade Pershing to work for the union at least in the beginning, since organizers were so few.

A full-page ad on April 4 in the Gastonia *Gazette* by so-called "Citizens of Gaston County" denounced the strike leaders as Communists, concluding as follows:

> Let every man and woman in Gaston County ask the question: Am I willing to allow the mob to control Gaston County? The mob whose leaders do not believe in God and who would destroy the government?
>
> The strike at the Loray is something more than merely a few men striking for better wages. It was not inaugurated for that purpose. It was started simply for the purpose of overthrowing this Government, to destroy property and to KILL, KILL, KILL. The time is at hand for every American to do his duty.

While I was inclined to smile at some of these lurid rantings, still I knew they indicated no favorable setting for our activities; a real wall of hate and an atmosphere of hysteria was being built up around us.

During these first few days I got to know the most active strikers who were already playing leading roles. Among the young men Kelly Hendricks, commonly known as "Red," stood out. Tall and very thin, with a shock of red hair, he remained pale in spite of sun exposure. He was a person who laughed readily and could get angry just as easily, but with his keen sense of humor a flare-up was quickly overcome. He had gone to work at the age of eleven as a gear-wiper. His courage was to be proven many times in this strike. "Red" often gave a talk at the "speakin'."

Lewis McLaughlin was in complete contrast. A short, stocky young man, he had a thick head of straight black hair. His family came originally from Georgia, where he had gone to work at age ten. He never earned more than $17. There was something intense and serious about Lewis, something brooding, even somber, in his face. He spoke little but was on hand for duty at all times.

Then there was Bill McGinnis, a lusty fellow, lively and talkative, part Indian, with coarse black hair, broad cheekbones, and swarthy skin. Bill had a fiery temper and if you really provoked him you were in for a fight. Russell Knight, tall and good-looking and more equable in temperament, was another good striker. All these young men, in their early or middle twenties, had gone to work as children. Bill McGinnis had practically no schooling; he could neither read nor write. Will Truet, somewhat older, a steady, determined, quiet man, as secretary of the local was responsible for signing up and registering union members and keeping records, all of which he did efficiently. Robert Allen was the only one who gave evidence of being very religious. He quoted the Bible so often we used to say he knew it backwards. In general, while there seemed to be little churchgoing among the people, there was much quiet religious feeling, which showed itself in hymn singing after the meetings or in the evenings when some of them would gather in the headquarters.

There was also an older man, Roy Stroud, who had come to Loray from South Carolina. I had noted the fact that mill workers moved around frequently, drawn I suppose by the illusion of greener pastures elsewhere. The Loray Mill, as a matter of fact, was known for hiring these drifters, as they could be gotten for lower pay. Stroud appeared to be in the middle forties, a short man with thin graying hair and fine lines in his face, a stable, mature man of good judgment. Once—much later—I asked Roy Stroud, "What did you think of us at first, at the beginning of the strike? How did we look to you?" After reflecting, Mr. Stroud answered chuckling, "To tell you the truth, Miss, we didn't know what to think." This dubiousness I had seen at the start in their faces, but it appeared that after a time we had won their confidence. Our poverty, though inconvenient for ourselves was in one way to our advantage: they didn't have to fear we'd run off with the funds, since there were none. In the long run sincerity, complete involvement, and tenacity won them over.

Among the women, there were Gladys Wallace and Mrs. McGinnis.

Gladys was a short woman in her middle twenties, fat, and sallow, she was generally sure of herself, blunt and direct, and never hesitated to speak up at meetings, where most of the women were shy. She had worked as a spinner in many Southern mills. Old Mrs. McGinnis, who except for her graying hair looked much like her son William, was another good striker. A skinny, bent little person, she was still full of vitality.

The woman who impressed me most was Ella Mae Wiggins from Bessemer City, a striker of the American Mill there, a spinner by trade who came sometimes to the mass meetings at Loray. She would write little ballads about the strike, set them to some well-known ballad tune, and sing them from the platform in a rich alto voice. Her rather gaunt face would light up and soften as she sang; her hazel eyes would shine; she became for the moment beautiful. She would often speak too, urging the strikers to remain firm. She appeared to be a person of unusual intelligence who grasped every feature of the strike and could explain it in her own words.

A group of young women in their late teens, already workers for several years, were in the front ranks at all the meetings. And then the children; many boys and girls in the lower teens were strikers. Typical was Binney Barnes, who said she was fourteen and had been working for two years, earning $4.95 a week for sixty hours work. Fourteen was the legal minimum age for employment: Binney looked no more than ten. The children were pathetic. What was their childhood like and what was youth here, deprived even of food to build a healthy body, with no opportunity for education, no energy for sports or play? What future could there be for them?

Having heard or read something of welfare work among the Loray workers and of a rest camp and sports activities sponsored by the mill owners, I questioned the strikers. With a funny look they would answer, "No'm, I ain't never been to that camp," as though it were ridiculous to ask since they had no vacation (paid vacations in those days being as yet undreamed of). And the welfare workers the mill supposedly maintained? "Why, they wuz people who snooped around if you didn't come to work, to see that they wasn't no absenteeism." I concluded the "welfare work" was altogether something of a bluff.

One day I was taken to a cottage to see a man sick with pellagra. The disease is due completely to malnutrition and vitamin shortage and, if left untreated, advances slowly, becomes chronic, and may ultimately be a cause of death. The victim was beyond working; he had peculiar-looking skin on his face—reddish-brown, thin, shiny skin as though stretched out; his mouth was full of sores. He said he felt weak and worried all the time because he couldn't work.

It became clear there was much illness among the strikers that was taken as a matter of course, unreported, and untreated. TB must have been common (Red Hendricks had it). Later on we had a case of small-pox. There was no quarantine, and nobody appeared perturbed any more than if it were a common cold. We provided services of a doctor when necessary. When one of the young women strikers became ill, we asked what ailed her. The doctor's answer was, "Too much free ridin'." VD was probably a menace also.

Soon after we started giving relief a rumor went around that Manville-Jenckes was going to reopen the Loray Mill. We put out great efforts in the meetings to hold the strikers firm, and above all to get them to picket the next day. Sure enough, at five the next morning the guts-deep but shrill and penetrating moan of the mill whistle sounded, which would now waken us every morning thereafter.

There was a picket line, a good one, of women, children, and some men. It hadn't gone far along the sidewalk parallel to Loray Mill when a group of troopers, bayonets in hand, as well as a few policemen were upon the people—chasing, probing, pushing women, children, and men, who ran in all directions. There were some bruises and some blackened eyes. One woman was poked with a bayonet on the arm enough to draw blood, but she didn't want to make a fuss about it; she insisted she was all right. There were some arrests, though the strikers were let out later. It appeared few people had gone into the mill, though the machinery thumped and crashed all day and night thereafter, a sort of orchestral accompaniment to our strike. And the whole building was lit up at night.

The breaking up of the line aroused excitement and resentment; the men wanted to fight, but with guns. The troopers were here now with weapons—let them carry *their* guns and they'd go out and picket! Beal reiterated patiently that they couldn't carry guns. It wasn't a war. We couldn't be violent in our strike. As this was something new to me, I thought we'd have to thrash it out privately among the organizers. I confined myself to some general remarks on the necessity of picketing as the chief recourse of a militant strike to keep the scabs out of the mill and show the boss we meant business.

Ellen Dawson told of the picket lines in Passaic and New Bedford that were carried on determinedly by thousands of unarmed workers despite beatings and police terror. There was no response except, "Just let us have our guns." These people were reserved, tight-lipped. As I looked at those blank faces, those dubious unresponsive eyes, I felt we weren't getting through to them on this matter. The strike committee meeting concluded without deciding the question.

It was a real obstacle. Although the setting up of the relief office had greatly increased the strikers' confidence, still on this question of weapons we made no dent in their resolve. To strengthen our position, Tom Jimison was called in. He was a Southern liberal whose sympathies were strongly with the strikers. Perhaps he saw them as "my people," reminiscent of the paternalistic attitude that the propertied classes display in the midst of all the cruelty toward the poor, whether white or black. Or it may have been that he came from a poor background originally; we didn't know. At any rate, Jimison's approach was familiar and genuinely friendly. It was certainly to his credit that he volunteered his services to the strikers led by Communists in this mill-dominated area. I believe he really appreciated what we were trying to do. He was a slim, well-dressed man in the late thirties. It was said he had been a minister before becoming a lawyer; he couldn't bear the control the mill owners exercised over the clergy.

Jimison said the same things we had said, but in the strikers' own language. Still the men remained obdurate. Privately Amy, Ellen, and I agreed that if Beal himself would say "Men, come out on the line with me," they'd go, but Beal stubbornly refused. He was the strike leader; it was not his job to picket.

In this picketing question Fred was showing one of his tendencies: he could be compared to a pillow. You can take a pillow and punch it real hard again and again. Will it change or be altered in any way? Not in the least: it remains exactly the same pillow. So when we privately pounded Fred with arguments, he would listen blandly, smiling, perhaps looking a little sheepish, but in the end he would only repeat his original position. Was it out of laziness, out of pride, or did he fear to fall into the hands of the police? Was it possible some jealousy of me was underlying this attitude? He had shown plenty of courage in coming down here, alone and unprotected, to begin the agitation and organization work. This we did not forget. Picketing remained a difficult matter throughout the strike.

One thing I had noticed as soon as I arrived was that the numbers of the strikers were nowhere near what they had been at the start. Beal had reported a thousand people in attendance at the protest meeting called when the union members had been fired. On April 1, when the mill was struck, eighteen hundred people had walked out. Where were they all now?

It was clear there were no eighteen hundred strikers, there were not one thousand, there were a few hundred at best. Beal had said people from other mills attended our mass meetings. A few from other states came too, sometimes in old beat-up cars. Beal had told me how on the first day of the strike there were at least two hundred people out to picket, but by afternoon the number had dwindled to only about thirty.

He had resorted to singing and with that drew many of them back to the line. Still, it seemed that in their situation, with their history of unsuccessful attempts to organize, and with the whole background of oppression one could hardly expect all of them to hold out for long.

Another mystery was the constitution of the strike committee, this important body that met every morning at nine o'clock. We would look over the faces, familiar now; sometimes one or two would be missing. Had they gone in to scab? For us, the organizers, there was worry in this apparently shifting nature of our committee; we seemed to be treading on ground that gave way under our feet. Days would pass; then after a week or longer, when we had given them up as lost, the departed members would reappear cheerful and unconcerned.

"Where were you? Did you go into the mill?"

"No'm, I wasn't scabbin'. I just went back to the hills to see my folks for a spell. Git me some home cookin'." Or, "Oh, I done went in to work for a week, just to git me a bit of foldin' money."

Never for one moment did it occur to them to notify the staff of their departures. Hill people turned mill workers, they were complete individualists. The union was all right if it could win their strike, but of union discipline they had no conception. At least we could be sure now that the noise of machinery and the lights were largely bluff. Some departments were completely empty, the machinery ran for nothing. There could be little production with the scanty work force they had.

In these early days spirits still ran high. The great euphoria of the successful walkout still sustained people, hopes were strong of winning the strike, and for those of us in charge there was great stimulation from this situation, where difficulties became challenges. As for the missing hundreds, it was becoming clear that they had simply drifted on either to stay with relatives in the hills or to work in a mill elsewhere. Few were scabbing.

Most pressing at this time was the lack of money. Each staff member was supposed to receive $15 a week for his or her personal sustenance. The week after my arrival this weekly stipend was not forthcoming. Beal always appeared skeptical in spite of Albert's explanation. I was beginning to see what Albert called Fred Beal's "rank and filism." He had the anarcho-syndicalist's distrust of all leaders, whom he saw only as lolling around some office, fattening themselves at the workers' expense. In speaking to me he would refer to Albert as "your husband," which irritated me. When I received a letter from Albert, Beal would immediately ask, "Did he send you any money?" I was as poor as anyone: I remember Pershing and I sharing a meal of biscuits and gravy with a striker's family —and this happened more than once.

When Ellen's week at the hotel was up, the problem of shelter for the three of us was solved by Amy and Ellen sharing a room in the big mill boardinghouse near the mill, while I rented a room with Roy Stroud and his family. Their company cottage was actually one of the better ones: three fairly large rooms, floors of planking, walls roughly plastered, electricity and running cold water, a toilet but no bath. The family of four slept in two large beds in one of the rooms. There were little fireplaces in the two bedrooms. I had a bed in a second room that was furnished as a sitting room; they generally rented this room to a millhand. Since the Strouds were better off than most, they could afford a beat-up old car. I shared breakfast with the family: the usual biscuits with Georgia cane syrup and coffee. I was there really only to sleep, since the strike took up practically all of my time.

Besides the strike committee and mass meetings, which were held daily, there were informal staff meetings from time to time; I also went down to Bessemer City occasionally. By this time an organizer had been sent to stay in Pineville: Bill Siroka, a YCL member formerly an active striker in Passaic.

I visited Pineville once. Beal's contact in Charlotte, a textile worker named Grier, took me down to Charlotte the night before. I had supper with the family in a little house they rented on a back street. From there in the early morning after a hearty breakfast of biscuits, grits, "meat" (fat sowbelly), and coffee, Grier and I drove ten miles out to Pineville.

The mill there was a spinning mill, No. 5 of the Chadwick-Hoskins chain. It was located out in the countryside near the South Carolina border. They used to talk in the South about the "mill-hill," which was equivalent to the "patch" in the coal camps of Pennsylvania. Here there was actually a hill, low and round with the cottages located in a circle at the top. We looked into some of them: ill-kept, dirty. Mill workers who work an eleven-hour day have no habit of housekeeping.

Because the mill was closed there was no picketing, but meetings were held daily and the workers received food relief, which Beal brought down from Loray. He tried to keep up their spirits by giving them news of our other strikes.

One aspect of this Pineville situation intrigued me. It seems that in some past period the employers had experimented with Negro help, had laid off the white workers, putting blacks in their places. Later on they had fired the Negroes and again all the help were white. Among the grievances of the strikers besides wage cuts and stretch-out was their being compelled to live in "nigger" cabins. This was all I could learn about it.

It was only a few days after my arrival—though those days felt more like weeks—that our national secretary, Albert Weisbord, my husband, came down to Gastonia.

Excitement and increased activity resulted: strike meetings were bet-

ter attended, reporters were about. Of course he visited and spoke at
Bessemer City and Pineville also. The speech he made to the mass meeting at Loray attracted attention throughout the South and was written up
in a number of leading papers in Charlotte, Raleigh, and Greensboro,
N.C., in Greenville, S.C., and in other cities. I quote parts of it here:

> This strike is the first shot in the battle that will be heard round the
> world. It will prove as important in transforming the social and political
> life of this country as the Civil War itself. Whereas the Civil War was
> between the slave-holding men of the South, who used the people as
> cannon fodder, and the manufacturing men of the North, who used the
> mill workers of the North as cannon fodder, the present fight is against
> those who exploit you in this new plantation system of the South.
>
> These same yellow aristocrats have ground you down for centuries.
> They went out to the farms and mountains to offer you high wages and
> good living conditions, but you've got a Chinese, a Japanese, an Asiatic
> standard of living. In 1880 the government of the country announced a
> ten-hour day in navy yards and for public work. Here you are so far behind
> them that you're working twelve hours a day.
>
> In 1888 we see in the North a big movement for an eight-hour day.
> The manufacturers began a systematic drive for European laborers. The
> workers there, driven under the lash of bloody aristocrats like you are
> here, came over.
>
> These fellows came over on the word of the same swindlers who prom-
> ised you money to come off the farms. Then they were driven into their
> hell-holes and into lower conditions. There they formed unions and be-
> came militant. That is why we have come to Gastonia to help you in your
> struggle for existence. . . .
>
> Our strike depends upon how we spread this movement to Green-
> ville, to Charlotte, and to all the mills. Go say "Come on brothers, white
> and black!" Our union knows no political or religious distinction. We
> have no color line, although the bosses wish you did. . . .
>
> Make this a flame that will sweep from Charlotte to Atlanta and
> beyond so that we can have at least 200,000 cotton mill workers on strike.
> You cannot go ahead by yourself. Stick together. Don't listen to the
> poison of the bosses. Extend the strike over the whole countryside. We
> need mass action.*

So much enthusiasm was generated that day by Weisbord's speech
and others that the mass meeting spontaneously organized itself into a

---

*Charlotte *Observer*, Apr. 8, 1929.

demonstration of perhaps three hundred and fifty people, who went marching around Loray Mill and the village, singing and cheering for nearly an hour.

The Charlotte *Observer*, under dateline Gastonia April 8, also came out with the following:

Infused with a new burst of extremist spirit with the arrival here of one of the nation's most famous radicals to command the Loray Mill union organization, strikers today opened the floodgates of defamatory propaganda against Governor Gardner, the late James B. Duke, the Cannons, the federal government and cotton manufacturers generally in redoubling their efforts to spread their disturbance throughout the South. . . .

On April 10 we read in the Gastonia *Gazette* some inflammatory statements, such as this one in an "impartial news column":

As long as the strike leaders Pershing and Beal and the two women, Dawson and Buch, are here to keep the spirit of the strikers flaming, the unsettled conditions will prevail; *if the source of the trouble could be removed* the whole thing would blow over in a few days. . . .

We also distributed a leaflet to the state troopers in an attempt to win them over to our cause. At the same time, the girls were urged to become friendly with the troopers; in fact all the strikers as far as possible were to make contact with the young men in khaki, most of whom came from families like their own. Following is the leaflet we gave out:

Workers in the National Guard: We, the striking workers, are your brothers. Our fight is your fight. Help us win the strike. You belong to the working class and must fight for the workers against the bosses.

The enlisted men in the guard are workers, the officers are the bosses or paid tools of the bosses. These tools of the bosses try to use the North Carolina National Guard as the textile bosses tried to use the National Guard of Massachusetts.

Max Gardner, the mill-owning slave-driving capitalist governor of North Carolina, has called out the National Guard in order to get them to break the strike, keep the stretch-out system and prevent the workers from getting an increase in wages.

The mill owners and the governor want you to smash the strike, shoot down innocent men and women so that the Manville-Jenckes company can continue to wring profits from the sweat of enslaved workers who labor from dawn to dark on machines that will smash a finger or an arm at a single clip, so that Manville-Jenckes' Max Gardner and other textile barons can drive children of ten and twelve years for the miserable wage of 10 cents an hour, sixty hours a week.

Inhuman conditions kill workers. The present conditions in the mills drive men, women, and children to an early grave. The strikers' demand and are fighting for better conditions, higher wages, shorter hours and against the enslaving of children.

This leaflet was widely circulated and the girls carried out their assignment of "fraternization."

Albert had announced that he wanted to take some strikers north with him to speak at a great relief and defense meeting in Madison Square Garden, New York City. Those selected were Dewey Martin, an active striker and a section foreman in the mill; Violet Jones, pretty and blonde, one of our most active young women; and Binney Barnes, the little girl striker.

While Weisbord was still there we held a Party fraction meeting. It was something that required a certain circumspection. It could obviously not be held in the mill village, where we had no private place, nor in hostile Gastonia. So we met at the home of Mr. Cohen, the Party member in Charlotte, driving down there in the early evening. Besides being refreshing in themselves, these trips around the countryside between Gastonia and Charlotte were helpful in understanding the background of the mill people. It was a section of small farms only, the big plantations being located further east. As it was April, some fields were being plowed, exposing the brick-red earth. There were many abandoned farms too, grown up in weeds, their houses almost in ruins, telling the story of poor farmers, renters, or sharecroppers, driven off the land into the mills.

Our meeting concerned itself first with the strike. Extension of the strike was the strategy Albert projected. As a matter of fact, another strike was occurring right then in the Florence Mill in nearby Forest City, where workers had requested our help. Their strike, as it turned out, was short-lived, but they did win abolition of the speed-up and transfer of the man who had instituted it.

Because of the wave of wage-cuts the whole textile South was seething with unrest. Small spontaneous strikes were being touched off in many places. The whole region was a tinderbox and a most fertile field for organizing. We agreed the policy made sense, but with our limited staff how could we possibly carry it out? Albert's answer was, "If you have another mill on strike, that will give me a talking point to get more money."

He reported also briefly on the Party situation. James P. Cannon had been expelled as a Trotskyite. Lovestone and Gitlow were probably on the way out as Bukharinites. With the turmoil prevailing in Party circles in New York that summer of 1929, it was difficult to get support from that source for mass work among suffering textile workers.

Privately Albert told me his own political situation was most precarious because of his opposition to the leadership; he might at any time be removed from his post. He said to me tenderly, "Don't think for one moment I don't worry about you, Vera, here in this difficult situation. I'm concerned about the others too. I admire your courage. You know I'll do my utmost to get help, but as far as money is concerned, my hands are tied."

As for our picketing problem, we had Albert's assurance we could not possibly allow the strikers to carry guns; there would be a shoot-out and the strike would end there and then. Before leaving he gave us some money that would enable us to carry on for a while.

One day soon after, Beal, Dawson, and I, with a striker as driver, went to a little town called Marion, where we had a contact. Marion was located at some distance northwest of us where the hills began. The town itself was pleasant enough (but so was Gastonia) with the great pine-clad slopes rising immediately beyond it. Very different were the mill villages on the outskirts. There were two small mills close together, the Clinchfield Mills and, not far away, another owned by the East Marion Manufacturing Company. Conditions were even more primitive here than in Loray: water had to be brought from a well; there were outside toilets in filthy condition. The cottages were even worse than in Loray. It was Sunday and the mill people were about. They had heard of our strike in Loray and were friendly enough, though not yet ready to join our union.

Then I had a bright idea. Manville-Jenckes owned another mill in nearby High Shoals, N.C., besides the seven they had in Rhode Island. Wouldn't it be tactically correct to get this mill out on strike? So we mimeographed and distributed a leaflet. The mill cottages here were located in a grove of trees, looking quite pleasant from the outside. All doors were left open; inside were the usual dirty, disorderly conditions: floors unswept, beds unmade, breakfast dishes and crumbs on the table. We made a pretty thorough distribution of the leaflet, calling for a meeting the next day after work.

When we arrived there a small group of unfriendly-looking men awaited us. We got out and Preacher-man stood on the running board and began to speak. With shouts of "Git out!" "Git out of here, we don't want no troublemakers!" and "We don't want no outside agitators!" the men crowded around. I got up on the running-board to speak next, but it was clear there was no use, these were not mill workers, they were bossmen, possibly also some sheriff's deputies. They began throwing things and we piled hastily into the car. As we drove away they pelted the car with tomatoes and rotten eggs, which smelled loudly. Needless to say, this ended any hope of organizing High Shoals.

Then there was the incident of the Armstrong Mill, one of the small Gastonia mills. One morning a striker came into the headquarters to inform Beal that Pershing had gone alone there to meet some workers during the lunch hour. Beal quickly found a car; I went with him, Dawson also. Sure enough, in front of the dingy little building there was Pershing with some half dozen mill workers. One could always tell them by their overalls, and they didn't wear hats. There was also a group of four or five other men in regular suits who were shouting angrily. As we got out of the car these men—bossmen, no doubt (foremen or even employers)—turned to us. They became threatening, shaking their fists at us.

"We'll run you out of town," they yelled at Beal. One of them turned to me: "We'll run you out, too." With things looking risky, we piled into the car and took off. At the last minute, with the car already in motion, Pershing jumped on the running board.

This affair was built up in the Party press as though Pershing had been in danger of lynching and Beal had saved him. "A large group of armed men" supposedly had attacked Pershing. As the event had occurred in broad daylight on a city street with people about, to talk of lynching seemed a great exaggeration.

The next day Beal failed to show up for the strike committee meeting. His home base was a furnished room in Charlotte. No one knew exactly where he lived, nor did we have any telephone connection with him. He was carried back and forth by a striker, a youth of nineteen named K. O. Byers, who had a car. The secrecy of Beal's arrangements was never questioned: for him to have stayed in Loray or Gastonia would have been obviously unsafe.

In Beal's absence, as second-in-command I had to open and carry on the strike committee meeting, beside inventing some excuse for his absence. I saw the doubting, anxious expressions on the strikers' faces, and the fact that nobody said anything only made it worse. Showing up late in the day, Beal gave no excuse—and the same thing happened the next day. At the time it never occurred to me to connect Beal's absenteeism with the incident at the Armstrong Mill. It was only later it came out that he and Pershing were scared; they were hiding in Charlotte those days.

Besides this matter there was a decision of the Party fraction that I was to lead the picket lines, if any. We had now a staff of six people, of whom three were men. Siroka was tied up at Pineville, which had no picketing because the mill was shut down; Pershing was at Bessemer City though he came to Loray every afternoon. Beal as always refused to picket. So Buch had to do it. Because of all this friction and the gun controversy our picketing had fallen off.

Still, with some effort one day we did mobilize a group of women and children and started out with a few signs to meet the night shift coming in at seven, the end of the working day. With Schechter beside me I headed the line marching down the broken sidewalk toward the mill, which loomed up ahead to our right. We hadn't gone far when we were met by Police Chief Aderholt of Gastonia blocking the sidewalk, in front of four or five troopers with drawn bayonets. Chief Aderholt was a very tall, very lean and lanky man, strong-featured with the hard-bitten look of the South. He always wore a black suit and a big black ten-gallon Texas hat. A short dialogue ensued between him and me about as follows:

Chief: Now where d' yah think y'all's goin'?

Buch: We are carrying on a peaceful picket line.

Chief: Don't you know this town has passed an ordinance against paradin'?

Buch: We are not a parade. We simply want to picket, to walk quietly up and down as we have a legal right to do.

Chief: Break it up, boys! [Jerking an elbow.]

Our pickets scattered, the troopers after them. Amy and I, stepping down to the roughly paved roadway, started toward the other side. The scene was a confused one, with shouts and screams as the women and children ran quickly back toward the headquarters, the troopers after them, pushing them, dealing blows, using their guns as clubs. A number of arrests were made including Schechter and myself, ten or twelve women altogether. We were all herded into a waiting paddy wagon, driven into town, and taken into what we learned later was Gaston County Jail.

We were led upstairs and were pushed all together into one large cell containing two or three cots with bare mattresses. Behind a partition in back were a toilet and wash basin. We were all much excited, talking and laughing together. We settled in, some on the cots, others on the floor. Among us were Gladys Wallace, Violet Jones, Mrs. McGinnis, Mrs. Totherow, Bertha Tompkins, and a few other active women. We were held overnight without charges and without supper. We stayed up nearly all night. Once in a while if one of us felt tired she would stretch out on a cot for a spell; otherwise we squatted on the floor or on the edges of the cots. We sang a lot: "Solidarity Forever" and "The Red Flag": "Though cowards flinch and traitors sneer / We'll keep the red flag flying here." The strikers sang their own beautiful plaintive ballads, "Barbry Allen," "Red River Valley," and many more. It was a time too for unburdening a lot of grievances, personal histories, and confessions, all very revelatory and important for Amy and me. We became much closer to the Loray strikers during that long night.

Some of the women had come directly from mountain homes to Loray; others had previously been mill workers out of work in South Carolina or Georgia. Those who were mountain-born retained some of the pride, vigor, and independence of their origin, but a generation or two as millhands—low-paid, sick, degraded, and ignorant—had reduced them to a sense of inborn inferiority. This we saw in Violet Jones, still a pretty young woman, though showing signs of wear and tear. She admitted being very soft on "Mr. Perishin'. Oh, he's so handsome, so kind . . . but he wouldn't ever look at me, I'm nothin' but a millhand." This was said with quiet humility and resignation as though such a fate were inevitable.

The women talked about the stretch-out, how you needed roller skates (this, I remember, had been the cry in Passaic also) to run from one side to another, you couldn't cover so many. They talked about how their children would get sick and it was so hard to give them any care. They preferred the night shift, though it was twelve hours, but only five nights. That left you two days "to ketch up on the housework, the washin', and a little cleanin' mebbe." That way you could give the little ones a bit of care during the day. And when do you sleep? "Well, you try to ketch a little sleep durin' the afternoon, mebbe." They told how every single woman or young girl that wanted to get a job in Loray Mill had to sleep with the bossman first. There was no two ways about that.

Violet told about a girl who brought an abortion on herself, "just went out to the toilet and it was all washed down there and she went back to work." Gladys Wallace told her own story: She had started work at age ten so that by now she had had sixteen years of experience, going from one mill to another, maybe seventy-five altogether. "Knocked around and slapped around," working twelve hours a day. She had been five years in the Loray Mill. She had got married, was infected with VD by her husband, had to have a hysterectomy; and then her husband had left her. "I had a kid first, but now I ain't got nothin' here no more," she said, patting her belly. "Hit don't matter now whut I do," and everybody laughed at that.

They told a story about a Loray superintendent they used to have. Oh, how they hated that man, he was so mean; "Stretch-out" was his middle name. "The Loray workers held a parade through the streets of Gastonia, that was back a year or so ago. They carried a man in a coffin. He had a sign on him, 'Superintendent So and So.' Eight men was carryin' the coffin. Every once in a while Super would rise up in the coffin and say, 'Six kin do it.' Then two of the men carryin' would drop out. Well, maybe that helped. They fired that man end of 1928, then they let down the stretch-out. We paraded again celebratin'. But with the new man they've got it's as bad as ever. Seems like there's nothin' to do but go out on strike, all of us. The weave room, fifty people, had a strike once. Then Mr. Beal come this year and talked to us. He was the man that got us all organized and out on strike here."

Late at night, weary and talked out, we lay down either on the three cots or on the floor and uneasily slept a little. In the morning we were all let out without arraignment. At the strike committee meeting we rejoined the other pickets and the whole event was reviewed. There had been a few bruises and scratches from the bayonets, nothing serious.

There was anger at the troopers, and above all against Manville-Jenckes, or its local representatives who had the full cooperation of the state forces, mayor, sheriff, and Governor Gardner. Amy got out a story for the *Daily Worker* and a news release. The spirit of the workers was raised rather than dampened by this skirmish with the troops.

Soon we made another attempt to picket the Loray Mill. I had noticed a side entrance where there seemed to be no guards. Five men volunteered to picket with me there, so we went out one afternoon with a couple of signs. A little unpaved street with mill cottages on one side led up the hill to the mill. These cottages, if I remember correctly, were painted brown and were a little better than most, perhaps occupied by bossmen or office workers. We hadn't gone more than halfway up that block when the troopers stationed at the front of the mill (actually some distance away) spied us, came running, and charged down the hill with their bayonets fixed.

My pickets vanished so quickly I couldn't see where they had gone. An organizer can't run away I told myself as I started to walk. One of the troopers poked at me with his bayonet—it didn't hurt any more than a stick—yelling "Git along thar, y'all." I replied with dignity, "I can walk, I don't have to be pushed," and very deliberately walked up the steps of one of the cottages and stood on the porch until the troopers quieted down and went back to their post.

So ran our days, those busy, purposeful, frustrating Loray days.

9

The Rolling Wave of Strikes

IT WAS ON APRIL 18, ABOUT A WEEK AFTER THE NATIONAL SECRETARY'S VISIT, that we came to a crisis, the first really that we had faced.

I was away at the time in Lexington, North Carolina, where we had a nucleus of mill workers. As it was pretty far and had to be an overnight stay, I went in a car with a striker and his wife. We arrived in time for an after-work meeting next to a railroad station. A man coming up to shake my hand afterward said, "You should be a lawyer, Miss. You talk just like a lawyer." This rather dubious compliment bothered me a little. Did I really speak like a lawyer?

I met then with a small group in a worker's home to discuss organization. It was already quite late when a man brought a telephone message: There had been a raid on our headquarters in Loray. A mob had come and had torn it all down. I wanted to rush right back but the others convinced me this was not feasible, so I stayed overnight with a worker's family. The man and wife went upstairs, and I had a big bed in the main room with a bright patchwork quilt. With a blaze in the fireplace it was a cozy cheerful scene, but there was little sleep for me as I lay picturing my comrades in Loray jailed, beaten, or worse.

Returning early the next morning, I found a good-sized crowd at the spot where our little shack had stood. Some rubble on the ground, a bit of roof hanging crazily from a remnant of a wall was all that remained of it in the gap between two buildings. All our people were unharmed, including the nine unarmed guards who slept in the place. They had been simply overpowered.

First the electricity had been cut off in the village. Then a mob of masked men had come (estimates of their numbers ran as high as one hundred and fifty). With hatchets, pickaxes, and crowbars, the intruders had torn the shack down. At the very last minute some of the troopers came along and arrested—whom? Our nine guards. Later on, when they were released on fifty dollars bond each, the arrestees reported they had been told at the police station if they would tear up their union cards they could have their jobs back in the mill. Needless to say, they declined. The men also said they had recognized some policemen among the mob, as well as some Loray bossmen. Lewis McLaughlin told his story of the raid:

"Nine of us was settin' up watchin' and sleepin' in the relief store. Ten masked men broke in and put flashlights and guns in our faces and told us to git out. There was upwards to a hundred and fifty more of these masked men outside. We went across the street, two masked men guarding us. I recognized Will Painter, a mill police.

"Major Dolley and two National Guardsmen came along and the leader of the mob, him with a green mask, hollered 'fifty in the back,' and they all run back of the buildings but two. A man in a mask passed between Major Dolley and a guardsman so close he coulda put out his hand and arrested him."

The mob had also raided our relief store. They had smashed one of the front windows to get in and had torn our fine new union sign.

We had stocks of food there that they completely ruined: flour, rice, and beans were strewn over the floor and into the street. Kerosene had been poured over it all. With dismay we saw this mess, all a complete loss. There was nothing to salvage from the wrecked headquarters. Fortunately the store could now serve for all purposes. A lot of people all talking and exclaiming at once piled in there and created quite a hubbub as they viewed the ruined food. It took some time to get enough quiet to hold a strike committee meeting.

Beal reported he had sent a wire to New York advising the national office. The destroyed food would be replaced at once (luckily we had money left from what Albert had given us). The mess in the store and in the street would be left to be photographed. A press release would be drawn up by Schechter and Beal and sent out immediately.

A salient feature of this mob attack was that the National Guard troops, who had been called in to Loray ostensibly to "protect property," had been in their tents beside the mill, a block away from our shack, but had made no effort whatever to interfere though the loud noise of the demolition must surely have awakened them.

The whole incident was seen as one more employers' attack. Bringing in troops had scared nobody. Neither had court injunctions against "parading" (picketing). Now came this outrageous assault.

We soon settled into our new routine in the store. In the long run the employers' excess brutality redounded to our advantage. Our mass meetings were much better attended now. For a few days we talked of the raid in all its aspects.

The event resulted in publicity throughout the country, something lacking until now. Relief contributions began to increase. There was strong reaction among Southern liberals. The Raleigh *News and Observer* forcefully denounced the raid. So too did the Greensboro, N.C., *Daily News* and other important Southern papers. Of course the Gastonia *Gazette*, ever ready to fan the fires of local hostility, was not only fulsome in its praise of the demolition but pressed even harder for driving out the organizers altogether.

Even in Gastonia and in our immediate surroundings came signs of improvement. A couple named Lodge who owned a big house on West Airline Avenue between Loray and Gastonia came around offering help. Perry Lodge was a union carpenter. His presence did not mean his union had changed its position of opposition, but Lodge bravely declared his personal sympathy for our cause. He and his wife Helen offered their home for accommodating members of our staff if needed; they also let us use a room for our occasional "staff" meetings (really the C.P. fraction). Then Helen Lodge began to cook for the staff a Sunday dinner, which we paid for, but such a dinner was unobtainable anywhere around there. Eating poorly as we did during the week, we lingered long over her ham, chicken, or roast lamb, her black-eyed peas, sweet corn, grits, and corn-bread, topped off with layer cake or pie and ice cream. Also the owner of the little restaurant where we used to eat on Loray's Franklin Street had perhaps noted some skipped meals, and he made us a generous offer: if we couldn't pay, any member of our staff could come in and eat without charge. This we sometimes took advantage of, always paying when we had the wherewithal.

On April 10 a division of cavalry left; then on April 20 the state militia was withdrawn. Although we had become accustomed to seeing the troops around, still it was a relief to have them gone. An investigator was sent in from Governor Gardner's office and a grand jury was convened, which after deliberation found itself unable to place any responsibility for the raid. Nor did the investigator succeed. Some of our guards who had seen the mob felt sure some of the grand jury members had been among them.

The destruction of our headquarters was really a sort of blood trans-fusion for our strike. Crowds were coming around now to the meetings. The spirit of the workers was so aroused that on April 22 a large picket line including men as well as women was organized. It didn't take long to see that the withdrawal of the troops made no difference, for the sheriff's deputies who took their place also carried guns equipped with bayonets.

This military equipment, we learned later, was provided from the state's arsenal.

The deputies together with the "laws" broke up the line and not only chased the picketers down the street, but even charged into our headquarters, where I happened to be at the time. Aderholt himself was among the intruders, who harassed the strikers receiving relief there and forced them to leave. There were flesh cuts and torn clothing from the bayonets. K. Y. Hendricks received a bad leg wound and his pants were ruined. We had the strikers exhibit their torn and bloodstained clothing and some of their wounds at the mass meeting. April 22 was thereafter referred to as "Bloody Monday."

There were some other attacks besides those on the picket line. A striker named James Ballentyne, who had been arrested, was beaten in the jail and punched in the stomach so badly that he had hemorrhages for some hours afterward. A further outrage that day was an attack on an elderly woman, Ada Howell, who was not even picketing but was on her way to the store to buy her supper. She was first cut, her dress torn and bloodied by the bayonets. Then two policemen named Praether and Jackson assaulted her, beating her on the face till her eyes were swollen closed and her whole face black and blue. It was clear we had gained nothing by the withdrawal of the troops.

My trip to Lexington had been part of our efforts to extend the strike; however, with the turmoil that followed the raid, it was not possible to keep an organizer there permanently. The local managed to carry on by itself, with occasional advice via telephone. Later the Wenonah Mill in Lexington went on strike using the same demands as the Loray strikers.

In Loray there was some legal harassment, and attacks on strikers continued. Apparently the authorities had had us all investigated and had found that Ellen Dawson, Scotch by birth, was a naturalized citizen. Dawson was arrested on a federal bench warrant, charged with obtaining citizens' papers on false pretenses, and held in jail in Charlotte until the bail of $2,000 could be raised in New York. "Red" Hendricks was arrested without charge or cause and was brutally beaten to the point of unconsciousness in jail. Shortly afterward Russell Knight was given the same treatment.

The American Civil Liberties Union sent the following telegram of protest to North Carolina Governor Gardner:

> State troops called to service in Gastonia on pretext of protecting public order were used to oppress striking textile workers and further the interest of the mill operators. They were not used to protect workers against

masked armed rioters who set up a reign of anarchy by destroying relief stores and committing acts of violence. The American Civil Liberties Union, with a large membership throughout the country, denounces this disgraceful partisanship of state and community and demands an executive intervention to restore human and civil rights under orderly government.*

The ACLU also offered a reward of $100 for the arrest and conviction of any or all of the raiders.

By this time we were receiving bundles of the *Daily Worker* several times a week and of the *Labor Defender*, the ILD monthly magazine. While the *Worker* carried publicity on the strike, sometimes imagination, Communist zeal, and an obvious desire to impress Moscow perverted reality to such an extent that the exaggerated accounts of our strike were better not read by the strikers. We withheld some issues. We also received a *Textile Worker* put out by the union. It was common to see the strikers sitting about the headquarters reading Communist literature. I don't recall anyone objecting to it.

On April 26 Tom Jimison filed an injunction petition with Judge Stack of superior court on behalf of the strikers in an effort to have the anti-parade ordinance rescinded. Jimison also sent a telegram to Senator Burton K. Wheeler of Montana calling for a Senate investigation of the conditions of Southern textile workers.

There was some strike activity too in Bessemer City, where the spinners of the small Osage Mill came out on strike and the mill was shut down. In the larger Gambrill-Melville Mill, which was reputed to have somewhat better working conditions than most (it had at least a fifty-five-hour week), a walkout principally of weavers occurred. Their demands had evidently been influenced by those in the Loray strike, although they set up a strike committee and organized relief for themselves and carried on their strike independently, rejecting any "interference."

For a time there was an influx of outsiders in Loray—not merely of newspaper reporters, but of writers like Mary Heaton Vorse, and of liberals and friends of the labor movement. Some of our own people came also. The International Labor Defense sent Karl Reeve, a recent graduate of the Lenin School in Moscow and the son of Ella Reeve Bloor, who remained about a week handling legal cases and getting publicity and photographs for the *Labor Defender*, of which he was now the editor. Reeve helped out too by speaking at our mass meetings. He was

---

*Charlotte *Observer*, Apr. 27, 1929.

one of the leaders of the picket line on April 22, was arrested, and was held briefly in jail.

Mary Heaton Vorse was staying now in a hotel in Gastonia, coming out to Loray for most of the day. She mingled with the strikers, getting statements from them about their wages, the mill conditions, their life histories, and the attacks they had experienced from the police. Vorse had been with her friend Elizabeth Gurley Flynn in the 1912 strike in Lawrence, Mass., as well as in the 1919 strike there. Those strikes were her models of what strikes should be. By comparison with them our strike no doubt appeared small and inadequate. Mary Vorse had arrived a couple of days after the Armstrong Mill affair, when our morale was at its worst. We told her we didn't have any money, but I doubt if she realized how literally true this was. Put out literature, circulate leaflets, send organizers to spread the strike? Didn't we know these things should be done? She wanted us to organize committees of middle-class women to collect money for a milk fund for the children. Lacking money even for our own food sometimes, we found the most elementary organization efforts impossible. Our enthusiasm was constantly dampened by our pitiful lack of means. While the relief contributions must surely have increased, the WIR still allowed only a mere trickle of money to reach the Loray strike.

Why were we so poor? Our union had no treasury because it was a new one, composed of poorly-paid workers, many of whom had been recently on strike. Strikers would sit all day in the store waiting. Amy Schechter called the New York office every day, and by late afternoon there would usually be some money telegraphed in to her. She would then rush to Gastonia to buy food and would give out packages of beans, flour, and other staples to the strikers. She would often give the organizers supper money too. It was a hand-to-mouth affair, a wretched situation, beyond our control and also beyond our understanding.

As for me, in a way I had come into my own there in Loray. I felt well; the fresh air and sun exposure had done me good. Here, where there was no one better than I, I had overcome my self-doubt. The Gastonia *Gazette* once referred to me as "the most important of the organizers." I was on the road to becoming a good public speaker; my voice was clear though never strong, but I knew how to project it. I was learning not to be afraid; to think on my feet; and, what is most important, to establish a rapport with the audience. As for organizing the work, it must be said that even if Beal or any one of us had been the best organizer in the world, without a cent to carry out plans the result might have been no better.

On Friday, April 26, the Chamber of Commerce brought Joe Mitchell Chapple to Gastonia to combat Bolshevism. As the town had no meeting hall large enough for the expected crowd, a flag-decorated platform was put up in front of the courthouse, with the street roped off. At the strikers' afternoon mass meeting Beal advised the people to go to Chapple's meeting. A group of older men who had seen service in World War I was selected to try to present the union point of view. They were told there would be only one speaker. Many hundreds of people turned out, including mill workers.

Mr. Chapple's subject was Americanism vs. Communism. He was an enormously fat man in evening clothes. Looking down on the gaunt shabby mill workers and other ordinary people of the town, Mr. Chapple gave a long rambling flowery harangue on the glories of individualism which had built up their splendid country. He praised especially a few local citizens who had risen from humble backgrounds to become mill owners and leaders of this beautiful city. As the speech was in progress and afterward, our committee of strikers quietly circulated among the crowd making their own propaganda for our strike.

We were actually able to counteract the Chapple meeting in a very impressive way. A letter from the Manville-Jenckes Company had fallen into our hands. We put it before the strikers:

> Member of the Cotton Textile Institute, Inc.
> Manville-Jenckes Company
> Pawtucket, Rhode Island
> November 8, 1927

Mr. G.A. Johnstone, Resident Agent
Manville-Jenckes Company
Loray Division
Gastonia, North Carolina

Dear Mr. Johnstone:

I have been keeping close tab on your payroll and production at Loray Division, and I am glad to say, it is very gratifying to see your payroll come down and your production go up. I am frank to say I was skeptical about you being able to cut $500,000 a year on the Loray payroll and keep your production up. I want to apologize now for this skepticism. Now I think you can cut out $1,000,000 a year and still keep your production up.

I am in hopes of getting South but you are making such a good job of it that I am only afraid I will upset things rather than help.

> Yours very truly,
> (signed) F.L. Jenckes

FLJ:evg

We knew, and the workers well knew, what lay behind these economic facts. The increased profit over which Mr. Jenckes so rejoiced had been squeezed out of the very blood, marrow, and bones of the workers. Their lives were being shortened. There were times when I had a peculiar strangled sensation, wanting at the same time to weep with sorrow at the workers' plight and to bellow with rage at the utter callous indifference to human life that is inherent in the profit system. Of course we publicized this find as well as we could.

April 26 became an important day for us for a quite different reason than the Chapple meeting. Previously the word had got around that the mill on strike in Pineville and the one in Bessemer City were going to open up on that day. This is always a most critical point in a strike. Then, if ever, the organizer must be at hand trying to hold the union people together, to prevent a mass stampede back into the mill. On just that day the annual convention of the Young Communist League was to open in New York. For a week beforehand our two organizers Pershing and Siroka, members of the League, talked of nothing else. They wanted to go to that convention. They telephoned daily to New York to get permission to leave. It was on the very day before the reopening of the mills that they finally received the consent of their chiefs to leave their posts in the South and return to New York. They took the evening train and were seen among us no more. Karl Reeve left too, but he was not so essential, nor was he responsible to the union. We were now only three organizers, Beal, Dawson and me. I was assigned to take over both of the abandoned posts.

Mr. Grier took me out to Pineville the next morning. Mill number five was running full blast. Left out and blacklisted were a handful of activists, an angry and resentful group. I had to tell them we could continue their relief and someone would get down to them once in a while, but we could not keep an organizer there. Then as soon as possible I went to Bessemer City, to find the same situation. Here, however, the excluded group was larger, ten or a dozen, chiefly women, among them a few real stalwarts such as Ella Mae Wiggins, who was as good as an organizer; her cousin Charley; and a short, vigorous middle-aged man named Wes Williams.

Now I had a new schedule: every morning at eight I would take the bus down to Bessemer City, a fifteen-minute trip to a small, drab town containing several cotton mills. I tried to encourage the strikers of the American Mill to keep in contact with those working, in hope that they might come out later on strike. Also, I led a picket line of strikers around the mill. After a few turns the women would complain of being "all tah'd out." I would ask them, "Didn't you stand twelve hours every night in the mill?" But I couldn't push them. Probably they were feeling the futility of the march, though in this they were not entirely right. The sight of the excluded ones picketing was still a link with those inside, which we needed to maintain.

On the street that ran past one side of the American Mill was a place, a store probably, with double doors always standing open. There were narrow beds inside kept made up. This was a place for single millhands to sleep. Completely bare, without chairs, bureaus, or tables, the place gave an idea of the life of the single worker—work and sleep, work and sleep, not even a family or home.

I was not very happy in this new assignment. Not only was I somewhat isolated now from the situation in Loray, but the whole incident of Siroka and Pershing rankled deeply within me. It was not simply because I had to take over a difficult situation, not merely that the two YCLers had deserted their posts; more than anything else I resented that they had authorization to do so by their leaders.

The struggle for funds went on unremittingly. Beal had occasionally appealed to Party leaders for help. In the early period in Charlotte he had written to Jay Lovestone describing the condition of his clothes, hoping to receive some money, but Lovestone had merely sent him a worn-out suit, which he had promptly returned. Now, at this point we decided to appeal to Robert Minor, acting Party secretary, most of the other leaders being in Moscow. Beal called him in New York. Minor, quite complacent, showed no concern for our plight, said he hadn't any money, and closed the conversation with a cheerful "Carry on, Comrades." We were much disgruntled and resentful at this rebuff. Beal never had any use for leaders, Party or otherwise. As for me, whatever illusions I may have had were wearing thin by now. There were times when we seemed to be at the end of our rope financially. All we could do was appeal to Amy, who had control of the relief money, never more than barely adequate to feed the strikers.

It was just at this time that our national secretary came down from New York again. We had a good big meeting for Albert beside the railroad tracks the day he arrived. The grass was completely worn off now on the lot by the daily trampling of feet. Previously Albert had spoken of extending the strike, unionizing all Southern textiles. Now it was on the question of racial equality that he spoke with his usual eloquence; equality of black and white in our union was his principal theme.

This speech was quoted throughout the South with reverberations among all propertied people. At these words, at this insult to Southern honor, what white man would not rise in horror! The Gastonia *Daily Gazette* frothed as usual. Among our own union members too there were repercussions: they were not prepared for such extremes. We did see some union people tearing up their cards. As we talked of it among the people and discussed it in the strike committee, it seemed the more intelligent of the workers could see the inclusion of the Negroes (even though they didn't want to associate with them personally) would strengthen the union.

With Albert had come down a Negro organizer; I believe he gave his name as Owen, sent down by the Party. He made one brief, scared appearance in Loray. I recall him standing by the car looking apprehensively at all those white people surrounding him. He then retreated to Charlotte, where he remained in a room Beal rented for him. We could hardly blame him: if ever anyone had a dangerous assignment, it was he.

With Albert had come another person whom we had barely noticed at the start. One morning as Beal, the other staff members, and I were consulting in the little office, a striker came to tell us there was a spy outside. To our astonishment we found the newcomer to be none other than Jack Johnstone, a Fosterite Central Committee member of the Party, a reputed trade union leader. He was a short stocky man with a Scotch accent. He acted at first so furtively that we could understand why he was creating such an impression. It didn't take long for us to realize that Johnstone had come unwillingly as the Party rep.

Within hearing of the strikers (there was no privacy whatever in our arrangements), he loudly proclaimed his objections: "Why in hell did they send *me* here? I'm no textile worker!"

Soon, however, a change took place in him; he was found sitting with the strikers, chatting amicably, comparing notes on their occupations. Johnstone insisted the boiler factory where he used to work was the noisiest place on earth (it had made him a little deaf); the cotton workers told him he should experience the weave room, where the thunder of the looms resulted in deafening many weavers. (Our Ellen Dawson, a weaver from Passaic, also had this affliction.) Johnstone did speak at one mass meeting. After a few days of telephone calls to New York he got the desired permission, took his departure, and was quickly forgotten.

At a Party fraction meeting, held this time at the Lodges' house, Albert stressed two points: a new strike strategy and Negro work. The new strategy was based on the news that textile workers were coming out spontaneously all over the South, protesting the wage cuts and stretch-out. He called it "The Rolling Wave of Strikes." Here in Loray and Bessemer City we were to make the greatest effort to get those working in the mills to join the union and come out on strike. By alternating work and strike the workers would be able to carry on in this situation where money was lacking. As staff, we could not feel enthusiastic at the prospect

of a long continuation of this assignment. Perhaps we were just getting
weary. However, by individual contacts we had already started the penetration of the mills, though it was too soon to have achieved results. Now
we would make it more systematic by setting up committees of strikers
to visit the scabs.

While we agreed in principle on the Negro question, its applications
here were difficult. Albert said we must fraternize with the Negroes;
rather hard in Loray since we never saw one there. They had made only one
brief appearance. One day early in the strike as I sat in a corner of the
headquarters, never a very light place, suddenly it seemed to me I saw two
black men standing by the counter. By the time I could get to where they
were, like shadows they had disappeared. Probably seeing only white
faces there, they had lost confidence and fled.

Some independent organization was being carried on in Bessemer
City by Ella Mae Wiggins. That unfortunate incident of the rope had
handicapped us from the start. On the first day of the strike when some
black workers were present with the white in the meeting hall, the whites
had insisted that a rope be stretched down the middle, separating them
from the blacks. There had always been a few Negro employees in the
American Mill, not working on machinery but doing heavy unskilled
labor—cleaning, toting bales—only outside the mill. Mrs. Wiggins got
around among them; she knew where they lived, for she lived there too.

"I know the colored don't like us," she said once. "But if they see
you're poor and humble like themselves, they'll listen to you."

I made one attempt to reach some black workers. There was in Bessemer City a small factory, a waste mill, located near the American Mill.
I used to see a few black women sitting in the sun by the doorway sorting
over heaps of rags. The pay for such a job must have been minimal, perhaps three dollars a week. I stopped to speak to them once. It was strange
talking to people who wouldn't even look at me. Not one glanced up
from her work or gave any sign she knew someone was talking to her about
a union that was for all the workers regardless of skin color, that might
help her get more money. A bossman inside watching may have inhibited
them.

It was during Albert's visit that Ella Mae Wiggins thought she had
enough cards signed among the blacks to call a meeting; I had to see a
black barber to get some information. He too wouldn't look at me. With
his eyes on the ceiling he said something like this:

"No'm. I didn't get to see that man Miz Ella Mae done tole me 'bout.
But we's gon' have a meetin' shoh nuf."

The place was Stumptown, a hamlet where the black folks lived on the
outskirts of Bessemer City. Albert and I went down there in the early

evening, walking between woods along the railroad tracks for about a mile. The heat of the sun was tempered. It was good for us to be alone and once more to be engaged in work together. Opportunities for privacy in our situation were few. The Lodges' had provided a bedroom for us, but we had been aware of a certain lack of rapport, as though there had been a long separation, though actually it was less than three weeks. Perhaps I had changed more than I realized in the sense that I was more independent now. At any rate, in that half hour of walking along the tracks I was able to recapture the feeling of oneness, and with it the old happiness of being together in the work we both wanted to do. That walk left a precious memory with me.

When we reached Stumptown we found a tiny railroad station, a little store, and a number of cabins, none ever painted, some dilapidated, but hardly one that didn't have flowers planted around it. The shacks were all alight with geraniums, nasturtiums, phlox, and goldenglow. Near the station house were two black men. A group of at least fifteen more stood perhaps thirty feet away, eyeing us, and women stood in the doorways of the shacks. Albert got up on the box and in a ringing voice urged them to come closer. And come closer they did, but not all at once; as he spoke, they gradually edged nearer. By the time my turn came they were around us in a circle. When I got down we shook hands; now they were smiling as we welcomed them to our union. What I felt then was something like the joy of reunion with members of a family long separated. Soon after this Albert left for New York.

On April 29 the workers again organized a fine picket line of about seventy-five men, women, and youth. This time the line tried a new tactic: evasion. At first they headed directly for the mill; then to fool the cops, who began to attack the head of the line, the rear end became the head and turned off on a side street past one end of the mill; then they again changed their direction. The three "laws" on duty, bewildered, rushed into Gastonia and quickly returned with several carloads of police, deputies, and thugs armed with guns, blackjacks, and clubs, headed by Chief Aderholt. Even with this force it took some time to disperse the picket line, with the usual blows, bayonet scratches, and arrests.

All of Loray Village and its environs were in turmoil for about an hour.

In the meantime the employers were not idle. On April 29 a number of strikers living in company houses received eviction notices from the Manville-Jenckes Company. On a test case of Manville-Jenckes *v.* J. A. Valentine, Magistrate Bismarck Capps handed down the decision that former employees of the Loray Mill still occupying the company houses must vacate the houses unless they arranged bond to cover rental for a period of a year, with a dollar per month added for water and still more for lights. In addition they were ordered to pay rent from April 1 to the present date.

Even though the shacks had previously rented for twenty-five cents per room per week, Judge Capps ruled that the rent now be set at a dollar per room per week. Furthermore, the bond must be posted before appeal of the case could be made. Attorneys Jimison and Gresham of Charlotte represented the mill workers, while the mill company's case was handled by Major A. L. Bulwinkle. The money needed for bond for sixty-two families was considerable. It appeared that the mill owners here were doing more than harass the strikers. They seemed to be wreaking vengeance upon them for daring to defy their employers.

Then suddenly, before anything could possibly be done, on May 6 the blow fell. On that day a large number of strikers were evicted from their company-owned houses: eighty-five families in all. The sheriff of Gastonia came with some sworn-in deputies and without the slightest regard for crying babies, sick people, resisting women, they set all the poor possessions in a heap outside and padlocked the doors. It was a scene of great confusion and distress. They spread the evictions widely about the village, as they said, "to show 'em what they'll be up against."

For the staff this situation was the most serious crisis we had faced yet. Of course Beal immediately called the national secretary in New York; Albert said he would contact the relief organization, whose province this was. Meanwhile we tried desperately to find shelter for whomever we could and to get some tarpaulins or oilcloth to cover at least the beds. It was a long hectic day with strikers constantly coming to the headquarters to report eviction. We had no way to solve the problem immediately, but the people bravely endured the new hardship. To make it worse, with nightfall a light rain started to fall. Some of the people crawled under the cabins for shelter.

I left the headquarters about nine o'clock, tired and ready for bed, and walked over to the Stroud house. There I found that they had been evicted also. All their belongings were out in front of the house. It was already dark. I managed to find my little suitcase and picked it up. For a moment I felt completely disoriented. Where could I go? I didn't have money for a hotel room. The Lodges'? It was too far to walk in the rain. Starting to return to the headquarters in the hope of finding it still open, I remembered that Amy and Ellen had a room in the mill boardinghouse close by. So I went there. There were rooms on the ground floor as well as on a gallery which ran around the second floor. I went up to the women's room. Amy was there. She was sympathetic and had no objection to putting me up. I got undressed and lay down in the center of the bed. Soon Ellen came. When she saw me she exclaimed, "What's this, we're sleeping three to a bed again?" I explained my predicament. She didn't answer but flounced out in a huff, slamming the door. In the morning we learned she had found an unoccupied room in which she slept till early morning, when she left. Our problem was solved by her renting a room in the dormitory for herself (they charged $2.50 a week for a room with a single bed) while I bunked in with Amy for a while.

Because of the crisis in Loray I didn't go down to Bessemer City as usual. That morning I went with Mary Vorse for a tour of the evicted families. The sight was appalling. Beds were everywhere beside the straggly gravel paths called streets. There were chairs too, tables, an occasional dresser, pots and pans, clothing, trinkets, all jumbled in a mess. Some tarpaulins had been provided, but not enough for all. Luckily last night's drizzle had been no more than intermittent; still, everything was damp. The hot sun would soon dry it all out. All around there were people coughing; there were babies in arms and many small children. People seemed still dazed by the event. All we could do was to give encouragement that the relief man from New York would be here soon to take care of them. Some of the leading strikers were among those evicted as well as others not so prominent.*

The next morning train brought Alfred Wagenknecht, businesslike, competent, and cheerful as always, accompanied by his secretary. They met with our strike committee and staff for a practical discussion. It was clear there was no possibility of placing the evicted families in houses, since none were available; the only possibility was tents. Where could we rent a piece of land to place some tents? The strikers explained: beyond the railroad tracks where there were a few streets and cottages, it was called "free" land. Our good friend in Charlotte, Mr. Cohen, had a friend who owned a plot of land in this free section. Upon Cohen's offer of some land he owned in Charlotte as security, this plot was given us for use rent-free. It was a flat field of good size at the edge of Loray Village where the woods began. North Loray was the name of the street, West Gastonia the place. Beyond the field ran a wooded gully with a little stream. This spot would do for the tents.

Then the idea arose that since we had this field without paying rent, why not build ourselves a new headquarters? On May 13 a permit was issued for the erection of a small cheap building on North Loray Street as headquarters for the NTWU. Lumber was ordered and some tools, as well as the tents. There were plenty of men with building skills; soon the reassuring sound of hammers and saws rang out. The tents were pitched

---

*For a fuller account, see Mary Heaton Vorse's news release, Federated Press Eastern Bureau, May 9, 1929.

on the slope of the gully, out of sight of the field, a quiet private place. Some kerosene stoves had to be bought for cooking, a pit dug, and an outhouse erected downstream. The cabin, our new headquarters, was located in the left front corner of the lot. It was neatly built, had the good smell of fresh-sawn lumber, and was commodious enough, perhaps twenty by thirty feet. A small space was partitioned off in the front corner for an office. Behind the building in the back were two tents for the guards and for relief supplies.

The evictions had brought a temporary influx of visitors: reporters, magazine writers, liberals of various stripes. They came to talk to us and to the strikers, to stand about at the meetings, to take pictures and tour Loray Village. They would stay a day or two, would pass on, and be forgotten.

While the new headquarters was being built, Karl Reeve returned, and with him came three members of the YCL, all of whom had been in the Passaic strike. Clarence Miller, a tall, heavy-set, sandy-haired, studious-looking young man wearing glasses, was the first. He was a member of the National Committee of the League. His stay was brief, a few days only. He spoke at the strikers' meetings, and was photographed several times with strikers' groups. With him came his wife, Edith Saunders, from Passaic, a young woman of good education and some sophistication, who remained to help in organizing and educating the youth. Sophie Melvin, a remarkably pretty girl of nineteen years, sturdy, cheerful and cooperative, came to work with the children. Caroline Drew, Wag's secretary, remained to take charge of the relief, while Amy Schechter was put on publicity.

Amy and I got along well together in the dormitory. I had learned to appreciate her reasonableness, her courage, her humor and wit, her cheerfulness. Amy was a good sport. Ask her to get up at three in the morning and walk five miles—if it was for the good of the union or Party, she would do it.

Living in the boardinghouse was in itself something of an experience. There was a bathroom next door, but the tub was used as storage space for boxes, rags, and other nondescript items. In any case there was no hot water. Whatever bathing we did was at the not-too-clean cold water wash basin. It was also a little annoying, whenever I opened a bureau drawer, to find some piece of Amy's dirty underwear stuffed in there. She let her clothes accumulate and at rare intervals gave them out to a laundry in Gastonia.

Then it happened that Mary Heaton Vorse, who had decided to remain in Loray, notified me there was a vacancy in her place. A widow had a little house in the free land section right by the railroad tracks, a pleasant, normal home where I could have a good-sized room to myself, and there was a bathroom too. Breakfast and supper also were furnished for a modest price. Feeling that at last there was some hope of permanence in my domestic arrangements, I wrote my mother to send my summer clothes down. Seeing my old dress, my only dress, hanging out on the washline, the women thought, "Vera must surely be staying in bed."

Defense became once more a concern. Threats had been heard. We weren't going to have this new headquarters destroyed like the other. The strikers took great pride in this building erected by their own hands. They put up a new union sign outside. They also collected a number of guns, shotguns, and old rifles, which were stacked in a corner at the back. The national secretary recommended that we make a public announcement that we would defend our new headquarters.

Accordingly, after discussion with the strike committee, the following letter was drawn up and sent to the governor of the state. It was naturally publicized in the newspapers.

> National Textile Workers Union of America
> Gastonia Local
> May 16, 1929

Max Gardner
Governor of the State of North Carolina
Raleigh, North Carolina

Sir:

The textile strikers of Gastonia are building with their own hands new union headquarters to take the place of the one demolished by thugs while the state militiamen were looking on. The new building is about to be finished and the dedication will take place next Saturday evening, May 18, before thousands of workers.

It is rumored around Gastonia that enemies of the workers, inspired by the mill owners, are plotting to wreck our new headquarters within three days after completion.

The strike committee took the matter up today and decided that it is useless to expect the onesided Manville-Jenckes law to protect the life and property of the many striking textile workers of Gastonia. Every striker is determined to defend the new union headquarters at all costs.

> Very truly yours,
> Roy Stroud
> Chairman of Strike Committee

From time to time that spring we would hear or would read in the newspapers something of the strike in Elizabethton, Tennessee, which had started on March 12.

When we read in the papers on May 26 that a labor conciliator named Anna Weinstock was ending the strike by arbitration, we feared another sellout, and the staff in Loray made a quick decision: we would take the message of our union to those beleaguered strikers in Elizabethton.

The strike at Elizabethton was in some ways very different from our Loray strike. There were two rather new big mills in the little town, both controlled by German industrialists. German operatives had trained American help that came from the nearby mountain valleys. For most of the native workers this was their first factory job. Enough anti-German feeling survived from World War I for the workers to resent the foreign influence, accompanied as it was by a fifty-five-hour work week with average pay of ten to fifteen dollars a week. High rent and food costs took most of that.

The strike had started in one department with a walkout of girls who earned less than nine dollars a week. Within a few days the entire force of five thousand men, women, and youth in both plants had joined the strike. The rayon workers of Happy Valley, Tennessee, soon found that their patriotism was not shared by the business people of the town, nor by the state authorities, all of whom supported the German employers. Sweeping injunctions were issued by the Tennessee courts, depriving the workers of practically all their civil rights. When a circuit judge and a chancellor of the division appealed for soldiers, Governor Horton sent in no fewer than eight hundred militiamen with uniforms and materiel supplied by the federal army. Soldiers were everywhere, and strikers were arrested in large batches. They had gone back to work after a verbal settlement, and finding they had gained nothing, they walked out again on April 15. Governor Horton openly warned that state troopers would be used to protect the property of the corporation.*

On May 26 a small group including Dawson, two strikers, Beal, and me left Loray after the afternoon meeting. Cliff Saylors, one of the older men ("old" in Loray meaning above thirty-five), drove the car; the other striker was Bill McGinnis.

It was already after sundown when we reached Lake Lure in the foothills of the Appalachians. The placid surface of the lake reflected the afterglow, the ranges beyond appearing to float in the purple twilight. Had I known what it meant to cross the Smokies by night, with their unending hairpin turns, their steep slopes, I might have hesitated. With songs

---

*For details of the Elizabethton strike, see Tom Tippett, *When Southern Labor Stirs* (New York: Jonathan Cape and Harrison Smith, 1931).

and jokes we kept ourselves awake during that long night over a narrow bumpy road lit only by our headlights. By early morning, as we entered Happy Valley (so the place was misnamed) and the town of Elizabethton, every single person in the car was asleep, including the driver. We ran off the road and into a tree, but luckily the speed was low, and we experienced merely a jolt and some bruises.

The two big, new mill buildings dominated the town. The American flag was flying in the yards; there were machine guns and searchlights on the roof and armed guards posted around the buildings. The center of union activity was a large tent in a big, open field. The workers were also clotted about on the streets in angry discussion. We mingled; they didn't repel us, they listened, but they were in no mood for union propaganda. Although they didn't yet know the terms of the settlement, they were resentful and suspicious in view of their previous experience.

To our surprise we found Albert there. He and William F. Dunne, one of the Party leaders had come from New York by train. Mary Vorse also put in an appearance. There was scarcely a moment for Albert and me even to talk together; we all had to make the most of this critical day for union contacts.

Beal and the two strikers were on the platform in the tent; Beal brought the greetings of the Loray strikers, told a little of our strike, and urged the people to continue to fight for their demands and not to accept an agreement made without participation of the strikers. Beal's easy, simple way of speaking, his open sunburned countenance, his characteristic look of surprise made a good impression. I was wearing a green silk dress that I considered too grand for Loray and Mary Vorse criticized me. The dress was too conspicuous; I was being talked about as "the girl in green."

The next morning a table was set up in the street where the company was registering strikers to return to work. We made an unsuccessful attempt to prevent them from signing up. Seeing nothing more to be done, we started back to Gastonia.

Whether we had achieved anything was doubtful; workers betrayed by one union are not likely to rush into the arms of another. We had done what we could. The trip home was a holiday. Now we felt free for one day to enjoy ourselves, to breathe that sweet mountain air, to stop in a wooded spot and enjoy the stillness and to pick the mountain laurel then in full bloom. We would ask for a drink of water at some mountain cabin perched high on a hill with its cornfield so perpendicular we wondered how anyone managed to defy gravity enough to plow. The mountain people were friendly and hospitable, appeared glad to see us. At one place we were given a drink of buttermilk. Come evening, we took up our duties in Loray again.

I O

"God Save the State and Its Hon'rable Co't"

WHEN THE RENEWED ACTIVITY FOLLOWING THE EVICTIONS HAD SUBSIDED, WE surveyed our forces and realized that the number of strikers had considerably dwindled. With no less than a hundred and twenty-five notices issued, those evictions had been a body blow, forcing some people back into the mill, while other families simply drifted quietly away.

Our staff was now composed of organizers: Beal, Ellen Dawson, and me; relief: Caroline Drew; publicity: Amy Schechter; youth and children: Edith Saunders Miller and Sophie Melvin of the YCL; defense: Karl Reeve for the ILD. The staff was now looked upon with confidence, even with affection, by the hard core of strikers that remained. I was now being called Miss Vera, Southern style—the first name a real advance for these characteristically reserved people. Mr. Perishin', so popular in the old days, was never mentioned.

During this time two volunteers appeared who had hitchhiked down from New Jersey. One was Joseph Harrison from Lodi, who had taken part in the strike in the dye mill in 1926. Joe was a short, muscular, quiet, and thoughtful fellow with a whimsical smile. He was a loyal union and Party member, eager to help. The other was George Carter of Mizpah, New Jersey, who showed a Party card from Atlantic City. He was a very tall, raw-boned, black-haired fellow, who evidently had some education as his English was good. Beal sent Carter to apply for a job in the mill, but his Northern accent barred him, so both young men were assigned to guard duty and received strike relief.

Another newcomer was Paul Sheppard, a young divinity student on vacation from Duke University, who had come to Loray to see the strike,

216

felt a great sympathy for it, and decided to stay. I believe he was put up at the Lodges'.

Our slim forces were further reduced when Ellen Dawson's case came up. The authorities had intended to have Dawson deported as an undesirable alien; failing this, they succeeded in getting her extradited to New Jersey. Ellen had not been so active since her arrest; still it was something just to have her there. Now full of smiles, she bade us goodbye. I couldn't help thinking, did she have to be so completely joyful to get out of it? Could there not have been one moment of regret, one thought for those left behind? Every departure brought its trauma, where so few were willing to come. I used to have dreams at times of myself left all alone there, all other staff members having fled.

Activity continued; the committees were visiting the scabs and we never missed the daily mass meeting. Attendance on Saturday evening, when workers from other mills were in the habit of coming around, was always large—several hundred at times.

On May 30 Edith Saunders and Sophie Melvin organized a Decoration Day parade of children and youth. Picketing had been abandoned completely a couple of weeks earlier when lawyer Jimison had got an adverse decision on his action challenging the city ordinance forbidding parades. Not merely was the ordinance upheld, but Judge Hoyle Sink slapped on a fifty-dollar fine or a thirty-day jail or road penalty (polite for chain gang). This was a strong deterrent.

Though the children's parade walked in a direction away from the mill, this did not protect them from the deputies and police, who were soon upon them. Half a dozen boys and girls were arrested and held overnight in jail. Carrie Jones was attacked by several deputies, who twisted her arms and pulled her hair. She was not even a picket but had come to get her little boy out of the line.

I counted my chief advantage in Bessemer City to be the opportunity to get acquainted with the group of activists, especially their leader Ella Mae Wiggins. Little by little Ella Mae's personal history came out. She had grown up and had married Wiggins "back in the hills," bearing nine children in ten years; with the last birth "Pappy done tuk off." Ella Mae then left with her brood, coming to Bessemer City to work in the American Mill. The older children had to stay at home to care for the babies. The oldest, eleven-year-old Myrtle, took mother's place. "They couldn't get no schoolin'." Then had come that dreadful time when the children were all down with the croup. She had asked the bossman's permission to stay home to care for them; it had been denied. Four of the children had died. Now, with Cousin Charley's help, she was raising the remaining five.

Ella Mae Wiggins was a short, sturdy woman of about thirty, with broad cheekbones, clear hazel eyes, and bobbed light brown hair. She had the deep-toned, chesty voice often heard in Slavic women. There was something in her features and especially in Charley's that recalled a girl I used to know in the sanatorium, a native of Galicia, Poland. When I asked Ella Mae about her family origin, sure enough, that was it.

One day when I went down to Bessemer City there was excitement among the usually quiet people. There had been an attempt to poison Mrs. Wiggins' water supply. She lived with her children in a little shack at the outskirts of town, getting water from a nearby spring. That morning the water looked blue and had a chemical smell. A neighbor told of having seen a man there earlier. Though they hadn't used any of the water, the matter was very disturbing. Mrs. Wiggins came to Loray to report on it later in the day. Because of prowlers around the tent colony at night, the strikers had increased the guard. We were holding the meetings later now, taking advantage of the cooling off that accompanied the lowering sun. With June coming on, the heat of the day was great.

We were not so busy now; I could generally have a break in the afternoon for a nap or for sitting around talking with Mary Vorse in her room at our little boardinghouse.

Mary Vorse was a sophisticated person, a trusted sympathizer to whom I felt I could talk more or less freely. Often she referred to "Bobby" (Robert Minor, her former husband), and I think she felt some reflected glory in that association. She had a long history of association with radical causes. An air of self-pity, an apologetic manner were part of her under-stated personality. She was tall, slim, with sallow skin, thin brownish hair, and heavy eyelids. She had a gravelly voice.

We had meals at our little boardinghouse. Our landlady made soup, something almost unknown in Loray—who had time to make soup?—and she made delicious deep dish berry pies baked in a bread pan as they are in England.

All our hopes now centered on the people working in the Loray Mill, that fortress that loomed always in the background. We were working toward the second strike, the new wave, to pull out those inside whom I always hesitated to call scabs. Many had been brought from a distance, unaware of the strike. Even those who went back to work did so only under great pressure. Our committees reported many had signed cards even though armed guards were stationed inside and any known union man or woman was quickly rooted out. Finally Beal and the strike committee set a definite date, a Friday evening since that was pay night. Pledges had been given to come out if we would send a picket line to the gate to meet them. Of course, I was to lead that picket line.

I left the boardinghouse after supper that day, the seventh of June, to stroll down the unpaved street by the railroad tracks toward the headquarters. The mill was to my right, clattering away as usual, and to the left beyond some cottages were open fields and woods. With the sun already set the heat was tempered and the air was sweet with summer odors. Somewhere a radio wafted out a sentimental tune of the day, "Carolina moon keep shining, shining on the one who waits for me. . . ."

A couple of days before, Mary Vorse had taken me aside outside the headquarters to warn me of some trouble she was sure was brewing. "Something's going to happen, Vera," she said seriously. "And perhaps soon. I've been in so many of these situations, I can smell it. I smell danger here." I told her it had always been dangerous; we had been threatened from the beginning. She insisted this was something special. It is true there had been the attempt to poison Ella Mae Wiggins' spring; there had been the prowlers at night around the tent colony. The *Gazette* was running stories of terrible slummy conditions in the tent colony, intolerable they called them—a gross exaggeration. The strikers felt quite satisfied living there. They had generally improved in health, freed as they were from work, out of doors all day, and eating probably almost as well as usual. The strikers kept the tent colony in pretty good shape. They called it "New Town." As one went down the steep path from the union field, the first thing one saw was a table full of blossoming plants in tin cans. Two "streets" among the tents were named *Union* and *WIR*. The tents could hardly be worse than the shacks the strikers had called home before. But the *Gazette* was pressing to get rid of the tent colony and to drive out the organizers. And yet all this didn't seem to me more than the usual harassment.

Perhaps Vorse had really heard something, but I didn't feel disturbed, nor did I worry. But Mary Vorse was gone the next morning; she had left without saying goodbye. Karl Reeve and Clarence Miller had also disappeared. Still, what I was thinking that evening was of the picket line I would have to lead and of how I could persuade the people to come forward and join me.

It was our last meeting; I would never see Loray again after that night . . . but I must try to piece together the series of events that were to put an end to our strike, turning this tranquil, almost bucolic scene into one of violence, of terror, of bloodshed.

The crowd of one hundred or more people was as usual filling the field. The treetops beyond indicated the gully that was the tent colony. Beal was there, as well as the women staffers. We lost no time in opening the meeting. Paul Sheppard, the divinity student, was the first speaker. Gravely, he stressed that a serious action would take place tonight: everyone must listen carefully to the directions the speakers would give.

I spoke next. I told how the workers inside the mill were ready to come out to join us; we had been assured they would come out tonight. We must get together a fine picket line to go down to the mill to meet them at the gate. I had not been speaking long when suddenly a disturbance broke out in the farthest corner of the field near the gully. There were shouts, people milling about. Mary Vorse's warning came back; I thought, "This is it! They're trying to break up our meeting!" I saw our guards moving toward the back. Beal went there too. At one point there was the sound in the rear of a dull explosion. Some men were scuffling but I couldn't see what was happening. Now they began throwing missiles, but none hit me. I couldn't see what they were, but I heard them plopping against the building behind me. Then I heard sharper sounds. I kept on talking as loud as I could, telling about our picket line. People were turning their heads to look toward the rear, but no one left; the meeting didn't break up. The disturbance was quieting down as I kept on shouting. Beal came up toward the platform. The guards wanted me to get down, so I let Beal take over. He referred first to the disturbance and stressed that we wouldn't let anybody break up our meeting. "If you see anybody trying to start something, just bring them to me," he said, "and I'll take care of them." He urged people to join the picket line and go down to the mill. When he finished, I rounded up the pickets.

It was as usual just a small group of women, youth, and children. No men came forward. People began leaving the field to go home and everything was quiet now. I had hoped for this important occasion the men might join us. But not one stepped forward. It was disappointing. I doubted whether such a small line would be effective. Still, we had to go through with it. I got my pickets lined up. Gladys Wallace was there, and Mrs. Totherow and her son Henry, Ruby MacMahon, Jennie Harkness, Viola Hampton, Marie Hunsinger, Mrs. McGinnis, Mrs. Tompkinson and her fourteen-year-old son Earl, and a dozen or so others besides our staff women.

We started out in the direction of the mill in the beginning twilight, myself leading the line with Amy Schechter beside me, over the gravelly, bumpy dirt road between the woods and the last of the cottages. We hadn't gone far, not even to the railroad tracks, when three "laws" appeared coming toward us. And I thought, "It'll be the same old thing; they'll break up the line; we'll be arrested again." But no, it was quite different this time. One of the cops, a huge, burly man advanced toward me, cursing. His eyes were bulging, his face was red, he glared at me hatefully as he uttered those obscene words. Then he raised his arm and with his big hand grabbed me by the throat, squeezed it, and shook me.

If there is anything that can render a person helpless it is having one's wind cut off. You can't scream, you can't utter a sound, you can't think of anything but getting your breath back. The big brute continued to curse, squeeze, and shake me. I wondered, did he mean to kill me then and there? How long this lasted I can't say; it seemed long. When he let go, I found Amy still beside me. The cops had gone after the others. The women and children were scattering in all directions, the cops chasing them, meting out blows with their sticks as they ran. Tom Gilbert and another cop were dragging poor old Mrs. McGinnis on the ground by the hair and were hitting her. Amy helped me locate one of my shoes that had come off; I put it on and felt my neck, which was hurting. Gladys Wallace came up saying, "That was Bill Whitlow done that to you, Miss Vera."

We started back toward the headquarters. A car passed us loaded with cops some standing on the running board, guns in hand. Inside I saw Aderholt's black hat. I expected the car to be waiting when we reached the building, but it was not in sight. Edith Miller, Caroline Drew, and Sophie Melvin, who had been on the picket line too, joined us. We were all excited and talking about what had just happened.

We went into the office. Beal was there with a couple of strikers. It was getting dark inside. They already had the light on in the office. I sat down at the typewriter by the window and started to dash off a story for the *Daily Worker* about the breaking up of the picket line. I had written only a few lines when shots began to ring out outside. Someone said, "Put out the light." Another voice said, "Get down on the floor!" They were all crawling under the table, Beal last, his backside sticking out. I got down and crouched as the explosions continued. During those long moments, just seconds probably, I had a strange unaccountable sensation: I was acutely conscious of my *skin* all over my body. I was all skin. Perhaps it was the same reaction as that of the animal whose back hairs are erected in the presence of danger. The shots stopped; there were a few moments of silence. We didn't dare move. Then the sound of a car driving off. Silence again.

At last we got up and groped about, not venturing to put on the light, still holding our breath. Some of us went out into the big room, empty now. Beal and I looked out of the window. It was dark outside. At first it looked as though the field were completely empty. Then in the far corner near where the path went down to the tent colony we saw an arm in a white shirtsleeve raised, heard a faint cry. Beal went out with one of the strikers; between them they brought back Joe Harrison, white-faced and shaken, his shirtsleeve bloody. He had been hit in his right arm and thigh. A few people were standing around.

They got Joe into a car. I got in and Edith Saunders followed me. Not a word was said. I was thinking, "A comrade is wounded, bleeding, someone must stand by him." Edith and I sat on either side of Joe Harrison. A striker named Polson was driving. Joe didn't feel like talking. It was only a short run to the hospital, and we took him directly into a little emergency room. We stood by while a nurse got Joe onto a table, cut off his sleeve with a big pair of sheers, and dressed his arm. Then she said, "You'll have to leave now. I have to take his pants off." As we went out, through the open door of a room opposite we saw a big man lying under a sheet. White-faced, he appeared unconscious though he was groaning.

Polson, a thin little man, was nervous and visibly shaking. "I'll take y'all wherever y'all wants to go," he said, "but make it quick."

For an instant I felt completely disoriented. What to do? Where to go? We seemed to have come to the end of everything and in the first instant I could think of no place to go. Then the Lodges' house came to mind; it had often seemed a refuge. The man drove in a zig-zag, dropped us like hot potatoes, and took off at top speed. It was quite dark now. We found the front door open, a dim light in the back hall. The big house appeared to be empty. I hung my coat on a peg under the stairs. We didn't know what to do. Then another woman came in, perhaps Caroline Drew. We began to hear steps outside; there were voices and flashlights. It seemed the building was surrounded. Obeying some instinct of the pursued to hide, we stepped into the little butler's pantry between the kitchen and dining room and closed both doors. Then after a minute or so I said, "We'll have to be taken. We shouldn't be found hiding." So we went out into the back hall just as three "laws" came in, one of them holding a paper. He read out my name. I admitted being Vera Buch. He said, "You're under arrest."

"I just want to get my coat."

"Y'all won't need no coat where you're goin'."

I got the coat nevertheless. They motioned to Saunders and Drew, "Y'all come along too."

We got into a car with one of the cops and started off. I thought: "This is it now. It's what we always expected. We'll be driven out of town. And then . . .?" I was bracing myself for some unknown fate when a few minutes later I saw we were stopping at the city jail. So we were just being arrested after all! My relief was great, and the walls of the jail looked good to me that night.

We were put into a cell, one of two that were used Saturday nights for women pick-ups, mainly drunks and prostitutes. The cells were empty; ours was next to the big outside window, which overlapped the cell and corridor. The front was just bars. At one end opposite the window was a toilet; against the back wall was a bench. We sat down. It wasn't long before they brought in Amy Schechter; a little later Sophie Melvin. Amy said Beal had started out for Charlotte to see lawyer Jimison. At that moment we weren't looking ahead at all, nor did we speculate about what we hadn't seen, nor did we really know as yet what had happened. We were just living from moment to moment, completely absorbed in the tensions of the present.

We were at the beginning of a long night, a night unparalleled in my experience, in which more than once I was grateful for the protection of the jail walls. They kept bringing in women singly, or by two's and three's. Some they put in the next cell, others in ours. Beyond the wall that faced the two cells we kept hearing footsteps and the trampling of feet and the clanging of doors; we assumed the cells for the men were there. Voices were heard from the courtyard outside; soon there were many of them. We pictured a crowd swarming out there in the night.

As they were brought in, the women told of the manhunt and woman-hunt going on in Loray; people in the tents had taken refuge in the woods; anyone who had a car had gotten out the minute they heard the shots. It was a real reign of terror outside: cops and deputies everywhere arresting anyone they could lay their hands on. One woman came in weeping: they had taken both her and her husband, leaving three little ones crying at home. We tried to comfort her; the neighbors would surely hear and would take care of the children. We didn't talk much except when they brought in a new prisoner who would tell her story. One of them told us the chief and two cops had been shot.

Outside men were standing on each other's shoulders to look in the window at us—to get a look at those devils, those snakes, those Bolsheviks they had been reading about for two months in the Gastonia *Daily Gazette*. It was good I had my coat. I tied one sleeve to a bar, and with someone holding the coat up it gave us some privacy when one of us had to use the toilet. At one point we heard screams and thudding sounds from behind the wall. They're beating up the men, we told each other. They kept bringing in women. Our cell was full now, and probably the other was too; we couldn't see. We were all close together, some of us sitting on the bench, some squatting on the floor, others standing. The rumble of voices and scuffling of feet from the yard was getting louder and louder.

Now from outside I heard a loud voice saying, "You take this thing in your hand like this, and you go into the union hall or any other place, and you go like this." There was a swoosh, a click inside the corridor, a slight explosion; then our eyes began to smart and tear, our noses to run. My throat, still sore from the policeman's squeezing, felt raw, and the burning went down into my chest. We had been teargassed. Soon most of us were coughing. The noise outside grew even louder. Several times I wondered, is it possible they'll turn us over to the mob? I didn't believe they would, but I was glad to be inside.

We commiserated with each other, and there was a certain sustenance in our numbers. These women were the pick of the strikers; they were strong, brave people. We could only wonder what had really happened for each of us knew only what she had experienced alone. At long last in the early morning hours they ceased to bring people in; both cells were jammed full. The mob outside had finally dispersed. We realized we were weary, needing rest. We gave the bench to a pregnant woman among us. We were so crowded there was not room for all of us to lie down, so we curled up as best we could side by side on the cement floor, some squatting by the wall. It wasn't possible to stretch out even for a minute. We remained quiet, sleeping brokenly.

The next morning, as we were getting up unrefreshed from the floor, an officer came with two buckets of water and shoved one with a dipper into each cell. Later he brought bags of sandwiches, one apiece. Our discomforts were great, some of us nursing bruises from the cops' clubs, all of us still with sore eyes and mucous membranes from the teargas; the woman whose babies were left behind fretted. How long we would have to stay here was our principal concern. Sophie and Edith started some singing to cheer the strikers up; we staff kept our worries to ourselves. Saturday was a long, anxious, uneventful day. With evening came another bag of sandwiches.

But the next morning we heard a long, slow tolling of the church bells. And later the word leaked in that Chief Aderholt had died the night before. Two other cops had been shot too. As staff members, we knew we were in for something serious. And why was there no word, no sign from outside? Surely the news of the shooting must have been in the papers. Surely the ILD must have gone into action.

The day passed with no word of any sort.

Then Monday at one point we heard a commotion behind the partition; later we learned they had brought in Fred Beal. Day after day the sandwiches, the uneasy sleep at night bunched together on the cement floor. By day we took turns sitting on the bench. Our weariness increased, so too our hunger, and the discomforts of going unwashed, uncared for, never taking off our clothes. Each human body quickly accumulates its own particular odor. With ten people constantly in contact with each others' bodies. . . . There is, however, some moral support in the bond that is created by a suffering shared and identical. No one really complained. It all came to seem inevitable, since there was nothing we could do.

For me there was one break. One day—I haven't the slightest idea which day it was—the officer came and said I was to come out with him. We must have had some fruit that day at least, for I remember distinctly that I was eating an orange. I finished it as we went down the hall, and holding the orange peel in my hand, I felt embarrassed at my messiness when the cop took me into a room. A number of men sat around a big table. I was told to sit down.

"Your name is Vera Buch?"

"Yes."

"You are an organizer of the National Textile Workers Union?"

"Yes, I am."

"We want to get your permission to take down those tents that you have out there."

"I don't own those tents; they are the property of the strike committee. I can't give permission; I don't own them and have no authority over them."

"Take her back to the cell."

My answer was impromptu. As a matter of fact, since the International Workers Aid had put up the money for the tents, they probably had the ownership. We always thought of them as union tents or the strikers' tents. My way of clearing myself of responsibility and avoiding giving permission to take down the tents was probably as good as any.

We passed the interminable days with talk and with ballad singing. Gladys Wallace, whose voice was normally somewhat raucous, sang the entire ballad of Barbry Allen musically and with feeling. I remembered how my mother used to sing that ballad long ago. All of the women knew any number of ballads, most of them rather mournful . . . or was it the misery, the uncertainty, the worry of our circumstances that made them seem so?

How lustily we sang, all joining in, all crowded together as we were in that little cell, how much feeling we threw into each verse! Anything to forget for a moment our bodily aches and discomforts, above all our anxiety. For, as the days passed, still we were left entirely alone, seeing only the cop who twice a day brought sandwiches and water. I devised elaborate curses against the ILD and the Party—why in . . . didn't someone show up? What were they doing? Didn't they know we were being held in jail? We tried to keep cheerful. That we were being held incommunicado did not dawn on us, though we were experiencing the reality of this procedure every waking moment.

We were avoiding demoralization, though we sometimes felt like a pack of dirty, smelly, helpless, and forgotten animals. We had completely lost track of the days. Five days, a week? Surely it was a week, perhaps longer, when at last the cop opened the door, saying, "Y'all kin git out now. You and you," designating Schechter, Melvin, Drew, and me, "kin come with me. The rest of you kin go home." As the others ran down the hall, he led the four of us to a washroom where we could wash our hands and faces and smooth our hair. Then outside to be herded with a large group of the men prisoners into a police van. Edith Miller was allowed to go—why and where she went we hardly had time to consider.

Relief that the ordeal of the cage was over was paramount. The van jolted off. We had no inkling as to where we were being taken. If you were loading some hogs or beef cattle into a truck you wouldn't bother to notify them whether they were being transported to the feeding lot or the slaughterhouse, would you? We'd surmised it was to some other prison. We were all smiling to be together and out, but we were a sorry-looking lot. Our sunburn completely faded, pale, haggard, hollow-eyed, our clothing mussed, definitely thinner, all of us. The men had evidently been allowed to shave. Joe Harrison was not with us; I assumed he was still in the hospital. Beal said with his old grin, "Jimison thought I was in danger of being lynched. He told me, 'Get out of here as fast as you can.' So K. O. Byers and I headed south. We were near Greenville when they caught up with us. By the way, I got Owen out. Can you imagine a Negro organizer in this situation? I got some of the fellows to fetch him from his room. Jimison gave me the money, and they got him on a train for New York.

"When those cops caught us, they put us in jail overnight in Monroe, a little place. When we got near Gastonia, there were some cars following. The police thought they wanted to lynch me and escaped by making a detour."

McLaughlin's shirt had dark, dried stains; in his thatch of dark hair was a spot of dried blood. Bill McGinnis' shirt too had bloodstains. "They done cracked down on us good that first night," he said.

"Did you hear the chief died? Where does that leave us?" Fred whispered to me as we got out of the wagon.

It proved to be a legal hearing that we were taken to in Charlotte, a habeas corpus hearing. Only later, too, did we find out that this hearing was held on Friday, June 14, which would make it a week that we were held in the city jail. Judge Harding presided. Major Bulwinkle, the same attorney for the mill owners who handled the eviction cases, was present, apparently leading the prosecution forces. Tom Jimison and Attorney J. K. Flowers, his associate, were there. We were glad to see Joe Harrison, who was there with his right arm in a sling. Reporters and photographers were present. There were probably some legal proceedings, but what I recall most is that Amy Schechter was questioned at some length as to whether she believed in God. She was clever in evading direct answers to their questions, and she avoided admitting she wanted a Russian form of government by stating she believed in government by the majority of the population, who were workers and farmers. Under pressure, however, she did admit she didn't believe in God or a supreme being. Man controlled his own destiny, she said.

Then back into the paddy wagon and to Gastonia, this time to the county jail, a large building on a square which also contained the city jail and the courthouse. It was on this square that the mob had gathered the night of June 7. Men and women prisoners were separated. The men left with the jailer, while we four women (Amy Schechter, Sophie Melvin, Caroline Drew, and me) followed a policeman upstairs. We were locked into a cell opposite the one in which Schechter and the women strikers and I had spent that night for picketing—so long ago it seemed now.

We inspected our new premises. The cell was a large rectangle, perhaps eighteen feet long and twelve wide, with four large heavily barred windows. One end of the cell was partitioned off with a toilet and wash basin inside. In the other corner at that end were half-partitions enclosing a cold water shower. In the fourth wall was the entrance, a door of heavy vertical bars. I went around feeling the window bars; their coldness filled my hands; there was no doubt of their strength. The windows also had a grating behind the bars which darkened the room. The sole furniture in the cell was four narrow cots, each equipped with a mattress and a folded blanket, reasonably clean. After our previous incarceration, this big cell for four seemed almost luxurious. We could move around freely, walk, sleep on beds!

The excitement of the morning and the novelty of a new location buoyed us for a while. There had to come a letdown, and it came when, seated on our cots in the quiet of that wing, surrounded by those heavy bars, we became aware above all of our isolation. In the days since the shooting, no word, no token had reached us from the outside. Where was Albert, the ILD, Wagenknecht, and others who should have helped? What had happened? Were they also in jail? Nothing had been explained to us.

The following day we had company in the cell opposite. They brought in some women strikers who had been with us in the city jail. What they were there for now they didn't know any more than we knew why we were being held. They made things lively with songs and talk, but the next day they were taken out.

The following day the jailer came into the cell to announce, "Miss Drew, you're free. You don't have to stay here any more. You may leave now." Overjoyed, we bade Caroline goodbye. When she had made her smiling exit, the three of us began to wonder on what grounds she had been released. She was involved as a staff member, and while she generally kept close to the office, still she had picketed that last day. She had mentioned in the confidences of those two days that she was born in Alabama, of a well-to-do family. A Southern girl . . . Was it Southern chivalry that had set her free? This hardly seemed likely. We wondered, too, why Edith Miller was not among us. The reason for Drew's release remained a mystery. After Caroline Drew had left, as we sat together in the silence the three of us became keenly aware that we were not going to be let out. Whatever the fate awaiting us, there would be no escape.

A few days later there were shuffling footsteps coming down the corridor, then a man appeared at the door who said he was Charley, the trusty, a shabbily dressed, good-natured fellow with a look of surprise on his sallow, unshaven face. "Does y'all want somethin' from the outside I kin git y'all?" We pooled some of our resources to order towels, soap, and a few other necessities. At last to get under a shower and to feel once more clean, even though we had to get back into the same dirty clothes!

It soon became apparent too that we had one great advantage here, a friendly jailer. The youngish sheriff Tom Hanna was like ourselves a Northerner, coming from Rhode Island. He spoke our language and it looked as though he had taken a liking to us. He would spend many a half hour standing outside the door conversing with us. Amy did most of the talking. Unless my memory is playing a trick, Tom Hanna bore a surprising resemblance to Humphrey Bogart. He used to refer to us as "the girls," and visited us almost daily. His wife came too once in a while: we took advantage of her friendliness to get some things we didn't want to ask the trusty to get, such as underwear, Kotex, and such.

Food is important where life is so empty. Our meals were completely alike six days a week. Breakfast at seven: the trusty appears with a cart; three bread tins, not too clean, are handed in. Each contains a couple of stale biscuits resting in a layer of mixed pork grease and Georgia cane syrup. Tin cups of hot, brown, never-identified liquid. Dinner at noon: similar bread tins containing an ample portion of stewed red pinto beans with a small cube of boiled "meat" (fat sowbelly) and a spoon. Supper between six and seven: a square of cornbread and a cup of buttermilk. There were seconds on the buttermilk, which we often took. It arrived in a big tall can fresh from the farm—thick, with bits of butter in it. The cornbread was not the sweetened fluffy kind one makes at home; it was heavy, soggy, greasy. Still, the supper was filling and nutritious enough. Sundays the dinner was stew-beef with rice and gravy, a delicious break in the monotony. Such meals are no doubt the diet of poor whites in the South. For a jail it was good food.

The lack of cleanliness in the cell bothered us. The former inhabitants had apparently been snuff-users, for the walls up to about five feet were spattered with brown spots. The floor too was dirty. With cooperation of jailer and trusty we obtained a broom, a scrubbing brush, and a large washtub of water. Taking turns, we spent a whole day at scrubbing the place up. Then Charley got us some orange crates to serve as tables and shelves, and a length of cord which, attached across the corner and tied to the window bars, was a clothesline. The place was cleaner. One thing, however, couldn't be scrubbed away: the jail smell, that unique, indefinable combination of stale, repulsive odors which, strange to say, is the same in all jails, North and South. We couldn't afford pillows and sheets and didn't really feel the need of them. After the ordeal of the cage, to be able to rest on a bed was enough for us.

When we indicated to the jailer that some reading material, especially newspapers, would be welcome, he informed us we weren't allowed to have newspapers or current magazines but he would try to scrape up some old periodicals. So Charley came with a stack of *Ladies Home Journal's*, *Collier's*, *True Love*, *True Confessions*, and similar pulps. We spent a week or more lying on our cots stupefying ourselves with the sort of stuff we would never look at outside.

After perhaps a week or ten days in the cell, the jailer came in holding a document, which he proceeded to read aloud. Fifteen people including ourselves were listed as having "willfully, wrongfully, unlawfully murdered and conspired to murder the Chief of Police of Gastonia, O. F. Aderholt." First-degree murder and conspiracy were the charges. Strange and unexpected was our reaction to this rather lengthy document. It seemed just awfully funny; as we sat listening on our cots we laughed; so did the jailer. I suppose most of all what was involved was the defense reaction of the mind when receiving a blow. To absorb the reality at once is too great a shock; the mind creates a shield to protect itself. We continued to make jokes after the jailer left. We had ample time thereafter to absorb all the implications of that document.

The most pressing and immediate worry of those first weeks was the failure to receive any word or token whatever from the outside. What in the world had happened? I told the women then what I hadn't mentioned before, Albert's confidential description of his position in the Party. He might have been ousted from his post in the union by that time. But what of the ILD, the WIR? Had everything collapsed? The most likely explanation appeared to be that a few people had come down to help, had been arrested themselves, and were being held in a jail somewhere else, perhaps in Charlotte. That no strikers tried to contact us we could understand: they would only risk being involved themselves.

Nevertheless, as the days piled up into weeks the feeling of loneliness, of isolation and abandonment grew and grew. In the cage, miserable as it was, there had been a certain sustenance in being closely surrounded by so many other people. That we were the leaders of the strike meant a certain responsibility for us; we had to think always of keeping up the others' spirits, and thereby we sustained our own. Here in this big locked cell, enclosed by thick walls and bars of heavy steel, seeing only Charley, the jailer, and occasionally the wife, we three sat alone, abandoned it seemed by the whole world.

It was at night in the wakeful darkness, with the light outside casting the stark shadow of the bars across cots and floor, that the stern realities of our situation pressed on me most. Sophie, nineteen years old, slept well. She did have a habit of grinding and gnashing her teeth in her sleep, an eerie sound in those surroundings. One night from Amy's cot I heard a quiet sobbing. Should I get up, try to comfort her? I decided not to. Were it I, out of pride I'd rather not be found weeping. And couldn't we all weep? Hadn't we all loved ones far away, infinitely remote they seemed now?

The cell opposite us housed temporary occupants picked up for "vagrancy" (for prostitution), "caught with a man under a tree" (for drunkenness), etc. We managed some communication back and forth, hearing their stories and occasionally singing together.

One day in the weary silence came a new sound from downstairs, where the jailer and his wife lived. A rich baritone on record, faint but clear, singing "The Water Boy."

> Water boy, where is yuh hidin'?
> If yuh don' come, gwine tell-a yoh mammy.
>
> Dere ain't no hammer dis side o' de mountain
> Dat ringa like mine, boys, dat ringa like mine.
>
> Done bust dis rock, boys, from here to Macon,
> Way back to de jail, boys, way back to de jail.
>
> You jack o' diamonds, you jack o' diamonds,
> I knowed you of old. . . .
>
> Done robba mah pocket, done robba mah pocket
> Done robba mah pocket of silver and gold.
>
> Water boy. . . .

How strange it sounded, how poignant, how unforgettable! The same voice sometimes also sang "Old Man River," that rich expression from the poorest of the poor.

During the period of isolation, when time hung heavy on our hands, talking was our chief recourse. Our talks ranged far and wide, so that sometimes we could even forget for a moment where we were, coming back with a jolt to the grim reality. We became thoroughly acquainted with one another, and we got along very well. I cannot recall a single instance of a quarrel or even a misunderstanding. Sophie was stockily built, a small young woman with a cherubic, pretty face. She had a rosy complexion, curly brown hair, and big blue eyes. Her appearance belied her character; she was sturdy and tough as anyone, insensitive in a way; still, to conceive of this little angel as a murderer would always make us laugh. We thought she would be an asset facing a jury. Her parents were born in Russia. She had got into the movement early, into the Pioneers, and from there had moved up to the YCL. These young people would rent an apartment together, girls and boys, and their relations were more or less promiscuous, though Sophie had a "steady" at the present time. I recalled that the YCL people used to live similarly in Passaic; I had been in their apartment and used to wonder sometimes who slept with whom.

Amy Schechter, about thirty-seven, was born in England, her father an Oxford professor. Her childhood had been spent in a refined, cultured, rather prim environment. She told of the fluffy white dresses with blue ribbon sashes she and her sister used to wear on Sundays. Amy was a graduate of Barnard College and had spent some time working for the labor bureau in London. From her English days she had a stock of songs with a Cockney accent:

> Oh girls, oh girls, take warning and never let it be.
> Never let a sailor go higher than your knee.

How she had got into the movement was not accounted for. We were all such disciplined dyed-in-the-wool comrades that it hardly seemed necessary to explain. She had been living with her husband in Chicago, sharing a house with Earl Browder, a prominent Fosterite I knew by sight and reputation only. Amy's devotion and admiration for Earl Browder were complete.

In the field Amy had proved her worth, her staunchness, her courage, her capacity to endure hardships. Now in jail she enlivened our talks with witty remarks. I had become accustomed to her little peculiarities. She refused to comb her hair, which was long and a hopeless mass of tangles. She liked to brush it, she said, but she had no brush. All of us had only

one dress apiece, which had been worn continuously at the start for over
a week. After a while I began to understand Amy's sloppiness: to be well-
educated, to come from a background of refinement and culture were not
assets in our movement. No doubt she just wanted to appear proletarian.

At last, after what seemed an interminable period, we had visitors.
Juliet Stuart Poyntz, representing the ILD, and Jimison were admitted to
our cell. Poyntz was her usual poised and confident self though she looked
rather pale and tired. Her story was: On June 8 the *New York Times* had
carried a small item on the shooting. The Party had alerted the ILD,
which had sent down to Charlotte a small group consisting of Albert
Weisbord, Jack Johnstone, and her. Gastonia had been in a state of siege,
guarded by hundreds of troopers as well as by police and deputy sheriffs.
To get in there was difficult, and when she did get in on the tenth, the
authorities refused her permission to see the prisoners—and so it had continued.

The ILD was mobilized; defense was being prepared, publicity put
out; we didn't need to worry; we would be taken care of now. And much
union activity was going on, she said. She was evasive about Albert, saying only that he had gone back to New York. As they left, Poyntz gave
me one of her penetrating, enigmatic looks. She seemed to feel sorry for
me. Was she thinking, poor Buch, you're really in a spot now? Or was it
that old thing of her knowing more than I, something about the Party,
about Albert perhaps? And now, withal the relief that our isolation was
at last broken, I had the added worry as to what had become of my
husband.

With Poyntz's help I later got back my little suitcase containing only
my clothes. The police had raided the room where I stayed and had taken
everything. I had kept a little diary of the strike and some notes on
language characteristics of the South, things of value to me. My papers
were never returned, but at any rate it was now possible to have the
pleasure of more than one dress.

From now on our dull routine was enlivened by visitors and our Spartan conditions alleviated by some amenities. The next Sunday our friend
Mr. Cohen from Charlotte came with some members of his family, bringing us big chicken dinners with ice cream and cake, a favor to be repeated
every week. Ingratitude must be inborn in the human race. Were we
overjoyed to have this dinner? Of course; much more than the dinner we
were warmed by the human contact. And at the same time I for one
secretly wished we could have the chicken some other day to relieve the
six-day beany monotony. I did like the Sunday stew beef with rice and
gravy, which from now on I missed.

We could now have papers and reading material, letters, and an occasional caller. From time to time I received letters from Ella Mae Wiggins simply enclosing a new poem she had written. These I at once dispatched to the *Daily Worker*. Then came a letter from my mother. I had written to her from Loray and to my father too, emphasizing the dreadful conditions of the Loray workers. Papa had answered me at the time, his letter ending with this statement: "I appreciate what you are doing, but *get out of Gastonia.*" Mother's letter began, "I never thought I would have to write to my daughter in a jail." Poor Nellie, a daughter in jail must have seemed to her the ultimate disgrace. Still she remained loyal; my parents did not abandon me.

When I wrote Mother, I asked her to send me materials and findings for a dress. In time came a piece of blue linen and one of green silk, a pattern, sewing thread, needles, and scissors. With them I whiled away some hours sewing, making myself two new dresses.

One important visitor was Attorney Leon Josephson of Trenton, New Jersey, a Party member and one of the defense lawyers. Josephson interrogated us in great detail regarding the events of June 7; in preparing our case he had to determine a line of defense, summon witnesses, and so on. He was the only one who questioned us. He intimated there was some ongoing controversy in New York over the line of defense, especially over whether or not to admit and defend the Communist background of the strike. We whose lives were at stake had nothing whatever to say about it. Nor were we really informed on the progress of our case except what Josephson told us and what we could divine from the occasional *Daily Worker* that drifted our way.

Finally in July came a letter from my husband from some place in Connecticut stating merely that he had been working on a farm and would come down to see me in a couple of weeks. At last we had a reunion in the cell sitting side by side on my cot. Albert was thinner and looked strained in spite of his joy at our reunion. Even though in his last visit he had given some intimation of the deplorable conditions in the Party, it was still shocking to learn what had really happened.

It was he who had first seen the notice of the shooting in the *New York Times*; it was he who had alerted the Party. Two groups had gone down to Charlotte, first Albert with Jim Reid of Providence, Rhode Island (president of the NTWU), and Ellen Dawson (a vice president of the union). The other group consisted of Poyntz, Jack Johnstone, Bill Dunne, Paul Crouch, Wagenknecht, and Walter Trumbull. In Charlotte, Albert had wanted to try at once to get into Gastonia, but he was overruled. Then a telegram had come from the Central Committee: he was to return immediately to New York under pain of expulsion. "What could I do, Vera?" he asked. "This was the hardest thing I ever did in my life, to leave then. But alone in Charlotte I could have done nothing."

This was not all. He had been literally and physically ejected from the office of the National Textile Workers Union. "Just think, the union I founded and built. Four people came in, Fosterites I suppose, and literally pushed me out. I couldn't call the police against Party members. Yes, these goons were comrades. They have all the records now.

"The Party is on the verge of splits following involvement with the Russian factions. All the leaders are in Moscow fighting for their political lives. I don't know whether I'm still a Party member or not; they're not speaking to me in New York. So I got this job. It was good to work hard out of doors; it was good to have a job that didn't carry a hundred worries per square inch. Very low pay—three dollars a week. Farmer tried to withhold it. I don't know what I'll do now. Probably get another job. And I can't help you, Vera. I admire your courage. I know you'll be able to carry on." We had to part having not the least idea of when or where we would meet again.

I didn't know whether the other women had heard what Albert had to say; he had spoken in low tones. And when he left they didn't say anything. For me there was a feeling of disgrace in what had happened, though surely I could not blame Albert. We women hadn't discussed the Party factional situation; it was in fact too unclear for discussion. And now began for me a feeling of isolation in relation to my comrades where before there had seemed to be unity.

In the earlier period of being incommunicado, Amy, Sophie and I had never squarely faced our situation as prisoners, keeping our forebodings to ourselves and joking openly about being murderers. Now, especially after Josephson's visit, we began to discuss our position more realistically. Was there any possibility of acquittal? To all of us it seemed unlikely. We knew too well what sort of territory we were in, what prejudice had been stirred up. People were really thirsting for our blood.

But on the other hand would they succeed in convicting us? Were we really facing the electric chair? Here I felt the prosecution had overreached itself in indicting fifteen people. With two or three they might have succeeded, as had been done so many times before. But fifteen? They were now beginning to learn, since our defense was building up, that we had broad support. Through Charley we learned that Beal was receiving telegrams from various organizations in the USA, even some from abroad. No, the most probable outcome would be long jail sentences.

Some things read during this period induced more pessimistic reactions. A pamphlet on the Mooney and Billings conviction in California gave me some gloomy private hours. These two poor men had, it was proven, been nowhere near the alleged crime; they had plainly been framed up. And what of Sacco and Vanzetti similarly convicted? The conspiracy charge against us was a palpable frame-up; there had been nothing of the sort. But the fact remained that Aderholt had been shot on our premises and that he had died of his wounds. We women had been inside the buildings; so had Beal, but most of the defendants had been outside during the shooting and some had fired guns. Inexperienced and ignorant as we were in legal matters, we thought then simply in terms of either conviction or acquittal for all fifteen. I was not always optimistic. There were times when awake at night shudderingly I tried to face the threat of my own unwilling and violent exit from this world.

Then I read the poignant story of Vera Figner's life and imprisonment. Here was something that really hit home. If it came, I would have to bear it; there would be no getting away from it, but I thought of Christ in Gethsemane—I had no one to pray to, having learned long ago that prayer is just the wish of the human being in extremity, and in that sense I could echo the prayer in that old story.

Now that we were allowed communication, we kept in touch with the men prisoners via the trusty.

One day Beal sent word by Charley that his pants were worn out; they had holes in them. What should he do? I sent back word: Don't worry, Fred, I'll make you a pair of pants. So from scraps of material left from my blue linen dress, I cut and sewed up a doll-size pair of pants. I stretched this task over a week, sending news of it every day. Then I made a big package stuffed with newspaper and conveyed the "pants" to Beal. With such deadly parlor tricks did the "murderers" while away their leisure hours.

When once in a while a *Daily Worker* reached us, we would look for news of the Party situation and would find little indeed. The editor was now William F. Dunne from Minneapolis, a Fosterite. There were, however, occasional mentions of our own case, some rather sensational. In one piece we were referred to as the "Gastonia martyrs." This we resented. Are not martyrs people who have died for a cause? Did they consider us as good as dead? What kind of augury was this for the defense that would soon have to be made? There were other references to the danger of lynching for the Gastonia prisoners. It had never occurred to us except on that first night to fear mob action. We felt safe enough in our cell.

Still, when a couple of days later we heard sounds in the street like people marching from a distance, shouts, then the thud of footsteps coming closer, we began to feel uneasy. We asked ourselves what we could do if a mob came. Outside our door to the right was an unused staircase leading upward. If we could rush up that staircase . . . but how could we possibly do that while the mob was opening the door? We were really joking; at the same time the tumult of a crowd was coming close, my heart was beating faster, and I had a brief moment of apprehension. Then suddenly a band began to play some patriotic tune. We learned later the "mob" was a patriotic parade.

Finally the date of the trial was set: July 29. It was not far off. Our long uncertainty ended, our days became exciting, taken up not merely by visitors but by a turmoil of emotion: anxiety underlying relief and anticipation of a change, no matter what it might be.

A reporter came to photograph us. Her chief interest seemed to be: what were we going to wear at the trial? We smiled, looking at our mussed, soiled attire. Then came Juliet Poyntz with boxes full of clothes for us . . . better clothes than any one of us was accustomed to wear. How quickly our human interest in attire revived! Fell to my lot a lovely sheer wool lavender suit and a white knitted dress and jacket with red and black trimming.

The great day came. I in the blue linen dress I had made, Amy and Sophie in their new outfits, we were escorted by the jailer across the courtyard. I had so looked forward to getting out but now how glaring was the sunlight, how weak my legs! And what was this strange sensation of walking on eggs as we crossed the cobblestone pavement?

We were taken by a side door into the courthouse. Inside the courtroom we were turned over to an usher, who led us to our places in a long row of seats up front facing the judge's bench and reserved for the prisoners. The seats for visitors were filled. Many mill workers, some of them our strikers, were present in the courtroom. We learned later that there were black workers among the crowds on the sidewalk in front of the courthouse. In those days of strict segregation they were not admitted inside. About thirty reporters and magazine writers had a place on the platform to the right. Batteries of lawyers for the prosecution and the defense were at their separate tables.

The scene was a colorful one, with women in their light summer dresses, the Southern lawyers togged out in white linen suits with a flower in each buttonhole. The sheriff then led in the row of men prisoners. Among them to my surprise was Clarence Miller. We had heard nothing about his being there. Judge Barnhill, young, dignified, and serious, took his place and the usher opened court with the statement we were to hear so often thereafter: "Oyez, Oyez, Oyez! The co't of the State of No'th Ca'lina is now in session! God save the state and its hon'rable co't." Then came the roll call of the sixteen defendants. Having given my response, I could relax to enjoy the spectacle of the crowded room, with myself and my comrades the center of attention. Having every expectation of remaining a prisoner, I made an effort to overcome the feeling of unreality and to live fully this brief moment of freedom.

As we learned later, up to the very morning of the opening of court no indictment had been prepared, no grand jury had met on the case. Only hastily that morning before court opened had the grand jury got together to produce the indictments in relation to Aderholt's death and the shooting of police officers and one plainclothesman. The haste of the whole procedure would appear to confirm that the prosecution felt certain of obtaining an indictment . . . it was as good as guaranteed in advance.

This first trial of the "Gastonia case," as it came to be known, lasted two days. Governor Max Gardner himself had ordered a special term of court to sit at Gastonia. It turned out to be more a hearing than a trial. The defense moved for a change of venue, which had to be substantiated by evidence.

The prosecution presented one hundred and fifty affidavits to support the possibility of a just trial in Gaston County. The defense had one hundred affidavits. Our lawyers read selections from twenty-four issues of the Gastonia *Gazette* and reviewed episodes of violence. Following is a typical example of the sort of stuff the *Gazette* had been printing every day:

> The blood of these men cries out to the high heavens for vengeance. This community has been too lenient with these despicable curs and snakes from the dives of Passaic, Hoboken and New York. For weeks and weeks we have put up with insult and injury; we have tolerated their insults and abuses. Our officers have taken unspeakable abuse from these folks day after day. We have put up with it, hoping that they would wear themselves out, although fingers were twitching to get at them. The blood of these officers shot down in the dark from behind cries aloud. This display of gang law must not go unavenged.*

Recently the *Gazette* had begun to change its tune. On July 23 an editorial had stated: "Southern cotton mill men might as well realize that they must get ready to treat with union labor or be forever embroiled in labor troubles and strikes." Such a statement was probably related to the efforts of the prosecution to keep the trial in Gaston County.

Among the defense affidavits documenting the terrorization of defense witnesses was a typical one from Viola Hampton, a striker. Viola

---

*Gastonia *Daily Gazette*, June 8, 1929.

swore she knew the man who fired the shot that killed Aderholt the night of June 7 but was afraid to testify because she had been warned by several persons she would spend the rest of her life in jail if she appeared in court.* There was evidence of much such terrorization of possible witnesses, including efforts on the part of the mill owners to drive out all strikers from the vicinity.

At one point I was called upon to testify how, in the crowded cell on the night of June 7, with the mob outside, I had heard from behind the partition sounds of scuffling, blows, and a scream. After hearing all the evidence, Judge Barnhill said he would take the defense motion under advisement. Finally court adjourned. Following the adjournment all sixteen defendants were escorted out behind the courthouse to be photographed.

We managed during the day to contact the strikers in the courtroom. Let me quote here from a letter I wrote to Mary Vorse at the time:

> I wish you had seen the spontaneous demonstration of the union members in the courtroom. At every recess of the court they flocked around us and nearly ate us up in their joy at seeing us.†

The following day the change of venue to Charlotte in nearby Mecklenburg County was granted. Automatically by North Carolina law this meant a delay of at least twenty days, giving more time to prepare the case.‡ As a matter of fact, Charlotte was also a mill-dominated town, but perhaps less hysterical than Gastonia.

Then came an unexpected move of the prosecution. Solicitor Carpenter got up to say the state was not asking for the death penalty for the three women. Was it to Southern chivalry we owed this sudden magnanimity? In any case, the result was that we three were now admitted to bail.

The ILD issued the following statement in the name of Amy Schechter:

> We object to any favored treatment on account of our sex. The others are no more guilty than we and if we are released on bail, they should also be released. We do not regard the change of venue or any of the gestures of the prosecution as any sort of guarantee that we will have a fair trial.

---

*ILD release, July 3, 1929.

†Dated Aug. 1, 1929, Gaston County jail. From personal papers, Mary Heaton Vorse, Labor History Archives, Wayne State University, Detroit.

‡New York *Telegram*, July 30, 1929.

Our bail was set at $5,000 each, and such a sum could not be raised locally. The American Civil Liberties Union in New York applied to the Garland Fund, which granted the necessary $15,000.* Because it was not till August 3 that bail was posted, the jail was our hotel for the remaining few days. I remember Poyntz asking us whether we three could go on a speaking tour together. Amy answered, "Vera is the only one who can carry a meeting."

The trial in Charlotte was set for August 26, about three weeks away, and a speaking tour for the defense was considered the best use of the time for us. As soon as possible we set out for New York.

---

*The Garland Fund was set up in the 1920s as the result of a donation of a million dollars to socialist and radical causes by a socially-minded millionaire named Garland. Norman Thomas was on the board of the fund, as well as a few Communists.

I I

A Tissue of Vague Allegations

HOW CLEAR, HOW PROUD IS THE MEMORY OF THAT MEETING IN CENTRAL Opera House, New York City, on August 12, 1929! Going up the side aisle I received applause, and again as I appeared on the platform. There were other speakers, men representing the ILD and WIR which shared the auspices with the NTWU, but I believe I was considered the principal speaker. Fully confident and in control of the situation, my voice clear and ringing, I could make myself heard by the many hundreds of people in the great hall.

I had chosen to speak of what was then known in the Party as the "Third Period," supposedly an epoch when the masses everywhere were surging forward against capitalism, as illustrated in the Gastonia strike. I also made a plea on behalf of the Gastonia prisoners:

> We say, if it should happen that things go badly through this coming month, and if we're not strong enough to defeat the frame-up, and if it is necessary for us to pay the penalty for the fight, we will pay it. We are ready.
>
> But it is for you to give your answer. It is for you to say: "We must not pay the penalty." We want to be free. We want our lives to give the service of the working class. It is up to you to show by your strength that the State of North Carolina dare not convict us. It is up to you to say that there shall not be one electrocution, not one prison sentence, not one day or week in prison for any of the defendants.

Following me, Amy Schechter gave a short talk; people came up on the platform to hear her better. She told earnestly of the terrible conditions in Loray.

A happy surprise it was to look over the audience and spot my own father in the ranks. I believe Papa felt some pride in his daughter as we met later . . . a strange experience for a parent to see the quiet, studious nestling suddenly fledging out into some sort of eaglet daring the skies. This I could only surmise, for Papa didn't say much.

The New York meeting was a high point of my speaking tour and, alas, it is the only meeting which I can truthfully say I recall. Vaguely, very vaguely comes back a poorly attended gathering in a small hall in Chicago (this one the *Daily Worker* had heralded as a "tremendous mass meeting" to be held at the Ashland Auditorium).

Strange and disquieting it is to read in the newspapers items concerning Gastonia defense meetings ranging far and wide, with the women defendants as speakers. The Charlotte *Observer* of August 11 carried a description of a meeting at which Vera Buch and Amy Schechter spoke in Washington, D.C. The Pittsburgh *Sun Telegraph* of August 18, 1929, recounts how Vera Buch, "New York college woman," spoke in Labor Lyceum, 35 Miller Street, about the Gastonia strike. Coal miners whom I knew were present, yet not one iota of this event can I bring to mind. The *Daily Worker* of August 14 stated that Buch and Schechter would tour eighteen more cities after the New York meeting: Paterson and Passaic, N.J.; Allentown, Pittsburgh, and Philadelphia, Pa.; Pawtucket and Providence, R.I.; New Bedford, Fall River, and Lawrence, Mass., were among the towns later reported where "vast crowds" greeted the women defendants. Not one shed of recollection of all this activity survives. I do not even know if I saw my husband during this period. The "Third Period" as a speech topic sounds more like Albert's choice than mine; I believe he wanted me to appear as a political person, no mere trade unionist.

For most of the happenings and background of Gastonia my recall is good; in some cases, as in the events of June 7, it is excellent. Other circumstances come back when I read of them. Then comes this baffling lacuna. A psychiatrist friend tells me such memory lapses may be due to deep psychological trauma.

For Albert all personal aspects of life during that summer and fall are obliterated; he recalls only the political developments, and certainly his trauma was great, perhaps even greater than mine. Never before had brutal gangster tactics been used against comrades in the U.S. (During the strikes in the garment and fur trades in New York, thugs had been hired by Communist organizers against scabs, but these were justified since the scab was seen as an enemy.) Stalin's tactics in Russia were to culminate in liquidation (cold-blooded murder) of many thousands of Party leaders and hundreds of thousands of people, not merely in Russia but in other countries. Trumped-up charges, slander, torture, farcical trials became the order of the day there.

The ouster of Weisbord from the NTWU office was part of a campaign in the U.S.A. against all elements who failed to line up behind Foster in support of Stalin; the dissenters were then ostracized, slandered, branded as "renegades," and driven out of the Party. Whereas I in my difficult moments had the companionship of workers and fellow staff members, Albert alone had to think of his wife in a far-away jail facing a possible death sentence. He asks himself today . . . what was I doing then, where did I go, how did I make a living? There is no answer.

I can at least clarify some aspects of the shooting as well as its aftermath locally in Gastonia and elsewhere. People at once began comparing the Gastonia shooting with the case of the IWW in 1919 in Centralia. Correspondents wrote about the "raid on the union headquarters," the "forced entry into the union hall." At no time that evening did the police try to get into the union hall. Nor did they "attack" or "destroy" the tent colony. It was of course very difficult for reporters to get at the truth. After the shooting on June 7 Roy Stroud, chairman of the strike committee, with his family and Will Truet, secretary of the Loray local, were able to get away because they had cars. Striker Polson, the man who drove Joe Harrison, Edith Miller, and me to the hospital and then took Miller and me to the Lodges' house, may also have escaped, as his name did not turn up in any reports. Paul Sheppard, who was not arrested on June 7, probably got away then but returned to activity later.

A slim, blue-eyed seventeen-year-old named J. C. Hefner, who was on guard duty that Friday, had been in the strike only a few days when the shooting occurred. He wanted to hop a freight afterward, but fell asleep by the railroad tracks with his gun beside him. There he was arrested and brought before Major Bulwinkle, who tried to get Hefner to promise to testify he had heard Beal say, "Shoot and shoot to kill." Bulwinkle threatened him with the electric chair if he refused. Hefner remained firm and was one of the fifteen indicted.[*]

Even after the terror had subsided somewhat, the continuing harassment made it practically impossible for the remaining women and children to sleep in their tents. They were homeless and dependent on the charity of neighbors for lodging. Around June 12 Wagenknecht was arrested and the police tried to get his permission to remove the tents. Finally, with the joint efforts of the WIR and ILD, the strikers' tent colony was moved to a location near the Arlington Mill.[†]

---

[*]Fred E. Beal, *Proletarian Journey* (New York: Hillman-Curl, 1937), pp. 179-80.

[†]Full accounts of the union's many activities during this period are given in releases of the ILD (Aug. 17, 1929, and others).

On July 28 a successful union conference had been held in Bessemer City bringing together 227 delegates representing 53 textile mills in 29 towns in Gaston County and other parts of North Carolina and endorsing the program of the NTWU. Among the speakers were William Z. Foster and Dr. John Randolph Neal of Scopes trial fame. Foster's presence was widely heralded in the South, his picture and articles concerning him appeared in many newspapers.

Of interest too is the disposition of the seventy-one people who were arrested on the night of June 7 and held for a week incommunicado in the city jail. We knew that nineteen of us had been taken to Charlotte for a habeas corpus hearing. Though state solicitor Carpenter wanted to have a special session of the superior court of Gaston County open on July 22 for the trial of all seventy-one, it did not materialize.* The prosecution had at first such an *embarras de richesse* of prisoners that they simply didn't know what to do with them all and juggled them around for a while. At first fourteen were charged with murder and with assault with a deadly weapon with intent to kill. They were Fred E. Beal, K. O. Byers, Lewis McLaughlin, William McGinnis, Vera Buch, Joseph Harrison, J. C. Hefner, Robert Allen, Russell Knight, N. F. Gibson, K. Y. Hendricks, Amy Schechter, Sophie Melvin, and George Carter.

Later the fourteen became fifteen. A striker named Delmar Hampton trying to get away in a car had got as far as Gaffney, N.C., was caught, brought back,† put in jail and indicted with the others.

Others charged with assault with a deadly weapon with intent to kill and then dismissed at or before the hearing of June 14 were J. O. Hinsley, Dewey Ward, Earl Tomkinson, Caroline Drew, Edith Saunders, Gladys Wallace, C. M. Lell, C. D. Saylors, Clarence Miller, and a few others. The disposition of this case no doubt accounts for the release of Caroline Drew from the county jail around June 16. There was also some harassment of active women strikers. Ruby MacMahon had to serve a month's sentence in the city jail. Viola Hampton, Lina Keater, and Jennie Harkness were jailed for three weeks on a vagrancy charge.

Our efforts in the South were having far-reaching effects. It was our activity from the beginning that had spurred both the United Textile Workers and the AFL center into some effort. As a result of the Loray strike, other union activity, and our hearing, the state legislature of North Carolina passed an act on August 10 limiting working hours to fifty-five. Mill owners of Gaston County and elsewhere then reduced working hours from sixty and sixty-five a week to fifty-five without reduction in

---

New York Times, June 13, 1929.
†Raleigh *News and Observer*, July 28, 1929.

pay. The wage-cutting campaign had been definitely stopped. The union was strong enough now so that an attempted wage cut or other aggression might have precipitated a general strike of the whole region.

The Loray strike in itself was enough of a scare, but now these avowed Communist organizers were spreading farther and farther. (George Pershing, YCL representative, had warned at the very start that the Communists were there to organize the entire South). Not merely the NTWU but the TUUL, the ILD, the WIR, and YCL, and the Pioneers, all Communist-controlled, were busily organizing under the very noses of mill owners and state authorities. Two prominent Communist leaders, Albert Weisbord and William Z. Foster, had appeared on the scene. To the mill owners and the state forces it probably appeared as though some giant octopus was slowly but surely choking them in its tentacles. Did these people really fear an end to their slave system, to the starvation wages combined with long hours and speed-up, to the repression of civil rights and all the brutal treatment that accompanied their monstrous exploitation of the workers? Did this fear reach as far as Washington?

That the federal government was indeed aroused, but not by the sufferings of the workers, is suggested by its nationwide policy to suppress Gastonia defense meetings. ILD and other meetings were not allowed to be held in Chicago. Fourteen workers were arrested there in late July and brought to trial for having attempted to hold a Gastonia defense meeting in a park. In New York too, in Pittsburgh, and in many other industrial centers such meetings were banned. In early July a leaflet entitled "Smash the Frame-up in Gastonia" was mailed out by the ILD. Because the envelopes were stamped with the slogan "Smash the Murder Frame-up," the circular was banned from the mails.

Back in Charlotte after my tour, I found the ILD had arranged for living quarters and meals in a boardinghouse for the women defendants. As soon as I was installed there, I reported to the nearby ILD headquarters. It was centrally located near the courthouse, which would be the hub of activities for some time to come. Ensconced in the office was William F. Dunne, a Party leader whom I met for the first time. He was short and enormous about the middle, while a big band of fat encircled his neck, meeting heavy jowls. He was one of those men who look unshaven even when they are not.

Learning that a union picnic was to be held that Sunday afternoon, August 25, at Mt. Holly, I took a bus down there. In a grove of tall trees I found Hugo Oehler, then leader of the union, sitting at a small table with union cards. Knowing little about Oehler except his failure to have visited us in jail but having heard he had TB, I was still inclined to be sympathetic. While not exactly unfriendly, he seemed reserved and uncommunicative, asked me nothing about my trip, and did not seem to want to talk about what he was doing.

What I experienced at this picnic is hard to describe, though I remember it well. As it was still early, the crowds hadn't turned out yet, though there were some people about. In one spot under the trees I saw a group digging a pit for a pork barbecue. A speaking stand was also prepared. I hadn't been asked by the Charlotte office to speak there; in fact, they hadn't even told me about the picnic; I had simply noticed a leaflet about it. The strikers I met were glad to see me, the staff members negative. While not formulated in words, my perception was sure. There was no welcome for me; I was ignored. I knew I wouldn't be asked to speak. I am a sensitive person and when I am hurt I withdraw. I didn't stay long at the picnic. Back in the office in Charlotte I tried to pick up whatever orientation I could for the events ahead.

A few days before the opening of the trial the Charlotte *News and Observer* had carried the following statement: "The leaders of the NTWU are Communists and are a menace to all that we hold most sacred. They believe in violence, arson, murder. . . . They are undermining all morality, all religion. But nevertheless they must be given a fair trial, although everyone knows they deserve to be shot at sunrise." Such comment gave cause to wonder whether much had been gained by transferring the trial from Gastonia to this other mill town. Still, the imminence of the trial had built up a hopeful excitement in the defense camp, an attitude that the course of the trial in the first few days was to tend to confirm.

Now our big day was at hand: August 26. No jailer leading us across the cobblestones this time; we three women left the boardinghouse together. It was a bright hot day; groups of people were standing about in the area in front of the fine, new Mecklenburg County courthouse. In the sidewalk squarely in front of the building was a bronze plaque with a model of a rattlesnake and the words (the state motto) DON'T TREAD ON ME. Somehow this plaque was always associated in my mind with Albert, in whose company I had seen it that first time he had come down to the South. Perhaps I thought of him that morning with a pang at our separation, but it could have been only briefly for this was an engrossing day. We found the courtroom crowded.

The trial had been advertised as an historical one—according to some writers, the most important ever held in the state. Mill workers and strikers were among the audience, but there was no chance to greet them. An usher guided us up the aisle to the three steps leading to the platform, where we sat down at the end of the row of empty chairs facing the judge's bench, seats reserved for the defendants. Between us and the judge's bench were the lawyers' tables; to our left was the empty jury box. At least twenty-eight newspapers had reporters there.

The courtroom presented a lively scene—women's bright summer dresses, lawyers seated or standing by their two tables, all the Southerners in white linen suits. Among the prosecution forces I could distinguish Solicitor Carpenter, tall, dark, and sardonic-looking; Clyde Hoey, dapper and trim with a high collar covered by his long gray locks; Major Bulwinkle, a short, stocky, burly man. At the defense table only Tom Jimison and Leon Josephson (ILD) were familiar and I greeted them.

The thirteen men prisoners filed in led by their jailer, Sheriff John Erwin, and we exchanged smiles as they took their places beside us. They looked neat and well-groomed, but pale with that special pasty hue of people long confined. Next appeared Judge Barnhill in his robes; as he took his seat an usher in a ringing voice intoned the old formula "Oyez, Oyez, Oyez! The co't of the State of No'th Ca'lina is now in session! God save the State and its hon'rable co't!" Once more the roll call, and as I answered to my name I began to feel with a throb of the heart that I was really part of this historical process, and I made every effort to be alert and miss nothing. Again we were arraigned as a group, all sixteen of us, on a charge of first-degree murder and conspiracy to murder. There was tension now in the courtroom as Tom Jimison answered Solicitor Carpenter's question: "By whom will you be tried?" with the old formula "By God and my country." And the Solicitor's reply: "May God grant you a true deliverance." Jimison also answered for all of us, "Not guilty."

The defense brought in a routine motion to quash the indictment and bill of particulars which predictably was overruled. Then Judge Barnhill said that he was dissatisfied with the bill of particulars and ordered the prosecution to amplify that part of the bill dealing with the events of June 7 and to specify what occurred at the headquarters that night.

According to this first bill, the conspiracy charge stemmed from the disturbance during our last meeting when Beal had ordered the guards to arrest anyone causing trouble and bring them to him. This bill charged also that by shouting "Shoot him! shoot him!" when Aderholt was about to leave the grounds, Fred Beal and Vera Buch gave the orders to the armed guards to kill the chief. The judge next took under advisement the defense motion to strike out large portions of the bill dealing with preceding events said to have led up to the alleged conspiracy.

In response to the judge's ruling, the prosecution overnight completed the redrafting of the bill and brought it in the next morning, August 27. The second bill charged specifically that Fred Erwin Beal, organizer for the National Textile Workers Union and leading defendant, ordered his codefendants, all heavily armed, "to resist and prevent at all hazards the police from entering the union headquarters" and that subsequently armed men were "encouraged by Vera Buch, Amy Schechter, and Sophie Melvin stationed at the door of the headquarters to shoot and kill Aderholt and others of his subordinates."

The second bill of particulars also charged that Beal ordered his co-defendants and other workers to drag employees from the Loray Mill by force if necessary and compel them to join the strike, an attempt then blocked by Aderholt and his men. In addition to instructing his associates to resist by force any entry of the police on June 7, the redrafted bill alleged, Beal ordered them "to arrest any other persons who might come upon the grounds and bring them before him and his codefendants for the purpose of inflicting such punishment as they might deem proper."

The amended bill disclosed that the state would seek to prove that Aderholt's death was the result of a conspiracy that had its inception on April 1, when the strike at the Loray Mill began, and that "led to violence, force, and intimidation to stop the operation of the Loray Mill. Many attempts to storm the mill resulted."*

In the first bill of particulars the call that brought the police to the union grounds was from a striker; in the second bill it was a neighbor who had made the call. After hearing this second bill of particulars, Judge Barnhill declared that he was still not satisfied; the prosecution had failed to comply with his order (to amplify and specify). Carpenter and Cansler wanted to present still another bill but this the judge denied. Too much time was being wasted; he wanted to get on with the case; he would therefore admit both bills. He ruled, however, that no evidence would be permitted to go before the jury on such parts of the bills as the defense might object to. He also ruled that he would restrict all evidence to the events on the eve of the slaying, would bar all evidence of prior events, and would confine the evidence of conspiracy to the alleged agreement of the defendants to keep all persons, including the officers of the law, off the grounds of the union headquarters.

One more advantage accrued to the defense this second day. North Carolina law had a provision that in capital cases the defense may be permitted to interview state witnesses in advance of the trial, provided a representative of the prosecution is present. This privilege was granted our lawyers. Solicitor Carpenter furnished them with a complete list of state witnesses. With Solicitor Carpenter presiding and a stenographic record kept, our lawyers interviewed fifteen state witnesses that evening, among them policemen Gilbert and Ferguson. Not one person interviewed could tell who fired the shots that fatally wounded Aderholt.

New York Times, Aug. 27, 1929.

After adjournment that day Arthur G. Hays made a statement to the press labeling the murder and conspiracy charges "a tissue of vague allegations."

The next day, August 28, the trial entered a new phase: the selection of the jury. How simple to state, how complicated in practice, how long and tedious! Because of the seriousness of the charge and the number of the defendants, the total challenges of selection permitted was very large. The law allowed in a first-degree murder charge four challenges for the state and twelve for the defense. Multiplied by sixteen, this gives a total of 64 for the state and 192 for the defense.* Besides this, North Carolina law had a property qualification for jury service that would disqualify many. As a man's name was called out, the prospective juror would come to the front. The first panel of two hundred veniremen waited in back of the hall. (In those days, of course, no woman juror was even considered.) The ranks of the journalists had thinned; the audience too was sparser.

Attorney E. T. Cansler for the prosecution would ask the first question, "Have you paid your taxes for the last year?" If the answer was no, no more time was wasted. "The state will excuse him." This question speedily eliminated many. Working in a cotton mill, or having ever worked in one, was at first enough to cause the state to challenge. Having a relative working in a mill or having ever been caught with a piece of Communist literature in one's hands also brought a challenge. We knew our lawyers were employing a detective or two to investigate the veniremen. So did the prosecution. Following a man's examination, if there was yet no challenge, the clerk would intone: "Juror, look upon the prisoners. Prisoners, look upon the juror. Do you like him?" Any one of us had the right to answer; however, in practice it was left for lawyers Jimison or Josephson to reply for us.

It also had to be determined if the prospective juror had formed any opinion in the case. Perhaps we should not have been surprised, knowing as we did the newspaper bias, to find many of the veniremen's minds already made up. "That fellow Beal is guilty," or even "They are all guilty," was a frequent response that automatically resulted in dismissal "for cause" by Judge Barnhill. Sometimes over a hundred veniremen would be called in a day to select three. A local florist had donated pink carnations for the jury; slowly these distinguishing marks multiplied, blossoming in the jury box as more and more jurors took their places.

One morning I was a little late and arrived only in time to rush up to the platform and answer to my name just as I was taking my seat. As I left for the noon recess, the usher stopped me. "Lucky you got here in

*Nell Battle Lewis, "Tar Heel Justice," The Nation (Sept. 11, 1929).

time to answer, Miss Buch," he said. "If you'd 'a been late it would 'a made it a mistrial." The same man once said to me as I was coming down from the platform, "Miss Buch, they tell me you're almost thirty years old. Don't ever tell anyone, Ma'm, you don't look a day over twenty-two."

Day after day these proceedings went on with increasing monotony and boredom. It was hot and stifling in the courtroom; to pay attention became a great effort. I must admit to having fallen asleep once—it was on the fifth day. Succumbing to heat and fatigue, I slept beautifully till the end of the session.

At long last, by slow degrees—it actually took eight days to pick the jury—our twelve "good men and true," our "jury of our peers" were assembled. All together, they looked surprisingly alike. There was one prevailing type: the Southern worker or poor farmer—tall, gaunt, neatly but plainly dressed. No white linen suits here, but dark clothing, faces all dour and unsmiling. Actually, we felt the best possible had been accomplished under the circumstances: our jury included seven working men: a steel worker, a railroad clerk, a railroad repairman, a grocery clerk; even a textile worker and a cotton mill worker had been able to slip by toward the end as the prosecution relaxed its vigilance a little. There were also four tenant farmers. Two were union members, all but two were married, and all but two were church members. The state had used 54 of its 64 challenges, the defense 128 of its 192. A total of 408 veniremen had been examined.*

As for the legal staff, our own lawyers had been busy unearthing information concerning these ten men (the prosecution) who had declared when the trial opened that "they represented the State of North Carolina and nothing else." Influence of the textile industry was predominant. A few were mill attorneys, one was a special counsel of the Manville-Jenckes Co., others were themselves mill owners or relatives of mill owners. A state commander of the American Legion was among them, as well as a state militia officer who had commanded a howitzer company in Gastonia during the strike.†

Counsel for the defense did not present such a unified picture. Its kernel was Tom Jimison with his Charlotte law partners Frank Flowers and W. H. Abernathy, to whom were added later J. D. McCall of Charlotte and R. L. Sigmon of Gaston County. Leon Josephson of Trenton, New Jersey, and now Joseph Brodsky of New York were both Communist

---

*From Liston Pope and Gilbert L. Starke, *Mill Hands and Preachers* (New Haven: Yale Univ. Press, 1942).

†For details see ILD news release, July 30, 1929.

Party members representing the ILD. At the start of the trial a prominent North Carolina attorney, former Judge Frank Carter of Asheville, had been brought in to head the case, or that at least was the intention of the Charlotte group. Perhaps objecting to the domination of the lawyers by the ILD or disagreeing with their opinions, Judge Carter soon withdrew. The ILD then replaced him with Thaddeus Adams, a prominent member of the Charlotte bar with over ten years experience in criminal cases.

The American Civil Liberties Union also had some involvement with the case. The eminent Dr. John Randolph Neal from Knoxville, Tenn., of Scopes trial fame had come in, but soon left, either unable to agree with the ILD policy or possibly deterred by the Communist Party domination. Then appeared Arthur Garfield Hays, prominant Eastern liberal, who had considerable experience in trying civil rights cases. It seems the ILD at first resisted having Hays come into the case, but after protests were made by New York liberals, they admitted him as a "consultant." Later he was called a regular counselor and refused to say he had any differences with the ILD.

Of course the ILD reflected Party policy, but policy at that time represented the different factions rather than one unified point of view. To some of the leaders the case was a frame-up; others like Foster and Dunne wanted to base the defense solely on the right of the strikers to defend themselves and their headquarters against attacks by the mill owners and their agents. Some leaders wanted openly to admit and defend the Communist direction of the strike.

All the particulars concerning the defense came out gradually during the evenings that I spent at the ILD headquarters at 112 Court Arcade. No one gave us a report on policy in the case. We got our information either from the press or from gossip passed along in the office. Never were we all present at any meeting at which the policy for conducting our defense was thoroughly and officially discussed and determined.

In the meantime we had to leave our boardinghouse. The place was one of those handsome, commodious old homes with bay windows, a wide porch, and a tree-shaded lawn. Our quarters were comfortable enough, though it was rather disconcerting to Northerners like us to find while taking a bath an inch-and-a-quarter-long black roach or two slithering up the wall. The food was excellent, resembling those Sunday feasts we used to enjoy at Helen Lodge's in the old days. But what was our discomfiture the first day of court to find that Solicitor Carpenter and Attorney Clyde Hoey were our dinner table mates! We hoped it was incidental, but no, they were regular guests at the midday meal. The roaches we could have put up with, but prosecution lawyers...! No beaten biscuits, Virginia baked ham, corn pudding, black-eyed peas, pecan pie, or any other Southern delicacies were that delicious! Schechter and Melvin moved to the Walton Hotel, where the other defense people were staying. I had other plans.

On a quiet back street only one block off the main drag in a racially mixed neighborhood I had noticed a "room to rent" sign. Giving an assumed name—it may have been Leona Smith, my old Passaic pseudonym—telling no one, I rented a satisfactory room at the back of the house. My motivations were so obscure as to seem instinctive. The summer's experiences had left me with an acute awareness of safety, or the lack of it. There was besides a subtle change in the relationship btween the other women defendants and me, as well as with the people in the office: they were not openly unfriendly, did not overtly slight me, but the easy familiarity and trust of the jail days was no longer there. That "left-out" feeling of which I had been so poignantly aware at the August 25 picnic was increasing. More and more I had to feel that I was under a shadow and alone.

It was at this time also that I had to decide the important question whether I should testify at the trial. No one had said a word to me about this matter. That I would be a good witness I felt sure. I was among the most important of the participants in the strike; I was the only union organizer involved besides Beal. I could have testified about the brutality of the policeman's assault on me in that last picket line, of Mary Vorse's warning. At the same time I had to consider my personal situation: the fact that I was not legally married to Albert Weisbord. We had stayed together during his two visits to Gastonia, which the prosecution surely knew. The prosecution lawyers could have made me appear some sort of whore, and I would have been discredited as a witness. So at any rate it appeared to me. I seem to recall that I did bring this up with Amy, but she gave no answer one way or the other.

I well remember the occasion when I reported to Comrade Dunne that I had decided not to testify. It was in his room at the Walton Hotel with some other comrades present. I simply told him that for personal reasons I felt it would be better if I didn't take the stand. His immediate reaction was one of surprise. He gave a start, there was a look of incredulity, then quickly a gleam of joy, of exultation in his slits of eyes. He said nothing, but I felt sure I had given him some great advantage. At the time I thought it was just that I would be deprived of a prominent role in the case. That the spider's web was much more intricate, more sinister than this, that I was assisting Dunne in carrying out schemes which I in my innocence at the time could not have conceived of, I could not then foresee.

Another aspect was the fact that defense lawyers had decided that I should not speak at union or defense meetings, that it would hurt our case if I did. At the time I accepted this decision without question or distrust. The matter came up in connection with a meeting held in Charlotte on the evening of August 27 where I had been advertised as a speaker along with Schechter, Melvin, Poyntz, Hugo Oehler, and some others. The prohibition did not extend to the other women defendants; it was only me. The following telegram from Mary Vorse to her newspaper, the New York *Evening Graphic*, has a bearing on this matter:

Night letter August 29

Louis Weitzenkorn
Evening Graphic
350 Hudson Street
New York

In my evening dispatch of August twenty seven I stated definitely lawyers would not allow Vera Buch to attend union meeting stop Such distortion is inexcusable in a trial where peoples lives are at stake stop I have no knowledge of what misstatement you may next make stop Kindly wire me assurance that you will at least not print the reverse of what I have written stop

Mary Heaton Vorse

Meanwhile on September 5 the trial began in earnest with the prosecution presenting its witnesses and evidence. To describe the happenings of the fatal evening they called four people: two women and one man who lived in the nearby cottages and had been present at our last meeting, plus A. J. Roach, who had accompanied the police on their raid. A man named Otto Mason described how a "rumpus" had broken out at the edge of the field and people began throwing rocks and rotten eggs at the speaker on the stand. He said that Beal had said when he was on the platform, "Go to the mill. Go to the mill and get them out." Then he told how a picket line composed of girls and women had set out toward the mill and was broken up by the police.* Mrs. Walter Griggs told how a little girl had come running up to her telling that a boy had been hit in the eye. It was then, she said, that she put in a call to the police.

Shortly afterward, according to Mason, the car containing Chief of Police Aderholt and the other officers drove up. "What is going on

---

*New York *Evening Graphic*, Sept. 5, 1929.

here?" said the chief. "None of your damn business," the guard answered. "We haven't come here for any trouble," the chief answered.

At this point Joseph Harrison, an armed striker, came forward. The chief ordered him disarmed and put under arrest. This was done by Officer Gilbert after a scuffle. Mason said that Vera Buch and Fred Beal, standing by the headquarters door, then called out: "Shoot him! Shoot him!"

This last point was repeated by Mason's wife, who, when asked how she could tell who had shouted these words, said, "I recognized them by their Yankee brogue." Following this, witnesses told of the shooting of the three officers and A. J. Roach. Cross-examination brought out that Roach had not been deputized, was in civilian clothes, had a gun but no warrant, and didn't know whether anyone else had a warrant. Further cross-examination brought out that the police knew that the strikers were in the habit of patroling their grounds at night, armed with shotguns. It was made clear the police had found no disturbance at the grounds when they arrived there. Not one single point of evidence was produced as to who had fired the shot or shots that caused Aderholt's death.*

The sessions of the court now took up most of the day. In the August heat we sat there hour after hour making the greatest effort to concentrate. Then one day we saw stationed in the first ranks of the audience, right below the jury box, the chief's widow, Mamie Aderholt, and her daughter, Ethel, both dressed in complete mourning.

That day testimony focused on the wounds of the deceased. Dr. H. R. McConnell testified on the large number of pellets that had penetrated the chief's body, all in the back; sixteen No. 4 "duck" shot were lodged in the right scapula, with a total of sixty pellets in various places over the entire body. Then an exhibit was produced and accepted: the union suit Aderholt had been wearing on his last day, his winter underwear it, seemed, for the bloodstained garment had long legs and sleeves. As this exhibit was handed from one juror to another, Mrs. Aderholt and her daughter took out their handkerchiefs and audibly sobbed.

Then Ethel was called to the stand to testify to her father's alleged deathbed statement. Tearfully she reported he had said, "I do not know why they shot me. I had done nothing wrong." Judge Barnhill ordered this testimony stricken from the record. The testimony on Aderholt's wounds continued on the next day, September 7. It was then that the prosecution asked leave to bring in another exhibit. A large object at least six feet high, covered by a black cloth, and mounted on a platform was wheeled into the courtroom by Sheriff Erwin and one of the ushers.

---

*Ibid.

They placed it directly in front of the judge. Solicitor Carpenter pulled the cover partly away: there stood an effigy of Chief Aderholt complete with black suit, big ten gallon black hat, and all. The angular features of the image were realistic enough, but the fixed staring black eyes of it were strange and shocking. Judge Barnhill's reaction was immediate.

"Take that thing out!" he ordered.

Carpenter hesitated, fussing with the black cover.

"I said, take that out!" the judge repeated louder and more emphatically, and the exhibit was trundled out.

It was on the following Monday, September 9, that court opened with a surprise announcement by the prosecution. As a consequence of viewing the image of Aderholt on Saturday, one of the jurors had gone violently insane; it had taken five men to control him and get him into a padded cell. The juror, J. C. Campbell, was a tenant farmer. As a result of his breakdown a mistrial was declared. Other statements had to be made, legal procedures gone through, so that actually court was in session until 2:30 P.M., when it adjourned with an announcement that court would reconvene on September 30 and a new jury would be impaneled.

Some conversation with the jurors during the noon recess and after adjournment revealed that although only state's evidence had been presented, if nothing stronger were to be produced, the jury would have been for acquittal.

For me personally the events following the announcement of a mistrial were simple enough. That evening the women defendants were invited out to dinner by Attorney Arthur Garfield Hays. This was a real occasion, the first and only one of that long period. Hays took us to the Walton, the best hotel in town. I wore my prettiest dress, an ivory chiffon with a black design that Albert had gotten for me in Passaic, and a string of jade beads. In a holiday mood we discussed the trial as it had developed so far; the indictment, the bills of particulars, the flimsy, falsified evidence. We could laugh at the grotesque image of Aderholt. How desperate the prosecution must be to resort to such a tactic! Sophie told of her conversation with four jurymen that morning; they had all been for acquittal. Gaily we chatted as we consumed oysters and other unaccustomed delicacies.

The next day for me brought indigestion. Though I had been up all night, I went over to the office as usual in the morning, but felt really sick and soon returned to my room, where I stayed for the remainder of the day.

Coming around to the office the following morning, Wednesday, September 11, I found the door open and the office empty. What could have happened? Finally one of the office workers showed up, then another. Bit by bit, as others came, I got the story. There had been a raid. Luckily our people in the office had been warned by a call from Gastonia and had all left. From the Charlotte newspaper and from what the comrades could tell I finally put together the whole outrageous story.

This had been no ordinary raid. It had started in Gastonia in the early evening of the ninth. A huge cavalcade of cars rallied, filled with vigilantes, the old Committee of One Hundred led by Manville-Jenckes people and by two prosecution witnesses named Tom Carver and Will Goff.

They first attacked a taxi containing union people on their way to a meeting at the Pinckney Mill in South Gastonia. The occupants were Hugo Oehler, Dewey Martin (a striker), Simon Gerson (a YCLer from New York), one other union man, and the driver. The mobsters smashed the windows, hit Oehler over the head with bottles, beat the other men, and nearly succeeded in dragging Dewey Martin bodily from the car. The car was surrounded by a swarm of shouting men and other cars, but finally the driver succeeded in pushing through the crowd. The union people escaped and went on to a workers' meeting scheduled at a mill in McAdensville.

Meanwhile, the caravan proceeded to raid and wreck the Gastonia union headquarters, then the one in Bessemer City. From there—it was now about nine in the evening—they returned to 512 West Airline Avenue, the Lodges' home, where I had been arrested on June 7. It was still used as a rooming house for union people. The Lodge family were all there, including a little granddaughter; with them were two strikers, C. M. Lell and Cliff Saylors. Also present was a young man named Ben Wells, an Englishman temporarily in the States and a C.P. member who had come down to Gastonia to help the textile strikers.

With hooting horns the cars stopped in front of the Lodges'; the men got out and noisily invaded the premises. A group of about a hundred pushed into the hall and living room, where the family and union men had taken refuge; other hundreds jammed the porch and front yard, all shouting and milling about. A number of those inside began singing loudly, "Praise God from whom all blessings flow. . . ." Some outside were yelling, "We're all one hundred percent Americans here. Anyone that don't like it can go back to Russia!" Others cursed the union and threatened to shoot anyone connected with it. They were going to go down to the Charlotte jail and bring that red-headed bastard Fred Beal out and lynch him.

When Ben Wells got up and started to speak, they pulled him out on the crowded porch, stuck an American flag in his hand, and ordered him to denounce the union. Wells said he was a British textile worker who had come there to help Southern textile workers on strike against unbearable conditions.

"That's enough," one man shouted. "We know you're an organizer," and they shoved him back into the room. Then the leaders consulted. There was talk of "taking care of them . . . Let's do it now."

Finally they seized Wells, Saylors, and Lell, took them outside, and put Wells into one car and the other two men into another. Accompanied by several other cars, they all drove off, some probably going home. As they drove through Gastonia, the kidnappers punched their victims, trying to get information out of them concerning the union. They threatened to throw them into the river, to hang them from a limb. They said they had beaten Oehler up and were going to finish him off when they could get their hands on him again. They would shoot any worker who tried to join the union. They cursed the women staff members, mentioning them all by name—Buch, Schechter, Drew, and Melvin. They weren't going to have such people around there anymore.

The mobsters drove until they reached a lonely woodsy spot between Concord and Monroe in Cabarrus County where there was a little iron bridge. It was late at night now and completely dark. They forced Wells to take off his clothes, then handed a leather belt to Saylors and told him to beat Wells, whom they made bend over. When Saylors refused, they gave the belt to Lell, who struck a few blows. It wasn't hard enough, so the vigilantes took over the beating themselves. They broke branches from the trees, held the victim down on the ground, and with belts and fagots flogged him all over, holding his mouth to stifle his cries.

At last the lights of a car were seen coming around a bend. Someone cried out, "It's the law!" and the attackers quickly piled into their cars and fled. It was not the law, only some 'possum hunters, but the kidnapped men were saved. Saylors and Lell lifted up the barely conscious Wells and with the help of the hunters they went to Concord, where they reported to the local police what had happened. Then at 5 A.M. they took a train back to Charlotte.

Still it wasn't over. The next morning, September 10, the cavalcade reassembled and proceeded to Charlotte, where with honking and yelling they cruised the town looking for their prey. They hoped to get Beal from the jail, but Sheriff Erwin would not admit them. They looked for Tom Jimison in both his home and his office but he was not to be found in either place. They went to the Walton Hotel but were kept away from Dunne and our other people who stayed there. Then they raided ILD headquarters at 110 Court Arcade. I was told my name was mentioned, they wanted me, but I was not there and no one knew where I was.

There were immediate reactions. On September 11 Governor Max Gardner ordered prosecuting authorities and police to bring to justice the kidnappers of the three strike leaders and the raiders on union headquarters in Gastonia, Bessemer City, and various places in Charlotte. Solicitor John Carpenter said in Gastonia that he would order a special grand jury to investigate the outrage. A fine ironic touch and typical of all the developments of this affair, considering that Carpenter was possibly one of the perpetrators of the raid.*

Fourteen men of the kidnapping mob were arrested, their bail set at $1,000 each. Among them were three Loray Mill superintendents plus Roach and Ferguson, Gastonia policemen. The warrants charged kidnapping and conspiracy to kidnap, assault with intent to kill, imprisonment and false arrest.†

A statement was issued by Dr. John Randolph Neal of the ACLU denouncing the raids as part of a massive drive to crush unionism in the South and linking the events of June 7 with this effort. He made the important point that the kidnapping had the further effect of scattering and eliminating defense witnesses for the trial. The NTWU also issued a protest.

For those of us at the center of things these were anxious days. Schechter and I once went to visit Ben Wells, who was recuperating in a room at the Walton Hotel. We found him lying in bed, a well-built fellow in his mid-twenties, blond and blue-eyed. He opened his pajama top to show us some of the scratches, which he said covered his entire body, from the tree branches they had beaten him with. There were bruises, he said, on his back left by the belts. He looked pale and his eyes still showed the shock of his ordeal. Since his voice was weak and it appeared hard for him to talk, we didn't question him or stay long.

Determined not to succumb to the brutal blows its people had received, the union rallied its forces once more to defy Manville-Jenckes and its allies, the state forces. The NTWU announced a great rally of all union people in Gaston County to be held in South Gastonia on September 14. The Gastonia *Gazette* warned people to stay away from that meeting.

On September 13 eight union leaders were seized in Gastonia on a

---

*Some people swore to have recognized both Solicitor Carpenter and Major Bulwinkle of the prosecution among the leaders of the vigilantes. Affidavits were taken by the ILD and were never convincingly denied. It was stated also that Major Bulwinkle was in charge of the militia that had been brought into Gastonia. The details of these raids are taken from newspapers of the day and from sworn statements by the kidnapped men.

†*New York Times*, Sept. 13, 1929.

Red Plot charge. They included Lell and Saylors (they didn't get bed-ridden Wells in Charlotte). The charge made against these men was conspiracy to revolt against the government of North Carolina! A little later this charge was dismissed for lack of evidence. The ACLU then sued Sheriff Erwin for false arrest.

The forces now were aligned for another confrontation. When the day for the rally came, a massive mobilization was made by the millowner–state group. Two thousand men (the vigilantes, sworn-in deputies, mill bosses and others) were ready to drive away all who showed up for the meeting in South Gastonia. Roadblocks were set up in all directions.

Shortly before the time scheduled for the meeting some defense people who were in a car heading for South Gastonia were arrested. They included Liston Oaks (then publicity director of the ILD), his wife Margaret Larkin, a magazine writer, Mary Heaton Vorse, a defense detective, and the driver A. A. Grier, our Charlotte textile friend. Oaks was charged with carrying a concealed weapon and Grier with reckless driving.

Tragedy lurked in ambush. A truck was coming from Bessemer City loaded with peaceful unarmed union people, Ella Mae Wiggins among them. At a road junction the truck was halted by the vigilantes and forced to turn back. As it proceeded toward Bessemer City, they stopped it again and there Ella Mae Wiggins was shot in cold blood and died.

The news of this heinous crime was most distressing to me. I went down on the bus one evening to Bessemer City. Actually I hadn't been there since the morning of June 7. Huddled in the old store that was still the union headquarters I found a few union people, sitting there with the window shades pulled all the way down. As it was getting dark, they lighted some candles. They said they were "acting quiet-like" since the raid; they didn't want any lights to show. They were all obviously glad to see me, in fact, welcomed me as an old friend. We talked chiefly of the murder of our dear Ella Mae. Her cousin Charley was the chief narrator.

"We was on this truck goin' to the speakin' at South Gastonia, Ella Mae an' me an' Wes an' a good bunch o' people. We'd got about halfway down past the Arlington Mill where they got the tent colony now, then they was a lot o' cars standin' in the road an' a great crowd o' men, the Loray Mill gang, the deputies, the same ones that raided this headquarters. An' they told our driver he'd got to turn the truck back. What could we do, ma'm, we didn't have no guns an' they was all armed. So the truck turned back for Bessemer City. About five o' the cars was followin' us. We'd got as fur as Gamble's Crossin' where they's a iron bridge. We'd just got over the bridge when this Essex coach run right around in front o' us an' we collided with it. So we was stopped an' it was then Ella Mae was standin' at the railin' of the track leanin' against it, an' a man come up not fifteen feet away and raised a gun an' fired at her.

"She turned to me an' said, 'O my Lord, they've done shot and killed me.' I caught her in my arms and Ella Mae died right then. They shot her straight through the heart and killed her."

All Charley's love and devotion came out in his voice, in his face. The others added their versions, telling how they all ran across the fields with the deputies hunting them down like rabbits. I asked what would become of the children.

"The ILD is lookin' for a home for them," replied Charley. "Till then I'm carin' for 'em."

Sitting there all close together in the dim store, with the light of the faltering candles touching our faces and throwing shadows on the wall, we talked in low tones hardly above a whisper. Strangely enough, I don't remember anything being said about a funeral. Had it already taken place? If they had spoken of it as yet to come, I would surely have been there. It was actually only much later that I read about Ella Mae Wiggins' funeral. A simple affair it was. Many of her fellow workers accompanied her to her last resting place. I don't believe it was even a cemetery, perhaps there was no money for that. She was buried in a cornfield on the side of a hill. Just a plain wooden coffin. And Gladys Wallace sang Ella Mae's own ballad "The Mill Mothers' Song" as they laid her in the ground.

We leave our home in the morning,
We kiss our children goodbye,
While we slave for the bosses,
Our children scream and cry.

And when we draw our money,
Our grocery bills to pay,
Not a cent to spend for clothing,
Not a cent to lay away.

And on that very evening,
Our little son will say,
"I need some shoes, dear mother,
And so does sister May."

How it grieves the heart of a mother,
You every one must know,
But we can't buy for our children,
Our wages are too low.

A few words were spoken by the mill workers who had become organizers now. What could they say of her? "You all knew our sister, Ella Mae. She was one of our best workers, and we'll feel her loss, I reckon. Her death is on Manville-Jenckes, and on North Carolina too. She died for us and the union. We must go on fighting, we must get our union."*

And what can I add? Shall I speak of this woman's courage, of her steadfastness, of her clear mind, of her hopes of a better life? What had she ever known but grinding poverty, overwork, and deprivation? The care of a brood of children had fallen upon her shoulders. For all her heroic efforts, four out of nine of them had died.

Genius is no respecter of social rank, and many exceptional minds are submerged in the multitude of those for whom the denial of opportunity is complete and daily toil exhausts all energies of body and intellect. Ella Mae Wiggins was such a one until the strike gave her the opportunity briefly to blossom out, to be a human being, to devote her talents to the struggle for a union. From the first day I met her I had appreciated Mrs. Wiggins' great qualities, and never could I think of her death without pain.

Much has been written of Ella Mae Wiggins as striker and especially as ballad singer. Was it for her ballads that she was singled out to be killed? Practically all of the women strikers sang ballads. But Ella Mae Wiggins was more than that. She understood immediately without argument the value of our union principle of racial equality. What is more, she set about of her own accord to organize the black people in Bessemer City, where she lived. Even more than Communism, it was the appeal to the black people, and especially her role in their organization, that incensed mill owners and like-minded people in the South. I am certain it was as an organizer of the Negroes that Mrs. Wiggins was killed.

For the killing of Ella Mae Wiggins seven men were arrested, six of them employees of Loray Mill. Their bond of $1,000 each was paid by the manager of the Loray. The charge was second-degree murder or manslaughter. The driver of the strikers' truck was also charged.†

Having leisure now for a few weeks, I tried to find a place in the work that was going on. The headquarters in Charlotte was ILD: there was at that time no union office in Charlotte, so we were not directly in touch with the union activities. No one asked me to do anything or informed me of what was going on. My isolation had now become systematic. I knew that I was in disfavor for political reasons, now that Foster had been

---

*Margaret Larkin, "Ella Mae's Songs," The Nation, Oct. 29, 1929.
†New York Times, Sept. 16, 1929.

given the Party. They could not push me out physically, as they had done to Albert, since I was a Gastonia defendant, on the payroll as such.

Here our pay—I believe it was twenty-five dollars a week—came regularly. Had we all received that amount of money weekly in the old days, what could we not have accomplished? How we could have extended the strike as we wanted to! Loray might have been a different story. Apparently the old days were of no concern to the staff who were there now. But the workers remembered.*

I had been sent to the South as an organizer of the NTWU, and I hadn't been removed from this post. Yet I had been quietly pushed out of the union here. The publicity of that summer, news releases of the Federated Press and ILD in referring to the women prisoners, focused on Melvin and Schechter. Melvin was sent out to address meetings and conferences, and there were full reports of every word she said. Buch was not allowed to speak, was barely referred to, and was included only when it was unavoidable. The *Labor Defender* of September 1929 published résumés of the life stories of the sixteen defendants, which we had been asked to provide. My account was not given as written. Most of my activities were omitted. Schechter's, on the other hand, was built up and full of inaccuracies. Though she was said to have been an organizer for the Save the Union Committee in 1927-28, I know she was not in the coal fields while I was there during 1928. If she was there in 1927, it is strange she never referred to this while we were in jail. To Bill Dunne, the Party representative, I had probably become a "renegade," the term now applied to all who disagreed with the Stalin-Foster line.

Why did I not protest all this discrimination, fight to get back into the union work? An obvious question, the answers to which are obscure. My position could not be easily grasped at the time. I was getting what is popularly called "the works." In spite of many subsequent repetitions, I never really learned to like it. But this first time I don't believe I realized the full import of what was going on. I did in a modest way attempt to build some opposition to Bill Dunne on the day-to-day issues (the really big issues were never taken up in weekly fraction meetings). I remember that the comrades would agree with me privately but in the meeting they would all knuckle under, not a peep out of them.

During this period of comparative leisure I had found time to do a little swimming at the YWCA pool. In preliminary physical examination it appeared my pulse rate was much above normal. The doctor hesitated, seemed concerned. I recalled that my pulse had always been high in the

---

*See Ella Mae Wiggins' ballad, in *The Nation*, Oct. 29, 1929, p. 8.

old TB days. Actually I had avoided doctors since then: my pulse hadn't been checked in years. Finally the woman said I could swim in moderation, never fast or very long.

For my first dip I resolved to overcome a handicap: because I had learned to swim in a shallow river, I feared deep water. Resolving to end this fear, I forced myself to swim all around the pool—deep water and all—without stopping. My heart was racing; it was in a small way an ordeal, but when it was over my fear of deep water had vanished forever. I enjoyed my occasional dips and hoped to build myself up with them because I was feeling quite tired.

In Gastonia, North Carolina. Left to right:
Vera, Ellen Dawson, Albert Weisbord, Fred Beal

The Gastonia defendants as pictured on the cover of the *Labor Defender*, September 1929. Vera is in the first row, third from left. On her left is Sophie Melvin, on her right Fred Beal. Amy Schechter is in the second row, behind Beal.

I 2

A Peculiar Trial

MEANWHILE, WE HAD ARRIVED AT SEPTEMBER 30 AND THE REOPENING OF the trial. The courtroom was the same, but Arthur G. Hays, was no longer among us. He had withdrawn from the case; perhaps he could no longer spare the time.

At the start of the trial, perhaps in the interest of maintaining an appearance of impartiality, Governor Gardner issued a statement calling for higher wages and shorter hours and abolition of all mill villages and company houses, but he denounced Communism and commended close cooperation of Capitol, labor, and the state.*

Now a real surprise: the prosecution had completely reorganized the case. Nine people including myself were nol-prossed with leave. For the remaining seven, Fred Beal, George Carter, Joe Harrison, Kelly Hendricks, William McGinnis, Lewis McLaughlin, and Clarence Miller, the charge was reduced to second-degree murder plus assault with a deadly weapon with intent to kill for each of the three men allegedly wounded on June 7 besides Chief Aderholt, namely, officers Gilbert and Ferguson, and Mr. Roach.

My natural relief to be more or less out of the case was tempered with the realization that the prosecution had given themselves a big advantage in this new disposal of the case. That the first jury favored the defense was clear. In fact, rumors had gone about that Campbell had been paid to "go insane," though they were never to my knowledge really checked out. Obviously it would be easier for the state to send seven men to the penitentiary than thirteen men to the chair and three women to prison.

*New York Times, Sept. 30, 1929.

263

Furthermore, the defense was less favored now in picking a jury; with the reduction of the charge and number of the prisoners, our challenges fell to twenty-eight, with fourteen for the state. As the trial progressed, it became clear also that Judge Barnhill's liberalism had somehow undergone some attrition in the interval. It was altogether clear the state would spare no means fair or foul to convict the seven men.

The jury this time was composed of nine farmers, a retired merchant, a postal clerk, and a Ford assembly plant worker. Except for this last man, they might be said to represent the most backward population of Mecklenburg County. With faces stolid to the point of stoniness they looked down upon a trial in which farce jostled tragedy and falsehood mingled freely with truth—in short, a trial astounding in many ways.

Again the events of June 7 had to be detailed. This time both McGinnis and McLaughlin were identified by different witnesses as having fired the opening shot, which didn't hit anyone. This time a purported "confession" of McLaughlin naming himself as the one who fired the second shot was introduced; also a "confession" of George Carter that he was the guard disarmed by the police before the shooting. Again Beal and I were identified as having shouted "Shoot him! Shoot him!" from the front door of the headquarters. Once more Dr. McConnell testified on Aderholt's wounds, but was not permitted to include the chief's dying statement. He testified also that Roach had over one hundred "duck" shot in him—all in front and ranging from his eyes to his ankles. Again Otto Mason and his wife took the stand, though this time lawyer Jimison unearthed the fact in cross-examination that Mason was in the pay of the Manville-Jenckes Co. George Moore, a grocer who lived near the union shack, corroborated the Mason's testimony, though they disagreed on who fired the first shot. Moore said he witnessed the shooting from a distance of about 175 feet.*

The prosecution's trump card was the introduction of Aderholt's daughter and wife. Miss Ethel told with sobs of her father's last hours. Then the widow, weeping too, quoted her husband. "Stay by me and hold my hand. I won't be here many hours," he had said.

Now Clyde Hoey asked, "What did he say about the shooting?"

"He said, 'I don't know why they shot me in the back and killed me. I have always tried to keep the peace and never done anyone any harm,'" the widow replied between sobs.†

Just about this time strike events in Marion, North Carolina, came to a tragic head with the result that most of the press people packed their

---

*New York Times, Oct. 4, 1929.
†New York Times, Oct. 5, 1929.

bags and rushed off to Marion. After a summer-long strike of the Baldwin and Clinchfield mills, negotiations between the bosses and the strikers had not produced any lasting reforms. On October 2 the local sheriff, eight deputies, and some armed bossmen were waiting in front of the mill when a teargas bomb was exploded. The deputies began firing randomly. The workers ran, but thirty-one of them were shot in the back. Two of them died on the spot, four more died in the hospital later, and twenty-five others were hospitalized.* The massacre of the unarmed Marion strikers aroused national indignation. Our courtroom in Charlotte was now comparatively deserted; we were no longer the center of attention.

Came the turn of the defense to present its evidence. Our first witness was a middle-aged man named Henry Strange, a carpenter. Mr. Strange was at the railroad crossing that evening of June 7 and had witnessed the assault by the "laws" on the picket line. He testified to having heard the drunken Gilbert say to Chief Aderholt, "Let's go down and kill them all off. This is the best time we'll ever get."

Attorney Clyde Hoey, who conducted the cross-examination, was unable to shake this witness' testimony. He did, however, after much probing, get him to admit that he had intercourse with a prostitute. What this act had to do with the death of Chief O. F. Aderholt of Gastonia was clear only to the interrogating attorney. Judge Barnhill interrupted to state that the details of the event were not material. Apparently, however, the report of the act was enough to destroy the credibility of the witness.

Next was called our good Gladys Wallace, who had been present at the meeting on June 7, had walked on the picket line, and had been arrested that evening. Her inquisitor was Attorney Jake Newell, a blunt, blustering fellow quite different from the suave, sophisticated Clyde Hoey, but nonetheless prurient. He tried to impugn Gladys' virtue as well as her truthfulness. He questioned her about the various towns she had lived in, as though she were engaged in some shady activity wherever she went. In every case Gladys' blunt answer to the question, "What were you doing there?" was only, "I spun."

Several defense witnesses, among them Marie Hunsinger, a fifteen-year-old striker who had picketed on the fatal night, testified to the brutality of the officers, particularly Gilbert, in breaking up the picket line. She had seen Gilbert and another officer dragging "Granny" McGinnis on the ground. Miss Hunsinger also testified that the first shot was fired

---

*For a fuller account of Marion, see Tom Tippett, *When Southern Labor Stirs* (New York: Jonathan Cape and Harrison Smith, 1931).

from the place where Gilbert and a guard were scuffling. She and other witnesses testified to the scuffle of officers with the guards which had led to the shooting. Defense witnesses were consistent in placing the shooting on the grounds. Prosecution witnesses had located the shots as coming from the union hall.

Meanwhile, on the outside active union work was continuing. NTWU's next planned move was a big Southern conference to be held in Charlotte on October 12 and 13. Because the interracial aspect of this affair seemed very important to me, I undertook to distribute leaflets in the Negro quarters of Charlotte. I teamed up in this work with George Saul, the ILD worker from Denver, who drove a car. He was a big man, slow-moving, somewhat stolid. We went out every day around Charlotte to cover the Negro neighborhoods. I remember particularly a small mill with all black help which pressed oil out of cottonseeds. Near it was a block-long row of identical cottages, presumably company houses. We distributed the leaflets there as well as at the mill gate when the workers came out. As we were walking away from the cottages, a black man came running after us, holding one of the leaflets.

"Does you really mean it? Is this for us?" he asked eagerly. "We wants to know, does you really mean it?"

We assured him we did.

"Then you'd better tell it better so's everyone can feel sure," he said.

We reported the incident at headquarters and a new leaflet was printed, spelling out in greater detail that black workers were invited on equal terms with white. We distributed at the same location.

On the afternoon of October 12, a Saturday, I was ready and waiting in the old City Auditorium on College Street as delegates were beginning to arrive, when I saw at the door three black men. I ran over to greet them. When they asked which way to the gallery, I assured them there was no sitting in the gallery for them here, all workers were to be together on the floor. To my astonishment the men turned around and left. How did I drive them away, I wondered in dismay. But no, in a few minutes they returned with five others. Actually the representation of black workers was good. It was a well-attended conference, with a total of around three hundred delegates representing one hundred and fifty-one mills in five Southern states: North Carolina, South Carolina, Virginia, Georgia, and Tennessee.

Needless to say, I had no role in that conference. I was on no committee, I was not on the platform, I made no speech. It was an extremely painful situation for me, and I didn't know how to deal with it. That I was a Party member was really the difficult kernel of my dilemma—a Party member could not criticize the Party or its actions or its officials to non-Party people. In the few fraction meetings that had been held I had displayed a critical point of view and found myself deserted by the same comrades who had privately agreed with me. The Party situation affected everyone. The *Daily Worker* had mentioned recently that Albert was to be expelled as a Lovestonite, which he never had been. The pressure on the ordinary member was tremendous; it was the pressure not merely of loyalty and discipline, but behind it all was the power of the C.I. backed up by the prestige of the Russian Revolution.

There in Charlotte we were chiefly absorbed in the trial, in the violence that had been committed by the millowner-state forces, in the union activities. Only ripples of the events in New York reached us. But Party representative Bill Dunne must have telephoned New York daily. Perhaps I was being slandered. Nothing in my situation was clear: I was just groping; uncertainty, a sort of grayness instead of clarity, handicapped me. It is never easy to buck authority, to go against the stream, and few will do this—so I was learning. I must surely have heard from Albert during this time, but he was not in a position easier than mine, nor could he help me at all.

Of course I had to miss some sessions of the trial during the preparation for the conference. The defense at last began presenting the defendants as witnesses.

George Carter testified he had come down as a volunteer and did guard duty. During the confrontation with the police, Roach clubbed him on the head and he remained unconscious until later.

Hendricks, thinner and paler than ever, testified he had left the grounds directly after the meeting and was arrested in his home at four the next morning. He brought out also the drunken condition of Officer Gilbert.

On the morning of October 14 Fred Beal was put on the witness stand. Here was the man who had started the Loray union and had been instrumental in calling the strike, who more than all the rest had been singled out for attack, and who to most people was synonymous with Communist leadership. Attendance was larger than usual, the ranks of the reporters' seats were well filled, and an unusual tension prevailed.

Very clearly I remember Beal on the stand. It seemed to me he was holding up well in his difficult situation. Trim and neat, freshly groomed, pale but calm and composed, he appeared to be bracing himself for a most important moment in his life. I could see signs of strain, of trouble as the day wore on. Still he remained unperturbed and answered deliberately in a soft, high-pitched voice that didn't carry too well in the courtroom. (Actually I couldn't hear all he said.)

Jimison brought out in great detail in an hour's questioning Beal's past history—his work in Lawrence textile mills and his union activities in Loray. This testimony in regard to our guarding the union grounds seemed to bring out a rather curious detachment in Beal as leader of the strike. It was true that in our formal arrangements there was a certain looseness. Authority was not openly designated. Beal's words prevailed because the workers had complete confidence in him. Our arrangements, completely democratic, enabled us to function pretty well.

Beal then testified to his habitual emphasis on nonviolence, denying he told anyone to drag people out of the mill or to shoot or kill anyone. Jimison asked:

Q. What did you tell your crowd that night to do?
A. I told the workers this—We have gotten in touch with the delegation of workers that were working inside of Loray at this time. They wanted us to come down and picket the mill on this night around nine o'clock, because they were going to get their pay around eight-thirty and they wanted to wait until they got their pay envelope before going out on strike. They told me they had the bonus taken off of them and they were not going to stay any longer, and they thought their place was with the other strikers that were out on strike, and they wanted the picket line to come down there and cheer them up as they came out of the mill.

Beal stated that the speakers the night of June 7 were Paul Sheppard, Clarence Miller, Vera Buch, and himself. He affirmed that the attempt to break up the meeting, the throwing of missiles, and the firing of a gun all took place while he was on the platform. He stated that all the men, women, and children on the lot went on the picket line. He said he didn't know who led it.

When asked if anyone was in the office when he went there after the meeting, Beal replied, "I saw Clarence Miller in there bathing his eye after getting blackjacked." He went on to tell how some women came back from the picket line: Vera Buch, Amy Schechter, Sophie Melvin, Edith Saunders Miller. All of them described how they had been choked on the picket line. Then he heard a shot fired "from outside somewhere."*

When the shooting stopped, according to Beal, Edith Miller went out to the window and discovered Joe Harrison wounded. And it was Beal now who took Joe to the hospital, accompanied by Paul Sheppard, K. O. Byers, and Ruby MacMahon, as well as the driver.

In detail the questions brought out how Beal, accompanied by K. O.

---

*Charlotte *Observer*, Oct. 15, 1929.

Byers, went in to Gastonia afterward to get a taxi and was driven out to Charlotte to Jimison's house. After sleeping there the night, Beal left at 10 A.M. Saturday, June 8, for Spartanburg, South Carolina, where he was to remain until Jimison would send for him. He told of his arrest in Spartanburg on that day, of his jailing in that town, and of his being brought back to North Carolina that night and being held in jail overnight in Monroe.

Now the question of Communism came up. Cansler focused on two things that the prosecution hoped would have an effect on the jury: Beal's membership in the Communist Party and his advocacy of racial equality. After considerable debate on whether to allow testimony on Communism, during which the jury was excused, the court tabled a decision until a later time. What seemed to irritate the prosecution most was Beal's racial views. Cansler said, "I submit if there is any question in the world that ought to impeach this man's testimony (I don't know what this man's views are about it) it is to open a notorious advocacy of social equality among the races, which means death and destruction of the two races. Wherever there has been an attempt on the part of one race to force its social rights upon social rights of another, one or the other of the two races has gone down. Your Honor knows that is the history of North Carolina and the entire South."

Cansler's grueling cross-examination went on for hours. At one time he evidently intended to trap Beal into some admission that he felt hostility toward the police or toward Aderholt or wanted to kill them. In general Beal evaded the trap quite well. He did, however, make one admission.

Cansler (reading from a letter of the strikers to Governor Gardner): "Every striker is determined to defend the new Union headquarters at all costs." Now what did you mean by that?

A.   That means if these same thugs that came fom that mill and smashed down these headquarters in the same way that they would defend themselves.
Q.   What did you mean by "all cost"?
A.   That is what I mean. They will protect themselves against them.
Q.   Do you mean to the extent of killing someone?
A.   If they come down to shoot them and kill them, yes.

Beal was holding up well under his ordeal even though his voice was sounding tired at times. Cansler probed persistently about the events of June 7. But the worst was yet to come. Apparently Judge Barnhill had decided affirmatively on the question of admitting testimony on Communism, for Cansler suddenly opened up on that question.

"Do you advocate the abolition of the government of the United States by force and violence and the establishment of a dictatorship formed by the workers?"

To this came the rather astonishing answer from a Party member: "No."

"Do you advocate the abolition of the Constitution of the United States?"

"No."

"I ask you if you don't advocate the abolition by force or violence of private property and turning it over to all the people of the United States for their use?"

"No."*

The next morning after a brief final redirect questioning of Beal, the outcome of the trial was indeed at stake when Edith Saunders Miller was called to the stand by the defense. I hadn't seen Edith nor heard any word of her since June 14, when the rest of us were taken to Charlotte for the habeas corpus hearing. With her very short, boyish haircut, her rather swarthy complexion, and her generally tough appearance she may have looked a little odd and unfeminine to the Southerners. She was, however, completely composed and articulate.

First, on direct examination by Attorney Jimison, Edith Miller stated that she had come South with her husband in May. She told of hearing Beal make his address the night of June 7 and denied he had said anything about going into the Loray Mill or "Shoot and shoot to kill." She said she went on the picket line and was choked when the officers broke it up. She had come back to the inner office with her husband, Beal, and some other women. They all lay on the floor until the shooting was over. No one there had fired a shot nor was anyone armed.

An issue of the *Young Pioneer* was brought out, and Edith insisted on reading some parts of it to the jury. She said she had taught that "the government stands for the slavery of the workers."

"What side did you tell the government was on?"

"On the side of the mill bosses."

"You taught the children to hate the government because it tried to break up strikes?"

"No. They could see that for themselves."

"Did you teach that private property should be abolished?"

"I taught that private property in this country was protected for the

---

*Greensboro *Daily News*, Oct. 15, 1929.

bosses by the government and that in Russia there is no private property and everything is for the mass of the workers."

"You mean you want a revolution?"

"Well, no great change has ever occurred unless the great mass of the people use every means in their possession."

"You mean revolution?"

"Yes. History has taught that revolution is needed."

"You also taught that what is needed here is the Soviet form of government?"

"Yes."

The defense attorneys were constantly objecting to these questions, but Judge Barnhill in most cases ruled against the defense.

When Attorney Newell asked Edith Miller if she believed in God, immediate objections arose from the defense and again the jury was excluded from the room. Judge Barnhill ruled he would allow the jury to hear a question about Mrs. Miller's belief in a supreme being to "impeach" her testimony, but would not allow it for the purpose of disqualifying her as a witness. "The Supreme Court of the state has held that belief in a supreme being is necessary in testifying but the prosecution declared no attempt would be made to disqualify this witness."* When the jury was again present, Edith declared that she believed in no supreme being and would as readily take an oath on an almanac as she would on the Bible.

The trial was drawing to its close; there would be no more testimony. Although court procedure in North Carolina allowed only two hours of argument on each side, at the request of the defense Judge Barnhill announced he would permit six hours. Four speakers would be allowed on each side. The prosecution speakers would be Clyde Hoey, Jake Newell, E. T. Cansler, and Solicitor Carpenter. For the defense T. A. Adams would open, with J. D. McCall, Tom Jimison, and J. K. Flowers following.

Now at last the final confrontation: prisoners and the "jury of their peers" faced each other. The jurors represented the old South, the defendants the new industrialized North Carolina just coming into being. Now the jury became the center of attention as they sat there, with an occasional look of mild astonishment or incredulity as they submitted to a six-hour bombardment of lawyers' words.

The courtroom was not so warm now; the audience was thinned out; the ranks of the reporters had dwindled; people had just gotten tired.

Clyde Hoey, looking like a caricature of some old Southern gentleman, with his aquiline profile and long, gray locks, his chocolate-colored

---

*Greensboro *Daily News*, Oct. 15, 1929.

morning coat and flower in his buttonhole, began in low tones by review-
ing the state's arguments. They considered the conspiracy proved so it
was not necessary to show who fired the fatal shot, but only to know that
the union leaders acted in concert and all were equally guilty. The whole
affair, according to him, was a war between law and lawlessness. "Has the
time come?" he asked, "when it is a disgrace for a man to wear the uni-
form of the law in North Carolina? I saw the sneers of contempt were
not directed against Chief Aderholt and Tom Gilbert, but at the law."

He turned his rhetoric against Beal. "Before Fred Beal came, Gastonia
was a peaceful city. There were no riots, no bloodshed. Beal came down
from Massachusetts. He had a right to do that. But, remember, gentle-
men, violence and rioting began the second day afterward, and yet he
would have you believe he did not counsel violence."* Joseph Harrison
was shot by his own comrades was Hoey's astonishing conclusion. Beal,
lying on the floor of the office, was a coward.

Opening for the defense, Attorney Adams brought up the rumor that
had circulated during the trial that Aderholt had been shot by one of
his own men, Adam Hord, who was next in line to succeed the chief.
Holding up Chief Aderholt's pellet-ridden clothes, "peppered with shot
in the back from his head to his feet . . . he concluded that the only way
he could have been shot in that manner is by a sawed-off shotgun. The
only man on the grounds that might have had one was one of his own
officers."†

Adam Hord had been on the stand as a prosecution witness. I recall
him as a middle-aged man, rather stolid and not very quick. He testified
that he had gone behind the building in search of a man he saw with a
gun, and had been there when the chief was shot. This apparently was
accepted as a sufficient alibi.

After four hours only half the arguments were presented that day.
Another two hours were to follow in the morning, October 18. Somehow
I missed Solicitor Carpenter's summing up. Whether I had something
necessary to do or was simply exhausted by the long verbiage I don't
recall. That I could never have imagined the sort of performance Carpenter put on was proof that I didn't know the South. Solicitor Carpenter, however, knew his South very well; he knew this was Holy Roller
country; there in the backwoods and in the textile towns and mill villages flourished numerous small religious sects meeting every week in the
homes of the poor. Orgies and paroxysms of sentiment released the ac-

---

*Greensboro *Daily News,* Oct. 17, 1929.
†Ibid.

cumulated tensions of cotton mill workers and poor farmers.* Carpenter knew his jury was composed of four Methodists, four Baptists, three Presbyterians, and only one non-church member.

He knelt before the jury, impersonating now the dying Aderholt, now the chief's weeping wife. He seized the hand of black-clad Mrs. Aderholt, exclaiming, "Moses paid for his act by wandering and doing penance for forty years. Do your duty, men. Make these men do penance for their crime by thirty years in the penitentiary." With that he threw Aderholt's coat at the widow shouting, "Take it home, take it home."

When he rolled on the floor like a frenzied performer in a revival meeting, Judge Barnhill finally called him to order. And Carpenter terminated his appeal with this gem of rhetoric:

> Do you believe in the flag of your country floating in the breeze, kissing the sunlight, singing the song of freedom? Do you believe in North Carolina? Do you believe in good roads, the good roads of North Carolina on which the heaven-bannered hosts could walk as far as San Francisco? Gastonia into which the union organizers came, fiends incarnate, stripped of their hoofs and horns, bearing guns instead of pitchforks. They came into peaceful, contented Gastonia with its flowers, birds and churches—sweeping like a cyclone and tornado to sink damnable fangs into the heart and life blood of my community. They stood it till the great God looked down from the battlements of Heaven and broke the chains and traces of their patience and caused them to call the officers to the lot and stop the infernal scenes that came sweeping down from the wild plains of Soviet Russia into the peaceful community of Gastonia bringing bloodshed and death, creeping like the hellish serpent into the Garden of Eden. Do your duty, men!†

It was with these words ringing in the jury's ears that court adjourned that day. There had been titters among the reporters and the audience during Carpenter's speech, so it was reported, and the stony-faced jury may have registered at least some slight reaction.

On the next day, June 21, the courtroom was packed, with many mill workers present. Judge Barnhill had stationed twenty uniformed police and plainclothesmen at various places with instructions to make arrests at the first sign of a demonstration. Immediately after convening court Judge Barnhill began his instructions to the jury and completed them in

---

*See Liston Pope, *Millhands and Preachers* (New Haven: Yale Univ. Press, 1942).
†Ibid.

two hours and fourteen minutes. The jury was then sent out and remained out for fifty-seven minutes. The foreman informed Avery W. Johnson, the deputy sheriff, that a verdict had been reached.

The prisoners were then brought in. The foreman of the jury reported, "We find all the defendants guilty of murder in the first degree."

Judge Barnhill stared in astonishment. "They are not charged with murder in the first degree," he said. "The charge is second-degree murder."

It was actually more complicated than that. Originally, in addition to second-degree murder there had been charges of assault upon two police officers (Gilbert and Ferguson) and upon plainclothesman Roach, but Judge Barnhill had quashed the assault charge upon Ferguson, finding no evidence to support it. There still remained three charges against each of the prisoners. Upon the jury's return each juror had to be polled on each of the charges for each defendant. That took over an hour. Guilty on all counts was the result.

Before passing sentence the judge questioned three of the defendants who had not been called to the witness stand. McGinnis brought out that he was a Gastonia boy who had never been in trouble before except for a fistfight. McLaughlin said he had never been in court before, had fired his gun after a man standing near the automobile had fired his, and that Hendricks was not on the grounds at the time. Harrison showed the judge his arm still scarred from the bullet wounds. Asked why he had come South, he replied, "Just to look around." He had taken no part in the shooting, he said. Clarence Miller, who also had not testified, was not questioned.

Judge Barnhill was now ready to sentence. Fred Beal of Lawrence, Massachusetts, Clarence Miller of New York, George Carter of Mizpah, New Jersey, and Joseph Harrison of Passaic, New Jersey, were sentenced to seventeen to twenty years in the state prison at Raleigh on the charge of second-degree murder; William McGinnis and Lewis McLaughlin, both of Gastonia, were each sentenced to twelve to fifteen years on the murder charge. Beal, Miller, Carter, and Harrison were given ten years each to run concurrently with the murder sentence for the assault on Gilbert. McGinnis and McLaughlin were given five to seven years on the same charge, Hendricks five years. (The judge had stated he was convinced Hendricks was not at the scene of the crime; still he sentenced him.) No sentence was given on the charges of assault against Roach and Ferguson.

Other formalities followed: the defense attorneys gave notice of appeal, whereupon Judge Barnhill fixed the appeal bond at $500 and the appearance bonds as follows: Beal, Miller, Carter, and Harrison $5,000 each; McLaughlin and McGinnis $3,500 each; Hendricks $2,000. Solicitor Carpenter complained the bail was too light in view of the sentences, but after hearing defense attorneys on the question, the judge retained those figures.

The audience and defendants appeared more stunned than anything else, though young K. O. Byers, Beal's close friend, was seen weeping. Only Clarence Miller glared angrily at the judge and prosecution, his face reddened, and when Solicitor Carpenter said he himself would run away on such low bail if he had seventeen years staring him in the face, Miller exclaimed, "We are not guilty." In arguing for lighter sentences, Attorney McCall declared he had never seen a case in North Carolina in which there was so much prejudice exhibited. "It is utterly impossible," he said, "to get a fair trial for these defendants, at least in this end of the state."

So the court adjourned at last.

And for me the Gastonia chapter now came to an unexpected, abrupt ending. I had been kept on the payroll because of the legal requirement implied in "nol-prossed with leave." I had surmised I would not be kept much longer. So I was not surprised but nevertheless shocked when I went to the ILD office that evening and was told that the two women office workers were leaving by car for Philadelphia early the next morning and if I wished I could go with them. There was really no choice. I had saved some money there and, since I had no other resources, I didn't want to spend half of it for fare to New York. So without the opportunity to say goodbye to striker friends or to mull over the outcome of the trial or to get reactions of others or to in any way conclude the experience there, hastily I had to pack my few belongings and depart.

II

At the conclusion of the trial editorials in the liberal press dealt with the civil liberties aspects of the case. I shall not go into them at length since I am concerned more with the matter of perjury during the trial. Looking critically into procedures we find not merely some inadequacies on the part of the defense, but actual distortions of the truth by both defense as well as prosecution witnesses. Some astonishing contradictions in the evidence come to light, which to my knowledge have never been uncovered, much less accounted for.

First, the defense failed to prove exactly where on the grounds the shooting took place. Defense testimony for the most part placed it toward the back of the field; prosecution witnesses located it at the front, where the building was. Never was this point settled. Never was a diagram of the scene produced which might have helped challenge the prosecution's testimony.

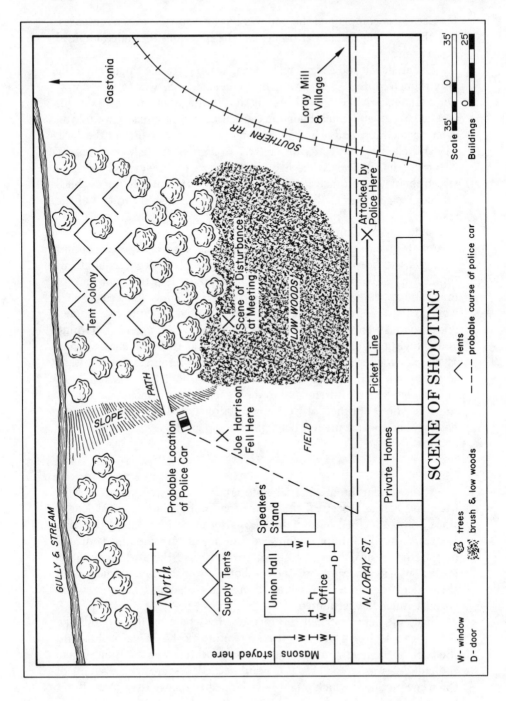

SCENE OF SHOOTING

The prosecution had to locate the shooting near the union shack in order to implicate four defendants who were inside the office at the time the chief was shot, namely Beal, Buch, Schechter, and Melvin. In the original bill of particulars introduced at the first trial on August 26, the prosecution stated that Buch, Schechter, and Melvin stood in the doorway of the building and shouted, "Shoot him! Shoot him!" which incited the union guards to shoot Chief Aderholt. The second bill of particulars presented different facts: now it was Beal and Buch who shouted from the doorway, "Shoot him! Shoot him!" The prosecution even produced a witness who testified that shots had come from inside the building.

A close examination of the facts as I recall them will enable us to pinpoint the location. With Gilbert, Ferguson, Roach, and Hord, Chief Aderholt came in a car to the grounds just after the picket line had been broken up by police. The car passed Schechter, Melvin, and me as we went along North Loray Street back to the union shack. When we reached that point, the car was nowhere to be seen. What had become of it? The five officers were looking for Beal. He was not seen around the grounds (they did not look inside the building), so they drove straight across the field to the back and went down into the gully where the tent colony was. Not locating Beal there either, they returned to the field, where the union guards were now clustered. The guards may have used that brief interval to go into the building to get their guns if they did not already have them. The police must have parked their car there and got out, and there followed the confrontation at the back of the field.

After the police car had driven away with the wounded officers, Beal and I went out of the office and to the window of the shack. Looking out on the darkened field, we found it quite empty, cleared of people and cars. Then, away in a far corner of the field dimly we saw an arm raised, heard a faint cry. Beal went out with a striker who had been with us in the office to where Joe Harrison was lying wounded. They helped him get to his feet and to walk between them to the front. He had been shot in the arm and thigh, had fallen to the ground, and was unable to move without assistance. Because Harrison had been in the thick of the skirmish (all testimony shows officers and guards in close confrontation), one can feel certain the point where he lay marked the location of the shooting. (See my diagram.) These facts were not brought out at all in the trial.

Witness George Moore testified he stood on North Loray Street and saw everything from a distance of 175 feet. This would clearly place the shooting at the back of the field. Further, in a twilight situation, with poor visibility, at a distance of 175 feet or even less, how could positive identification be made? Also, among the defendants named as taking part in the confrontation were three—Joe Harrison, Lewis McLaughlin, and William McGinnis—who happened to resemble each other: all three short and sturdy in build, all three with black hair. At close range facial characteristics would have differentiated them, but at that distance in a dim light they could have been easily mistaken for one another. This point was not made by the defense.

It had been rumored during the trial that Hord, next in line to succeed the chief, was the one who shot him. In the final summing up defense attorney Adams had created a sensation by accusing Adam Hord of shooting the chief, an assumption based chiefly on the sort of wounds Aderholt had received, sixty shots in all, throughout his body, all entering from the rear. Only a sawed-off shotgun could have produced such wounds, said Adams, and Hord was the man who had such a gun. Had the defense been equipped with a diagram locating the shooting in the back part of the field, it could easily have been proved that from behind the building where Hord said he went there was a clear range and not too great a distance to have shot the chief from there. As a matter of fact, witness Rathbone testified that shots came from the woods behind the building. The possibility that they also could have come from Hord's gun was overlooked by the defense. If it is true that Chief Aderholt could have been shot only by a sawed-off shotgun, who had one and how many persons had such guns? If the guards had none, it would be clear that only Hord could have shot Aderholt. It was strange that no guns were produced in evidence and that the matter was not examined ballistically and in depth.

The declaration of a mistrial was another matter in which the defense defaulted. Apparently they accepted without challenge the "insanity" of juror Campbell that was allegedly induced by seeing the image of Aderholt; at least I find no record of such a challenge, nor was anything heard of one at the time. Why did they not demand that their own physician examine Campbell? Why was there no probe on his subsequent hospitalization and the continuation of his derangement? The state had motive to obtain a mistrial because the first trial was going favorably for the defense. The defense offered no contest to the motion for a mistrial.

Now we reach the mystery of Clarence Miller. Here was a defendant who was not present in Loray at the time of the alleged crime. He was drawn into the case only at the last minute, on the morning of July 29 when the grand jury met in Gastonia to work out the indictments just in time for the opening of the hearing.

How can it be proved that Miller was not there on June 7? None of the newspaper accounts of the arrests mention Miller. Nor did any of the witnesses' testimony place him at the scene. In fact, except for the roll call, the name of Clarence Miller was not mentioned in any of the hearings or trials until October 14, when Fred Beal stated that Miller spoke at the meeting on June 7 and later was in the union shack bathing his eye after being blackjacked.*

Let us examine for a moment Beal's statement. Who blackjacked Miller, when, where, and why? There were no police on the lot at that time, nor was any disturbance going on. The picket line had barely left for the mill. Suddenly Miller is blackjacked in the eye. And "bathing his eye." With what? The shack was the plainest sort of little building, with electric wiring but no plumbing. Nor did we have bowls of water standing around for the convenience of ghosts suddenly descended from somewhere with injured eyes. And if Miller's eye had been blackjacked, would there not have been something said about it or would we (the others in the office later) not have also been able to see it? How did Beal know it was blackjacked if he didn't ask Miller? Furthermore, at a moment that was very critical for our Loray strike, at the very moment a picket line was going down to the mill to meet new strikers coming out, an event long planned for, Beal finds nothing better to do than secretarial work on union cards and books in a little inside office in a shack far away from the scene of action. With secretarial help Beal did not have to work on cards at all.

The examination had further brought out that after about twenty minutes some people returned: Vera Buch, Amy Schechter, Sophie Melvin, and Edith Miller came into the office from the line. About five minutes later a shot was heard from outside:

Q. What did you do then?

A. It only seemed to be about one minute after that—or a second after that when a great number of shots were fired—and Clarence Miller said, "It must be the Committee of One Hundred coming down to shoot us up, we better lay down on the floor so the shots don't hit us as they come through the building."

Did it not occur to anyone that this alleged speech of Miller was an extraordinarily long one for anyone to make at such a moment of tension and danger? Also, no one objected that this speech played into the hands of the prosecution because it placed the shooting at the front of the lot,

---

*In his "Trial by Prejudice" Arthur G. Hays originally made the point that Miller was not present in Loray on June 7. Later in his discussion, however, he stated that Miller was in the office during the shooting.

right outside the building, whereas all defense testimony so far had located the confrontation further back in the field.

It is interesting to compare this part of the testimony at the trial with the account given later in Fred Beal's *Proletarian Journey* of the events of June 7. There Miller is not mentioned as a speaker at the union meeting; only Sheppard, Buch, and Beal. In this account Beal was not working on union cards when he went into the office but was "trying to type a report" and lamented his fate of being in the office instead of down by the mill where the danger was. Then the people from the picket line came back, and it was after this that Beal noticed Miller bathing his eye "already blackened and swollen." But Miller here makes no speech. "Just then someone shouted 'The Committee of One Hundred is coming!' and looking out they see two cars and Roach and Chief Aderholt outside the door."* Another point: although Edith Miller testified that she had returned to the office "with her husband" after the picket line was dispersed, no witnesses mentioned Miller on the picket line. A big fellow, he would have been conspicuous among the thirty-five or forty women, children, and undersized youth who constituted that last line.

The first indictment of July 29 charged the sixteen defendants with first-degree murder and conspiracy. The conspiracy charge could have been stretched to cover Clarence Miller in New York, or wherever he was. However, the application of this charge was greatly limited when Judge Barnhill ruled on August 27 that he would limit evidence of conspiracy to the events of June 7 preceding the shooting, namely the disturbance that took place at the meeting and whatever Beal may have said at that time.

In the last trial, beginning September 30 and entailing a complete reorganization of the case, the conspiracy charge was dropped entirely. So now without a shred of evidence locating Miller on the scene of the crime, his indictment became completely unsubstantiated.

Returning to Beal's testimony, if we compare that given on the matter of our last meeting on June 7 with his account of the same event in *Proletarian Journey*, we find definite discrepancies. In the testimony he pictured the entire disturbance as taking place while he was on the platform, but in his book he said:

Vera Buch started to tell the strikers how they were to form the picket line, eggs came flying through the air, splashing against the wall of the union building behind the speaker's stand. Then came bottles and rocks.

Proletarian Journey (New York: DaCapo, 1971), pp. 167-68. Originally published in 1937.

A great disturbance was created and Vera was forced down by the guards although she wanted to stand up against the missiles. I jumped up on the stand in an effort to quiet things. Above the noise of the disturbance I shouted to the strikers why they had been specially called together that night. I was about to go on and give them the instructions regarding the march to the mill gates when from the rear I saw a pistol pointing straight at me. Before I had time to duck or do anything, someone in the crowd pulled the arm of the gunman. The shot went into the ground. Then bedlam broke loose.

The disturbance did indeed take place while I was on the platform, but the discharge of a weapon in the rear also took place then. By the time Beal came up to the platform things were comparatively quiet. *Our meeting did not break up.* There was no bedlam. Had there been, no picket line would have been possible, and the police would surely have been summoned then and there.

The significance of the attempt to break up this union meeting was not made use of by the defense. There definitely was a conspiracy but not on the part of the defendants. The attempt to break up the meeting was a planned effort of the Manville-Jenckes bossmen to prevent the union picket line from going to the mill that night. They knew the unrest that prevailed among the workers in the mill and feared a second strike wave.

Under direct examination by Jimison, Beal said the following:

Q. When the shooting was over what did you do?
A. After the shooting was over we heard no more shots fired and we got up off the floor and Edith Sanders [sic] Miller opened the door of the inner office and looked out the window and said "Oh, Joe Harrison has been shot and someone is bringing him in." I went to the door and looked out and someone was holding him right there. I said "I will take him to the hospital." I took Joe and put him in a car and went to the hospital with him.
Q. Now what did you do with Joe?
A. Carried him to the hospital.
Q. What hospital?
A. I don't know the name of it, somewhere in the center of town.
Q. Who went with you?
A. Paul Sheppard, K. O. Byers, Ruby MacMahon and I believe the driver was a fellow named Polson. Stayed there only long enough to put Joe in charge of the nurse who was there.*

---

*Charlotte *Observer*, Oct. 15, 1929.

The likelihood is that Beal left for Charlotte as soon as we departed for the hospital, K. O. Byers taking him in Byers' car. I recall definitely that when Amy Schechter was brought into that city jail cell on the night of June 7, only a short while after Drew, Edith Miller, and I were put in there, she reported that Beal had gone to Charlotte to contact our lawyer.

Beal then described how he went to the Lodges' house, then on by taxi to Jimison's house in Charlotte.

There are some things quite unrealistic about this story. Beal sets out for the hospital in a car with the following people: Joe Harrison wounded, Polson the driver, plus Paul Sheppard, K. O. Byers, and Ruby MacMahon —a total of five people besides himself. He leaves Harrison at the hospital. Three people and the car now drop out of sight, though Beal said K. O. Byers was with him. No means of transportation is indicated. How did they get to the Lodges' house in West Gastonia, a distance of at least two miles from the center of a town swarming with vigilantes?

Jimison continued the questions:

Q. Where did you go?
A. Spartanburg, South Carolina.
Q. How came you to go there?
A. By automobile.
Q. Who took you?
A. A fellow named Grier.
Q. Was he one of your members?
A. Yes, a union member.
Q. Who was with you when you came to my house?
A. K. O. Byers.

Grier was our Charlotte textile contact who had taken me twice to Pineville. Grier's home was nowhere near Jimison's; he had a car but no telephone in his home. How was it arranged that he come with his car? Furthermore, if Grier was the one with whom Beal set out for Spartanburg, how can we explain that it was K. O. Byers who was arrested with Beal in that town when the police caught up with them the next day? This event was reported in all the papers; there was no mystery about it. Why did Jimison bring out that K. O. Byers came with Beal? In my opinion, it was to call attention to the false testimony in regard to Grier.

At the conclusion of the evidence before the final summing up, Judge Barnhill called up the defendants who had not appeared as witnesses. Besides Beal, only Hendricks and Carter had taken the stand. So one by one McGinnis, Harrison, and McLaughlin appeared before the judge, who briefly questioned them about their personal history. But Miller was also a defendant who had not appeared on the witness stand. Why did Judge Barnhill not question him? To anyone knowing the history of the case, the answer to this is obvious: The judge knew, as the prosecution knew, that Miller was not in Loray on June 7, and they carefully avoided his taking the stand in fear that this fact might come out. But if one of their defendants was unjustly accused, why did they not call him to the stand to prove his innocence? The answer is simple: the defense wanted him to have been present. This can be explained in the light of Party policy, which was fairly intricate, involving not merely the standing of the leaders with Moscow, but also something important to them, to discredit Vera Buch, the wife of a "renegade" (they could see me only in such terms; women in themselves had no importance to them).

Bill Dunne, ostensibly representing the ILD in Charlotte, was really the C.P. rep in the field. It was he who was running the defense. Dunne had broken with Cannon (who had been expelled as a Trotskyite) and was now with Foster. The situation in October at the Party center was changed greatly from what it had been in April and in May, when Robert Minor had been in charge as acting secretary while the bigger leaders were in Moscow. Minor evidently had an eye to survival and had switched his allegiance in time (as did Jack Stachel and William Weinstone). All three had been relegated to minor posts. The Party was now entering the "monolithic" phase, everybody automatically obeying Stalin's orders, all opposition inside crushed, all comrades toeing the line.

We must try to establish first why Clarence Miller went to Gastonia as he did for a few days in May while the new headquarters were being built. Was it out of a pure urge to help in the effort to organize the exploited textile workers? Such a motive he may indeed have had, but Miller as a Central Executive Committee member of the Young Communist League was not free to follow his urges, to flit about the country here or there as he willed. The policy of the League and of the Party was involved. Party leaders did nothing, said nothing, wrote nothing, without an eye to the effects on Moscow, upon which their political survival depended.

When the Passaic Strike in 1926 achieved national and even international fame, the leaders in Moscow must have said to the American Party leaders: Who is this Weisbord, leader of that important strike? *Where were all you people?* The Gastonia strike, like the Passaic strike, received no support from the Party leaders. Foster, in spite of all the C.I. decisions to build new unions under Party leadership (see chapter 7), remained AFL-oriented. Industrial unionism was his cause. Alfred Wagenknecht, head of the WIR in the U.S. who controlled the funds raised for relief of the strikers, was a committed Fosterite. He permitted only a mere trickle of funds to reach the relief of the Gastonia strikers. The Fosterites had attempted to send one of their leaders, Jack Johnstone, early in the strike, but he remained only a few days and fled. The YCL sent Pershing at the start and Siroka a little later, but after a few weeks they too quit their posts.* As Clarence Miller had switched over from the Lovestone faction to the winning side in time, and as he had had some experience in the Passaic strike, he could be used in the situation.

Now why did Miller make a second visit to Loray on June 11 or thereabouts, ostensibly to look after his wife? He may have indeed felt worried about Edith, but a Communist, especially one in a leadership position, cannot act solely on sentimental grounds. The Party and the League must have felt it absolutely necessary, now that the Gastonia case was an affair of international importance, to impress Moscow by having one of "their" leaders in it. Since no evidence could be brought forth that Miller had actually been there on June 7, it had to be manufactured. A leadership role was also to be contrived. Hence the rather silly "evidence" of Miller in the office bathing a blackjacked eye and spouting lengthy speeches of advice and playing leader, wounded in the cause. Was Miller just to pull the chestnuts out of the fire for the leaders and then serve a long jail sentence? If we are to believe Beal's account in *Proletarian Journey*, Clarence Miller was to be rewarded by the Party. Beal writes:

> We paced our cells. We paced the "bull pen." The International Labor Defense raised $5,000 bail for each of us while the case was appealed to the State Supreme Court. Five thousand dollars was extremely low bail under the circumstances. . . . It was significant that one of our local lawyers suggested that we "skip" to Soviet Russia. And soon after that, as we paced the bull pen, "Bill" Dunne visited us with Juliet Stuart Poyntz.
>
> "Take it easy, fellas" said Dunne, "You'll leave for over there as soon as you're out of here on bail."
>
> "Over there" meant Soviet Russia. . . . I was so pleased with the prospect of seeing Soviet Russia that all else left my mind. Clarence Miller, usually non-committal, was positively enraptured. He rose to ecstatic heights as he led prisoners in a march round and round the bull pen singing the "International."†

---

*Pershing soon afterward left the movement to become a businessman, according to Beal in *Proletarian Journey*, p. 155.

†*Proletarian Journey*, p. 209.

Yes, Miller would see the Workers' Fatherland, the Mecca of every United States Communist at that time. Later Miller with the help of his wife was the chief instrument for getting the prisoners out of the country and to their cherished haven. All of them managed eventually to jump bail and flee.*

And what of Edith Miller? It seems to me that the distinction of having gone to the office window after the shooting was awarded to Edith to compensate her for being deprived of the role which she actually had fulfilled of accompanying Joe Harrison, with me, to the hospital. Perhaps Edith had objected to being left out altogether.

Beal's testimony carries out Party policy in not merely locating Miller at the scene of the crime but at the same time giving Miller a leadership role. And he helped the Party in the goal of discrediting me and depriving me of the role I really had played that night. To this end the things I did were assigned to others.

Beal had another reason for aiding the prosecution by testifying that the shooting was at the front of the field. In his book he tells in lurid detail of the shooting, embellishing the danger, placing himself squarely in the thick of it. All of his description—the splintered glass, the bullets penetrating the door, the rifle smoke in the room—is pure fabrication. Most likely it was all to prove that Beal was not a coward.

It is somehow hard to reconcile all this distortion with the character Beal had seemed to have. Even with his timidity Beal had his good qualities. His friendliness with the workers was genuine; he appeared to be a modest, unassuming fellow. His honesty, too, I would have vouched for. But facing a long prison term and under great Party pressure, he apparently let his fears win out.

The testimony that was really crucial to the outcome of this trial was that relating to Communism. We have seen how Beal denied advocating the "abolition of the government of the United States by force and violence and the establishment of a dictatorship formed by the workers." He denied also his advocacy of the abolition by force and violence of private property and turning it over to all the people of the United States for their use.

But when it came to the testimony the next day of Edith Saunders Miller, we heard something quite opposite. Edith Miller insisted on reading to the jury certain sections of the *Young Pioneer*, which had been brought out in evidence. When questioned as to what she taught the children in Loray, she handed out a very nice little lesson on Communism to jury, judge, and audience.

---

*See *Proletarian Journey*, pp. 213ff., for details.

Beal, in *Proletarian Journey*, gives this explanation:

the leaders had debated whether to use the courtroom as a rostrum for propagating Communist principles or to avoid propaganda in order not to antagonize the jury. It was decided, so the defendants were informed, to take the latter course. We were instructed not to discuss the issues of the strike, not to attack the mill bosses, the Committee of One Hundred, or the police for their violence and acts of provocation—the testimony was to be merely one of defense against the charges and was to be given in a way which would win the sympathy of the jury for all of us. But we were not told that exactly the opposite instructions had been issued to Edith Miller, who, though no longer one of the defendants,* was still to appear as a witness. The result of this brilliant "compromise" between the factions which held different views on what should be the Communist policy at the trial, was to discredit the defendants. If we denied our beliefs for fear of the consequences, would we not, therefore, deny the facts?†

Edith Miller was a collaborator in the fabrications of the Party, but in her testimony it seems to me likely that she acted under the instructions of her organization, the Young Communist League, rather than the C.P. itself. The League in general was known to be much more radical than the Party. Its members had been inspired by the Passaic strike; they were militant, outspoken, and what might be termed "leftist." Party instructions may have accounted also for the negative nature of Beal's responses to the questions regarding the tent colony, guard protection, and so on.

The role of Judge Barnhill was of course important, perhaps decisive, in determining the outcome of the trial. Barnhill had appeared at the beginning to be a very fortunate choice from the defense point of view. He had a reputation for liberalism in the state since he had recently ruled that Negroes in North Carolina must be given adequate seats in buses. He made a fine impression on the nation's liberals. "This tall, kindly-faced and informal-mannered jurist, who is the youngest judge on the circuit bench of his state, impressed observers with his independence and common sense."‡

Addressing the grand jury (July 29), Judge Barnhill stated that no prisoner should receive "either more or less than is just on account of his race, color, or condition in life, or on account of his convictions upon social, economic, industrial, political, or religious matters. These matters

---

*She never was a defendant—V.B.W.
†P. 196.
‡*The Nation*, Editorial, Aug. 11, 1929.

have no place in a criminal trial, and should not and will not be permitted to becloud the one issue we are to try.* And he granted the change of venue to Charlotte.

The last trial revealed a quite different Judge Barnhill. He permitted a life history of Fred Beal to be brought out going back to his childhood. Past events such as the organization of the strike, the tearing down of the first headquarters, and the erection of the tent colony were thoroughly aired. He refused to allow the two bills of particulars of the other trials to be admitted as evidence or to consider as evidence of innocence of the seven defendants the fact that nine of the defendants under the same charge had been nol-prossed from the case. Most important, he admitted testimony on religious belief and on Communism, although he excluded the black-white issue.

During the trial John Randolph Neal of Knoxville, who was one of the defense lawyers at the start and withdrew probably because of the domination by the ILD (the Party), returned, and we find him addressing Judge Barnhill in protest, declaring that the "prosecution had dragged Communism in the cases" to prejudice the jury, and asking Judge Barnhill to "reserve the ordinary technical rules of testimony" and exclude all reference to Communism and religion. This Judge Barnhill refused to do.†

Any attempt to explain Barnhill's diversion from his original position can be only speculative. Perhaps it was simply the overwhelming pressure of the environment, the press, the predominance of mill owners in the upper-class society in which a judge would move, our work organizing blacks, the conviction that we were really Communist agitators—all of these factors combined could have persuaded Barnhill to line up finally with his peers.

When all is said and done, we get back in the end to trial by prejudice. Perhaps that is all the Gastonia trials ever were. Perhaps, after all, the evidence whether true or false simply didn't matter. As the last trial progressed, a feeling of fatalism grew and grew in the courtroom. The jury, so anachronistic they probably didn't know the Civil War was over, looking down with faces of stone on the dandified Southern lawyers in their tailored white linen suits, strutting, posing, getting their pictures in the papers, speechifying, playacting—all this was posed against the sinister background of the terror launched on oppressed millhands struggling for a little more to eat, a little relief from unbearably long hours. Everything culminated on September 14 with the murder of Ella Mae Wiggins. Per-

---

*Ibid.
†Greensboro *Daily News*, Oct. 16, 1929.

haps the trial was after all just a charade, as much farce as tragedy, which had to be gone through to comply with the law of the land. Who shot Chief Aderholt? Did anyone really care? Communists must be convicted, and they were convicted; that was the essence of the case.

So in the end, though Judge Barnhill had stated at the Gastonia hearing that this would be no Sacco-Vanzetti case, Gastonia took its place in the long roster of labor cases: Haymarket, Centralia, Eugene V. Debs, Bill Haywood, and many others that stand as testaments to the indestructible urge of the exploited to rebel as well as to the might of the forces arrayed against them.

While the Loray strike was not successful enough to win its demands, it was instrumental in bringing about a reduction of hours for all textile workers in the state. And, more than we knew at the time, it did cripple the Loray Mill. In the summer of 1929 the mill failed to deliver orders to its chief customers, and they canceled their contracts. From then on, Loray Mill and Village steadily deteriorated even further. In 1936 Firestone Rubber Co. bought the mill and village, spent several hundreds of thousands of dollars in new machinery and rehabilitation of the village, and Loray became a captive mill.*

We cannot leave the story of Gastonia without giving the outcome of the trial of the men charged with the shooting of Ella Mae Wiggins. At a hearing in Gastonia on November 5 "a little wiry, gray-haired man named D. L. Case, probably fifty-five years of age," positively identified the killer as Horace Wheeler, a Loray Mill worker. Horace Wheeler's bond was set at $5,000, the others' at $2,500.† Their bail was met by the Loray Mill.

The grand jury in Gastonia on January 13, 1930, had before it more than sixty persons willing to testify to having witnessed the crime. Indictments were returned against five men, all employees of the Loray Mill. A change of venue was granted to Mecklenburg County, and the trial opened on February 24, 1930, in Charlotte. Attempts were made to blacken Mrs. Wiggins' reputation by calling her children "bastards." Despite the testimony of witnesses to the shooting, which took place on an open highway in broad daylight, and the positive identification of the killer as Horace Wheeler, a verdict of not guilty was returned on March 6, 1930.

So the death of Ella Mae Wiggins went unavenged. Brave heart, songstress of mill workers, pioneer organizer of the blacks, Ella Mae Wiggins took her place among labor's martyrs. May she be long remembered!

Yet after all the human effort and travail, the dedication and the

---

*Pope, *Millhands and Preachers*, p. 310.
†Greensboro *Daily News*, Nov. 5, 1929.

heroism of the Loray strike in the end found a repository in the dusty files of libraries, in the labor history archives of universities, where now and then a student, degree-oriented, will stir among these old bones for material to write a thesis. But again this is not the whole picture. The workers remember. Seeds are planted that lie dormant, but will spring to life later.

Revolt, defeated in one place at one time, breaks out again later elsewhere, and again and again as long as there is exploitation. The forces of reaction grow more clever in their senility but their internal weaknesses and contradictions advance also, and as long as there are voices to be lifted in protest and brave men and women ready to lay their lives on the line to fight them, there is hope.

13

Against the Stream

THE SAME TRAUMA-INDUCED MEMORY LAPSE THAT HAD BLOTTED OUT MOST of my speaking tour of the summer of 1929 prevents any recollection of my reunion with Albert, of what he was doing then, or of where we located. Albert thinks he was in New Jersey, but surely after the seven-month separation we would have wanted above all to be together.

I can recall my teacher friends in New York telling me that with the publicity of the Gastonia trial, my pictures in the papers, and people talking about me in the high schools, there was little chance of employment for me in the public school system. With many small plants in New York and Brooklyn, a job in a knit goods factory was still possible, even though jobs in general were getting scarcer. Luckily, I had had the foresight the winter before to protect myself by an assumed name. What boss in a New York factory would ever associate the quiet, reliable, competent Merrow operator known as Anna Miller with the notorious Southern agitator Vera Buch?

Out of the dimness of that period two scenes emerge. In one of them some people, Party members, a small room somewhere in New Jersey. . . . Behind the table in front Fred Beal speaking; of his words only these can I recall: "Albert Weisbord deserted his post in the South. . . ." I learned then the meaning of the word "dumbfounded." Did I jump to my feet, did I shout, "That is a damn lie!" No, I was literally stricken dumb with astonishment, with disbelief. Of course afterward I denounced the slanderous statement among the comrades present, which does not excuse my failure. Again Beal was letting himself be used for the purposes of that same party he despised.

Another meeting comes to mind, one for the Gastonia defense held in some small hall in New York. I sat in the audience; on the platform

290

were Beal and the three Loray defendants McGinnis, McLaughlin, and Hendricks. They all greeted me with friendliness, even affection, beckoning me to join them on the platform. Of course I had not been asked to speak. In my refusal I meant to disassociate myself from both Beal and the Party leadership. When Fred called attention to me in his speech, there was applause but I remained where I was.

Soon I joined the Party unit of the section where we lived, a small group composed almost entirely of workers. The prestige of the Gastonia strike was great, and the rank and file comrades were not yet infected with the poison of slander. I was treated warmly and with respect. The political situation was not discussed. There was no fighting at all, nor any creative activity either . . . only routine business.

A notable member of the unit was Comrade Robert Minor, who never appeared at meetings. His wife, Lydia Gibson, a rather handsome and dignified, dark-haired, tall young woman, who had a reputation in Greenwich Village as an artist, attended regularly. I used to introduce a motion, passed with gusto every week, that Comrade Minor should attend unit meetings. Of course we knew he never would; this was simply a game we played.

A principal activity of the comrades then was "building up the mass organizations," the WIR and ILD. This meant giving up two evenings every week to attend the meetings of these groups, finding there only a few besides our own members. Routine Party meetings of one sort or another might require an additional evening or two. I saw how the comrades' time was being taken up futilely, preventing their making contact with the masses, which should have been their chief effort, especially now that the economic situation of the country was worsening.

With Herbert Hoover as President the country at the end of 1929 was entering into the great Depression. On October 29, following the failure of an Austrian bank, the Credit Anstalt Bankverein, came an unprecedented stock market crash, then panic and a run on the banks. The events affected not merely the workers but the middle class: small manufacturers, storekeepers, and professional people, who after years of work, having saved up some thousands of dollars, found themselves at one stroke left penniless. While we ourselves were not personally involved, headlines and pictures in the newspaper conveyed stunned shock and anguish, followed by hysteria, stampeding, and injuries. Remembering previous depressions, people had been asking, "How long will this one last?" But now the calamity created an atmosphere of apprehension; it was becoming clear this was no ordinary depression, but a crisis of capitalism on a global scale.

For Albert and myself these months were among our most important and critical; it was the time of our separation from the Party. A year before how indignantly would we have repudiated any suggestion that we might ever leave it! Yes, we who were so devoted, so totally committed. Not in the least had we changed our basic opinions; the road to Communism was the only road out for the working class, in fact for all humanity.

The process was not simply deciding to leave and resigning. It had been in the previous June that Albert had come to the conclusion that because of the leaders' sabotage of our work in the South he would have to resign his post as head of the C.E.C. Textile Committee. Before he could carry out this decision, the shooting of June 7 broke out in Loray; then, withholding his resignation pending some solution of the crisis there, Albert left for Charlotte on June 9, waiting only for the meeting of the NTWU executive committee, which was held in New York that very morning. He left with Reid and Dawson on the evening train. Arriving in Charlotte on Monday morning, June 10, they found a large Party group already there, including Poyntz, Wagenknecht, Dunne, Johnstone, Crouch, and Trumbull.

Dunne moved that Poyntz should go into Gastonia ahead of the others on the grounds that, first, as a woman she would be less likely to be lynched, and, second, since it was now a defense case, the ILD representative should be there. When this motion was defeated, Albert decided as textile representative that the union people should go in first. Before they could leave, however, came the telegram signed by Robert Minor recalling Albert. The fraction unanimously decided he should not return, but then came two phone calls threatening him with expulsion and he felt compelled to obey. Reporting to the secretariat in New York, he found himself charged with "running away from the South." This frame-up was to lay the basis for his later removal from the Central Committee and his suspension from the Party.

Soon afterward the secretariat ordered a fraction meeting of the NTWU. At this meeting appeared Foster who, in the name of the secretariat, demanded that Weisbord resign as secretary of the union and that the fraction approve this step. The comrades were by no means all in agreement, but when Albert said he would not fight the order of the secretariat, they agreed.* Albert recalls that after he had been kicked out of the union office, Foster had approached him saying, "Weisbord, why don't you just give in and join me. You can have your post back." Albert knew that Foster, the "eclectic trimmer," had nothing of principle to offer. His leadership could lead only to stifling the Party.

---

*Albert Weisbord, "My Expulsion from the Communist Party," *Class Struggle*, Aug.-Sept. 1931.

All during the summer of 1929 Albert had maintained his confidence in the Comintern itself. He had in fact sent an appeal to Moscow denouncing the frame-up that had been designed to get rid of him and demanding a trial and the right to appear personally before the Russian leaders. He even wrote a statement to the Party secretariat on June 19, 1929, saying that "the CI called upon every party member to finish what the CI had begun: the elimination of the present leadership fundamentally vitiated by petty-bourgeois politician tendencies and rotten diplomacy and for the creation of a leadership actually tested in the fire of proletarian struggles."

It was through the *New York Times* that he learned his loyalty was rewarded with expulsion by the CI. In *Inprecor* a completely unproved article by Losofsky appeared, denouncing him as "a white chauvinist." Jack Johnstone, who fled from Gastonia in less than a week, actually proposed that the NTWU build two unions in the South, one white, one black.

Sometime during that confusing summer a cablegram was sent from Moscow by Jay Lovestone stating that the CI was appointing a secretariat to head the American party consisting of Weisbord, Wicks, and Weinstone, these three having been chosen because they were the least involved in factional struggles. Albert could feel for a brief period that he had been vindicated; however, nothing more was heard of this alleged decision.

Another interesting episode of that summer was the escape of Lovestone and Gitlow, who, as often happened to those in opposition, were being detained in Moscow ("detention" being the prelude to "liquidation"). It was through the cooperation of the American Embassy that both escaped.

It was not possible for the membership to know all the maneuvers and decisions in Moscow by which the leadership of the American Party was being shuffled around. We ourselves had seen enough and experienced enough to feel complete lack of confidence in all the American leaders. Our original view that the Party could be so influenced by mass work as to create a new leadership had been shown to be unfounded. It was upon this conclusion that we drew up a statement of resignation from the Party, charging the leaders with total involvement with and domination by Moscow and utter incompetence in building the American Party.

We never had cause to regret our decision. This did not mean, however, that the transition was easy. In our devotion we had cut off practically all ties with non-Party people. It was necessary now not merely to build a new life but to learn new ways of thinking. We decided as a fundamental policy to get jobs in some basic industry and live among the workers. Under an assumed name, Albert found an opportunity in a Ford assembly plant located in Newark, New Jersey. So we moved there. We stayed first with a Party family, renting a bedroom with kitchen privileges.

Albert's first job was as a stevedore loading automobiles in their cases onto barges at a wharf on the Passaic River. From there they were transported to Newark Bay to be loaded on ships for overseas. It was a heavy, dangerous job. The Ford plant worked an eight-hour, five-day week and paid twenty-five dollars a week. These were unusually good hours and pay for those times, but everybody knew Ford got his money's worth. Albert was a healthy young man, never had had a seriously sick day (though he did have tension headaches sometimes in Passaic), and had built up a good muscular system by athletics in his youth. Still, he would come home exhausted every day and would spend the weekend recuperating.

For me the brief period till I found a job was pretty unsatisfactory. After the long separation, there seemed to be no opportunity for personal communication of any sort. The struggle for survival was uppermost; there was no time to talk, and, indeed, as far as the political situation was concerned, there were too many unknown factors for us to be able to find clarity. And what of Gastonia, our great experience? Was there no time to speak of that, to analyze it, to achieve an historical perspective? Like the Passaic strike, when it ended Gastonia was thrust into some limbo of the mind, the ordeal perhaps too great to stand revival. I recall at that time frequent dreams of being pursued by unknown enemies. With the withdrawal into a merely personal life, something of my old insecurity had returned.

Soon, however, I obtained a job in an important textile mill, the Clark Thread Company, a Scotch firm long established in Newark that made ONT (Our New Thread). The plant employed five thousand people, many of them women. Like some medieval castle, it had massive high walls of gray stone, with turrets posed at intervals on top . . . for what purpose, to conceal machine guns? Two wide gates stood open between 6:45 and 7:15 A.M., as seven was the hour for beginning work. Arriving there once at 7:20, I had to go into a little gate house at the right to fill out a pass, which I had to take first to my building superintendent to be countersigned, then to my department foreman, the lost time being deducted from my pay.

Within the walls were many large buildings spread around a cobblestone courtyard. I had to climb big flights of stairs to get to my department, where enormous spinning frames made in Birmingham, England, perhaps thirty feet long and seven feet high, were ranged down a long room. Some ten or twelve new "girls" were receiving instruction from a forelady. Finding myself on the outer fringes of the group, I couldn't see how the knots had to be tied in the "ends," and I believe throughout my employment there I tied them the wrong way. Rows of threads close together, moving upward over the frames, were the object of one's attention. Each of the new girls had to attend to about twelve feet of frame. The thread would break and the ends had to be quickly tied; that was the job, not hard but demanding. Standing for long periods was always hard for me. Backache quickly developed. My fatigue was great. For the noon hour there was no place to eat, not even a chair to sit on (such luxuries as plant cafeterias and coffee breaks being unheard of in those days). The older workers had their own little folding camp chairs on which they sat to eat a lunch brought from home. The newcomers went out to some slop joint in the neighborhood.

Saturday at eleven-thirty the power was shut off. We then had to spend a full half hour cleaning the machinery. Textile work always produces dust as the friction of the machinery erodes the cotton fibers. We had to clean an inch-high layer of dust from all the parts of a big complicated machine, using swabs of cotton waste which lay in piles on the floor. Under the dust was the black grease that protected the machinery. It was a filthy task. Because some of the women were on piecework, this half-hour every week was just a present they had to hand over to the company. The pay for learners was fifteen dollars, for experienced workers twenty to twenty-five dollars.

I had not been long at Clark Thread Company when we made a change in our domestic arrangements; we rented a room with a Negro family, the Newcombs, who owned a small cottage at the edge of a Negro quarter. Part of our general plan was to make contact with the black people; this seemed a modest beginning. The room was big and cozy, with a carpet and cretonne curtains; at the two sunny windows were plants and a rocking chair. We had not been ten minutes in the room unpacking when the landlady's little boy knocked on the door. His mamma said, could we lend her five dollars? Foreseeing a bad precedent, we simply told him we didn't have five dollars.

As soon as I had gotten somewhat used to the job at Clark, I began to think of organizing in the department where I worked. Here were employed possibly fifty women, the majority old-timers; some of them had even come from Scotland with the company. A few approaches to them showed them to be unresponsive, even hostile. Some of the beginners intended to remain. Poor as the job was, it gave promise of being steady if you could stick to it. As the beginners were all discontented with the low pay and conditions, they listened to me. Within a couple of weeks, feeling I had made enough progress, I told the women I had a contact with a union in New York which might send someone out to help us organize.

With that I wrote two letters, one to the office of the NTWU in New York, the other to the organization committee of the Party (District 2 included New Jersey). I described fully the Clark plant, its location and layout. I drew a ground plan showing where the exit was and gave the time the workers came out. Then I suggested they put out a leaflet, send in some people to get jobs in different departments, and assign an organizer to cooperate with me in an attempt to organize the plant. Fully expecting a response and waiting daily to see a leaflet crew when I got out from work, I allowed a week to pass.

Because it was remotely possible my letters had gone astray, at the end of ten days I dispatched two similar letters. Again no reply, none whatever. I was forced to conclude that rather than cooperate with Vera Buch, rather than give her a chance to function effectively among the workers, my ex-Party would pass up an opportunity to penetrate a big textile plant right at their doors, a half-hour away from downtown to New York. Alone now in the plant, with no contact outside I could do little.

Meanwhile our arrangement with the Negro family terminated unexpectedly. Coming home from work one Saturday afternoon, I found a group of strange people outside the house. We had always noticed that our hosts seemed to have a lot of friends; people were always dropping by. Now the Newcombs were arrested for running a numbers racket. Later, when Albert got home, we obtained the services of a lawyer and got the arrestees out on bail. We felt, though, that it was inadvisable to continue living there. (It was lucky we weren't home when the raid took place.) We decided to move to Jersey City, nearer to Albert's job than most locations in Newark. I quit the thread mill job, for which I no longer had any motivation.

Our location in Jersey City was a pleasant furnished apartment; a large room with a bed and dresser in an alcove; three big windows on a quiet street, in a closet at the back a sink, a little electric stove, and cupboards. And I spent time in that place, for we had decided I was to take a month off to read the three volumes of Marx's *Capital*. So now every morning at eight o'clock or even earlier I would sit down at the table and remain hunched over my task for most of the day. As I progressed through this tremendous work, so detailed yet so profound, so completely thorough and all-inclusive in its analysis of the functioning of the capitalist system as it was in Marx's day, I seemed to find at last that truth which I had been seeking all my life. Marx's system did not touch on the old questions of the immortality of the soul or man's relations to the sidereal universe, but since such problems are in all likelihood unsolvable, I found enough inspiration in comprehending the objective world in which I lived; here at last was my key to that world. Reading Marx wasn't easy; I had been so long away from study, for months having read little except the newspaper, that at first mere concentration was hard. There was nothing, however, that could not be understood with enough effort, and steadily I progressed to the end.

The fragmentary and unfinished Volume III, edited by Engels, was disappointing, and it left a keen sense of the limitations of all human efforts, even the greatest of which must be defeated in the end by death. Of course such a massive work as Marx's *Capital* was not something to remember; it was rather to be referred to often and constantly applied to current developments, economic and political, national and international, with a gradual deepening of one's understanding of Marx's thought and the laying of a firm basis for the interpretation of events.

Albert was gradually upgraded in the Ford plant. From the loading dock he progressed to a job of closing packing cases containing completed cars; the wood had to be sawn to size and nailed in place, the nails being held in the mouth. Everything had to be done with the greatest speed; it was another hard and exhausting job. Later he was put on a slushing job; machine parts had to be loaded into baskets, this heavy load lifted up to a container where the parts were flushed with oil before being packed to be sent abroad. He sustained a few accidents on these jobs, luckily none too serious. Finally his good service and reliability, perfect attendance, and ability to keep up with the pace of work were rewarded by his being made a stock picker, a less arduous and more interesting job that enabled him to get around the plant and meet more of the workers. Really he had accomplished a feat of survival rare in the Ford plant, where only two or three out of one hundred men lasted that long.

Our life was now a secluded and narrow one; the prevailing hostility excluded us further from contact with Party members. Albert did, however, go into New York one Sunday, returning with a copy of the Cannon group newspaper, *The Militant*. I remember my shocked reaction: "What, you're reading that . . . that *sheet*?" Strangely enough, though we were ourselves expelled, we looked upon the other groups thrown out of the Party as untouchable. Albert replied that we simply had to investigate all opinions and begin to reorient ourselves to political life. It was not long afterward that we had a visitor in our hideout, no less than James P. Cannon himself.

Discussion brought out first that Albert was not a Lovestonite as had been charged. It also began to open our eyes to the violence that had been done to Leon Trotsky, who a few years before had been forcibly expelled from the Soviet Union and taken in exile to Alma Ata, a remote place in

Asia (actually beyond the Pamir Mountains, so far that it was near the
borders of China). Merely faint echoes of slander had reached the
American membership. Trotsky's eminent record since 1905 had been
erased from Russian histories; his name was anathema. We learned now
of Lenin's Testament asking for the removal of Stalin as general secretary
of the Russian Party and suggesting Trotsky in his place. Max Eastman,
a liberal writer, was beginning to translate Trotsky's many writings.

While we were grateful for the information concerning Trotsky, we
were not persuaded to join Cannon's group. Perhaps the chief deterrent
was Cannon himself. He was considered in the Party not merely to be an
unprincipled factionalist like the others but to be inefficient as well. In
all those months of turmoil in Passaic that had brought innumerable
arrests, not once did James Cannon appear in the field. His paper, the
Labor Defender, gave very poor coverage of the strike. (In the New Bedford strike his defense policy was in effect strikebreaking.) Cannon would
go out once a year for a tour of the few ILD branches that existed. This
he called a "refreshing plunge among the masses," as though he were
jumping into a swimming pool. He was a fairly large man of thirty-five
with reddish sandy hair, shifty blue eyes, a high-pitched voice, and a rather
theatrical manner. Some compared him to a preacher. (See Appendix E.)

Cannon's visit with us was brief; he did not argue or attempt to persuade. It is possible he came only to probe, or if he had hopes of winning
an adherent, he may have sensed from Albert's coolness there would be
no support for him in our quarter. He touched only briefly on the history of his relations with Trotsky, and he did not attempt to exaggerate
his following in New York, saying they had only a small group too weak
to attempt mass work.

Not long afterward came another pilgrim to our humble retreat: Jay
Lovestone of the majority group, which now functioned as a separate
entity with more members than Cannon had. It was amusing to see
people who had had no use for Albert while we were all in the Party now
coming practically hat in hand to our door. Lovestone fared no better
than Cannon. It probably would have been difficult if not impossible for
these Party leaders to realize that they themselves were the chief reason
for our leaving the Party.

Lovestone was a young man, only about two years older than Albert.
Tall, blond, not sluggish like Cannon but energetic and quick, he spoke
fast and incisively. His contention was that his new grouping *was* the
Party, since he had the majority recognized by the Comintern. Of course
all his followers were not in the new group: many had remained with
Foster-Browder; others had simply dropped out. He said he had hundreds

of members and a functioning apparatus and was putting out a paper, *Revolutionary Age*. Lovestone offered Albert a chance to speak at their coming convention, to which Albert replied that if he spoke it could only be to criticize and attack the majority group. Lovestone left soon after that and we heard no more from him.

A final unexpected visitor there in Jersey City was my father, who came out one evening from New York. Long afterward Papa told me he had every intention that time of "telling us off," of "giving us a piece of his mind"—all this of course in relation to the lack of an official piece of paper in our marriage.

Ill feeling had prevailed in my family for years on this question. It all traced back to the one visit home Albert had made with me in the fall of 1926 after he had left Passaic. On that trip he insisted I acquaint my family with the fact of our living together. It was harder than Albert could imagine for me to break through the barrier my mother had built up between herself and her children on any matter concerning sex. I put it off until the very last minute. At last at ten o'clock I blurted out, "Albert and I are married. We'll stay in my room," and we went up to bed. When I came down early the next morning, Mother confronted me.

"Just when did you get married?" she asked.

It had to come out now. "We're not married. Albert is married to somebody else, so we're just living together."

She didn't say a word, but I could see her heart beating fast under her dress. Nellie's hair was all gray now, though her cheeks still showed a little color. In her gray-blue eyes that avoided mine was that look one sees sometimes in the eyes of those who have not known passion, an incongruous look of virginity. Later she sent me a letter stating I could come out there, *"but alone."* She never thought her daughter would do a thing like that, she said.

But now in Newark Papa evidently had a change of mind. We had a friendly chat over coffee cups; Albert and he seemed to get along well together. The soberness and happiness of our relationship must have been apparent to any sane mind, and if there was such a mind in my family, it was Papa's.

My Marxian vacation over, I returned to the little knit goods factory in the New York garment district where I had been employed briefly after leaving Gastonia. It was more than a year now that Albert had worked in the Ford assembly plant. As a stock picker he was one of the solid inner core of workers and was not laid off for the Christmas-New Year period as most of the plant was for inventory. He made an effort to organize the plant, but met with the same failure of the Party to cooperate as I had

experienced in the Clark Thread Co. Accordingly, he reached the conclusion, in which I concurred, that it was time he got back to political
life. We had saved up some money and could ride for a while. So Albert
quit his job and we returned to New York, locating in a small furnished
room downtown. Because we ate our meals out, I was free from housework and had my evenings. Albert gave full time now to study of whatever material was available in order to find a new political orientation and
above all to make contacts.

One of the results of the splits that divided the Communist movement into three sections was that many members, bewildered by the rapid
changes and the many unexplained decisions from Moscow and disgusted by the turmoil and unprincipled direction of the movement, had
simply dropped out. These were the people to be reached, as well as those
who had been expelled. To attend any official Party meeting in those days
would have meant physical attack ("renegades" were definitely not tol-
erated). However, in the ferment of the political life of which Fourteenth Street was the center there were meetings of the two other groups,
also of the Socialists, occasionally the IWW or anarchists, neutral for-
ums, and so on. Interested people were to be found also in the cafeterias,
where the unemployed would congregate to chew on political questions
by the hour over a cup of coffee.

Albert was coming to feel he had to set up his own political group.
There seemed to be no alternative; to join an existing group was impossible since we didn't agree with any of them. What were we to do, be
annihilated, drop out altogether from political life? I remember suggesting at one point that we might consider, for a while at least, working
within existing mass organizations until we could get more of a following
or until the situation clarified. To this Albert had a conclusive answer:
what was most necessary now was to provide a correct political line; for
this we must put out a paper, and to do that we had to have a group. He
was his old self once more, a dynamo waiting to be attached to a mecha-
nism, his mind teeming with ideas, talking incessantly as he worked out
his thoughts, absolutely sure of himself.

It was not long before he had gathered around himself a group of
like-thinking people. The conception we had of our group was not merely
one of theory but of action. In fact, it was clear that there could be no
theory of the working class struggle worthy the name without participation in the mass actions of the workers; activity and theory were inevitably intertwined. Had we been willing to accept as members all those who
agreed in principle, our group would have been much larger, but as actual
members we would take only those who agreed to take part in whatever
actions were possible and donated regularly ten percent of their wages.

The others were considered sympathizers who would donate money as they wished, attend public meetings, help distribute the paper, and provide a certain moral support as friends.

The question arises: why did Weisbord not draw a following out of the Party as the other leaders did? For one thing, the others were part of Russian groupings, which in itself carried prestige and protection. Also, in the Party Lovestone and Cannon spent most of their time winning adherents for their factions. Weisbord gave full attention to mass work, making no effort to build a personal following.* Our union was a new one, and there had not been time to build a base through it. In Passaic there were Party members among the textile workers, but they were attached to the foreign federations, which claimed their principal loyalty. As for the Cannon group, they survived chiefly through Trotsky's support and prestige; they were thus a parasitic group much like the Fosterites supported by Stalin. The Lovestonites, attached to Bukharin, with all their superior numbers and apparatus achieved little and in a few years crumbled apart.

On March 15, 1931, we launched a new organization which we called the Communist League of Struggle, combining two historic names: Karl Marx's Communist League and Lenin's early organization, the League of Struggle for the Emancipation of the Working Class. Soon we started publishing the *Class Struggle*. I was associate editor. The paper was at first printed, but that proved beyond our means financially, so we bought a secondhand mimeograph machine and ground out the sheets by hand. All members participated in getting the paper out, and the sympathizers helped to distribute it. The first issue of the paper contained a thesis written by Albert Weisbord and adopted after thorough discussion by the group. The CLS announced itself as an internationalist group adhering to the basic principles of the International Left Opposition, headed by Leon Trotsky. We were a Marxist group, involved in American life, understanding and utilizing the laws of motion that flow from the internal contradictions of capitalism. We stood for the close connection of theory and practice, for leadership based on participation in mass struggles, for a vanguard party.

We were what was then called a "splinter group." The workers' move-

---

*Keller and Dawson went with Lovestone, Murdoch with Foster. Jim Reid of Providence, Rhode Island, not a textile worker but a dentist who had been made president of the union because of years of devoted service, had solidarized himself with Weisbord to the extent of signing the telegram sent to Moscow protesting Albert's ouster. However, Reid was an older man, perhaps not equal to the rigors of the political struggle, and eventually dropped out.

ment was indeed fragmented. (See Appendix F.) We were pelted from the right and from the left; the U.S. government tried to deprive us of mailing privileges, which was to be expected; the Cannon group always referred to us disparagingly and finally raided our headquarters and stole our Marxist library. The official Party people physically attacked our members who attempted to distribute leaflets at their meetings. It was a steady warfare paralleling the theoretical bombardment in the press.

For a headquarters our group rented a sort of loft in a building at 212 East 9th Street, near Third Avenue. Well I remember when we went to look at this place, Albert and I and a couple of other comrades. It was a very large room occupying a whole second story, windows in front, entrance at the rear, and a tiny office partitioned off in back. A large round iron stove was the only provision for heat. It looked so poor, so barren. As the comrades cheerfully viewed the place and discussed its advantages, a cold grayness came over me, a presentiment: this cannot succeed. Of course I said nothing; it really was a good headquarters and the price was low. Overcoming my hesitation, I devoted myself completely to the new enterprise. The comrades built a set of wooden benches and bookshelves; all who had books of a Marxist nature donated them to the group. Later on in 1933 we were able to move to a better location on Second Avenue.

I had shifted my place of work to a factory in Brooklyn where I could in a way feel more at home because some of the workers knew me as Vera Buch. The regular working day at that time was nine hours; in the busy season one, two, or even three hours of overtime were added at only the regular rate of pay. With this fifty-five or sixty-five hours of work, the accumulation of fatigue was great. Exhaustion took its toll in sickness; there were always some machines vacant. It was hardest after five o'clock. How slowly that clockhand moved! After a while the aches and pains were replaced by numbness, one worked on as an automaton, the hands moved to put the pieces in place, to guide them through the machine, the knee pressed the pedal; shoulder seams, sleeves setting, collar, underarm seams—on and on, on and on. One was now really only a part of the machine, all thought gone, feeling reduced to one dull general ache, until at last it was 8:30 or 9:00 P.M.—quitting time! The young girls would laugh and giggle in the elevator. There was a need for release, to feel human again, to overcome this numbness that weighed one down.

There were two busy seasons a year and two slack; in the slack seasons most of the shop would be laid off, only a few relatives or bosses' favorites being kept on. In those periods I would sometimes pick up a job in another trade. Once I worked on pocketbooks. Another time I answered an ad for an operator on blouses. So many women applied for that miserable twenty-dollar-a-week job, crowding the stairs and pushing into the office, that the boss, wild-eyed, shouted, "Get out!" and shoved us all out of the room, locking the doors. Whether he hired anyone or not I didn't know, but surely at least two hundred applicants were there. So it was in the depression.

Under direction of the CP bureaucrats the knit-goods workers in the National Textile Workers Union were shifted into the Needle Trades Workers Industrial Union, which was the Party union in the needle trades at that time. The excuse for this move was that with the depression many cloakmakers and ladies' garment workers, union people, were finding employment in the knit goods, which was expanding with the invention of rayon yarn to make dresses and suits of knitted material as well as sweaters and bathing suits. In practice the move helped further to break down the NTWU. A small committee functioned for the organization of the knit-goods trade consisting chiefly of Party members working in the shops with a few others, of whom I was one. There was also an anarchist named Louis Nelson, who always treated me with respect. It was hard indeed after a long day's work to stay up for these committee meetings devoted to reports on shop conditions and discussion of ways and means to build the union. We all had to fight off sleep and fatigue. I remember the efforts to keep my heavy eyelids from closing.

Sometimes we called public meetings for the workers. While in the committee meetings I seemed to be accepted as one of the group, at the open workers' meetings it was a different story. Evidently the Party people had been instructed to attack me in public, to see to it that I couldn't build any influence. I would take the floor only to make some concrete proposal in relation to the workers' interests. And each time I spoke four or five of these Party people would jump up in succession to denounce me. I was a Lovestonite, a Trotskyite, a careerist, an intellectual who was using the workers for her own purposes, and so on. I would be given three minutes to reply. What could I do? Their tactics disrupted the union work and probably drove some workers away. There were times when I thought I might do better to stay away altogether, but that was just what they wanted. I couldn't capitulate.*

Who were the people around us in our group, the Communist League of Struggle? As New York was a financial and commercial center with variegated light industry, the only members from basic industry were a group of seamen. We also had a railroad worker, three cooks, a baker, a butcher, two teachers, a garage mechanic, some taxi drivers, a laundry

---

*Eventually in 1935 we called a general strike in the trade. It was fairly successful, with the result that we became Local 155 of the ILGWU, with Louis Nelson as president.

worker, several office workers, one knit-goods worker (myself), one mechanic in the Brooklyn Navy Yard, one plumber's helper, and a number
of unemployed youth. We had a German family who had belonged to a
left socialist German group (the *Allgemeine Union*). We had a Welsh-
man, formerly a coal miner, an English seaman, an Australian seaman, a
young Russian only a few years in this country, and one Negro from Paterson, so that our group was to a limited extent international. Though
the original founders of the group were chiefly male, eventually some
women were drawn in.

The English seaman Thomas Bunker had worked for years in the
British Navy. I wish I could recall the sailors' chanties Bunker used to
sing for us in spare moments. "Blow the Man Down," "Have a Little
Piece of My Wife's Cake," "She was a nice girl, she was a good girl, but
she was of the roving kind, ..." and others. Thomas Bunker was a slim,
wiry fellow in the early thirties, sunburned, cheerful, and a gifted as
well as companionable man, as could be seen from the articles he contributed to our paper. Later on in his life he went to Australia, where he
became head of a seamen's union. Seaman Joyce from Australia had been
a member of a sheep-shearer's union there. There was also Weser, an
American-Jewish seafarer. The seamen were sturdy fellows and were
among our most active people.

One of our unemployed was a slender, dark-eyed, handsome youth
named Sydney. A bad heart condition prevented him from working or
seeking work. He wanted so much to be active, to participate in our activities. When a great hunger march of the unemployed to Washington was
being organized, Sydney longed to go. Life was worth nothing to him,
he said, if he had to live only to take care of his health. So our comrades
voted that Sydney should go on the March. It was a rugged affair, in
winter, involving much hardship. Sydney didn't live long after that.

Phil Rosenberg, also unemployed, was a good-natured fellow who
often stayed around the headquarters. He was dark-skinned, fuzzy-haired,
hooknosed, rather awkward of movement. Phil contributed a long analyt-
ical article to our paper on the Hollywood film industry. In the second
winter, leaving his family, he rented a tiny flat on the lower East Side. It
was heatless, as such flats generally were. One morning a shocking announcement appeared in the paper: a Philip Rosenberg had been found
dead in his bed, asphyxiated. Another young man was with him, unidentified. Accompanied by Murray B., one of our sympathizers, I went to
the abandoned little flat. The bedroom held only the rumpled bed and
a small gas stove. This stove had a row of outlets at the bottom, which
were visible, and as I examined the thing, I found another row at the top

that could not be seen. Evidently the comrades had lit the lower outlets unaware of the existence of the others.

Now there was the question of who the other young man was. Murray and I went to the morgue, down a little stairway to a gruesome basement, where in tiers of large drawers in the wall they stored the unidentified dead. The attendant pulled out a drawer. I stared at the very dead-looking face of a young man. "No, I don't know this person," I said, and then all of a sudden in a flash I knew. I turned and ran out of the place, rushing blindly up the stairs. The dead man was Sam Rosen, a youth of about nineteen years, a friend of Phil's and a sympathizer of our group. Now there was the sad business of notifying the family. I was glad I didn't have to do that.

Another tragedy affected us all greatly. Sam Fisher, a young man of about twenty-one was one of the founders of our group. Expelled from the YCL as a Trotskyite, he took part in all the discussions and work and was well-grounded in theory. He was a little fellow, thin and pale, with a round, naive, smiling face and a remarkably equable, cheerful disposition. A certain resiliency, a quiet courage combined with optimism made Sam a person who could come up smiling after blows. Sturdy and dependable, he was one of the pillars of the group. He lived with his mother in an East Side slum, working when he could get a few days employment as a plumber's helper. When we formed the Passaic Valley Organization Committee, Sam was sent out to live in Passaic. Although we had the support of Norman Thomas in this venture, our efforts there did not achieve much success, but Sam held out, undaunted. He actually lived in the headquarters in a hand-to-mouth fashion, eating little because money was scarce. After a time he became ill and was found to have tuberculosis. He insisted on remaining at his post until he collapsed and was taken to a hospital in Jersey City, where after a time he died.

Despite these woes our life as a group was by no means one of unmitigated gloom. Albert contributed strength and enthusiasm. He was always full of plans, could inspire people to go along with him, could make jokes to cheer up a discouraged comrade.

The CLS ran a regular weekly forum, at first held at our headquarters on East 9th Street, later in the Labor Temple at 14th and Second Avenue. Current events and political questions were discussed. Attendance often ran to one hundred or more. One of the forum's notable events was advertised as a debate between A. Weisbord and A. J. Muste on the program of the CPLA (Conference for Progressive Labor Action, Muste's group). Muste was also scheduled to debate William Z. Foster the following week. When Foster heard of the projected debate with Weisbord, he threatened to cancel his debate with Muste. So in place of Muste, Louis Budenz debated Albert.

At another time Albert debated Arthur Garfield Hays, a prominent liberal and my attorney in Gastonia. The subject was "Democracy or Communism, Which Way Out for the American Workers?" We also ran classes in our headquarters. I taught Marx's *Capital*, volume I. Albert gave volumes II and III. I also contributed frequently to the paper. As the Depression continued, it became less and less possible to get other work in the off seasons of the knit goods; thus I had weeks of free time.

During those years since my mother's rejection of Albert I still maintained some contact with my family, going out to the country once in a while. Albert thought I should break altogether, but to me this seemed uncalled-for. How could I forget my mother's sacrifices to give me an education, her devotion to me in my early years? In spite of the Depression my father had managed to improve his situation; using his native talent for drawing, he had worked himself into poster designing. Now he was the artist in a small firm printing theatrical posters, was made foreman of the plant too. He would sometimes help out with the wood engraving. There was plenty of good food and Mother was saving money, something she had always wanted to do; perhaps she was at last free from financial worry. They had put in a bathroom and bought some shrubs for the front lawn. Otherwise the house was the same, the rooms generally untidy. I used to spend my holidays there housecleaning and, in the right seasons, working outdoors.

Having lost her job, my sister had appealed to our parents to let her come and stay with them. Years later Papa admitted that was one of the big mistakes of his life. She never left. The antagonism between Ora and Papa remained. He had to endure her slurs on weekends when he was there, and he would break out once in a while. For me she had jibes about Communism and my unmarried state. Ordinarily I tried not to get into conflict with her, but once she made such an insulting remark about Papa that I couldn't stand it and I hit her, dealing her a couple of blows and feeling very mean as I did so. She retaliated by going to the county sheriff and swearing out a warrant against me. I had to make myself scarce there for a long time afterward.

During this period Albert devoted a great deal of time to study, completing his knowledge of Marx's works, making outlines of them begun while he was in the Socialist Party, reading all of Lenin and Trotsky that was available, and extending his research on world conditions begun with the thesis of the CLS. It was then that he conceived the idea of writing a series of pamphlets for workers on the modern political movements: Liberalism, Anarchism, Syndicalism, Socialism, Communism, and Fascism. He had not gone far in his research before he came up against an important historical and philosophic concept: ideas have no history, ideas are but figments in the brains of people, it is people, humankind, who evolve and have a history.

For example, what is democracy? Liberals can fill pages with effusions on this word. However, if we start to examine the countries that profess to maintain democracy, we find them quite different in the details of their history and contemporary practices. Generalities exist only in the human mind; reality, truth, is all concrete and very particular. So Albert found himself involved in an immense task that took him five more years of delving into the history of the movements, starting with the English civil wars of the seventeenth century. From 1931 on, he devoted a good part of his time daily to research in the 42nd Street library, and he began the writing of *The Conquest of Power.**

In 1932, thinking to establish a closer relationship with Trotsky, the group raised money to send Weisbord to confer with this leader, who was then in exile in Prinkipo, Turkey. In the course of his visit of three weeks with the great Russian, Albert evidently made a favorable impression because thereafter Trotsky contributed articles to our paper and was eager for us to unite with the CLA (Cannon group). We did try to arrange for a series of discussion meetings with them, but when the time for the first meeting came, not one of them showed up. Later on in 1934, when Trotsky, who was then living illegally in France, harassed by the French police and in really desperate circumstances, advised his comrades to join the Socialist Party, Cannon took his group for a brief foray into Muste's short-lived American Workers Party.

Albert's trip included also a one-month stay in Germany at the time Hitler was coming to power. Albert lived there with a worker's family in Berlin, learning German well enough to give a talk in the language. In Paris he had an interview with a leader of the French Trotskyists, and he spent some time as an observer in Spain, which was involved in revolution. From that time on we had correspondence with and received publications of various left European groups. During Albert's absence I put out the paper as usual.†

Tired of furnished rooms, I rented a secluded nook in a rear building on Avenue A, just south of 14th Street, a little two-room, cold-water flat, only eight dollars a month. It had sun and cross-ventilation, two west windows in the kitchen-living room overlooking a big courtyard,

---

*2 vols. (New York: Covici Friede, 1937).

†The editor of the Greenwood edition gives me credit: "While he [Weisbord] was away, Vera Buch ably carried on the journal."

one window in the bedroom getting the East River breezes. There was no bathroom; the public bath nearby, a clean place with plenty of hot water, sufficed. A toilet between two flats was shared. I bought a small gas heater, some secondhand furniture, and fixed up the flat attractively. There were the usual set washtubs, over them a two-burner gas plate, cupboards above, and a sink in the corner.

The neighborhood was chiefly Italian. Pushcarts with cheap vegetables and fruits swarmed on First Avenue. Some of the peddlers were unlicensed and always kept an anxious eye out for the cops, ready to push off. Occasionally there were funerals, with people marching after the hearse and a band playing soul-touching dirges. And sometimes at night from the courtyard below my little flat would come a wine-rich male voice pouring out romantic Neapolitan songs in Italian. I would always think, "I'll remember this," but with the morning every trace of the song would be gone.

Some gypsies lived in the store in the front building, a large family, the men generally absent by day, the women with their big, dirty, colorful skirts and seductive dark eyes waiting for palm-reading customers. One of them was very pregnant. I passed her sitting by the door one morning as I left for work. When I returned twelve hours later there she sat in the same spot, her face wan and drawn now, her belly collapsed, while from the store inside came the wail of a newborn infant.

Moments of anguish which the mind shrinks to recall . . . instincts may be strong, overwhelming common sense as well as political expediency. Poor foolish me, I had always wanted to have a baby. I was getting on in my thirties. I didn't have much time. I remember Dolores' reaction—she must have visited me once in the rear flat—"To all this, to add the care of a baby!" Well, I tried. The pregnancy was confirmed in the osteopathic clinic where I was being treated for my lower back trouble. They didn't charge a fee but had a plate at the entrance where you put your quarter or fifty cents or dime, and if you had nothing it was all right. The two women doctors were solicitous, encouraging. "She must have the best care at the end." There was a nursery in the neighborhood where I could leave the baby while I worked.

One day in the headquarters, I began to spot. I told Albert what would happen and went home. I had to go through it all alone. He came at last, found me in the blood-soaked bed. He got a doctor, who tried to cheer me up: "Every woman has at least one miscarriage." They took me to Bellevue Hospital, to the charity ward. Long rows of beds, with women of all ages. . . . Some of the nurses did more than their share for there was a help shortage. Others spared themselves, were callous. Once they trundled a lot of us out into the hall on stretchers "for x-rays." We waited a long time in the chilly, drafty hall. Then they just took us all back in. It was Christmas time, and they had a tree for us there in the ward. . . .

With everthing else I had to do, somehow or other during that period of the early thirties I managed to write a novel. Always I had this urge to write. To one who had read so many novels and stories a novel seemed a natural expression. There was some urge in me that was not to be satisfied by political work or by the contributions I made to the *Class Struggle*. That novel, which I called *But Unbowed*, was an attempt to express the life of our CLS and of poor people during the Depression. I took a group of people who happened to live in a rear house like mine, a few others tangentially associated with them, some incidents that tied them together, much detail of life during the Depression, and behold—a novel.

My life was complicated, my difficulties increased by the fact that my health had deteriorated. A slight thing at first, it had been worsening: some pelvic difficulty, pain and inflammation at times, and discharge. We had no money for a doctor, so I went to one of the free clinics that functioned in the New York hospitals. They would have half a dozen women lined up on the tables, their feet in the stirrups, knees bent, without even a sheet thrown over them, waiting for the doctors to examine them. I don't really recall whether any treatment was given; at any rate I was getting worse. Finally we located a doctor sympathetic to the movement who would treat me without payment. It seems I had incurred a strep infection in the abortion two years earlier. That rapid pulse detected in Charlotte may have been a first symptom. My uterus was full of pus. I was given suppositories and douches that were supposed to lead up to an electric cautery of the cervix.

I also had at this time a heart disturbance, first noticed in Detroit, called paroxysmal tachycardia. I had occasional attacks of violent, uncontrolled beating of my heart, which was not considered dangerous but was distressing to experience. The Party physician in Detroit had advised, "Comrade Buch should never have to work very hard."

In 1935 began my first bout with arthritis, just in a foot and ankle, but I found myself again in a clinic, where they strapped the foot so that I could walk. When I asked the doctor, "How long will this last?" he said, "Two years," which prognostic proved to be correct.

Yes, Anna Miller's life was a hard one, but there were compensations. There was a camaraderie in the shop; the very act of working day after day with the same women at their machines on the long table created a certain familiarity, and conversation was not prohibited provided we kept up a steady pace of work. And there would be jokes and confidences exchanged. Evenings, of course, I would go over to the headquarters. Sometimes there were meetings, sometimes work on the paper, or else I just sat around talking with the comrades. Sundays, weather permitting, we would go out hiking. We would take the subway to Van Cortland Park, then hike to Hunter's Point, where there was a beach on Pelham Bay. We would go swimming in summer, carry lunch along, and hold discussions too. Those days in the open air compensated a little for the long hours at the machine. An occasional trip to Staten Island on the ferry was a big treat. The Depression brought people closer together; the common misfortune leveled differences, cooperation took the place of competition, and, as money was lacking for diversions (movies, shows, trips), people learned to get satisfaction out of being with one another. There was time now too for reading, for study, for thinking.

At least in those days prices were low and rents were low in the poor neighborhoods. There were cafeterias set up by MacFarlan, a humanitarian, where one could eat a small meal for as little as five cents; stewed raisins, one cent, stewed wheat berries and other cereals, one cent. A Child's restaurant on Fourteenth Street had a weekly bargain of "All You Can Eat for 60¢." We used to save up for that, dreaming of it all week. But I always lost out; never could I eat much more than usual without great discomfort for hours afterward; gorging could be only a fantasy for me.

It was no longer possible to have illusions; this was no ordinary depression. As the bread lines of the Salvation Army and other private charities grew, as hunger became a common phenomenon, people were beginning fearfully to ask, "What is going to become of us?" During 1931 the city belatedly had opened a relief station. It was, however, on a limited scale, for single men only. Unemployed men begging for food and sleeping on the streets at night had become a problem. At the relief station they were given fifteen cents to sleep in a flophouse; there was a bread line where, after long standing, a bowl of weak soup and a hunk of bread could be obtained once a day. Many were keeping themselves alive on that. During the summer of 1932 the applicants swarmed in such numbers to the station that the officials in desperation closed the place for a few days.

Truly capitalism had reached a low ebb. Under President Herbert Hoover the country went from bad to worse. Production fell and fell, banks were failing on all sides, the millions of unemployed were multiplying.

Then came a dramatic change. When Franklin D. Roosevelt took over with the resounding message, "We have nothing to fear but fear itself," with a coterie of advisers behind him, suddenly a new and strong leadership appeared. Daily new powers were handed to the President, and legislation from Washington setting up all sorts of bureaus never heard of before became the order of the day. The NIRA (National Industrial Recovery Act) attempted to put capitalism on its feet again by regulation; the WPA, the PWA, and the CCC (Works Progress Administration, Public Works Administration, Civilian Conservation Camps) were born. The domestic market had to be restored. So the able-bodied unemployed were put to work, either on massive public works (PWA dams, roads, bridges, etc.) or on make-work, "doodling" things such as clearing away rubbish, beautifying the parks, etc. (WPA). With a little money in their pockets people could spend again. Massive loans and subsidies to business and to farmers started the factory wheels turning and the farmers raising grains and animals.

That the powers of the President were being extraordinarily increased, that the public works might be really war preparations, that all this regulation of business and of people's lives was paving the way for Fascism, the final stage of capitalism, was not so easily recognized. Capitalism was being saved; that was the main thing. As for the poor, at last public assistance, or dole, was organized.

Now at last if you had no job, no money, and no food, you could go somewhere for help. You "got on the relief." And we too got on the relief. Well I remember that huge gymnasium of a public school somewhere downtown. The first hurdle was to get through the mob at the door. Then you joined the long lines waiting at some half dozen windows for a clerk to take down your pedigree. After the preliminary questioning you were sent to a room upstairs for another going over. Finally you would be told to wait at least a week or until an investigator came to interview you in your home (but you were supposed to be completely destitute, penniless, before you applied!). At least there was modest help; if you were approved, they paid your rent and gave you a check for groceries which could be used in only one store. Supplemental foods were handed out from special stores—once in a while a big slab of butter or some cabbages or potatoes. The canned beef from Argentina was really good. You were required to report every two weeks to the office, waiting interminably each time.

It was in those days too that Fred Beal returned. Rumors at first; then a visit to a hideout in New Jersey, a summer cottage of Roger Baldwin's; then a visit with Albert to the furnished room where Fred was staying with another man; then at last he came with his roommate to the flat we had then, a little bigger than the one on Avenue A, where he asked us for money. He was of course illegally in America. The tales he told of his Russian experience were shocking: of beggars in the streets, of workers under conditions worse than the U.S.A., above all of the farmers in the Ukraine, where he had seen a whole village of dead people starved to death. All this was hard to reconcile with the faith we still held in the

Workers' Fatherland. We thought perhaps it was just a partial view, an
unbalanced opinion, for Beal was reacting strongly now against the Soviet Union. After these brief contacts we heard no more from him and
never saw him again.

In the spring of 1935 the comrades raised five hundred dollars to send
me to Europe as an emissary to contact other groups of the left opposition. I went first to Glasgow, where we had a connection with an anarchist group (the Guy Aldred group). They arranged a mass meeting for
me in a large hall; I remember speaking among other things on anti-
imperialism. In London other anarchists and a few left Communists; in
Paris some Trotskyist groups; in Belgium again the anarchists; then to
Nîmes in the South of France, where I spent a few weeks at the home of
the Communist-anarchist André Prudhommeaux, who owned a printing
plant. I helped him and his comrades put out their paper and shared the
news from Spain.

I have poignant personal memories of this trip. Of the icebergs among
which our little ship crept slowly, losing a full day on the trip. Of an illness in Paris; sick with grippe I lay in a *mansarde* bedroom cared for by
two women comrades who debated whether to give me hot or cold drinks:
"Je lui ferai une boisson bien chaude, une tisane, parcequ'elle est en-
rhumée . . . Ah mais non, c'est le froid qu'il lui faut, puisqu'elle a le
fièvre. . . ." They compromised on a glass of hot wine and water with biscuits. Of flopping in the Salvation Army, quite broke, while waiting for a
reply to my cabled appeal to Albert for funds. It was a big barren place on
the outskirts of Paris, with iron-ribbed beds and cheap unwholesome food.
Of an entire day, a Sunday, spent alone on the Bois de Boulogne, nearly
penniless, just a roll for my day's food, dreaming all day of a chocolate
ice-cream soda! And of Victor, that gentle friendly medical student in
Paris who treated me sometimes to a meal in one of the students' restaurants and guided me on endless foot-trips through the city. He wanted
to take me to an autopsy, but at his description—"On met le cadavre sur
la table, les bras étendus comme le Christ sur le calvaire, et puis on lui
donne un coup de hache . . ."—I lost courage.

A reunion with George Padmore, the comrade of the old days in the
Harlem English branch, was precious. For two hours we compared notes
in the Café Rotonde, circling the world of ideas. Then I never saw George
again.*

My trip further connected our group with the international groupings,

---

*He eventually went to Ghana, where he made a place for himself as an adviser
to Nkrumah. When he died, the Ghanians erected a statute to his memory, so I have
been told.

not in an organizational sense for we found no group just like our own, but we kept up communication and received their papers.

As the years of the Roosevelt Administration progressed, it became clear America was entering an entirely new period. The first social legislation such as workmen's compensation was enacted in 1933. It was becoming plain that the day of immediate revolution was not yet at hand. The threat of Fascism was in the air, and we pointed out the germs of it in all the Roosevelt regulations, especially in the greatly increased powers of the President.

The threat of war too lay ahead.

Our group made little headway; the difficulties were always overwhelming. We were tired of the endless debates in the Fourteenth Street cafeterias that were the chief object in life of New York radicals. We began looking toward Chicago, center of basic industry and heartland of America, as to a mecca where our ideas might be sown in more fertile ground. "Westward Ho!" became once more a magnetic slogan. The question was discussed for some months among members and sympathizers. Some were tied to jobs, others to family obligations, some perhaps were glad of an excuse to drop out. Finally we sifted out those loyal and courageous people who were ready to go, made arrangements for those left to continue the work in New York, and westward we went, a close-bound handful of people illumined by hope and illusions, to Chicago.

Epilogue: The Long Wait

WHAT HAPPENED AFTERWARD? DID SUCCESS AWAIT US IN CHICAGO? AMERI-
can stories are traditionally success stories. We have been trained to expect that ultimately money and fame as well as the attainment of a goal
will be the reward of effort and sacrifice. Such an outcome has not been
mine . . . and success is such a relative thing after all. Remember the case
of the astronauts, that Gemini 6 projected trip to the moon which so
nearly missed complete collapse. The enterprise failed in its objective. In
any human sense, however, what an achievement it was and what a
triumph for science as well, just to have been able to return to earth, for
those three men trapped in the outer atmosphere in a failing apparatus,
with only directives from below and their own courage and ingenuity to
save them!

If one's objective is to help bring about a better life for all on this
earth, obviously this is not within easy reach, nor will it bring rewards in
the ordinary sense. It will take many lives and many years. That the movement progresses is reward enough if one must think in terms of reward.

Now a little of what happened since 1935. We never regretted coming to Chicago, "city of the broad shoulders," which may truly be said
to be America's heart. We located on the South Side among the numerous black population there, and we became involved in the Workers Alliance, an organization of the unemployed. The political climate of the
country was changing; war was looming closer. In 1937, with the hardships of maintaining a tiny opposition group becoming too formidable,
we disbanded the Communist League of Struggle after putting out a
final edition of our paper, *Class Struggle*. A few members returned to
New York, others found niches for themselves in Chicago.

In that year, during the Spanish civil war, Albert made his second trip

314

to Spain and renewed his contacts of 1932. Working with the PC (Partido Obrero de Unificación Marxista), he experienced the bombardment of Barcelona by the Germans, did guard duty, visited the trenches. Meanwhile in Chicago I was running a sewing machine again in a North Side factory. My chief interest was watching for the Spanish news in the papers, since communication from Spain was difficult.

Returning, Albert offered his services as organizer to the budding Congress of Industrial Organizations (CIO), but the Communist Party faction there prevented his being accepted. The American Federation of Labor and several of its international unions, however, did take him on. We relocated in Philadelphia, and Albert traveled constantly. Working under Frank Fenton, then director of the AFL Organization Department, he brought thousands of workers into the AFL. In the course of his work he argued cases before the National Defense Mediation Committee, the War Labor Board, the National Labor Relations Board, and several state industrial boards and arbitration bodies. At various times he appeared for the International Hat, Cap and Millinery Workers Union, the International Upholsterers Union, and the Brotherhood of Electrical Workers. In one case alone he won over twenty million dollars for the furniture workers of the South.

For me, often alone and often ill, the Philadelphia story was not a happy one. The strep infection incurred in my induced abortion of 1928 continued to spread. Not bedridden but suffering frequent periods of painful illness, I was not capable of sustained activity and could not think of professional work. I learned then, and subsequently have had to relearn, the lessons of the physically handicapped: not to feel sorry for oneself, not to complain, but to find satisfaction just in being alive; above all, to persist in whatever one is able to do. Not for us to leap forward like the swift and noble deer, though its spirit may be ours; still, our patient tortoise plodding may in the end achieve some of our goals.

During this period I began another novel, *Oil in the Corn,* and wrote some short stories (two of which were published). Albert and I got married in 1938 chiefly to console my mother. Her response was: Your marriage comes too late. She never relented.

In the early 1940s I worked with a beginning CORE committee (Congress of Racial Equality), mostly Quakers. We tested restaurants; if they would not serve blacks, we picketed them.

Now under pressure from the employers and no doubt also from the F.B.I., Albert was let go by William Green, then president of the AFL, but not without a good recommendation. For a while he worked as a railroad fireman on the Philadelphia and Reading Railroad under the name of Albert West until the company got wise to his pseudonym. I was employed part time then in a war plant. We used to run into each other occasionally coming in and out of the apartment—ships passing in the night.

The war took on overwhelming importance. Because we considered the war against Nazism a progressive war, we supported it but tried to convince the American people that such a war could best be fought as a noncapitalistic war. To that effect Albert wrote a thesis on how to mobilize the country against Fascism. Senator Claude Pepper sent a copy to Fiorella La Guardia, head of the country's civilian defense.

All through the World War II period, with the horrors of Stalin's purges followed by the extermination of the Jews heaped on the holocaust of the war, my disillusionment with Russia and the Communist International increased. Two books were landmarks: Dallin and Nicolaevsky's *Forced Labor in Soviet Russia* (New Haven: Yale University Press, 1947) and Anton Ciliga's *In the Country of the Perplexing Lie*.*

Ciliga was a young Yugoslav Communist leader whom Albert had met in Italy in 1948. As one of the leaders of the Yugoslav Communist Party, he had a great desire to see for himself what the Workers' Fatherland was like. He found out. In the prisons of Siberia, together with other captive politicals, he sought the reasons for the collapse of his dream. He came to discard all illusions and was driven to cut his wrists in a desperate suicide attempt before Stalin would let him out. Ciliga stressed the great vitality of the Russian people and showed how their persistent hopes and efforts were being crushed by the state under Stalin. Certainly it was unrealistic for anyone to have expected that socialism could be realized in one country alone, especially in such a vast, backward, peasant country as old Russia, and perhaps had we ourselves had more knowledge, we should have foreseen the degeneration. Still, there was never a complete reversion to private capitalism.

Returning to Chicago in 1946, we found ourselves in the midst of the Joe McCarthy period, with harassment from the F.B.I. making employment difficult. Employers would receive notice that they had a dangerous Red in their service. Goodbye job. Albert passed the civil service exam for Analyst No. 2 with the highest rating in the state but got no appointment. Frequently we would get phone calls from agents wanting to know where he worked. Once an agent came to our home when Albert was out. With the man at the door was Paul Crouch, whom I had met briefly in Gastonia. I saw through the ruse at once. "Crouch must be

---

Au Pays du Mensonge Déconcertant (Paris: Les Iles D'or, 1938, 1950). Ciliga also wrote *Sibérie, Terre de l'Exil et de l'Industrialisation* (*Siberia, Land of Exile and of Industrialization*) (Paris: Les Iles D'or, 1950).

cooperating," I thought. I didn't give any sign that I knew him, didn't ask them to come inside. They quickly left.

In 1950 the problems of my family came to a head. Papa had died in 1942 of lung cancer. He had come to a good job at last: foreman of a small printing plant that made theatrical posters, he designed the posters and helped out at times in wood engraving. As work had been irregular his last few years, when he applied for social security he could not fit into their quarters. So a man who had worked all his life since the age of twelve was cut off without a cent. When he died, Mother couldn't see that she had to sell the place, and she hung on till the mortgage was foreclosed. Having no more insurance money left, she had to make the ultimate sacrifice of her pride and go on social security. With her death in 1954 my sister, thrown at last on her own resources, was able to support herself and even to save some money. I was able to help very little in all of their difficulties; my family problems were always beyond my capacity to solve.

Less strenuous days finally came for my husband and me. During the Korean War, Albert as a last resort set up a management consultant firm as a way to avoid F.B.I. harassment, to earn some money, and at the same time to show employers and unions how to get wage increases despite the regulations freezing wages at the time. This he did for the next ten years, which enabled us to have a little economic security. During his leisure hours Albert had found a new interest in comparative language studies, and later he formed a Group Language Institute, in which he showed that four basically related languages may be learned at the same time. Thus he taught basic Romanic, basic Teutonic, and Russian (there was no call for his basic Slavonic).

I helped a little in this work, but I too had acquired a new interest. In 1952 I returned to my long-neglected art talent, went to the Art Institute of Chicago, and for the next twenty years was immersed in the study and practice of art. Over four hundred pictures resulted, giving much joy to me and perhaps some satisfaction to those who have my paintings.

From time to time, whenever possible, we took part in local actions in the antiwar movement and in the struggle of the blacks. Around 1957 we began the Afro-American Committee, an interracial group which issued a pamphlet entitled "Afro-American Manifesto." It enjoyed a pretty good circulation, not merely locally. Later on we followed it by "Afro-American Program of Action," another pamphlet.

Beginning in 1957, we made several foreign trips. Staying in the small, cheap hotels frequented by Europeans and using our familiarity with languages to get close to people, we expanded our knowledge of the world and of history. Having trekked from the fjords of Norway to the islands of the Mediterranean, twice through South America, often to Mexico, and finally in 1971 to some of the Arab countries, Greece, and Israel, we recall our trips as all fabulous. The memories of them spice many a day now.

With his retirement in 1962 Albert gave full time to study and writing in the fields of economics, history, and political analysis to which I made a small contribution. *Latin American Actuality* was published in 1964 and some articles saw the light, though most of the books, pamphlets, and articles remain in manuscript form.

During all this time, which I think of as "the long wait," we lived like so many others, on the fringes of society, never integrated into it, never having more than a toehold. The endeavors of the past in which we had expended our youth seemed buried, bypassed by generations participating in a "prosperity" in which 30 or more million people in this country were never included. The world continued to produce significant upheavals, such as the revolts of colonial peoples and the Chinese Revolution, while the USA went its own way maintaining its position of leadership, the voices of protest indeed crying in the wilderness.

At last, in 1965, came the long overdue uprising of the black people in the civil rights struggle. This was perhaps a turning point more decisive than it seemed at the time, followed as it was by the awakening of women, the antiwar struggles of the Vietnam period, and the student unrest of the late sixties. We felt something of a sense of reward when on October 16, 1976, a symposium commemorating the fiftieth anniversary of the Passaic strike was held in the William Paterson College at Wayne, New Jersey. It was sponsored by the New Jersey Historical Commission, the Essex County College Labor Studies Program, and the New Jersey Urban History Association. Albert was one of the principal speakers, and I took part in a participants' panel. Few indeed were the participants, but we did get to meet again our old colleagues Joe Magliacano and Martha Stone.

Finally, with another world depression threatening, we have come full cycle beyond 1932. But what a changed world! Capitalism has become truly international now in every respect—economic, financial, and political. The internal contradictions that formerly led to antagonism between individual nations now take the form of groups of nations rather than single ones. The capitalist world now confronts that other "socialist" world born in 1917. All questions must be considered on a global scale.

In our own country one interesting phenomenon among many others is a great ferment going on nationally at the ground level. Countless active groups exist, composed chiefly of youth, though they cut across age levels: black groups, women's groups, political groups, religious groups, nature-oriented groups, cooperative-living groups. Some operate only on a neighborhood basis; others are more widespread. Affected by the violation of the earth, the ruin of the environment, or disgusted by the corruption and duplicity revealed in scandals like Watergate, nature-oriented youth are returning to back-breaking toil on farms. The black groups show a great diversity; so do the political groups: some of them spring from the student youth leadership of 1968, and they are generally Marxist-oriented. Bewildered and dismayed at the enormity of the obstacles confronting them, perhaps they concentrate too much on the past, mulling over issues long bypassed by history, searching in the works of their god-heroes Lenin, Trotsky, and Mao for some magic formula that today may lead them to victory. We may also add perhaps the Radical Caucus of the universities, which has contributed much in the way of concrete studies to revive the lost history of the last few decades in the U.S.A. In all of this disparate activity there is at least one common thread: a disaffection with life as it is. Perhaps the youth, always more sensitive, feel that it is time for a change.

The nonparticipation of any large segments of the working class in all the upheavals, from civil rights to antiwar activity, is noteworthy. If they can see no farther than overtime pay, perhaps they will have to learn the hard way.

This recent period, especially the last two decades, has seen an enormous expansion of the human intelligence. Researches carried out in an unbelievable number of fields have given rise to a truly modern Renaissance. While technology achieves its miracles, we are still left with the painful contradiction that all this wealth of knowledge has been unable to solve human problems: people by the millions are dying of starvation; other millions lead brief and tortured lives, doomed by malnutrition to an early death. Even in the country of the greatest wealth, millions are deprived of education and livelihood. Other hundreds of thousands are confined in prisons, mental hospitals, and other institutions.

Chronic unemployment increases in the industrial countries with computerization and automation. Little is said about these factors, perhaps because they create a problem unsolvable within the framework of present social relations. One is reminded how in the very early days of capitalism in Europe and in England cottage weavers ekeing a poor living by their hand-worked looms were ready to destroy the machines to prevent their own displacement when power looms and spindles were invented. What to do with the surplus people is now a problem for experts to sweat over. The time-honored solution in the past was war.

The ultimate contradiction is present today: the world holds in its present condition the seeds both of despair and of hope, either complete destruction or the building of a new and better world. The next bloodbath, already being planned, will be atomic warfare, with nuclear power being within easy reach of any crackpot. But the same technology that makes possible the unspeakable agony of war, if properly controlled and directed, has the possibility never before present in human history of setting people free, no longer bound by many hours of toil to support a parasitic minority, but free to solve the human problems, to understand themselves and each other and the world about them, to realize a rich life for all never before dreamed of.

At times the scene of the present-day world is like some mad dance of death. How to find the clue, the way out? As my old friend Omar Khayyám said centuries ago,

> Ah love, could you and I but conspire
> To grasp this sorry scheme of things entire
> Would we not shatter it to bits
> And then remold it nearer to our heart's desire?

A poet's dream, or wisdom of a prophet?

Yes, Omar, it was too early for you, but the world has moved on, the time is ripe now. It will not be easy. It may take longer than we think, but we can make it. We can realize your dream.

APPENDIXES

APPENDIX A

Actually, the Left Wing had begun to emerge much earlier. "Within socialist ranks, the Left Wing had first appeared in 1905, supporting the launching of the IWW against the policy of the Right Wing, which favored the officials of the American Federation of Labor. Again, the Left Wing loomed large in 1912 when it fought against the adoption of Article II, Section 6 of the Socialist Party Constitution, expelling anyone who favored sabotage. In 1917 it compelled a strong resolution to be drafted against the War. Finally, if called to the support of the Soviet regime in Russia, and struggled for the adherence of the Socialist Party to the Communist International." Albert Weisbord, *The Conquest of Power*, vol. 2 (New York: Covici Friede, 1937), p. 1100.

APPENDIX B

The Associated Silk Workers of Paterson was an independent union resulting from work done in the silk mills by the IWW years before. The union was now under the influence of A. J. Muste, a clergyman interested in working people. Involved too, to a certain extent, was the attitude of Jewish Party rank and file members in both Paterson and Passaic, a few of whom belonged to the Associated Silk Workers. If they had asserted themselves on behalf of our policy, they might have won over the union to strike in solidarity with Passaic. Nothing of the sort had happened; when Albert spoke before the Paterson union earlier in the strike, the Party comrades never opened their mouths.

APPENDIX C

There were about twenty-five delegates from the U.S. They didn't travel together but by factions. Foster didn't go, but some Fosterites did. A few followers of James P. Cannon, who had recently set up his own group, went on a different boat. Albert found himself with Gitlow and the other Lovestonites, going second-class on still another steamer. Gitlow ignored him all the way. In Moscow most of the delegation was put up at the big Hotel Europa; a few, including Albert, stayed at the Metropole. Meals were excellent, such foods as the average Russian at that time could never hope to enjoy. Breakfast was sumptuous, including big chunks of ham and cheese, even partridges, and eggs and coffee.

Albert described the daily sessions of the Profintern Congress. Many nationalities were present, including a large Chinese delegation that had had a rough time getting out of their Chiang Kai-shek-dominated country. All delegates spoke their native tongues, which had to be interpreted into different languages, so the proceedings were not always easy to follow. Gitlow was too busy politicking to attend the sessions. He had an interview with Bukharin (Kamenev and Zinoviev were there too), which the other Lovestonites attended. Seeing no reason to align himself with Bukharin, Albert stayed away.

APPENDIX D

Browder had spent some time in China in 1927 as a Comintern representative. At the time of the Chiang Kai-shek takeover, Browder was a partisan of the general, whom the Party officially had supported at the time. To Amy, Earl Browder was about the ultimate in what a human being should be. I didn't know him personally at the time, so I said nothing. I had been determined from the start not to tolerate factionalism in Loray. To divide into factions would have been the last straw; it would have destroyed us completely.

APPENDIX E

Born in a small town in Kansas, son of a railroad worker, Cannon had been active in the IWW before joining the Socialist Party. In 1919 he was in the early Communist movement and was a leader in the Communist Labor Party in the Midwest. In 1922 he met Trotsky in Moscow, where he had gone to fight on behalf of the "liquidators" of the underground. Trotsky was at that time in favor of an open party in the U.S. and an end to the factional squabbles.

APPENDIX F

The Communists were split into the following groups: 1) The official Party controlled by Stalin, locally led by Foster and Browder; 2) the Communist Party (majority group), known as "the Lovestone group"; 3) the Communist League of America, referred to as "the Cannon group"; 4) the Communist League of Struggle, or "Weisbord group." Later there were two spin-offs from the Cannon group: 5) the Oehler-Stamm group, and 6) the Fields group. The Proletarian Party (7) formed in 1919 led a quiet, restricted life chiefly in the Midwest. In addition, the Socialist Labor Party, "DeLeon's group," (8) was still extant. There was also a "Mattick group" (9) limited to Chicago. Paul Mattick, a German who was the head of this group, seemed to be a German nationalist; at any rate he believed strongly in the technological superiority of the Germans. His tendencies otherwise were rather ultra-leftist. He believed, for example, that the trade unions in the U.S. were only reactionary and must be destroyed.

Allied with Mattick was a man named Bereiter, formerly of the Proletarian Party. At one time Albert made a trip to Chicago to hold a debate with this group. In addition the Socialist Party, much weakened by the tearing away of its militant leftists, still functioned as a right-wing parliamentary organization. The Industrial Workers of the World (IWW), also deprived of its function once the Communists began to engage in mass work, was still on the scene and was active chiefly among seamen and nomadic harvest workers. There were also some anarchist groupings. One heard something in those days too of the "Muste Group." A. J. Muste started out in the early twenties as a minister, a "do-gooder" interested in the reconciliation of labor and capital. "The Fellowship of Reconciliation" was his first group. He became interested in textile workers; he branched out with Brookwood Labor College and the Conference for Progressive Labor Action, which provided organizers for Southern textile strikes (Muste himself didn't go; he sent others); and finally in 1933 he entered the political field directly with the American Workers Party, in which for a brief period he was joined by James P. Cannon and the CLA (also by some split-offs from the Lovestone group such as Bert Miller and Benjamin Gitlow).

To thread one's way among the theoretical differences of these numerous groupings was indeed difficult, taxing the patience of the most valiant, the most knowledgeable. Some of the issues were basic to the movement—questions of internationalism, of reform vs. revolution, of the nature of the economic crisis. Some were American questions, such as the "Negro problem." While the conflict over Trotsky was raging, the Russian questions were much involved: socialism in one country, the nature of the Russian state, industrialization and the Five-Year Plan, "liquidation of the Kulaks," an so on. Whether Russia was a workers' state or not was argued for interminable hours in the cafeterias. For the average worker it was all too much. As some of our well-meaning sympathizers used to put it: "It's hard enough to get anyone to see Communism. How can you expect them to split hairs like this, or support a tiny group the real Party hates?" Indeed, we were not responsible for the thorniness of the path. Such was the historic reality to which we had to try to adjust ourselves.

I N D E X

Abernathy, W. H., 249
ACLU. *See* American Civil Liberties Union
Adams, Thaddeus A., 250, 271–72, 278
Aderholt, Ethel, 253
Aderholt, O. F., 195, 224, 237–38, 246–47, 252–54, 264–65, 273–78
Afro-American Committee, 317
Aldred, Guy, 312
Allen, Robert, 184, 243
Amalgamated Clothing Workers, 114
American Civil Liberties Union: and Passaic strike, 125, 127, 130, 134; protests troopers' attack in Gastonia, 201–202; bails out strike organizers, 239; involvement in Charlotte trial, 250
American Federation of Labor: Socialist Party support of, 83; and Passaic strike, 124, 129, 133; Albert Weisbord's organizing for, 315
American Workers Party, 307, 323
Ashkenudze, George, 113
Associated Silk Workers, 321
Auerbach, Rissie, 96
Auto plants unionization, 146–52

Bail, Alex, 143
Baldwin, Roger, 113, 311
Ballam, John, 82, 105
Barnes, Binney, 192
Barnhill, Judge, 236, 238, 246–48, 253, 264–74, 280–88
Beal, Fred Erwin, 105, 164, 172–99, 205–26, 234–35, 246–47, 252–53, 263–90, 311–12
Blacks. *See* Negroes
Bloor, Ella Reeve, 151–52
Borah, William, 130
Brezniak, Ma, 115
Brodsky, Joseph, 249
Bromley, Dorothy Dunbar, xiv
Brophy, John, 154, 160
Browder, Earl, 145, 322

Bryan, Jack, 108–109, 126
Buch, John Casper (father), 3–50, 233, 241, 299, 317
Buch, Nellie Crawford (mother), 3–50, 233, 241, 299, 306, 315, 317
Buch, Ora (sister), 16–17, 54, 57, 58–59, 68–69, 306, 317
Buch, Vera. *See* Weisbord, Vera Buch
Bukharin, Nikolai, 301
Bulwinkle, Major, 246, 257
Bunker, Thomas, 304
But Unbowed, 309
Byers, K. O., 243, 268–69, 275, 281–82

Campbell, J. C., 254, 263, 278
Cannon, James P., 83, 98, 121, 163–64, 192, 283, 297–302, 307, 321–23
Cansler, E. T., 248, 269, 271
Capital, 296–97, 306
Carpenter, John, 246, 250, 257, 271–75
Carter, Frank, 250
Carter, George, 216, 243, 263–67, 273–74, 282
Catholic Mediation Committee, 128–29
Central Committee of the Russian Cooperative Unions, 88–89
Centrosoyus, 88–89
Chapple, Joe Mitchell, 204–205
Charlotte *News and Observer*, 245
Charlotte, N.C. trials, 236–89
Chernenko, Lena, 112, 127, 131
Chiang Kai-shek, 145–46, 322
CI. *See* Comintern
Ciliga, Anton, 316
Clark Thread Co., 294–95
Class Struggle, 301, 309, 314
Cohen, Maximilian, 76, 82
Colby, Bainbridge, 126
Comintern: role in capitalist world, 122; policy on new unions, 164–65; expels Albert Weisbord, 293; *see also* Communist Party
Communism: early period of American,

325